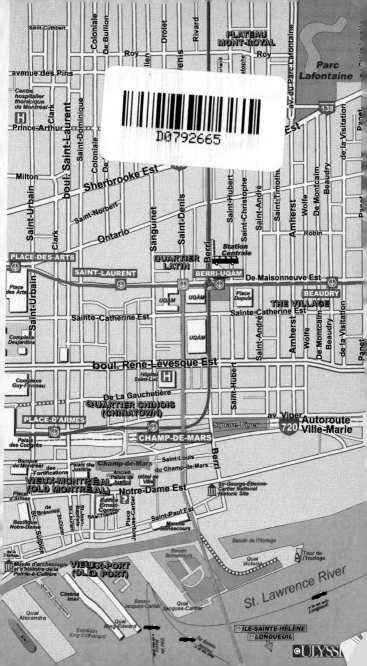

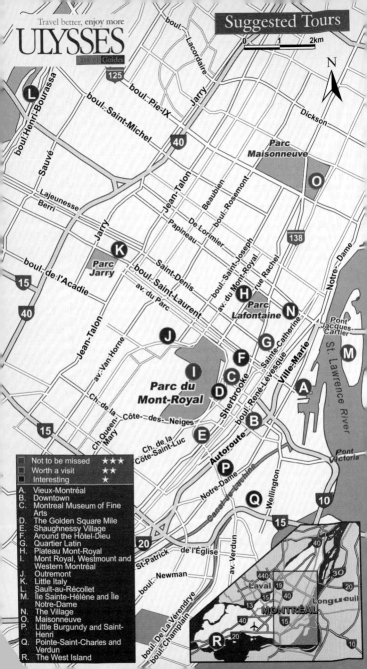

CHUNG

Montréal 2001

6th Edition

Travel better, enjoy more
ULYSSES
Travel Guides

Offices

CANADA: Ulysses Travel Guides, 4176 Saint-Denis, Montréal, Québec, H2W 2M5, ☎ (514) 843-9447 or 1-877-542-7247, ≈(514) 843-9448, info@ulysses.ca, www.ulyssesguides.com

EUROPE: Les Guides de Voyage Ulysse SARL, BP 159, 75523 Paris Cedex 11, France, ☎ 01 43 38 89 50, ≈01 43 38 89 52, voyage@ulysse.ca, www.ulyssesguides.com

U.S.A.: Ulysses Travel Guides, 305 Madison Avenue, Suite 1166, New York, NY 10165, ☎ 1-877-542-7247, info@ulysses.ca, www.ulyssesguides.com

Distributors

CANADA: Ulysses Books & Maps, 4176 Saint-Denis, Montréal, Québec, H2W 2M5, ☎ (514) 843-9882, ext.2232, 800-748-9171, Fax: 514-843-9448, info@ulysses.ca, www.ulyssesguides.com

GREAT BRITAIN AND IRELAND: World Leisure Marketing, Unit 11, Newmarket Court, Newmarket Drive, Derby DE24 8NW, ☎ 1 332 57 37 37, Fax: 1 332 57 33 99, office@wlmsales.co.uk

SCANDINAVIA: Scanvik, Esplanaden 8B, 1263 Copenhagen K, DK, ☎ (45) 33.12.77.66, Fax: (45) 33.91.28.82

SPAIN: Altaïr, Balmes 69, E-08007 Barcelona, ☎ 454 29 66, Fax: 451 25 59, altair@globalcom.es

SWITZERLAND: OLF, P.O. Box 1061, CH-1701 Fribourg, ☎ (026) 467.51.11, Fax: (026) 467.54.66

U.S.A.: The Globe Pequot Press, 246 Goose Lane, Guilford, CT 06437 - 0480, ☎1-800-243-0495, Fax: 800-820-2329, sales@globe-pequot.com

Other countries contact Ulysses Books & Maps, 4176 Saint-Denis, Montréal, Québec, H2W 2M5, ☎ (514) 843-9882, ext.2232, ☎ 800-748-9171, Fax: 514-843-9448, info@ulysses.ca, www.ulyssesguides.com

Canadian Cataloguing-in-Publication Data (see page 4)
© April 2001, Ulysses Travel Guides.
All rights reserved. Printed in Canada
ISBN 2-89464-335-7

"Between the St. Lawrence River
and its tributary...a lovely plateau...
is situated...amid grasslands...
with birds of many different colours
whose songs tamed our French people
in this wilderness."

*«Entre le fleuve de Saint-Laurent
et une petite rivière qui s'y décharge...
une prairie fort agréable...
il y avoit... dans la prairie...
tant d'oiseaux de différens ramages et couleurs,
qu'ils étoient fort propres à apprivoiser
nos François en ce pays sauvage.»*

Histoire du Montréal, 1640-1672
François Dollier de Casson (1636-1701),
Sulpicien and Seigneur of the Island of Montréal

The first historian of Montréal,
François Dollier de Casson, compiled the
Histoire du Montréal between 1672 and 1673,
from which this description of the site on which Montréal
was built (present-day Point-à-Callière) is taken.

James E. Caldwell
"Ottawa," 1907

Authors
François Rémillard
(Exploring)
Benoit Prieur
(Portrait)

Editors
Caroline Béliveau
Stéphane G. Marceau

Publisher
Pascale Couture

Copy Editing
Jacqueline Grekin
Eileen Connolly

Translation
Danielle Gauthier
Tara Salman
Sarah Kresh
S. Heidenreich
Tracey Kendrick

Page Layout
Caroline Béliveau
Rafaël Corbeil

Cartographers
André Duchesne
Patrick Thivierge
Yanik Landreville

Computer Graphics
Stéphanie Routhier

Artistic Director
Patrick Farei (Atoll)

Illustrations
Lorette Pierson
Marie-Annick Viatour
Myriam Gagné

Photography
Cover page
MTP Net-
work/Turgeon
Inside pages
Philippe Renault
Patrick Escudero

Collaboration: Marie-Josée Béliveau, Julie Brodeur, Benoît Caron, Daniel Desjardins, Jacqueline Grekin, Loïc Hamon, Elyse Leconte, Alain Legault, Christin Lemieux, Stéphane G. Marceau, Marc Rigole, Yves Séguin, Patrick Thivierge.

We acknowledge the financial support of the Government of Canada through the Book Publishing Industry Development Program (BPIDP) for our publishing activities.

We would also like to thank SODEC (Québec) for its financial support.

Canadian Cataloguing-in-Publication Data

Montréal

    (Ulysses travel guide)
    Includes index.

    ISSN 1-483-2666
    ISBN 2-89464-335-7

    1. Montréal (Québec) - Guidebooks. I. Series.

FC2947.18.M6613   917.14'28044   C97-302253-1
F1054.5.M83M6613

List of Maps

Around the Hôtel-Dieu 147
Downtown 101
      Accommodations 267
      Restaurants 295
General Orientation 51
Golden Square Mile 131
Îles Sainte-Hélène and île Notre-Dame 197
Island of Montréal and Surroundings 12
Lachine 233
Little Italy 189
Little Burgundy and St-Henri 217
Maisonneuve 210
Mont Royal, Westmount and Western Montréal 168
Montreal Museum of Fine Arts 121,123,125,127
Montréal's Fortifications circa 1750 17
Outremont 179
Plateau Mont-Royal 163
Pointe-St-Charles and Verdun 223
Quartier Latin 155
Restaurants on Boulevard Saint-Laurent 305
Sault-au-Récollet 193
Shaughnessy Village 143
Southern Québec 11
Suggested Tours of Montréal 78
Table of distances 47
The Montréal metro 53
The Village 203
Underground Montréal 109
Vieux-Montréal 81
West Island 231
Where is Montréal 10

Map Symbols

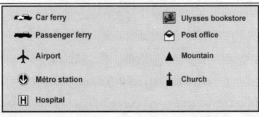

- Car ferry
- Passenger ferry
- Airport
- Métro station
- Hospital
- Ulysses bookstore
- Post office
- Mountain
- Church

Symbols

≈	Air Conditioning
bkfst incl.	Breakfast included
⊗	Fan
≈	Fax number
🔥	Fireplace
⊙	Fitness centre
K	Kitchenette
P	Parking
🐕	Pets allowed
pb	Private bathroom
≈	Pool
ℝ	Refrigerator
ℜ	Restaurant
△	Sauna
sb	Shared bathroom
✿	Spa
☎	Telephone number
⊛	Whirlpool
	Ulysses's favourite
♿	Wheelchair access
wine	Bring your own wine

ATTRACTION CLASSIFICATION

★	Interesting
★★	Worth a visit
★★★	Not to be missed

HOTEL CLASSIFICATION

Unless otherwise indicated, the prices in the guide are
for one standard room, double occupancy in high season.

RESTAURANT CLASSIFICATION

$	$10 or less
$$	$10 to $20
$$$	$20 to $30
$$$$	$30 or more

The prices in the guide are for a meal for one
person, not including drinks and tip.

All prices in this guide are in Canadian dollars.

Write to Us

The information contained in this guide was correct at press time. However, mistakes can slip in, omissions are always possible, places can disappear, etc. The authors and publisher hereby disclaim any liability for loss or damage resulting from omissions or errors.

We value your comments, corrections and suggestions, as they allow us to keep each guide up to date. The best contributions will be rewarded with a free book from Ulysses Travel Guides. All you have to do is write us at the following address and indicate which title you would be interested in receiving (see the list at the end of the guide).

Ulysses Travel Guides
4176 Saint-Denis
Montréal, Québec
Canada H2W 2M5
www.ulyssesguides.com
E-mail: text@ulysses.ca

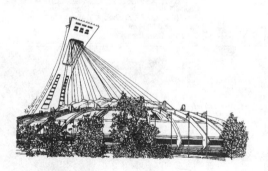

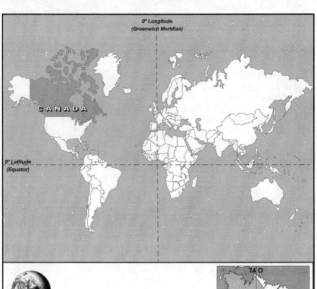

QUÉBEC	MONTRÉAL
Capital: Quebec City	Population: 3,200,000 inhab.
Population: 7,500,000 inhab.	Area: 176,74 km²
Area: 1,550,000 km²	
Currency: Canadian dollar	

©ULYSSES

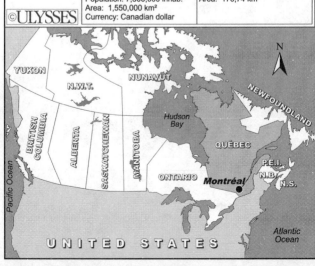

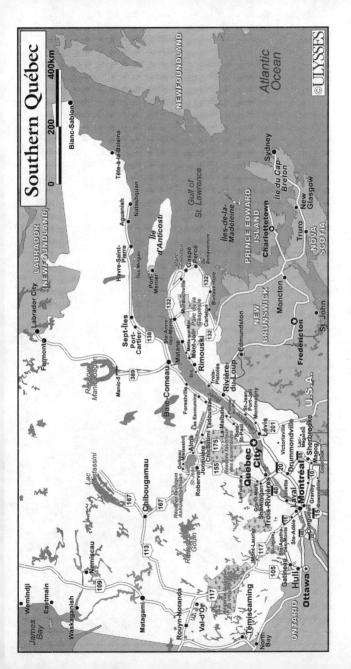

Southern Québec

© ULYSSES

0   200   400km

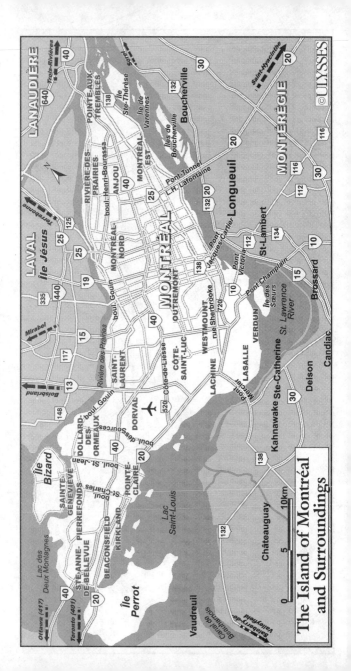

The Island of Montréal and Surroundings

Portrait

Seen as both Latin and northern, cosmopolitan and unmistakably the metropolis of Québec, the largest French-speaking city in the world after Paris, yet also bilingual, Montréal is definitely a city of paradoxes!

Visitors to the city appreciate it for many different reasons, for as it succeeds in delighting American tourists with its so-called European charm, it also manages to surprise overseas travellers with its haphazard character and nonchalance. Above all, Montréal holds nothing back and visitors find what they are looking for without having to search too far. Montréal is a city that exists in a balance between several different worlds: firmly planted in America yet with eyes looking toward Europe, claimed by two lands, Québec and Canada, and always, it would seem, in the middle of social, economic and demographic changes.

It is difficult to define this city, especially since no postcard or cliché truly succeeds in evoking an image of it that is even the slightest bit realistic or honest. If Paris has its great boulevards and squares, New York its skyscrapers and celebrated Statue of Liberty, what best symbolizes Montréal? Its many and beautiful churches? Its Olympic Stadium? Its opulent Victorian residences?

In fact, despite Montréal's rich architectural heritage, it is above all the city's unique, engaging atmosphere that appeals to people. Montréal is an enchanting city to visit, an exhilarating place to discover; it is generous, friendly and not at all mundane. And, when it comes time to celebrate jazz, film, comedy, francophone singers or Saint-Jean-Baptiste Day, hundreds of thousands of people flood into the streets, turning events into warm public gatherings.

There is no doubt that Montréal is a big city that has remained on a human scale. For while its towering glass and concrete silhouette give it the appearance of a North American metropolis, Montréal has trouble hiding the fact that it is primarily a city of little streets, of neighbourhoods, each with its own church, businesses, restaurants, brasseries — in short, each with its own personality, shaped over the years by the arrival of people from all corners of the globe.

Elusive and mysterious, Montréal's magic is nevertheless genuine, and is as mystical for those who experience it on a daily basis as it is for visitors immersed in it for only a few days.

History

To understand Montréal's place in the history of this continent, it is first of all necessary to consider the tremendous advantages afforded by its location. Occupying an island in the St. Lawrence River, the main route into northeastern North America, Montréal lies at the point where maritime traffic encounters its first major obstacle, a series of rapids known as the Rapides de Lachine or Lachine Rapids. From a commercial point of view, this geographical quirk worked to Montréal's advantage for many years, forcing vessels travelling on the river to stop here for transshipment. The city's commercial calling was further reinforced by the proximity of a number of other important waterways, guaranteeing it privileged access to the riches of an immense hinterland. These assets, moreover, have greatly favoured Montréal's growth and evolution throughout its history.

Origins

Before the regional balance was disrupted by the arrival of European explorers, what is known today as the island of Montréal was inhabited by the Iroquois nation. These people had probably recognized the location's exceptional qualities, which enabled them to flourish by dominating the St. Lawrence valley and by playing the role of commercial intermediary for the entire region.

In 1535 and 1541, Jacques Cartier, a navigator from Saint-Malo in the service of the king of France, became the first European to briefly explore the island. He took the opportunity to climb the mountain rising up out of its centre, which he christened Mont Royal. (Following Jacques Cartier's 1535 voyage, an Italian named Giovanni Battista Ramusio,

born in 1485, analysed Cartier's discoveries and published *Delle Navigationo et Viaggi* in 1556, a work which included a map called *La Terra de Hochelaga nella Nova Francia* of the surroundings of Mont Royal, which he translated in Italian as *Monte Real*, the origins of "Montréal.") In his ship's log, Cartier also mentioned a short visit to a large aboriginal village apparently located on the side of the mountain. Inhabited by approximately 1,500 Iroquoian people, this village consisted of about 50 large dwellings protected by a high wooden palisade.

All around, the villagers cultivated corn, squash and beans, thus meeting most of the dietary needs of their sedentary population. Unfortunately, Cartier left only a partial and sometimes contradictory account of this community, and thus even today the exact location of the village, as well as the name by which the Iroquois referred to it (Hochelaga or Tutonaguy?), remain unknown. Another enduring mystery that still gives rise to much specula-

Portrait

JACQUES CARTIER
1534

tion is the astonishing and rapid disappearance of this village after Cartier's visits. Some 70 years later, in 1603, when Samuel de Champlain travelled through the region, he found no trace of the Iroquoian community Cartier had spoken of. The most popular hypothesis is that the aboriginal people of the island of Montréal had, in the meantime, fallen victim to trade rivals and finally been driven from the island.

Be that as it may, Champlain, the founder of New France, quickly took an interest in the location's potential. In 1611, just three years after founding Québec City, he ordered that an area be cleared on the island. He viewed this spot, named Place Royale, as the starting point of a new colony or an outpost for the fur trade. The project had to be postponed, however, since at the time the French, allied with the Algonquins and Hurons, had to cope with attacks by the Five Nations of the Iroquois Confederacy . Supported by the merchants of New Amsterdam (which

Paul de Chomedey, Sieur de Maisonneuve

would later become New York), the Confederation was trying to seize complete control of the fur trade. The founding of Montréal was thus delayed for a number of years, and is not attributable to the efforts of Samuel de Champlain, who died in 1635.

Ville-Marie (1642-1665)

The fur trade was the primary reason for the French colonization of Canada in those years; however, it does not appear to have been at the origin of the founding of Montréal. The city, initially christened Ville-Marie, was established by a group of pious French men and women strongly influenced by the Jesuits' accounts of their time in America, as well as by the currents of religious revival then affecting Europe. Driven by idealism, they wanted to establish a small colony on the island, in hopes of converting natives and creating a new Christian society.

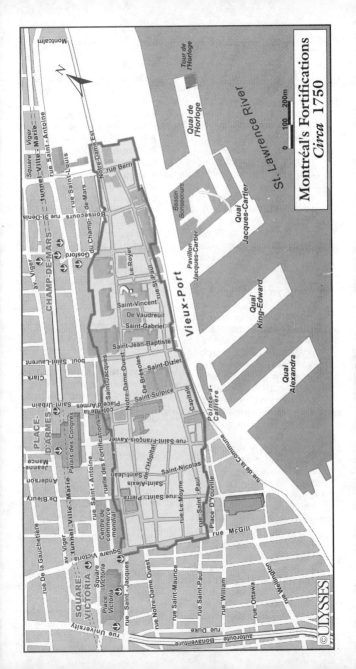

Montréal's Fortifications
Circa 1750

Paul de Chomedey, Sieur de Maisonneuve, was chosen to see this venture through, and was later designated governor of the new colony.

Heading an expedition of about 50 people, including Jeanne Mance, de Maisonneuve arrived in America in 1641 and founded Ville-Marie in May of the following year. From the beginning, a great effort was made to hasten the construction of the social and religious institutions that would form the heart of the town. In 1645, work was begun on the Hôtel-Dieu, the hospital Jeanne Mance had dreamed about. A few years later, the first school was opened, under the direction of Marguerite Bourgeoys. The year 1657 was marked by the arrival of the first priests from the Séminaire de Saint-Sulpice in Paris, who subsequently, and for many years to come, had a decisive influence on the city's development. Ironically, the primary goal behind the founding of Ville-Marie, the conversion of the Iroquois, had to be quickly abandoned or at least set aside for a certain period of time. In fact, just one year after their arrival, the French had to confront the Iroquois, who feared that the presence of colonists would

disrupt the fur trade and put them at a disadvantage.

Before long, a permanent state of war set in, threatening the very survival of the colony several times. Finally, however, after nearly a quarter-century of hanging by only a thread, the colony was provided with military protection by King Louis XIV, who had been governing New France himself for two years. From that point on, Ville-Marie, which had already come to be known as Montréal, began to flourish.

Fur Trade (1665-1760)

Although the church hierarchy still maintained its authority, and the spiritual vocation of the town endured in people's minds, the protection afforded by the royal administration enabled Montréal to prosper as a military and commercial centre from 1665 on. The arrival of French troops and the relative "pacification" of the Iroquois that ensued, especially from 1701 on with the signing of the Montréal peace treaty, finally made it possible to capitalize on the town's advantages as far as the fur trade was concerned. Since Montréal was the town located farthest up the St. Lawrence River, it soon surpassed Quebec City as the hub of this lucrative commerce. In addition, more and more young Montrealers called *coureurs des bois* were leaving the city and venturing deep into the hinterland to negotiate directly with native fur suppliers.

Legalized in 1681, this practice gradually became more organized and hierarchical, and the *coureurs des bois* became for the most part paid employees of important Montréal merchants. Montréal, located at the gateway to the continent, also served as the starting point for France's intensive exploration of North America. French expeditions, notably those led by Jolliet, Marquette, La Salle and La Vérendrye, kept pushing the borders of New France further and further. Pierre Le Moyne d'Iberville founded Louisiana in 1699 on one of these expeditions. In those years, France claimed the major part of present-day North America, an immense territory that enabled France to contain the expansion of the much more densely populated English colonies in the south, between the Atlantic and the Appalachians.

Supported by the royal administration, Montréal continued to grow slowly throughout this period. In 1672, a map was created, delimiting for the first time a number of the city's streets, the most important being Rue Notre-Dame and Rue Saint-Paul. Then, between 1717 and 1741, the wooden palisade surrounding the city was replaced by a stone wall over 5m high to reinforce the city's defences. While the populations grew somewhat slowly, it nevertheless spread beyond the areas outside the enclosure from the 1730s on. A clear social distinction gradually developed between the residents of these areas and those of the city centre, where, after a number of devastating fires, only stone buildings were permitted. The core of the city, protected by walls, was occupied mainly by members of the local aristocracy, wealthy merchants and social and religious institutions, while the outlying areas were inhabited primarily by artisans and peasants.

With its numerous multi-story stone houses, the centre of Montréal already had the appearance and atmosphere of a peaceful little French city by the middle of the 18th century.

The Seven Years' War, which raged through Europe between 1756 and 1763, was to have enormous repercussions in

Important Dates in Montréal's History

5th century: Nomadic tribes settle in the valley of the St. Lawrence and on the island known today as Montréal.

1535: On his second voyage to North America, Jacques Cartier sails up the river to the island of Montréal, where he visits an Amerindian village and climbs the mountain, naming it Mont Royal.

1642: Under the command of Paul de Chomedey, Sieur de Maisonneuve, a French colony, originally named Ville-Marie, is founded on the island. This small community survives with great difficulty for nearly a quarter of a century, and very quickly abandons its initial plans to convert the Amerindians to Christianity.

1672: The main roads of Montréal, a city whose survival is now assured, are delineated for the first time.

1701: The French and Amerindians sign a treaty, ushering in a period of peace and thus fostering the development of a fur trade centred around Montréal.

1760: Like Québec City the previous year, Montréal falls into the hands of British troops. The fate of the city and its inhabitants is drastically altered as a result.

1775-1776: While the American Revolution rages in the United States, an American army occupies Montréal for several months.

1831: Montréal surpasses Québec City in terms of population, thereby becoming the main urban centre in Canada.

1837: Riots break out in Montréal, with the Fils de la Liberté (Sons of Liberty), a movement made up of young French Canadians, opposing the Doric Club, composed of loyal British subjects.

1867: Canadian Confederation expands the domestic market, which, in the following years, is very beneficial to Montréal's development and industrialization.

1874: Creation of Parc du Mont-Royal, laid out by Frederick Law Olmsted, who designed New York's Central Park.

1911: Due to recent immigration, 10% of Montréal's population is of neither British nor French extraction.

1951: Montréal's population surpasses 1,000,000, not including the rapidly expanding suburbs.

1966: Inauguration of the Métro.

1967: The City of Montréal organizes the successful World Fair, Expo '67.

1970: In October, a crisis breaks out when the Front de Libération du Québec (FLQ) kidnaps British diplomat James Cross and minister Pierre Laporte. The Canadian government reacts by enforcing martial law, and the Canadian army takes up position in Montréal.

1976: The summer Olympic Games are held in Montréal.

1992: Montréal vibrantly celebrates the 350th anniversary of its founding.

Portrait

America, which quickly became a battlefield. The cities of Québec, in 1759, and Montréal, the following year, fell into the hands of British troops. And when the war ended in Europe, France officially ceded control of almost all its North American possessions to England under the Treaty of Paris, thereby signing New France's death sentence. The fate of Montréal and its francophone population, numbering 5,733 inhabitants, was significantly altered as a result.

chants of Scottish extraction who would go on to form the Northwest Company in 1787. In 1775-1776, the city was invaded once again, this time by American troops, who only stayed for a few months. It was therefore at the end of the American Revolution that Montréal and other parts of Canada were faced with the first large waves of English-speaking immigrants, made up of Loyalists (American colonists wishing to maintain their allegiance to the British Crown).

Transitional Years (1763-1850)

The first decades after the conquest (1760) were characterized by an atmosphere of uncertainty for the city's community. First of all, despite the return of a civilian government in 1764, French-speaking citizens continued to be edged out and excluded from the Public Administration and higher realms of decision-making, until 1774, when control of the lucrative fur trade passed into the hands of the conquerors, particularly a small group of mer-

Later, from 1815 on, these individuals were followed by large numbers of newcomers from the British Isles, especially Ireland, which at the time was severely stricken by famine. The French-Canadian population, meanwhile was growing at a remarkable pace, due to a very high birth rate. This rapid increase in the Canadian population had a positive effect on Montréal's economy as the urban and rural areas grew more and more dependent upon one another. The rapidly expanding rural areas, particularly in the part of the territory that would later become Ontario, formed a lucrative market for all sorts of products manufactured in Montréal. The country's agricultural production, particularly wheat, which inevitably passed through the port of Montréal before being shipped to Great Britain, ensured the growth of the city's port activities. And then in the 1820s, an old dream was realized with the inauguration of a canal that made it possible to bypass the Lachine rapids.

In fact, Montréal's economy was already so diversified by that time that it was barely affected when, in 1821, the Hudson's Bay Company took over the Northwest Company, which had represented the city's interests in the fur trade until then. For many years the mainspring of Montréal's economy, the fur trade had become but one industry among many.

During the 1830s, Montréal earned the title of the most populated city in the country, surpassing Quebec City. A massive influx of English-speaking colonists disrupted the balance between French and English, and for 35 years, starting in 1831, there was an anglophone majority in Montréal. Furthermore, the different ethnic communities had already started to group together in a pattern

that would endure for many years to come: the francophones mainly in the east end of the city, the Irish in the southwest and the Anglo-Scottish in the west. These various ethnic groups did not, however, share the territory without problems. When the Patriote rebellions broke out in 1837-1838, Montréal became the scene of violent confrontations between the members of the Doric Club, composed of loyal British subjects, and the Fils de la Liberté (Sons of Liberty), made up of young francophones. It was actually after an inter-ethnic riot, leading to a fire that destroyed the parliament building, that Montréal lost its six-year-old title of capital of United Canada in 1849.

Although Montréal's urban landscape did not undergo any major changes during the first years of the English Regime, British-style buildings gradually began to appear in the 1840s. It was also at this time that the city's wealthiest merchants, mainly of Anglo-Scottish descent, abandoned little by little the Saint-Antoine neighbourhood and settled at the foot of Mont Royal. From that point on, less than a century after the conquest (1760), the British presence was an undeniable part of the city's make-up. It was also at this time that a crucial phase of Montréal's development began.

Industrialization and Economic Power (1850-1914)

Montréal experienced the most important period of growth in its history from the second half of the 19th century until World War I, thanks to rapid industrialization that began in the 1840s and continued in waves. From then on, the city ranked as Canada's undisputed metropolis, and became the country's true centre of development.

The broadening of Canada's internal market — first with the creation of United Canada in 1840 and then, most importantly, the advent of Canadian Confederation in 1867 — reinforced Montréal's industrial sector, whose products were increasingly replacing imports. The main forces that would long lie at the heart of the city's economy were the shoe, clothing, textile and food industries, as well as certain heavy industries, particularly rolling stock and iron and steel products. The geographical concentration of these activities near the port facilities and railroad tracks significantly altered the city's appearance.

The area around the Lachine Canal, the cradle of Canada's industrial revolution, followed by the Sainte-Marie and Hochelaga neighbourhoods, filled up with factories and then inexpensive housing intended for workers. The industrialization of Montréal was intensified by the city's advantageous position as a transportation and communications hub for the entire Canadian territory, a position it worked to strengthen throughout this period. For example, starting in the 1850s, a channel was dug in the river between Montréal and Quebec City, thus enabling larger ships to go upriver to the metropolis, thereby eliminating most of the advantages enjoyed by Quebec City's port.

The rail network which was beginning to extend over the Canadian territory also benefitted Montréal by making the city the centre of its activities. Montréal's industries enjoyed privileged access to the markets of southern Québec and Ontario via the Grand Trunk network, and the west of the country via that of Canadian Pacific, which reached Vancouver in 1866. As far as both domestic and international trade were concerned, Montréal occupied a dominant position in the country during this period.

The city's rapid growth was equally exceptional from a demographic point of view; between 1852 and 1911, the population went from 58,000 to 468,000 (528,000 including the suburbs). This remarkable increase was due to the huge pull of the booming city. The massive waves of immigration from the British Isles, which had begun in the early 19th century, continued for several more years before slowing down appreciably during the 1860s. This deceleration was then amply compensated for by an exodus of peasants from the Québec countryside, attracted to Montréal by the work offered in its factories. The arrival of this mainly francophone population

also led to a new reversal of the balance between French and English in Montréal. By 1866, the population became, and remains to this day, mainly francophone.

An entirely new phenomenon began to take shape toward the end of the 19th century, when Montréal started attracting immigrants from places other than France and the British Isles. Initially, those who came in the greatest numbers were Eastern European Jews fleeing persecution in their own countries. At first, they grouped together mainly along Boulevard Saint-Laurent. A considerable number of Italians also settled in Montréal, mostly, for their part, in the northern section of the city. Thanks to these waves of immigration, Montréal already had a

Lachine Canal

decidedly multiethnic character by 1911, with more than 10% of its population of neither British nor French extraction.

The urbanization resulting from this population growth caused the city to spread out further, a phenomenon promoted by the creation of a streetcar network in 1892. The city thus expanded beyond its old limits on a number of occasions, annexing up to 31 new territories between 1883 and 1918. At the same time, efforts were being made to lay out areas where Montrealers could spend leisure time, such as Parc du Mont-Royal (1874) (see p 166). As far as residential construction was concerned, British-inspired styles were most prevalent, notably in working-class neighbourhoods, where row houses with flat roofs and brick fronts would predominate from then on.

Furthermore, in order to offer low-cost housing to working-class families, these buildings more frequently had two or three stories and were designed to accommodate at least that many families. Affluent Montrealers were increasingly settling on the sides of Mont Royal, in a neighbourhood that would soon be known as the Golden Square Mile, due to the great wealth of its residents. The industrial revolution had, for that matter, increased the socio-economic divisions within Montréal society. This phenomenon separated the main ethnic groups involved in an almost dichotomous fashion, since the upper middle class was almost entirely made up of Anglo-Protestants, while the majority of unspecialized workers consisted of French and Irish Catholics.

Between the Two Wars

From 1914 to 1945, a number of international-scale events hindered the city's growth and evolution. First of all, with the start of World War I in 1914, Montréal's economy stagnated due to a drop in investments. It regained strength very quickly, however, thanks to the exportation of agricultural products and military equipment to Great Britain. These years, however, were marked above all in Montréal by a political battle waged between anglophones and francophones on the subject of the war.

Francophones had mixed feelings about the British Empire and therefore protested at length against any Canadian participation in the British war effort. They were therefore fiercely opposed to the conscription of Canadian citizens. Anglophones, many of whom still had very strong ties with Great Britain, were in favour of Canada's full involvement. When, in 1917, the Canadian government finally made a decision and imposed conscription, the francophones exploded with anger, and Montréal was shaken by intense inter-ethnic tensions.

The war was followed by a few years of economic re-adjustment, and then the Roaring Twenties, a period of sustained growth stretching from 1921 to 1929. During this time, development in Montréal picked up where it had left off before the war, and the city maintained its role as Canada's metropolis. Toronto, however, thanks to American investment and the development of Western Canada, was already starting to claim a more important place for itself. Taller and taller buildings with designs reflecting American architectural trends gradually began to appear in Montréal's business centre. The city's population also started growing again, so much so that by the end of the 1920s, there were over 800,000 people living in Montréal, while the population of the island as a whole had already ex-

ceeded 1,000,000. Due to both the size of its population and the appearance of its business centre, therefore, Montréal already had all the attributes of a major North American city.

The crisis that struck the world economy in 1929 had a devastating effect on Montréal, a good part of whose wealth was based on exports. For an entire decade, poverty was widespread in the city, where up to a third of the population of working age was unemployed. This dark period did not end until the beginning of World War II in 1939. From the start of this conflict, however, the controversy surrounding the war effort was rekindled, once again dividing the city's francophone and anglophone populations. The mayor of Montréal, Camillien Houde, who was opposed to conscription, was imprisoned between 1940 and 1944. Ultimately, Canada became fully involved in the war, putting its industrial production and army of conscripts at Great Britain's disposition.

Renewed Growth (1945-1960)

After so many years of rationing and unfavourable upheavals, Montréal's economy emerged from the war

Portrait

stronger and more diversified than ever. What followed was a prosperous period during which the population's consumer demands could be met. For more than a decade, unemployment was almost non-existent in Montréal, and the overall standard of living improved radically. The growth of the Montréal urban area was equally remarkable from a demographic point of view, so much so that between 1941 and 1961, the population practically doubled, going from 1,140,000 to 2,110,000, while the population of the city itself passed the 1,000,000 mark in 1951. This population explosion had several causes. First of all, the century-old exodus of rural inhabitants to the city, more widespread than ever, resumed after coming to an almost complete halt during the Great Depression and World War II.

Immigration also recommenced, the largest groups now arriving from southern Europe, especially Italy and Greece. Finally, the increase in Montréal's population was also due to a sharp rise in the number of births, a veritable baby boom, which affected Québec as much as it did the rest of North America. To meet the housing needs of this population, neighbourhoods located slightly on the outskirts of the city were quickly covered with thousands of new homes. In addition, suburbs even further removed from the downtown area emerged, fostered by the popularity of the automobile as an object of mass consumption. Suburbs also began developing off the island on the south shore of the river, around the access bridges, and to the north, on Île Jésus, now known as Laval. At the same time, downtown Montréal underwent some important changes, as the business section gradually shifted from Vieux-Montréal to the area around Boulevard René-Lévesque (formerly Boulevard Dorchester), where ever more imposing skyscrapers were springing up.

During this same period, the city was affected by a wave of social reforms aiming, in particular, at putting an end to the "reign of the underground." For years, Montréal had had a well-deserved reputation as a place where prostitution and gambling clubs flourished, thanks to the blind-eye of some corrupt police officers and politicians. A public inquiry conducted between 1950 and 1954, during which lawyers Pacifique Plante and Jean Drapeau stood out in particular, led to a series of convictions and a significant improvement in the social climate. At the same time, a desire for change manifested itself in the strong protest by Montréal's francophone intellectuals, journalists and artists against the all-powerful Catholic Church and the pervading conservatism of the times. However, the most striking phenomenon of this period remained French-speaking Montrealers' nascent awareness of their socio-economic alienation. Indeed, over the years, save certain exceptions, a very clear socio-economic split had developed between the city's two main groups. Francophones earned lower average incomes than their anglophone colleagues, were more likely to hold subordinate positions and their attempts at climbing the social ladder were mocked. And though the francophone population formed a large majority, Montréal projected the image of an Anglo-Saxon city, due to its commercial signs and the supremacy of the English language in the main spheres of economic activity. Nevertheless, it wasn't until the early 1960s that the desire for change evolved into a series of accelerated transformations.

From 1960 to Today

The 1960s were marked by an unprecedented reform movement in Québec, a veritable race for modernization and change, which soon became known as the Quiet Revolution. Québec francophones, particularly those in Montréal, where the opposition between the two main ethnic groups was strongest, clearly expressed their desire to put an end to the anglophone minority's control over the province's societal development. A battery of changes were initiated with this aim in view. At the same time, the nationalist movement and its push for independence or increased political sovereignty for Québec, found very fertile ground in Montréal. The most important demonstrations in support of this cause were held there. It was also in Montréal that the **Front de Libération du Québec** (FLQ), a small cell of extremists wishing to "accelerate the decolonization of Québec," was most active.

Starting in 1963, the FLQ carried out a series of terrorist attacks in the city. Then, in October of 1970, a major political crisis broke out when certain members of the FLQ kidnapped British diplomat James Cross and Québec cabinet minister Pierre Laporte. On the pretext of curbing a dreaded climate of revolt, the federal government, headed by Pierre Elliot Trudeau, reacted quickly, enforcing martial law. The Canadian army took up position in Montréal, thousands of searches were conducted and hundreds of innocent people imprisoned. The crisis finally ended when James Cross's kidnappers obtained a safe-conduct to Cuba — not, however, before Pierre Laporte was found dead. The reaction of the Canadian government was harshly judged by many, who did not hesitate to accuse it of having used the political context not only to bring the FLQ under control, but above all to try to halt the rise of the nationalist movement in Québec.

Be that as it may, over the years, the francophone majority made its presence felt more audibly in Montréal. Furthermore, the image projected by the city changed noticeably when successive provincial governments adopted language laws requiring commercial signs, which had up until then been in English, or at best in both languages, to be written entirely in French. For many anglophones, however, these laws, combined with the rise of nationalism and en-

trepreneurship in Québec, were changes too difficult to accept, and a number of them left Montréal for good.

At the same time, Montréal, whose mayor in those years was Jean Drapeau, shone brightly on the international scene as it played host to a number of large-scale events, the most noteworthy being the 1967 World's Fair (Expo '67), the 1976 Summer Olympic Games and the 1980 Floralies Internationales (International Flower Show).

From an economic standpoint, Montréal underwent profound changes with the decline of many branches of activity that had shaped its industrial structure for over a century. These were then partially replaced by massive investments in such leading industries as aeronautics, computers and pharmaceutical products. In the mid-1960s, Montréal was also stripped of its title of Canadian metropolis by Toronto, which had been growing at a faster pace for several decades. The growing prominence of skyscrapers downtown, however, proved that Montréal's economy was nevertheless continuing to grow.

The city's population also increased, so much so that the number of inhabitants in the Montréal urban area reached about 3,000,000. This growth was mostly in the suburbs, however, which were becoming far removed from the city centre, while the population of the city of Montréal itself stagnated at around 1,000,000. Furthermore, with the influx of immigrants from around the world over the previous decades, Montréal became an increasingly complex, cultural mosaic. More than ever, it had become a true international crossroads, while remaining the North American metropolis of French culture.

Language Question

The coexistence of two distinct cultural ideologies is one of the most fundamental elements of Montréal's makeup. More than anywhere else in Québec or Canada, two language communities, francophone and anglo-phone share the same territory, the same city.

Montréal's language paradox is in fact much more complex than it seems, and has apparently been that way since the British Conquest of 1760. Visiting Montréal at the beginning of the 19th century, Alexis de Toqueville was surprised to observe the almost complete absence of the French language in public affairs

and commerce. In fact, although francophones have always been in the majority in Montréal, except for a short period in the middle of the last century, the city projected an image almost as typically Anglo-Saxon as London, Toronto or New York for nearly 200 years. On business signs, in downtown department stores or during encounters, unexpected or not, between anglophones and francophones, the English language triumphed. Eventually, however, a new awareness on the part of francophones led to bitter disputes during the 1960s and initiated the process of restoring French to favour in Montréal.

Later, when Québec governments instituted a battery of language laws, including the thenceforward famous (or infamous) Bill 101 in 1977, the presence of the French language grew stronger in Montréal.

The "Frenchifying" of the city did not, however, take place without greatly offending the sensibilities of the anglophone minority, who saw a complete disregard for their rights. Many anglophones left Montréal in the mid-1970s, while activists denounced certain provisions of Québec's language laws, particularly those requiring business signs to be written in French only (today amended) and the mandatory integration of children of new arrivals into French schools.

However, despite appearances, things are far from being as simple as some people would like to believe; the anglophone community feels threatened, but francophones still find themselves in a fairly precarious situation. The English language is still alive and well in Montréal. Downtown, for example, in the very heart of what people often like to refer to as the second largest francophone city in the world after Paris, English is used just as often as French. You have to venture farther east or north in the city to truly feel the francophone majority in Montréal. Though the anglophone community still succeeds in integrating many of the new arrivals into its world, the provincial government's efforts to reverse this trend are starting to have an impact. Since English is *the* international language, and is spoken by 98% of North Americans, its attraction as a means of cultural integration into North American society is tremendous. Convincing new residents of Québec to adopt French as a second language can be quite a challenge in this context.

In their own way, therefore, Montréal's francophones and anglophones share the same fear — that of disappearing. Under circumstances such as these, how can Montréal, and Québec for that matter, maintain a balance between French and English that is acceptable to everyone? This question, which has been posed countless times, has yet to be answered and presumably won't be by means of simple principles. Montréal's bilingual population has always played a crucial role in this debate, so, until the issue is resolved the precarious balance that exists between English- and French-speakers will continue.

Economy and Politics

Harshly affected over the past two decades by a loss of momentum in several primary industries that had long been the driving force behind its growth and wealth, Montréal's economy has neither the panache nor the power it once did. Many factories, some true symbols of Montréal's strength, have been swept away by technological changes or are quite simply only shadows of their former selves. And despite the growth of a number of other industries, particularly those related to high technology, the effects of this massive deindustrialization have not yet been entirely absorbed. This is revealed by statistics relating to the unemployment rate of some neighbourhoods, where almost a quarter of the population is out of work. These difficulties, reinforced by the middle-class exodus to the suburbs, a trend which has continued steadily since the 1950s, now project an image of a city leaning toward impoverishment. Of course, Montréal is not the only city affected by these problems; they are the lot of many big North American centres. The situation, moreover, is not hopeless, since this Québec metropolis has many assets capable of revitalizing its economy: the quality of its workforce, its bilingualism, the existing infrastructures and the possibilities of research and development offered by the four universities located within its limits.

On the other hand, before discussing economic recovery, it will be necessary to consider a malaise that has long been affecting Montréal — the seemingly unattainable consensus between the principal parties involved. On a regional level, Montréal is at daggers drawn more often than it should be with the adminis-

trations of the cities on its outskirts, which it regularly accuses of not paying their fair share. Furthermore, despite its size and importance, this city, the seat of neither the federal nor provincial government, is often the victim of politicians' incomprehension and, above all, the prevailing tensions between these two levels of government, leading to the development of plans of action that are frequently incoherent or ineffective. In fact, Montréal, more than anywhere else, is both the centre of the guerilla war between Québec and Canada and its victim. As pathetic as it might seem, the city now waits for some sort of political direction to establish a more well-defined role and position for it. Should Montréal join the Canadian sphere once and for all, or become the centre of an independent Québec? According to the 1995 referendum, a majority of Montrealers still have faith in the Canadian federal system. Greater Montréal is home to nearly half of Québec's population and it was not until Montréal's majority "ño" vote was factored in that the tide began to turn on referendum night.

Montréal's Communities

Saturday night, on Rue Durocher in Outremont, dozens of Hasidic (orthodox) Jews dressed in traditional garb hurry to the nearby synagogue. A few hours earlier, as usual, a portion of Montréal's large Italian community met at Marché Jean-Talon to negotiate the purchase of products imported directly from Italy or simply to socialize with compatriots and discuss the latest soccer game between Milan and Turin. These scenes, well known to all Montrealers, are only two examples among many of the very vital community life of a number of the city's ethnic groups. In fact, Montréal's different ethnic communities have countless meeting places and associations. And one need only take a brief stroll down Boulevard Saint-Laurent, the Main, which divides the city between east and west and is lined with restaurants, grocery stores and other businesses with an international flavour, selling specialties from around the world, to be convinced of the richness and diversity of Montréal's population.

Indeed, Montréal often seems like a heterogeneous group of villages, which, without being ghettos, are mainly inhabited by members of one or another ethnic community. In fact, this sectioning of the city was initiated back in the last century by Montrealers of French and English descent — a division which still marks the

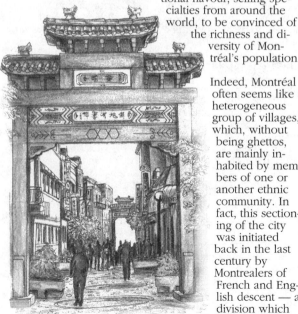

Chinatown

city to a certain degree. The east thus remains to a large extent francophone, while the west is anglophone. The most affluent members of the two communities live for the most part on opposite sides of Mont Royal, in Outremont and Westmount.

With the arrival of new people from different ethnic backgrounds, several new neighbourhoods gradually fit into this puzzle. Very early, a small Chinese community, whose members had come to work in Canada when the railroads were being built, took up residence around Rue de la Gauchetière, west of Boulevard Saint-Laurent. They created a Chinatown which still has a mysterious quality about it.

The city's large Jewish community, for its part, first gathered a little higher on Boulevard Saint-Laurent and then settled further west, particularly in certain parts of Outremont, Côte-des-Neiges and Snowdon and in the municipalities of Côte-Saint-Luc and Hampstead, where its institutions flourished.

Little Italy, often a very lively and colourful place, with its many cafés, restaurants and shops, occupies a large section in the northern part of the city, near Rue Jean-Talon and the Saint-Léonard area, where many Italians live. The Italians, for that matter, make up Montréal's largest ethnic community and add an undeniable energy to the city.

Finally, a number of other more recently established communities also tend to gather in certain areas, for example, the Greeks along Avenue du Parc, the Haitians in Montréal-Nord, the Portuguese around Rue Saint-Urbain and the Jamaicans in Griffintown. In Montréal, it seems as if you almost pass from one country to another, from one world to another, within the space of a few blocks.

Indeed, what would Montréal be without all its communities, without its famous smoked meat, a specialty developed by Eastern European Jews, or its countless little restaurants serving so-called "Canadian" cuisine, whose owners are, more often than not, Greek?

Four Seasons: As Many Faces

It is common knowledge that Montréal has at least as many different moods and personalities as there are seasons in a year. Indeed, this city truly lives in step with its often capricious climate, to which it has

Portrait

managed to adapt so well as to reap all the possible benefits the weather has to offer. In winter, for example, the season with which people most commonly identify this "Northern" city, the temperature often wavers well below freezing and tons of snow fall upon the city, yet it hardly misses a beat. This is because Montréal has become a world leader in "winter management," a veritable point of reference for a multitude of other big "cold" cities around the globe.

During the winter months, day and night, 3,000 workers are available on call to remove the approximately 6.5 million m³ of snow that, on average, obstruct the city's streets every year. To a large degree, Montrealers have also managed to circumvent the problems that can accompany a severe winter climate, notably by building an incredible underground city, one of the world's largest. Linked to one another by the métro system, these underground passageways, which cover almost 30km, make it possible to reach all sorts of office buildings, stores, restaurants, bars, hotels, cinemas, theatres and residential high-rises — without ever having to step outside! In short, be it the snow or the cold, nothing slows this city down. Of course, winter doesn't only bring problems; it also offers its share of pleasures, and helps shape Montréal's character.

Transformed by winter, the urban landscape lacks neither charm nor romanticism. The season's finest days offer an opportunity to enjoy a pleasant outing under the snow-laden trees, or a delightful visit to one of the city's outdoor skating rinks. In addition, winter marks the awakening of a veritable passion, as typical of Montréal as any ever was — the love of hockey. During the professional hockey season, the performance of Montréal's famous team, the Canadiens, is the topic of many conversations. Year after year, Montrealers manage to get through the long winters, sometimes grumbling a little, but also enjoying the marvellous pleasures the season has to offer.

Then, often abruptly, winter makes way for spring, an exhilarating season when Montréal takes on the appearance of a Mediterranean city. The first days of the season are always unforgettable, when the effect of the climate upon the city's inhabitants is most evident and Montrealers, transformed by the first rays of spring sun, seem to get back in touch with their Latin roots. It is finally possible to dress in lighter clothing, sit on a terrace or roam idly through the city streets. As if emerging from long months of hibernation, the crowds rush Rue Saint-Denis, Boulevard Saint-Laurent and Parc du Mont-Royal. This short, bucolic period of the year, when Montrealers are finally able to take advantage of the beautiful parks and main streets of their city, is only a prelude to the summer season — vacation time. Come summer, there is so much to do that Montrealers often choose to vacation in their own city.

With the warm weather, Montréal comes to life, hosting numerous festivals to celebrate jazz, comedy, Francophone singers and film, not to mention the traditional Saint-Jean-Baptiste Day, leading inevitably to gatherings of hundreds of thousands of people. In summer, Montréal is not exclusive, it is wide open. The festivities continue until September; then, slowly, autumn settles in, and before fluttering to the ground, the leaves change colour, turning brilliant yellow, orange and red. But just as Montrealers prepare to bundle themselves up for another long cold winter, they are given a brief respite known as Indian Summer, just to remind them how acutely their lives are lead by Mother Nature. Thus, the cycle starts anew.

Literature

As with much of modern literature in the Americas, Québec writing began with accounts of voyages by early explorers. These texts were meant to inform Europeans about the "new" lands, and often described in detail the life of indigenous peoples. Toward the end of the 18th century and the beginning of the 19th, the oral tradition still dominated literary life in the New World. Later, the legends from this era were committed to paper, but there was no true literary movement until the end of the 19th century in Québec. At this point, some of the major themes were survival and praise for a simple, religious, country lifestyle. With few exceptions, the novels of this period are mostly of socio-historical interest.

In French

Tradition continued to be the main characteristic of Québec literature well into the 1930s, though there were several innovative writers worth noting. **Émile Nelligan**, a poet in the early 20th century, was influenced by Baudelaire, Rimbaud and Verlaine. Producing much of his work early on in life, he then sank slowly into madness, and remains a mythic figure today. Though country life remained a main feature in novels of the time, it began to be represented more realistically, as in *Maria Chapdelaine* by **Louis Hémon**.

Literary works began to evolve toward modernism during the economic crisis and the Second World War. Novels set in the city, where the majority of the population now lived, began to appear. One of the most interesting of these is set in Montréal: *Bonheur d'occasion* (*The Tin Flute*) by **Gabrielle Roy**, a franco-Manitoban. Modernism took hold at the end of the Second World War, in spite of the strict political regime of Maurice Duplessis. Novels of the time were split into two categories: urban or psychological. Poetry flourished with the emrgence of a number of great writers such as **Alain Grandbois** and **Anne Hébert**. Important works by **Gratien Gélinas** and **Marcel Dubé** marked the birth of Québec theatre.

During the Quiet Revolution, in the 1960's, political and social changes affected literary creation, thus leading to the "demarginalization" of authors. The novel experienced a golden age, and new authors began to be established: **Marie-Claire Blais**, **Hubert Aquin**, and **Réjean Ducharme**. Theatre also went through an exciting period, with the emergence of **Michel Tremblay**. Many poets, novelists and playwrights began to use *joual*, which is the spoken, popular form of Québec French.

Contemporary literature is becoming richer and more diverse. Important names on the current scene include **Alice Parizeau**, **Roch Carrier**, **Yves Beauchemin**, and **Christian Mistral**. In the 1980s, theatre became a far more important genre, with many innovative new directors, such as **André Brassard**, **Robert Lepage**, **Lorraine Pintal**, and **René-Richard Cyr** coming into their own.

Humour has also always been an important part of Québec culture, and has been integral to the societal changes. In the 1960s, the comedy troupe **Les Cyniques** (The Cynics) produced biting criticisms of the clergy and political institutions, and so did their own part for the Quiet Revolution. In the 1970s, **Yvon Deschamps** created characters who typified the exploited but nice Québec everyman, and brought about painful self-awareness in the province. The years following the referendum in the early 1980s produced humour with elements of self-deprecation and the absurd – signs of a disillusioned generation. This type of humour is typified in groups such as **Ding et Dong, Rock et Belles Oreilles**, and by comedian **Daniel Lemire**.

In English

Mordecai Richler's sharply comic prose, as salty as a smoked meat on rye, depicts life in the cold water flats and Kosher delis of mid-town Montréal in the 1950s These novels portray a neighbourhood whose face is now changed but still recognizable on certain corners, such as Clark and Fairmount.

Richler is a frequent contributor to the *New Yorker*, with his crusty and controversial accounts of Québec politics, and to out-of-towners he along with poet **Irving Layton**, gravel-throated crooner/poet **Leonard Cohen**, novelist and essayist **Hugh MacLennan** and poet and novelist **Mavis Gallant**, may be the most familiar literary voice of English Montréal. Playwright **David Fennario's** *Balconville* examines the lives of middle-class anglophones and francophones in Montréal.

In the performing arts, English Montréal's best known singer is **Corey Hart**. His *Boy in the Box* album, released in the mid-1980s, was successful throughout North America. He recently reappeared on the music scene after a break of several years. The comedic duo **Bowser & Blue** find much to laugh about in the "plight" of anglophone Montrealers.

Cinema

While some full-length films were made earlier, the birth of Québec cinema really, also centred in Montréal, did not occur until after World War II. Between 1947 and 1953, independent producers brought a number of literary adaptations to the screen, including *Un Homme et Son Péché* (1948), *Seraphin* (1949), *La Petite Aurore l'Enfant Martyre* (1951) and *Tit-Coq* (1952). However, the arrival of television in the early 1950s resulted in a ten-year period of stagnation for the Québec film industry.

A cinematic renaissance during the 1960s occurred largely thanks to the support of the National Film Board (NFB-ONF). With documentaries and realistic films, directors focused primarily on a critique of Québec society. Later, the full-length feature film dominated with the success of certain directors like Claude Jutras (*Mon Oncle Antoine*, 1971), Jean-Claude Lord (*Les Colombes*, 1972), Gilles Carle (*La Vraie Nature de Bernadette*, 1972), Michel Brault (*Les Ordres*, 1974), Jean Beaudin (*J.A. Martin Photographe*, 1977) and Frank Mankiewicz (*Les Bons Débarras*, 1979). The NFB-ONF and other government agencies provided most of the funding for these largely uncommercial works.

Import feature films of recent years include those of Denys Arcand (*Le déclin de l'Empire américain*, 1986, and *Jésus de Montréal*, 1989, both available in English),

Jean-Claude Lauzon (*Un zoo la nuit*, 1987, and *Léolo*, 1992), Léa Pool (*À corps perdu*, 1988), Jean Beaudin (*Being at Home With Claude*, 1992) and François Girard (*The Red Violin*, 1998). Director Frédérick Back won an Academy Award in 1988 for his superbly animated film, *The Man who Planted Trees*.

Daniel Langlois has also made significant contributions to Québec cinema. A key player in the film industry, he has been very involved in the development of film centres and festivals. He founded Softimage, which designs special effects software that has been used in several well-known feature-length films over the past several years.

In addition to being the home of a booming moviemaking industry, Montréal has been featured in several feature-length films, mostly from the United States. International producers and directors choose Montréal because it is a beautiful city with skilled professionals and excellent services. So next time you watch a film, whether it is set in Boston or Munich, you might spot a part of Montréal!

Practical Information

There are 28 municipalities on the island of Montréal, which measures 32km at its longest point and 16km at its widest.

Montréal proper, with a population of about one million, is the main urban area in the Communauté Urbaine de Montréal (Montréal Urban Community), which encompasses all of the boroughs on the island. Greater Montréal also includes the Rive-Sud (South Shore), Laval and the Rive-Nord (North Shore), for a grand total of 3,200,000 inhabitants. The downtown area runs along the St. Lawrence, south of Mont Royal (234m), which is one of the seven hills of the Montérégie region.

Information in this chapter will help visitors better plan their trip to Montréal.

Area Codes

The area Code for Montréal is **514**.

The city's surrounding areas, which previously used the same code, were assigned the area code **450** in June 1998. Altough you must include the area code when dialing, you do not incur long-distance charges when calling between the two regions.

Entrance Formalities

Passport

A valid passport is usually sufficient for most visitors planning to stay less than three months; visas are not required. A three-month extension is possible, but a return ticket and proof of sufficient funds to cover this extension may be required.

Caution: some countries do not have an agreement with Canada concerning health and accident insurance, so it is advisable to have the appropriate coverage. For more information, see the section entitled "Health" (p 64).

European citizens who want to enter the United States will need a visa. It is best to apply for this visa from home, although it is obtainable at the border, usually without problems.

Extended Visits

Visitors must submit their request **in writing** and **before** the expiration of their visa (the date is usually written in your passport) to an Immigration Canada office. To make a request, you must have a valid passport, a return ticket, proof of sufficient funds to cover the stay, as well as the $65 non-refundable filing fee. In some cases (work, study), however, the request must be made **before** arriving in Canada.

Embassies and Consulates

Abroad

AUSTRALIA
Canadian Consulate General
5th Level, Quay West Bldg.
111 Harrington St.
Sydney, N.S.W. 2000, Australia
☎*(612) 364-3000*
⁼*(612) 364-3098*

BELGIUM
Canadian Embassy
Avenue de Tervueren, 2
1040 Brussels, Belgium
☎*2.741.06.11*
⁼*2.741.06.43*
Métro Mérode

DENMARK
Canadian Embassy
Kr. Bernikowsgade 1
DK-1105 Copenhagen K
Denmark
☎ *33.48.32.00*
⇌ *33.48.32.20*

FINLAND
Canadian Embassy
Pohjos Esplanadi 25 B
00100 Helsinki, Finland
☎ *17.11.41*
⇌ *60.10.60*

GERMANY
Canadian Embassy
Friedrich-Wilhelm Strasse 18
53113 Bonn, Germany
☎ *(49) 228 9680*

Canadian Consulate General
Internationales, Handelzentrum
Friedrichstrasse 95, 23rd Floor
10117 Berlin, Germany
☎ *261.11.61*
⇌ *262.92.06*

GREAT BRITAIN
Canada High Commission
Macdonald House
1 Grosvenor Square
London W1X 0AB, England
☎ *258-6600*
⇌ *258-6333*

NETHERLANDS
Parkstraat 25
2514 JD The Hague, Netherlands
☎ *361.41.11*

NORWAY
Canadian Embassy
Wergelandsveien 7,1244 Oslo, Norway
☎ *22.99.53.00*
⇌ *22.99.53.01*

SPAIN
Canadian Embassy
Edificio Goya
Calle Núñez de Balboa 35,
Madrid 28001
☎ *91.423.32.50*
⇌ *91.423.32.51*
www.canada-es.org

SWEDEN
Canadian Embassy
Tegelbacken 4, 7th floor
Stockholm, Sweden
☎ *(08) 453-3000*
⇌ *(08) 24 24 91*

SWITZERLAND
Canadian Embassy
Kirchenfeldstrasse 88, 3005 Berne 6
☎ *357.32.00*
⇌ *357.32.10*

UNITED STATES
Canadian Embassy
501 Pennsylvania Ave., NW
Washington DC, 20001
☎ *(202) 682-1740*
⇌ *(202) 682-7721*

Canadian Consulate General
1175 Peachtree St. N.W.
100 Colony Sq., Suite 1700
Atlanta, GA 30361-6205
☎ *(404) 532-2000*
⇌ *(404) 532-2050*
atnta@dfait-maeci.gc.ca

Canadian Consulate General
3 Copley Pl., Suite 400
Boston, MA 02116
☎ *(617) 262-3760*
⇌ *(617) 262-3415*
http://www.boston.gc.ca

Practical
Information

Canadian Consulate General
Two Prudential Plaza
180 N. Stetson Ave., Suite 2400,
Chicago, IL 60601
☎ *(312) 616-1860*
= *(312) 616-1877*
http://www.canadachicago.net

Canadian Consulate General
St. Paul Pl., 750 N. St. Paul St.,
Suite 1700, Dallas, TX 75201
☎ *(214) 922-9806*
= *(214) 922-9815*

Canadian Consulate General
600 Renaissance Center, Suite 1100
Detroit, MI 48234-1798
☎ *(313) 567-2340*
= *(313) 567-2164*

Canadian Consulate General
550 S. Hope St., 9th Floor
Los Angeles, CA 90071-2627
☎ *(213) 346-2700*
= *(213) 620-8827*
http://www.cdnconsulat-la.com

Canadian Consulate General
701 Fourth Ave. S., Suite 900
Minneapolis, MN 55415-1899
☎ *(612) 332-4641*
= *(612) 332-4061*
http://www.dfait-maeci.gc.ca/min
neapolis

Canadian Consulate General
1251 Ave. of the Americas, Concourse
Level, New York, NY 10020-1175
☎ *(212) 596-1628*
= *(212) 596-1790*
http://Canada-ny.org

Canadian Consulate General
One Marine Midland Center
Suite 3000, Buffalo, NY 14203-2884
☎ *(716) 858-9500*
= *(716) 852-4340*

http://www.canada-congenbuffalo.org

Canadian Consulate General
412 Plaza 600
Sixth and Stewart sts.
Seattle, Washington, 98101-1286
☎ *(206) 443-1777*
= *(206) 443-9662*

Canadian Consulate General
200 South Biscayne Blvd., Suite 1600
Miami, Fla 33131
☎ *(305) 579-1600*
= *(305) 374-6774*

In Montréal

Consulate General of the United States of America
Place Félix-Martin
1155 Rue Saint-Alexandre
Montréal
☎ *(514) 398-9695*
= *(514) 398-9748*

Australian High Commission
(no office in Montréal)
50 O'Connor Street, Suite 710
Ottawa, Ontario K1P 6L2
☎ *(613) 236-0841*
= *(613) 236-4376*

Consulate General of Belgium
999 Blvd. de Maisonneuve Ouest
suite 1250
Montréal H3A 3C8
☎ *(514) 849-7394*
= *(514)844-3170*

Consulate General of Great Britain
1000 De La Gauchetière Ouest
Suite 4200
Montréal, H3B 3A7
☎ *(514) 866-5863*
= *(514) 866-0202*

**Consulate General of
Federal Republic of Germany**
1250 Boulevard René-Lévesque Ouest
41st Floor, Marathon Building
Montréal, H3B 4X1
☎*(514) 931-2277*
⇰ *(514) 931-7239*

**Consulate General of the
Netherlands**
1002 Rue Sherbrooke Ouest,
Suite 2201, Montréal H3A 3L6
☎*(514) 849-4247*
⇰ *(514) 849-8260*

Consulate General of Norway
1155 Boulevard René-Lévesque Ouest
suite 3900, Montréal, H3B 3V2
☎*(514) 874-9087*

Consulate General of Sweden
8400 Boulevard Décarie
Montréal, H4P 2N2
☎*(514) 345-2727*
⇰ *(514) 345-7972*

**Consulate General of
Switzerland**
1572 Avenue Dr Penfield
Montréal H3G 1C4
☎*(514) 932-7181*
⇰ *(514) 932-9028*

Tourist Information

Tourist information is available from Tourisme Québec through the offices of the Délégation Générale du Québec located abroad, and from the tourist offices in Montréal. See below for the addresses:

Tourisme Québec
Case postale 979
Montréal H3C 2W3
☎*(514) 987-2015*
☎*800-363*-7777
⇰ *(514) 864-3838*
www.tourisme.gouv.qc.ca

Tourisme Québec
Abroad

Belgium
Avenue des Arts, 46
7th floor
1000 Bruxelles
☎*512.00.36*
⇰ *514.26.41*

Canada
Québec Government Office
20 Queen St. W.
Suite 1504
Toronto, Ontario
M5H 3S3
☎*(416) 977-6060*
⇰ *(416) 596-1407*

Germany
Canada Tourismus programm
Postfach 200 247
63469 Maintal 2
☎*49 6181 45178*
⇰ *49 6181 497558*

United States
Tours & Travel
140W 69th St.
New York, N.Y.
10023-5107
☎*(718) 579-8401*

**Practical
Information**

Switzerland
Welcome to Canada!
22, Freihofstrasse
8700 Küsnacht
☎ *910.90.01*
≈ *910.38.24*

Information
in Montréal

Centre Infotouriste
1001 Rue du Square-Dorchester
Métro Peel
☎ *873-2015*

The centre is open every day from 8:30am to 7:30pm from June 25 to Labour Day, and every day from 9am to 6pm from Labour Day to June 24. It provides detailed information, maps, flyers and accommodation information for Montréal and all the tourist regions of Québec.

Bureau du Vieux-Montréal (Old Montreal)
174 Rue Notre-Dame Est
Métro Champs-de-Mars
☎ *874-1696*
Information on the Montréal region only.

On the Internet

All sorts of information is available on the Web. Here are a few interesting sites:

Quebecers and visitors alike will want to visit the site posted by the **Ministère du Tourisme** (*www. tourisme.gouv.qc.ca*), which provides access to the various regional tourist associations and even gives a virtual tour of Québec.

Check the **Ulysses Travel Publications** site (*www. ulyssesguides.com)* for new information on Québec, updated regularly.

You could also check the following sites:

www.voyagez.com
www.canoe.ca
www.montrealplus.ca
www.quebecplus.ca
www.toile.qc.ca
www.petitmonde.ca

The site of the **Office des Congrès et du Tourisme du Grand Montréal (OCTGM)** (*www.tourisme-montreal.org*) is overflowing with practical and cultural information about the city of Montréal. It also has a calendar of the countless festivals and events that liven up the city in both summer and winter.

Do you want to see real-time images of the city? Well, the Réseau de **Caméras en Direct du Grand Montréal** (*www.montrealcam.com*) has a webcam that takes shots of the city at 10 different angles, plus gives the date, time and temperature.

As well, various Montréal magazines and newspapers

Table of distances (km)

Via the shortest route

1 mile = 1.62 kilometres
1 kilometre = 0.62 miles

	Baie-Comeau	Boston (Mass.)	Charlottetown (P.E.I.)	Chibougamau	Chicoutimi	Gaspé	Halifax (N.S.)	Hull / Ottawa	Montréal	New York (N.Y.)	Niagara Falls (Ont.)	Quebec City	Rouyn-Noranda	Sherbrooke	Toronto (Ont.)
Boston (Mass.)	1040														
Charlottetown (P.E.I.)	724	1081													
Chibougamau	679	1152	1347												
Chicoutimi	316	849	992	363											
Gaspé	337	1247	867	1039	649										
Halifax (N.S.)	807	1165	265	1430	1076	952									
Hull / Ottawa	869	701	1404	725	662	1124	1488								
Montréal	676	512	1194	700	464	930	1290	207							
New York (N.Y.)	1239	352	1421	1308	1045	1550	1508	814	608						
Niagara Falls (Ont.)	1334	767	1836	1298	1126	1590	1919	543	670	685					
Quebec City	422	648	984	515	211	700	1056	451	253	834	925				
Rouyn-Noranda	1304	1136	1833	493	831	1559	1916	536	638	1246	858	877			
Sherbrooke	662	426	1187	724	451	915	1271	347	147	657	827	240	782		
Toronto (Ont.)	1224	906	1746	1124	1000	1476	1828	399	546	823	141	802	606	693	
Trois-Rivières	545	566	1089	574	338	808	1173	331	142	750	814	130	747	158	688

Example: The distance between Montréal and Boston is 512 km.

have their own Web pages, such as the English weeklies, *Hour* (*www.afterhour. com*) and *Mirror* (*www. montrealmirror.com*), and Montréal's English daily newspaper, *The Gazette* (*www.montrealgazette.com*).

The *montrealplus.ca* site, which was inaugurated on November 25, 1999, allows people to explore or take a virtual tour of businesses and services like restaurants and bars, cinemas, music, culture, sports and hobbies, boutiques, hotels and tourist attractions. It provides access to *Ulysses Travel Guides* as well as guidebooks produced by *Voir*, a local weekly, in addition to direct and exclusive links with Radio-Canada for content in five key areas: news, sports, culture, television and radio. Other partners, such as Admission ticket office and Web Seduction, are directly accessible on the site.

Getting to Montréal

Access

When coming **from Quebec City**, there are two possible routes — take either Highway 20 West to the Champlain Bridge (*pont*), then Highway 10 (Autoroute Bonaventure), which leads directly downtown, or take Highway 40 West to Highway 15 South (the Autoroute Décarie), and then follow the signs for downtown (*centre-ville*).

From Ottawa, take Highway 40 East to Highway 15 South (the Autoroute Décarie), and then follow the signs for downtown (*centre-ville*). Visitors arriving **from Toronto** will arrive via Highway 20 East, continue along it and then take the 720 Autoroute (the Ville-Marie) and follow the signs for downtown (*centre-ville*).

From the United States, via either Highway 10 or Highway 15 you will use the Champlain Bridge and Highway 10 (the Autoroute Bonaventure).

Airports

There are two airports near Montréal: **Dorval** and **Mirabel**. Dorval Airport is intended for international and domestic flights whereas the Mirabel Airport handles chartered flights.

Dorval Airport

Dorval Airport is located approximately 20km from downtown Montréal, about 20min by car. To get downtown from here, take Highway 20 East to the junction of Highway 720 (the Auto-route Ville-Marie), then follow the signs for downtown (*centre-ville*).

Information

An information counter is open from 6am to 10pm seven days a week (☎514-633-3105, *www.admtl.com*) to provide information regarding airport services (arrivals, departures and other information).

Buses

From Dorval to downtown: with the bus company La Québécoise (*Mon to Fri, every 20min from 7am to 11pm and every 30min from 11pm to 1am; Sat to Sun, every 30min from 7am to 1pm;* ☎514-934-1222). The bus stops at the downtown air terminal (*777 De La Gauchetière, corner University*) and at the Station Centrale (*505 Boulevard de Maisonneuve Est, Métro Berri-UQAM*). Costs $11 one-way and $19.75 return.

You can also take public transportation from Dorval Airport to reach downtown. Take bus no. 204 going east to the Dorval terminus, then bus no. 211 going east to the Lionel-Groulx Métro station.

Taxis

Dorval Airport is served by 260 cars, as well as 12 minivans that can transport wheelchairs (the drivers were trained to transport passengers with disabilities). The service is offered from 6am until the last flight arrives. The fare is $28 plus $1 in airport fees for passengers travelling between Dorval and downtown Montréal. For shorter trips, the minimum fare is $10 plus $1 in airport fees. All taxis serving Dorval Airport accept major credit cards.

Foreign Exchange

A Thomas Cook counter is open from 6am to 11pm, but a high commission is charged. Better exchange rates are available in downtown Montréal (see p 60).

Taxes

A $10 departure tax is charged for everyone leaving Dorval Airport. You can pay this tax at any of the automatic machines in the airport or at the counter next to the boarding gates.

Lost and Found
☎(514) 636-0499

Mirabel Airport

This airport is located approximately 50 km north of

Practical Information

Montréal, in Mirabel. To reach downtown Montréal from Mirabel, follow Highway 15 South (the Autoroute des Laurentides) until it intersects with Highway 40 (the Autoroute Métropolitaine), which you follow for a few kilometres to the west, then continue once again on the 15 South (now called the Autoroute Décarie) until the 720 Autoroute (the Ville-Marie). Follow the signs for downtown (*centre-ville*). The trip takes 40 to 60 minutes.

Information

For information on airport services (arrivals, departures, and other information), visit the information counter, which is open every day from 8am to 11:30pm There is also a 24hr telephone service (☎*514-394-7377 or toll free 1-800-465-1213*).

Buses

From Mirabel to downtown Montréal: the La Québécoise bus company offers a service (☎*514-931-9002*). The bus stops at the Hôtel Reine-Elizabeth (Queen Elizabeth Hotel, Rue Mansfield, Métro Bonaventure) and at the Station Centrale (*505 Boulevard de Maisonneuve Est, Métro Berri-UQAM*). Cost: $18 one-way, $25 return (free for children under five).

From Dorval to Mirabel: with the La Québécoise bus company (*every day;* ☎*514-931-9002*).

Airport Limousine

Limousine service is provided by **Limousines Brenka** (*$80;* ☎*514-938-5466*) or **Limousines Montréal** (*$85;* ☎*514-333-5466*).

Taxis

Mirabel Airport is served by 45 cars, but the services are more limited and expensive (*about $70*) because of the longer distance between Mirabel and downtown Montréal. It is a better idea to take the shuttle service.

Foreign Exchange

The ICE Currency is open during flight arrivals and departures, but charges a high commission. Better exchange rates are available in downtown Montréal (see p 60).

Lost and Found

☎*(514) 394-7765*

By Train

The Montréal train station, **Gare Centrale** (*895 Rue De La Gauchetière Ouest*) is located right downtown. For information call ☎*871-7765* or

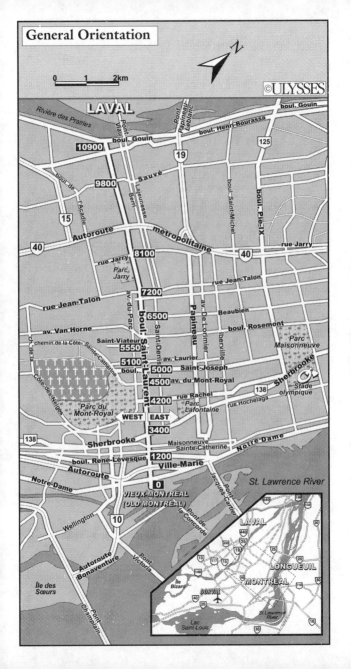

visit the web site of **VIA Rail**, Canada's main passenger train service at *www.viarail.ca*.

By Bus

Station Centrale *(505 Boulevard De Maisonneuve, at the corner of Rue Berri* ☎*842-2281)*, is Montréal's main bus station. Most big North American bus companies, such as Orléans from Québec, make use of this terminal. It is equipped with washrooms, lockers, snack bars, a tourist information desk and car rental counters. The terminal is in a building above the Berri-UQAM Métro station.

Getting Around

Montréal is an easy city to drive in. Its north-south and east-west grid of streets makes an almost perfect checkerboard.

The east-west arteries are divided by Boulevard Saint-Laurent, where street address numbers begin at zero and increase eastward and westward, with the direction usually designated in the address (33 Mont-Royal Est, 45 Boulevard De Maisonneuve Ouest).

On north-south arteries, addresses begin at zero at the river (south of the island).

No. 4176 on Rue Saint-Denis roughly corresponds to no. 4176 on Rue Papineau or on Rue Saint-Urbain. The map on p 51 provides a quick orientation to the city.

The only drawback to driving in Montréal is the dreaded one-way street! Montréal is full of one-way streets, and you may find yourself literally going around in circles. For example, a street may be one-way north for a section and then suddenly switch to one-way south. Luckily, however, streets usually alternate in direction; if one is one-way north, generally the next will be one-way south. Always check for traffic signs carefully!

Taxis

Co-op Taxi
☎*725-9885*

Diamond
☎*273-6331*

Taxi Lasalle
☎*277-2552*

You can expect to pay about $25 for a taxi from downtown to Dorval Airport.

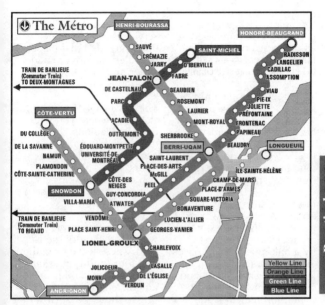

The Métro

HENRI-BOURASSA

SAUVÉ
CRÉMAZIE
JARRY
JEAN-TALON
DE CASTELNAU
PARC
ACADIE
OUTREMONT
ÉDOUARD-MONTPETIT
UNIVERSITÉ-DE-MONTRÉAL
CÔTE-DES-NEIGES
GUY-CONCORDIA
ATWATER

SAINT-MICHEL
D'IBERVILLE
FABRE
BEAUBIEN
ROSEMONT
LAURIER
MONT-ROYAL
SHERBROOKE
BERRI-UQAM
SAINT-LAURENT
PLACE-DES-ARTS
McGILL
PEEL

HONORÉ-BEAUGRAND
RADISSON
LANGELIER
CADILLAC
ASSOMPTION
VIAU
PIE-IX
JOLIETTE
PRÉFONTAINE
FRONTENAC
PAPINEAU
BEAUDRY
CHAMP-DE-MARS
PLACE-D'ARMES
SQUARE-VICTORIA
BONAVENTURE
LUCIEN-L'ALLIER
GEORGES-VANIER

LONGUEUIL
ÎLE-SAINTE-HÉLÈNE

CÔTE-VERTU
DU COLLÈGE
DE LA SAVANNE
NAMUR
PLAMONDON
CÔTE-SAINTE-CATHERINE
SNOWDON
VILLA-MARIA

TRAIN DE BANLIEUE
(Commuter Train)
TO DEUX-MONTAGNES

TRAIN DE BANLIEUE
(Commuter Train)
TO RIGAUD

VENDÔME
PLACE SAINT-HENRI
LIONEL-GROULX
CHARLEVOIX
JOLICOEUR
MONK
LASALLE
DE L'ÉGLISE
VERDUN
ANGRIGNON

Yellow Line
Orange Line
Green Line
Blue Line

Public Transportation

Visitors are strongly advised to take advantage of Montréal's public transportation system, which consists of an extensive network of buses and subway trains (the métro) that serve the region well. Métro stations are identified by a blue sign with a white arrow pointing downwards and the word "Métro." Bus stops, indicated by a blue and white sign, are usually located at street corners. Smoking is prohibited throughout the system.

A pass entitling the holder to unlimited use of the public transportation services for one month costs $48,50 for adults and $22.50 for students and seniors. Bus passes are on sale at the beginning of the month only. Another pass, valid for a week starting Monday until Sunday and also entitling the holder to unlimited use of the public transportation services is on sale for $13.50. For shorter stays, visitors can purchase six tickets for $8.50, or single tickets at $2 each. Children and seniors benefit from reduced fares. Tourist Cards could also be purchased: $7.00 for 1 day and $14.00

for 3 days. Tickets and passes can be purchased at all métro stations. **Take note that bus drivers do not sell tickets and do not give change.**

The green, orange and yellow metro lines are in operation from Sunday to Friday between 5:30am and 12:30am, and Saturday between 5:30am and 1am. The blue line operates every day from 5:30am to 11pm.

Most bus lines follow the same schedule. However, there are night buses, which are indicated at each stop by a half-moon. Night buses circulate more or less regularly between 12:30am and 5:30am along the city's main thoroughfares. All major stops on the bus network feature a small sign displaying schedules and routes.

If a trip involves a transfer (from one bus to another, from the bus to the métro or vice versa, for example), the passenger must ask the bus driver for a transfer ticket when getting on, or take one from a transfer machine in the métro station. Free subway maps are available inside all stations, as are timetables for the buses that stop at that station.

Note that there is a service offered to women who might need to get off the

bus between stops. This service is available after 9pm, provided that passengers alert the driver in advance and that the drop-off location is safe.

The Berri-UQAM métro station is where you will find the Planibus, the detailed schedule and route of each bus. During office hours, this is also where you can pick up objects that may have been lost in the métro or bus.

Commuter trains serve the western section of the island. These leave from the Vendôme and Bonaventure métro stations and provide an efficient means of getting to these areas. However, on weekends the service is less frequent, so it is a good idea to check the timetables carefully.

On the métro map, the dotted lines represent projected stations, the thin lines are commuter train lines, and the circles with squares inside are stations served by both commuter trains and métros.

For more information on the public transportation system, call ☎*288-6287* (which corresponds to the word AUTOBUS, French for bus, on a telephone dial) or visit the site www.stcum.ca.

By Car

Since Montréal is well served by public transportation and taxis, having a car is not essential to visit the city, especially since most of the sights are located relatively close to one another, and all of the suggested tours can be done on foot, except the one of the West Island. Nevertheless, it is quite easy to get around by car. Parking lots, though quite expensive, are numerous in the downtown area. Parking on the street is possible, but be sure to read the signs carefully. Ticketing of illegally parked cars is strict and expensive, and on certain major thoroughfares cars are towed during rush hour.

Things to Consider

Driver's License: As a general rule, foreign driver's licenses are valid for six months from the date of arrival in Canada.

Winter Driving: Although roads are generally in good condition, the dangers brought on by drastic climatic conditions must be taken into consideration.

During snow removal after a storm, special parking signs are placed on the side of the road for drivers to move their cars. As well, trucks with distinctive, blaring warning sirens go by while clearing the snow to remind drivers to move their cars.

Driving and the Highway Code: Signs marked "*Arrêt*" or "Stop" in white against a red background must always be respected. Come to a complete stop even if there is no apparent danger.

Turning right on a red light and turning from a one-way street onto another on a red light are both forbidden in Québec.

Traffic lights are often located on the opposite side of the intersection, so be careful to stop at the stop line, a white line on the pavement before the intersection.

When a school bus (usually yellow) has stopped and has its signals flashing, you must come to a complete stop, no matter what direction you are travelling in. Failing to stop at the flashing signals is considered a serious offense, and carries a heavy penalty.

Seat belts must be worn in both the front and back seats at all times.

There are no tolls on Québec highways, and the speed limit on highways (*autoroutes*) is 100km/h. The speed limit is usually 90km/h on secondary high-ways and 50km/h in urban areas.

Gas Stations: Because Canada produces its own crude oil, gasoline prices are less expensive than in Europe. However, due to hidden taxes, gas prices are considerably higher than those in the United States and in Western Canada. Some self-serve gas stations (especially in the downtown area) might ask for payment in advance as a security measure, especially after 11pm.

Car Rentals

Vacation packages that include flight, hotel and car, or simply hotel and car are generally less expensive than car rentals on the spot. Many travel agencies have agreements with the major car rental companies (Avis, Budget, Hertz, etc.) and offer good deals; contracts often include added bonuses (reduced show ticket prices for example). Packages usually prove to be a good deal.

Avis
Mirabel Airport
☎*(450)476-3481*
Dorval Airport
☎*636-1902*
1255 Rue Metcalfe
☎*866-2847*

505 Boulevard de Maisonneuve Est, at the bus terminal
☎*288-9934*

Budget
Mirabel Airport
☎*(450)476-2687*
Dorval Airport
☎*636-0052*
1240 Rue Guy
☎*937-9121*

895 Rue de La Gauchetière Ouest
☎*866-7675*
Complexe Desjardins,
170 Rue Sainte-Catherine Ouest
☎*842-9931*

Discount
607 Boulevard de Maisonneuve Ouest
☎*286-1554*

Hertz
Mirabel Airport
☎*(450) 476-3385*
Dorval Airport
☎*636-9530*
1073 Rue Drummond
☎*938-1717*
1475 Rue Aylmer
☎*842-8537*

National
Mirabel Airport
☎*(450) 476-3460*
Dorval Airport
☎*636-9030*
1200 Rue Stanley
☎*878-2771*

Via Route
1255 Rue Mackay
☎*871-1166*

When renting a car, find out if:

- the contract includes unlimited kilometres or not

- the insurance offered provides full coverage (accident, property damage, hospital costs for you and passengers, theft)

Remember:

- To rent a car in Québec, you must be at least 21 years of age and have had a driver's license for **at least** one year. If you are between 21 and 25, certain companies (for example Avis, Thrifty, Budget) will ask for a $500 deposit, and in some cases they will also charge an extra sum for each day you rent the car. These conditions do not apply for those over 25 years of age.

- A credit card is extremely useful for the deposit to avoid tying up large sums of money and can in some cases (gold cards) cover the insurance.

- Most rental cars have an automatic transmission; however, you can request a car with a manual shift.

- Child safety seats cost extra.

Accidents and Emergencies

In case of serious accident, fire or other emergency, dial ☎**911**.

If an accident occurs, always fill out an accident report. In case of a disagreement as to who is at fault, ask a police officer for assistance. Be sure to alert the car-rental company as soon as possible.

If you are planning a long trip and have decided to buy a car, it is a good idea to become a member of the Canadian Automobile Association, or CAA, which offers assistance throughout Canada. If you are a member of an equivalent association in your home country (U.S.A.: American Automobile Association; Switzerland: Automobile Club de Suisse; Belgium: Royal Automobile Touring Club de Belgique), you can benefit from some of the services offered. For more information, contact your association or the CAA in Montréal (☎*861-7111*).

Cycling in Montréal

One of the most enjoyable ways to get around in the summer is by bicycle. Bike paths have been set up to

Practical Information

allow cyclists to explore various neighbourhoods in the city. To help you find your way around, there are two booklets that show all the bike paths in Montréal: *The Great Montréal Bike Path*, and *Biking Montréal* (Ulysses Travel Guides, 1999). A small free map of the paths is also available from the tourist information office. Except during rush hour, bicycles can be taken on the Métro.

Since drivers are not always attentive, cyclists should be alert, respect road signs (as is required by law) and be careful at intersections. Bicycle helmets are not mandatory in Montréal, but wearing one is strongly recommended.

Ça roule Montréal
Mar to Oct
27 Est de la Commune
☎*866-0633*
www.caroulemontreal.com
Bicycles and in-line skates are rented here (*$20/day, May to Oct*).

Guided Tours

Various companies organize tours of Montréal, offering visitors interesting ways to explore the city. Walking tours lead to an intimate discovery of the city's neighbourhoods, while bus tours provide a perspective of the city as a whole. Boat cruises highlight another facet of the city, this time in relation to the river. Though the options are countless, consider the walking, bus and boat tours offered by the following companies.

On Foot

Architectours (Héritage Montréal)
☎*286-2662*
These walking tours criss-cross neighbourhoods focusing on architecture, history and town planning. Tours are organized on summer weekends; they last about two hours and cost $8 per person. Tickets are available at Infotouriste (the tourist office).

L'Autre Montréal
summer, $14/3hrs
winter, groups only
2000 St-Joseph E.
☎*521-7802*
This organization uncovers the hidden face of Montréal, through its hippest neighbourhoods and little known nooks and crannies. Some tours are thematic (for example, "Women in the City").

Guidatour
Jun to Oct, $11.50/1h30
winter, groups only
477 Rue Saint-François-Xavier Suite 300
☎*844-4021*
www.guidatour.qc.ca

This company organizes tours along the city's major arteries, allowing visitors to discover Montréal's history, its growth, its architecture and its culture. You can even tour the city in costume dress.

By Bus

Tours Imperial
1001 Rue du Square-Dorchester
(Centre Infotouriste)
☎871-4733
Offers guided tours including a three-hour general tour that costs $26 or a tour on a London-style double-decker bus. They give you the option of spending more time at an attraction and continuing the tour by joining a later group.

Connaisseur-Gray Line
1001 Rue du Square-Dorchester
(Centre Infotouriste)
☎934-1222
Regular city tours aboard comfortable buses. Each outing lasts six hours and costs $45. Three-hour tours aboard a trolley-style bus are also offered for $26.

By Boat

Croisières AML Montréal
Vieux-Port de Montréal
Quai de l'Horloge
☎842-3871 or (800) 667-3131
www.groupeaml.com
Visitors can enjoy various cruises on the river starting

at $14. The duration and the cost of these excursions varies depending on the package. You can even take a cruise on a New Orleans-style paddle-wheel boat with live entertainment by blues or jazz musicians. Evening dinner cruises are also offered.

Amphi-bus
Departure from the corner of Rue de La Commune and
Boulevard Saint-Laurent
☎849-5181
The Amphi-bus is an "amphibious" bus. From May to October, it offers guided tours of Old Montreal on land and water for $18 – an experience that is sure to please children!

Le Bateau-Mouche
Vieux-Port
Quai Jacques-Cartier
☎849-9952
www.bateau-mouche.com
Cruises along the river offer an interesting perspective of Montréal. During the day, a cruise costs $20 and lasts 1.5hrs. Departures every day at 10am, noon, 2pm and 4pm. Evening tours, during which dinner is served, last 3.5hrs and cost between $68 and $100.

Practical Information

Financial Services

Exchange Offices

Several banks in the down-town area readily exchange foreign currency, but almost all charge a commission. There are exchange offices, on the other hand, that do not charge commissions, but their rates are some-times less competitive. It is a good idea to shop around. The majority of banks can change U.S. currency.

Banque Nationale du Canada
1140 Sherbrooke Ouest
☎*394-5555*
www.bnc.ca

Banque Nationale du Canada
895 Rue de la Gauchetière Ouest
☎*394-5555*

Automatic teller machines that exchange currency have been installed at Complexe Desjardins (on Sainte-Catherine West, between Jeanne-Mance and Saint-Urbain). They are open every day from 6am to 2am. Various foreign currencies can be changed into Canadian dollars. Cana-dian dollars can also be changed into U.S. and French currency. Similar machines are located at Mirabel Airport.

Traveller's Cheques

Remember that Canadian dollars are different from U.S. dollars. If you do not plan on travelling to the United States on the same trip, it is best to get your traveller's cheques in Cana-dian dollars. Travellers' cheques are accepted in most large stores and ho-tels; however, it is easier and to your advantage to cash your cheques at an exchange office. Traveller's cheques in U.S. and Cana-dian dollars can be pur-chased at most banks in Montréal.

Credit Cards

Most credit cards are ac-cepted at stores, restaurants and hotels. Though the main advantage of credit cards is that they allow visitors to avoid carrying large sums of money, using a credit card also makes leaving a deposit for car rental much easier and some cards, gold cards for example, automatically insure you when you rent a car. In addition, the ex-change rate with a credit card is generally better. Cash advances can also be made on credit cards. The most commonly accepted credit cards are Visa, MasterCard, and American Express.

Banks

Banks can be found almost everywhere, and most offer the standard services to tourists. Visitors who choose to stay in Québec for a long period of time should note that **non-residents** cannot open bank accounts. If this is your case, the best way to have ready money is to use travellers' cheques. Visitors who have attained resident status, permanent or not (immigrants, students), can open a bank account. A passport and proof of resident status are required.

Money withdrawals from automatic teller machines are possible across Canada thanks to the Interac network, and are much less expensive than withdrawing through a teller. Most machines are open at all times. Many machines accept foreign bank cards, so that you can withdraw directly from your account (check before to make sure you have access). Cash advances on your credit card are another option, although interest charges accumulate quickly. Money orders are a final alternative for which no commission is charged. This option does, however, take more time.

Banks are generally open Monday to Friday, from 10am to 3pm. Many are also open Thursdays and Fridays until 6pm, and sometimes until 8pm.

A Few Addresses

Banque Nationale du Canada
895 Rue De La Gauchetière Ouest
☎*394-5555*
Complexe Desjardins
4506 Rue Saint-Denis

Caisse populaire Desjardins
482 Avenue du Mont-Royal Est
☎*288-5249*
1145 Avenue Bernard
☎*274-8221*
1760 Rue Amherst
☎*597-1613*

Banque Canadienne Impériale de Commerce
200 Boulevard René-Lévesque Ouest
☎*286-4000*
1155 Boulevard René-Lévesque Ouest
☎*876-2323*
550 Rue Sherbrooke Ouest
☎*845-5994*

Banque de Montréal
630 Boulevard René-Lévesque Ouest
☎*877-7146*
5060 Boulevard Saint-Laurent
☎*277-1060*
670 Rue Sainte-Catherine Ouest
☎*877-8010*

Practical Information

Exchange Rates*

$1 US	=	$1.50 CAN	$1 CAN	=	$0.66 US
$1 Euro	=	$1.39 CAN	$1 CAN	=	0.72 Euro
£1	=	$2.20 CAN	$1 CAN	=	£0.46
$1 Aust	=	$0.82 CAN	$1 CAN	=	$1.22 Aust
$ NZ	=	$0.66 CAN	$1 CAN	=	$1.52 NZ
1 fl	=	$0.63 CAN	$1 CAN	=	1.58 fl
1 SF	=	$0.91 CAN	$1 CAN	=	1.10 SF
10 BF	=	$0.34 CAN	$1 CAN	=	29 BF
1 DM	=	$0.71 CAN	$1 CAN	=	1.41 DM
100 PTA	=	$0.83 CAN	$1 CAN	=	119.65 PTA
1000 ITL	=	$0.72 CAN	$1 CAN	=	1,392 ITL

*Samples only: rates fluctuate.

Banque Nationale de Paris
1981 Avenue McGill College
☎ *285-6000*

Banque Royale
1 Place Ville-Marie
☎ *874-7222*
180 Avenue du Mont-Royal Est
☎ *599-2100*
2157 Rue Guy
☎ *874-8966*

Currency

The monetary unit is the dollar ($), which is divided into cents (¢). One dollar=100 cents.

Bills come in five-, 10-, 20-, 50- and 100-dollar denominations; coins come in one-, five-, 10- and 25-cent pieces and in one- and two-dollar coins.

Francophones sometimes speak of "*piastres*" and "*sous,*" which are dollars and cents respectively. On occasion, especially in everyday language, you might be asked for a "*trente sous*" (30-cent piece); what the person really wants is a 25-cent piece. A "*cenne noire,*" furthermore, is a one-cent piece! In English, Europeans may be surprised to hear "pennies" (1¢), "nickels" (5¢), "dimes" (10¢), "quarters" (25¢), "loonies" ($1), and even toonies ($2).

Telecommunications

The **area code** for the island of Montréal is **514**. The area code for the region around the island, which used to be the same as Montréal, was changed to **450** in June 1998. Calls between these two regions are still local (such as from most parts of Montréal to Laval, vice versa) but you must dial the area code (without the 1) before the number. You do not have to dial the area code when calling within the island of Montréal.

Areas that were long distance from Montréal to its surroundings are still long distance (Montréal to Sainte-Adèle, for example), and require that you dial the 1 followed by the area code then the number.

Telephone numbers preceded by 800 or 888 are toll-free. If the toll-free number you are dialing is in the United States, it is sometimes reachable from Canada. To reach an operator, dial 0.

Public telephones can be found pretty much everywhere. Some of these even accept credit cards. Local calls cost 25¢.

For long-distance calls, stock up on quarters or purchase a telephone card ("La Puce") – these are sold in $10, $15 and $20 denominations and are available at newsstands and some convenience stores. Calling Quebec City from a Montréal phone booth, for example, costs $2.50 for the first three minutes and $0.38 per additional minute. Phoning from a private residence is less expensive and can be done with a credit card, or with the prepaid "Allô" card, but be aware that these payment methods greatly increase.

Post Offices

Large post offices are open from 8am to 5:45pm. There are many smaller post offices throughout Québec, located in shopping malls, *dépanneurs* (convenience stores), and even pharmacies; these post offices are open much later than the larger ones.

1250 Rue University
☎*846-5401*

1695 Rue Sainte-Catherine Ouest
☎*522-3220*

Time Zone

Québec is in the Eastern Standard Time zone, as is most of the eastern United States. It is 3hrs ahead of the west coast of the continent. There is a 6hr time difference between Québec and most continental European countries and a difference of five hours between Québec and the United Kingdom. Daylight-savings time goes into effect in Québec on the first Sunday in April and ends on the last Sunday in October. All of Québec (except the Îles-de-la-Madeleine) is on the same time.

Business Hours and Public Holidays

Business Hours

By law, stores can be open the following hours:

- Monday to Wednesday from 8am to 9pm, though most stores open at 10am and close at 6pm.

- Thursday and Friday from 8am to 9pm, though most open at 10am.

- Saturday from 8am to 5pm, though most open at 10am.

- Sunday from 8am to 5pm, though most open at 11am; not all stores are open Sundays.

Dépanneurs (convenience stores that sell food) are found throughout Québec and are open later, sometimes 24hrs a day.

Public Holidays

The following is a list of public holidays in Québec. Most administrative offices and banks are closed on these days.

New Years
January 1st and 2nd

Easter Monday and/or Good Friday
Variable

Fête de Dollard or Victoria Day
3rd Monday in May

Saint-Jean-Baptiste Day
June 24
Québec's national holiday

Canada Day
July 1

Labour Day
1st Monday in September

Thanksgiving
2nd Monday in October

Remembrance Day
November 11
only banks and federal government services are closed

Christmas
December 25 and 26

Climate

Québec's seasonal extremes are something that set the province apart from much of the world. Temperatures can climb to above 30°C in summer and drop to - 25°C in winter. Visiting Québec during the two "main" seasons (summer and winter) is like visiting two totally different places, with the seasons influencing not only the scenery, but also the lifestyles and behaviour of the local population.

The winter of 1998 was probably the most devastating in the history of Montréal. For almost a week in early January, heavy freezing rain hit the city, causing a series of catastrophes. The accumulation of the freezing rain toppled electrical pylons, cut Montréal's electrical supply, and plunged almost half of Québec's population into a cold darkness for several days, and in some cases for several weeks. The downtown core was closed for about a week to clear the ice, interrupting all financial and commercial activity. Though the "Ice Storm of 1998 strongly affected Montrealers", it brought the community together in a show of support.

www.meteomadia.com

Health

Vaccinations are not necessary for people coming from Europe or the United States. On the other hand, it is strongly suggested, particularly for medium or long-term stays, that visitors take out health and accident insurance. There are different types, so it is best to shop around. Bring along all medication, especially prescription medicine. Unless otherwise stated, the water is drinkable throughout Québec.

For Emergencies, dial ☎911

Québec Cuisine

Although many restaurant dishes are similar to those served in France or the rest of North America, some of them are prepared in a typically *Québécois* way, making them unique; the following dishes should definitely be tasted.

La soupe aux pois
pea soup

La tourtière
meat pie

Le pâté chinois
also known as shepherd's pie; layered pie consisting of ground beef, potatoes, and corn

Practical Information

Les cretons
a type of pâté of ground pork cooked with onions in lard)

Le jambon au sirop d'érable
ham with maple syrup

Les fèves au lard
baked beans

Le ragoût de pattes de cochon
pig's-foot stew

Le cipaille
layered pie with different types of meat

Sugar shack

La tarte aux pacanes
pecan pie

La tarte au sucre
sugar pie

La tarte aux bleuets
blueberry pie

Le sucre à la crème
creamy sugar fudge squares

Taxes and Tipping

Taxes

The ticket price on items usually **does not include tax**. There are two taxes, the 7% GST (federal Goods and Services Tax, TPS in French) and the 7.5% PST (Provincial Sales Tax, TVQ in French) on goods and services. They are cumulative, so you must add 15% in taxes to the price of most goods and services.

There are some exceptions to this taxation system, such as books, which are only taxed at 7% and food (except for ready-made meals), which is not taxed at all.

Tax Refunds for Non-Residents

Non-residents can be refunded for taxes paid on purchases made while in Québec. To obtain a refund, it is important to keep your receipts. A separate form for each tax (federal and provincial) must be filled out to obtain a refund. The conditions under which refunds are awarded are different for the GST and the PST For more information of tax refunds check with Centre Infotouriste in Montréal.

In Montréal:

Forms are available at customs (at the airport) and certain department stores.

For further information, call ☎ *1-800-668-4748* (toll-free for the GST and the PST).

Tipping

In general, tipping applies to all table service: restaurants, bars and nightclubs (no tipping in fast-food restaurants). Tipping is also standard in taxis and hair salons.

The tip is usually about 15% of the bill before taxes, but varies, of course, depending on the quality of service.

Language

Quebecers are very proud of their language and have struggled long and hard to preserve it while surrounded on all sides by English. The accent and vocabulary are different from European French and have a charm all their own.

When writing a guide to a region where the use and preservation of language are a part of daily life, certain decisions have to be made. We have tried to keep our combined use of English and French consistent throughout this guide. The official language in Québec is French, so when listing attractions and addresses, we have kept the titles in French. This will allow readers to make the connection between the guide and the signs they will be seeing. The terms used in these titles are in the glossary, but we are confident that after a couple of days, you will not even need to check! English style has been used in the text itself, to preserve readability. In Montréal visitors will often hear English almost as much as French, and where English terms for attractions are common, we have included both. English-speaking visitors to Montréal will often be able to take a break from practising their French, if they want. Just remember, a valiant effort and a sincere smile go a long way!

A complete list of all the local expressions would be too long to include in the guide. Travellers interested in knowing a bit more on the subject can refer to *Le Québécois pour mieux voyager* published by Ulysses, le *Dictionnaire de la Langue Québécoise* by Léandre

Practical Information

Bergeron, published by
Éditions VLB, or the excellent *Dictionnaire Pratique des Expressions Québécoises*, published by Éditions Logiques.

Language Courses

Visitors who plan on spending a longer amount of time in Montréal may want to consider French lessons. A knowledge of French will reveal a whole other side of the city's vibrant culture. Canadian citizens can learn French for free at local CEGEPs (community colleges), while landed immigrants and refugees are offered French classes by Immigration Québec. Everybody else must take courses either from the universities, the YMCA or private language schools. Here are a few private schools to try:

Berlitz Language Centre
☎288-3111 or 387-2566

Centre Linguistica
☎397-1736

Language Studies Canada
☎939-9911

Insurance

Cancellation

Your travel agent will usually offer you cancellation insurance when you buy your airline ticket or vacation package. This insurance allows you to be reimbursed for the ticket or package deal if your trip must be cancelled due to serious illness or death.

Theft

Most residential insurance policies protect some of your goods from theft, even if the theft occurs in a foreign country. To make a claim, you must fill out a police report. It may not be necessary to take out further insurance, depending on the amount covered by your current home policy. As policies vary considerably, you are advised to check with your insurance company. European visitors should take out baggage insurance.

Health

This is the most useful kind of insurance for travellers, and should be purchased prior to departure. Your insurance plan should be as complete as possible because health-care costs add up quickly. When buying insurance, make sure it covers all types of medical costs, such as hospitalization, nursing services and doctor's fees. Make sure your limit is high enough, as these expenses can be costly. A repatriation clause is also vital in case the required care is not available on site. Furthermore, since you may have to pay immediately, check your policy to see what provisions it includes for such situations. To avoid any problems during your vacation, always keep proof of your insurance policy with you.

Wine, Beer and Spirits

In Québec, the sale of alcohol is regulated by a provincial authority, the Société des Alcools du Québec (SAQ). The best wines, beers and spirits are sold in SAQ stores. The shops are conveniently located throughout the Montréal area, but most have rather restricted business hours.

Some SAQ outlets:

4128 Rue Saint-Denis
☎845-5630

585 Rue Sainte-Catherine Ouest
☎844-7544

1108 Rue Sainte-Catherine Ouest
☎861-7908

1616 Rue Sainte-Catherine Ouest
☎935-5127

866 Rue Sainte-Catherine Est
☎842-3398

895 Rue De La Gauchetière Ouest
(Halles de la Gare)
☎876-4144

480 Boulevard Saint-Laurent
☎849-5015

3565 Boulevard Saint-Laurent
☎842-1660

440 Boulevard De Maisonneuve Ouest
☎873-2274

200 Rue Jean-Talon Est
☎276-1512

390 Avenue Laurier Est
☎271-7010

1 Westmount Square (Westmount Square mall)
☎931-4546

Complexe Desjardins
☎844-8721

One outlet, called **SAQ Sélection** (*440 Boulevard De Maisonneuve Ouest*, ☎873-2274), offers a greater selection of wines and spirits than the others as well as specialized advice.

The **SAQ Express** outlets offer a more limited selection but are open later. They stock about 400 of the most popular products. They are open seven days a week, from 11am to 9pm from Sunday to Wednesday, and from 11am to 10pm Thursday to Saturday. These outlets are located at 1034 Avenue du Mont-Royal Est (☎523-0503) and at 1108 Rue Sainte-Catherine Ouest (☎861-7908).

Finally, the **SAQ Whisky & Cie** (*Cours Mont-Royal, 1700 Metcalfe*, ☎282-9445) is a specialty shop for high-quality spirits: cognacs, scotches, whiskies, brandies and fine liqueurs.

Beer

Two large brewing companies, Labatt and Molson-O'Keefe, share the greater portion of the provincial market. Each produces various types of beer, mainly lagers, with varying levels of alcohol. In bars, restaurants and nightclubs, beer on tap, sometimes referred to as "draft" (even in French), is less expensive than bottled beer.

Beside these "macro-breweries," micro-breweries have been sprouting up over the last several years and their beers are very popular in Québec for their variety and flavour. Some of the better-known micro-breweries are Unibroue (Maudite, Fin du

Monde, Blanche de Chambly), McAuslan (Griffon, St-Ambroise), Cheval Blanc (Cap Tourmente, Berlue), Brasseurs du Nord (Boréale), and GMT (Belle Gueule).

N.B. The legal drinking age in Québec is **18 years**.

Advice for Smokers

Cigarette smoking is considered taboo and is being prohibited in more and more public places:

- in shopping centres
- in buses and métros
- in government offices

Many public places (restaurants, tearooms) have smoking and non-smoking sections. Cigarettes are sold in bars, grocery stores and newspaper and magazine shops.

Safety

Violence is far less prevalent in Québec than in the United States. A genuine non-violence policy is advocated throughout the province. The city of Montréal even boasts a peace monument built out of 12,700 war toys given up voluntarily by Montréal-area children. The monument, designed by Linda Covit, is on display at Jarry Park (Métro Jarry).

Visitors who take the normal precautions have no need to be overly worried about personal security. If trouble should arise, remember to call ☎911.

Senior Citizens

Seniors who would like to meet people their age can do so through the umbrella association below, which groups together most organizations for senior citizens' and provides information about activities and local clubs throughout Québec.

Fédération de l'Âge d'Or du Québec
4545 Avenue Pierre-de-Coubertin
C.P. 1000, Succursale M
Montréal H1V 3R2
☎*252-3017*
≈*252-3154*

Reduced transportation fares and entertainment tickets are often available to seniors. Do not hesitate to ask.

Gay and Lesbian Life

Montréal offers many services to the gay and lesbian community. These are mostly concentrated in the part of town known as **The Village**, located on Rue

Sainte-Catherine between Amherst and Papineau streets, as well as on the adjoining streets.

More information is available at the gay and lesbian bookstore **L'Androgyne** (*3636 Boulevard Saint-Laurent*) and at the **Centre Communautaire des Gais et Lesbiennes** (*2075 Plessis,* ☎*528-8424,* ≈*528-9708*). The latter, a community centre for gays and lesbians, organizes various activities, such as dances, language courses and music.

The **Défilé de la Fierté Gaie et Lesbienne** (Gay and Lesbian Pride March) takes place on the first weekend in August on Rue Sainte-Catherine and ends with various performances (*information: Divers Cité, 4067 Boulevard St-Laurent, H2W 1Y7,* ☎*285-4011,* ≈*285-8793*).

Three free magazines are available in bars: *RG*, *Fugues* and *Orientations*. They are monthly publications and contain information concerning the gay and lesbian communities.

Disabled People

Keroul, an organization devoted to tourism for people with disabilities, publishes a guide called *Accessible Québec*, which lists

Practical Information

Weights and Measures

Although the metric system has been in use in Canada for several years, some people continue to use the Imperial system in casual conversation. Here are some equivalents:

Weights
1 pound (lb) = 454 grams (g)
1 kilogram (kg) = 2.2 pounds (lbs)

Linear Measure
1 inch (in) = 2.54 centimetres (cm)
1 foot (ft) = 30 centimetres (cm)
1 mile (mi) = 1.6 kilometres (km)

Land Measure
1 acre = 0.4047 hectare (ha)
1 hectare (ha) = 2.471 acres

Volume Measure
1 U.S. gallon (gal) = 3.79 litres (L)
1 U.S. gallon (gal) = 0.83 imperial gallons

Temperature
To convert °F into °C: subtract 32, divide by 9, multiply by 5
To convert °C into °F: multiply by 9, divide by 5, add 32.

places accessible to disabled people throughout the province. These places are classed by tourist region. Most of the regions also have associations that organize leisure and sports activities for people with disabilities. Contact the following organization for the addresses of these associations.

Association Québécoise de Loisir pour Personnes Handicapées
4545 Avenue Pierre-de-Coubertin
C.P.1000, Succursale M
Montréal H1V 3R2
☎ *(514) 252-3144*
≠ *(514) 252-8363*

For further information:

KEROUL
4545 Avenue Pierre-de-Coubertin
C.P. 1000 Succursale M
Montréal H1V 3R2
☎ *(514) 252-3104*
≠ *(514) 252-0766*

Children

Children in Québec are treated like royalty. Facilities are available almost everywhere, whether it be transportation or leisure activities. Generally, children under five travel for free, and those under 12 are eligible for fare reductions. The same rules apply for various leisure activities and shows. Find out before you purchase tickets. High chairs and children's menus are available in most restaurants, while a few of the larger stores provide a babysitting service while parents shop. We suggest some attractions that are

likely to please children on page 213.

Pets

Dogs on a leash are permitted in most public parks in the city. Small pets are allowed on the public transportation system, as long as they are in a cage or well controlled by the owner. Pets are generally not allowed in stores, especially not food stores; however, many Montrealers tie their pets up near the entrance while they run in. Pets are not allowed in restaurants, although some establishments with terraces permit pets.

Drugs

Drugs are strictly forbidden (even "soft" drugs). Drug users and dealers caught with drugs in their possession risk severe consequences.

Electricity

Voltage is 110 volts throughout Canada, the same as in the United States.

Electrical plugs are two-pinned and flat, and adaptors are available here.

Practical Information

Folklore

Québec's rich folklore offers interesting insight into the history and culture of the province. The organization below regroups various regional committees aimed at the preservation and development of folklore. Activities are organized depending on the season and location.

For more information:

Association Québécoise des Loisirs Folkloriques
4545 Pierre-de-Coubertin
C.P. 1000 Succursale M
Montréal H1V 3R2
☎ *(514) 252-3022*
= *251-8038*

Hairdressers

A tip of 15% before taxes is standard, as in restaurants.

Laundromats

These are found almost everywhere. In most cases, detergent is sold on the spot. Although change machines are sometimes provided, it is best to bring plenty of quarters with you.

Museums

Most museums charge admission; however, permanent exhibits at some museums are free on Wednesday evenings from 6pm to 9pm, while reductions are offered for temporary exhibits. Reduced prices are available for seniors, children, and students. Call the museum for further details.

Newspapers

International newspapers can easily be found in Montréal. The major Montréal newspapers are: in French *Le Devoir, La Presse* and *Le Journal de Montréal,* and in English *The Gazette.* Four free weekly newspapers are also available: *Hour* and *The Mirror* in English and *Voir* and *Ici* in French.

Pharmacies

Apart from the smaller drug stores, there are large pharmacy chains that sell everything from chocolate to laundry detergent, as well as the more traditional items, such as cough drops and headache medications.

Religion

Almost all religions are represented in Montréal. Unlike English Canada, the majority of the Québec population is Catholic, although most Quebecers are not practising Catholics.

Telegrams

These are sent by private companies, so it is a good idea to consult the *Yellow Pages* under the heading "telegrams." Listed below are two companies:

American Telegram
☎*1-800-343-7363*

ATT Communications Inc.
☎*(514) 861-7311*

Weather

For weather forecasts, dial **Environment Canada** at ☎*283-3010*. You can also tune into **Météomédia**, channel 17 on cable television, or visit their web site at *www.meteomedia.com*. For road conditions, dial ☎*284-2363* in Montréal and ☎*877-393-2363* anywhere else in Québec.

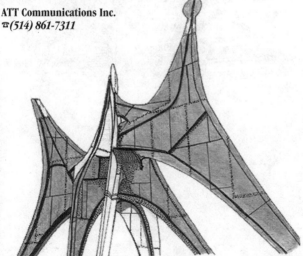

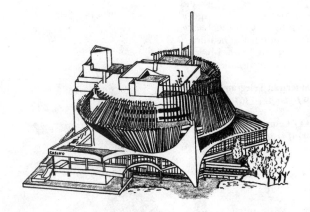

Exploring

To help you discover Montréal and its neighbouring municipalities, we have outlined below 17 walking tours and one longer tour that can be done by bike or by car.

Tour A: Vieux-Montréal

In the 18th century, Montréal, like Québec City, was surrounded by stone fortifications (see map of fortifications, p 17). Between 1801 and 1817, these ramparts were demolished due to the efforts of local merchants, who saw them as an obstacle to the city's development. The network of old streets, compressed after nearly a century of confinement, nevertheless remained in place. Today's Vieux-Montréal, or Old Montréal, thus corresponds quite closely to the area covered by the fortified city.

During the 19th century, this area became the hub of commercial and financial activity in Canada. Banks and insurance companies built sumptuous head offices here, leading to the demolition of almost all buildings erected under the French Regime. The area

was later abandoned for nearly 40 years in favour of the modern downtown area of today. Finally, the long process of putting new life into Old Montréal got underway during the preparations for Expo '67, and it continues today with numerous conversion and restoration projects.

Ulysses's Recommended Tours of Montréal

Tour A: Vieux-Montréal ★★★   77
Tour B: Downtown ★★★   100
Tour C: Montreal Museum of Fine Arts ★★   118
Tour D: The Golden Square Mile ★   129
Tour E: Shaughnessy Village ★★   141
Tour F: Around the Hôtel-Dieu ★   146
Tour G: Quartier Latin ★★   153
Tour H: Plateau Mont-Royal ★   160
Tour I: Mont Royal, Westmount and
          Western Montreal ★★   167
Tour J: Outremont ★   178
Tour K: Little Italy ★   187
Tour L: Sault-au-Récollet ★   191
Tour M: Île Sainte-Hélène and
          Île Notre-Dame ★★   195
Tour N: The Village ★   201
Tour O: Maisonneuve ★★★   208
Tour P: Little Burgundy and Saint-Henri ★   218
Tour Q: Pointe-Saint-Charles and Verdun ★   224
Tour R: The West Island ★★   232

The tour begins at the west end of Old Montréal, on Rue McGill, which marks the site of the surrounding wall that once separated the city from the Faubourg des Récollets (métro Square-Victoria). Visitors will notice a considerable difference between the urban fabric of the modern downtown area behind them, with its wide boulevards lined with glass and steel skyscrapers, and the old part of the city, whose narrow, compact streets are crowded with stone buildings.

The **Tour de la Bourse** ★ (*Place de la Bourse*, ☎871-2424*)*, or the stock exchange tower, dominates the surroundings. It was erected in 1964 according to a design by the famous Italian engineers Luigi Moretti and Pier Luigi Nervi, to whom we owe the Palazzo dello Sport (sports stadium) in Rome and the Exhibition Centre in Turin.

The elegant 47-floor black tower houses the offices and trading floor of the exchange. It is one of many buildings in this city designed by foreign talents. Its construction was intended to breathe new life into the business section of the old city, which was deserted after the stock market crash of 1929 in favour of the area around Square Dorchester. According to the initial plan, there were supposed to be two, or even three, identical towers.

In the 19th century, **Square Victoria** was a Victorian garden surrounded by Second Empire and Renaissance Revival stores and office buildings. Only the narrow building at 751 Rue McGill survives from that era. North of Rue Saint-Antoine, visitors will find a **statue of Queen Victoria**, executed in 1872 by English sculptor Marshall Wood, as well as an authentic Art Nouveau **Parisian métro railing**. The latter, designed by Hector Guimard in 1900 and given to the city of Montréal by the city of Paris for Expo '67, was installed at one of the entrances to the Square-Victoria métro station.

The headquarters of the two organizations that control civil aviation in the world, IATA (the International Air Transport Association) and ICOA (the International Civil Aviation Organization) are located in Montréal. The latter is a United Nations organization that was founded in 1947. It recently gained the new **Maison de l'OACI** (*at the corner of University and Saint-Antoine Ouest*) to house the delegations of its 183 member countries. The back of the building, which has been connected to the Cité Internationale de Montréal, is visible from Square Victoria. Completed in 1996, it was designed by architect Ken London, who was inspired somewhat by Scandinavian architecture of the 1930s.

Enter the covered passageway of the Centre de Commerce Mondial.

World trade centres are exchange organizations intended to promote international trade. Montréal's **Centre de Commerce Mondial / World Trade Centre** ★ (*Rue McGill, Square-Victoria métro*), completed in 1991, is a new structure hidden behind an entire block of old façades. An impressive glassed-in passageway stretches 180m through the centre of the building, along a portion of the Ruelle des Fortifications, a lane marking the former location of the northern wall of the fortified city. Alongside the passageway, visitors will find a fountain and an elegant stone stairway, which provide the setting for a statue of Amphitirite, Poseidon's wife, taken from the municipal fountain in Saint-Mihiel-de-la-Meuse, France. This work dates back to the mid-

Exploring

● ATTRACTIONS

1. Tour de la Bourse
2. Square Victoria
3. Maison de l'OACI
4. Centre de Commerce Mondial de Montréal
5. Banque Royale
6. Banque Molson
7. Place d'Armes
8. Banque de Montréal
9. Parc de La Presse
10. Basilique Notre-Dame
11. Vieux Séminaire
12. Cours Le Royer
13. Place Royale
14. Centre iSci / Imax
15. Musée d'Archéologie et d'Histoire de la Pointe-à-Callière
16. Place D'Youville
17. Hôpital Général des Sœurs Grises
18. Musée Marc-Aurèle-Fortin
19. Vieux-Port de Montréal
20. Auberge Saint-Gabriel
21. Palais de Justice (Courthouse)
22. Édifice Ernest-Cormier
23. Vieux Palais de Justice (Former Courthouse)
24. Place Jacques-Cartier
25. City hall
26. Château Ramezay
27. Sir-George-Étienne-Cartier National Historic Site
28. Gare Viger
29. Gare Dalhousie
30. Chapelle Notre-Dame-de-Bonsecours
31. Maison Papineau
32. Marché Bonsecours
33. Tour de l'Horloge

◯ ACCOMMODATIONS

1. Auberge Alternative
2. Auberge du Vieux-Port
3. Delta Centre-Ville
4. Gîte du Vieux-Montréal
5. Hotel Inter-Continental
6. Les Passants du Sans-Soucy
7. Maison Pierre du Calvet

● RESTAURANTS

1. Bio Train
2. Café Électronique
3. Cage aux Sports
4. Casa de Mateo
5. Chez Better
6. Chez Delmo
7. Chez Queux
8. Crémerie Saint-Vincent
9. Gibby's
10. La Gargote
11. La Marée
12. Le Bonaparte
13. Le Petit Moulinsart
14. Maison Pierre du Calvet
15. Modavie
16. Pavarotti
17. Soto
18. Stash's Café Bazar
19. Steak-Frites
20. Titanic
21. Vieux Saint-Gabriel

18th century; it was exe cuted by Barthélémy Gui-bal, a sculptor from Nîmes, France, who also designed the fountains gracing Place Stanislas in Nancy, France.

Climb the stairway, then walk along the passageway to the modest entrance of the lobby of the Hôtel Inter-Continental. Turn right onto the footbridge leading to the Nordheimer building.

This edifice was restored in order to accommodate the hotel's reception halls, which are linked to the trade centre. Erected in 1888, the building originally

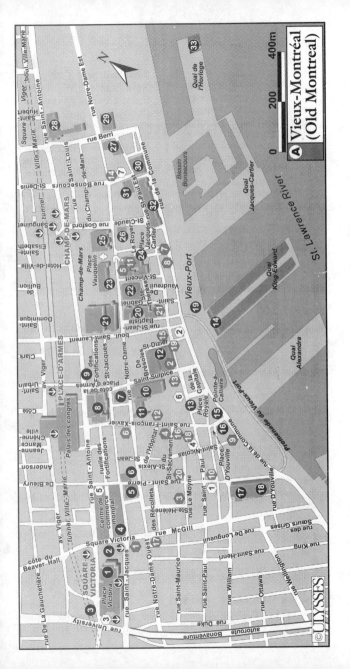

Vieux-Montréal
(Old Montreal)

St. Lawrence River

Quai de l'Horloge

Bassin
Bonsecours

Quai
Jacques-Cartier

Quai
King-Edward

Quai
Alexandra

Vieux-Port

Promenade du Vieux-Port

0   200   400m

© ULYSSES

housed a piano store and a small concert hall, where many great artists performed, including Maurice Ravel and Sarah Bernhardt. The interior, with its combination of dark woodwork, moulded plaster and mosaics, is typical of the late 19th century, characterized by exuberant eclecticism and lively polychromy. The façade, facing Rue Saint-Jacques, combines Romanesque Revival elements, as adapted by American architect Henry Hobson Richardson, with elements from the Chicago School, notably the many-windowed metallic roof.

Exit via 363 Rue Saint-Jacques.

Rue Saint-Jacques was the main artery of Canadian high finance for over a century. This role is reflected in its rich and varied architecture, which serves as a veritable encyclopedia of styles from 1830 to 1930. In those years, the banks, insurance companies and department stores, as well as the nation's railway and shipping companies, were largely controlled by Montrealers of Scottish extraction, who had come to the colonies to make their fortune.

Begun in 1928 according to plans by New York skyscraper specialists York and Sawyer, the former head office of the **Banque Royale** /

Royal Bank ★★ (*360 Rue Saint-Jacques*), was one of the last buildings erected during this era of prosperity. The 22-floor tower has a base inspired by Florentine palazzos, which corresponds to the scale of the neighbouring buildings. Inside the edifice, visitors can admire the high ceilings of this "temple of finance" built at a time when banks needed impressive buildings to win customers' confidence. The walls of the great hall are emblazoned with the heraldic insignia of eight of the 10 Canadian provinces, as well as those of Montréal (St. George's Cross) and Halifax (a yellow bird), where the bank was founded in 1861.

The **Banque Molson / Molson Bank** ★ (*288 Rue Saint-Jacques*), was founded in 1854 by the Molson family, famous for the brewery established by their ancestor, John Molson (1763-1836), in 1786. The Molson Bank, like other banks at the time, even printed its own paper money – an indication of the power wielded by its owners, who contributed greatly to the city's development. The head office of the family business looks more like a patrician residence than an anonymous bank. Completed in 1866, it is one of the earliest examples of the Second Empire, or Napoleon III, style to have been erected in Canada. This French style, modelled on the Louvre and the Paris Opera, was extremely popular in North America between 1865 and 1890. Above the entrance, visitors will see the sandstone carvings of the heads of William Molson and two of his children. The Molson Bank merged with the Bank of Montréal in 1925.

Walk along Rue Saint-Jacques; you'll soon come to Place d'Armes.

Under the French Regime, **Place d'Armes** ★ ★ was the heart of the city. Used for military manoeuvres and religious processions, the square was also the location of the Gadoys well, the city's main source of potable water. In 1847, the square was transformed into a lovely, fenced-in Victorian garden, which was destroyed at the beginning of the 20th century in order to make room for a tramway terminal. In the meantime, a **monument to Maisonneuve** was erected in 1895. Executed by sculptor Philippe Hébert, it shows the founder of Montréal, Paul de Chomedey, Sieur de Maisonneuve, surrounded by prominent figures from the city's early history, namely Jeanne Mance, founder of the Hôtel-Dieu (hospital), Lambert Closse, along with his dog Pilote,

and Charles Lemoyne, head of a family of famous explorers. An Iroquois warrior completes the tableau.

The square, which is in fact shaped more like a trapezoid, is surrounded by several noteworthy buildings. The **Banque de Montréal** ★ ★ (*119 Rue Saint-Jacques, Place-d'Armes métro*), or Bank of Montreal, founded in 1817 by a group of merchants, is the country's oldest banking institution. Its present head office takes up an entire block on the north side of Place d'Armes. A magnificent building by John Wells, built in 1847 and modelled after the Roman Pantheon, it occupies the place of honour in the centre of the block, and offers customer banking. Its Corinthian portico is a monument to the commercial power of the Scottish merchants who founded the institution. The capitals of the columns, severely damaged by pollution, were replaced in 1970 with aluminum replicas. The pediment includes a bas-relief depicting the bank's coat of arms carved out of Binney stone in Scotland by Her Majesty's sculptor, Sir John Steele.

The interior was almost entirely redone in 1904-05, according to plans by celebrated New York architects McKim, Mead and White

Exploring

(Boston Library, Columbia University in New York City). On this occasion, the bank was endowed with a splendid banking hall, designed in the style of a Roman basilica, with green syenite columns, gilded bronze ornamentation and beige marble counters. A small **Numismatic Museum** (*free admission; Mon to Fri 9am to 5pm*) located in the lobby of the more recent building displays bills from different eras, as well as an amusing collection of mechanical piggy banks. Across from the museum, visitors will find four bas-reliefs carved out of an artificial stone called *coade*, which once graced the façade of the bank's original head office. These were executed in 1819, after drawings by English sculptor John Bacon.

The surprising red sandstone tower at number 511 Place d'Armes was erected in 1888 for the New York Life insurance company according to a design by architects Babb, Cook and Willard. Although it only has eight floors, it is regarded as Montréal's first skyscraper. The stone used for the facing was imported from Scotland. At the time, this type of stone was transported in the holds of ships, where it served as ballast until it was sold to building contractors at the pier. The edifice next door (*507 Place-d'Armes*) is adorned with beautiful Art Deco details. It was one of the first buildings over 10 stories to be erected in Montréal after a regulation restricting the height of structures was repealed in 1927.

A short optional excursion from the bottom of Côte de la Place d'Armes provides a look at the **Parc de la Presse** (*free admission; Jun to end of Oct, every day 8am to 9pm; at the corner of Saint-Antoine Ouest and Saint-Urbain*). Set where old houses once stood, this private green space was laid out according to plans by *La Presse*, the newspaper whose offices adjoin the park to the east. This daily is one of four major papers published in Montréal. The tiny park is traversed by alleyways and dotted with panels relating the history of Old Montréal through reproductions of *La Presse* articles published since the paper's founding in 1884.

On the south side of the Place d'Armes, visitors will find the Basilique Notre-Dame and the Vieux Séminaire, which are described below.

In 1663, the seigneury of the island of Montréal was acquired by the Sulpicians from Paris, who remained its undisputed masters up until the British conquest of

1760. In addition to distributing land to colonists and laying out the city's first streets, the Sulpicians were responsible for the construction of a large number of buildings, including Montréal's first parish church (1673). Dedicated to *Notre Dame* (Our Lady), this church had a beautiful Baroque façade, which faced straight down the centre of the street of the same name, creating a pleasant perspective characteristic of classical French town-planning.

Basilique Notre-Dame

At the beginning of the 19th century, however, this rustic little church cut a sorry figure when compared to the Anglican cathedral on Rue Notre-Dame and the new Catholic cathedral on Rue Saint-Denis, neither of which remains today. The Sulpicians therefore decided to make a decisive move to surpass their rivals once and for all. In 1823, to the great displeasure of local architects, they commissioned New York architect James O'Donnell, who came from an Irish Protestant background, to design the largest and most original church north of Mexico.

Basilique Notre-Dame ★ ★ ★ (*$2;110 Rue Notre-Dame Ouest, Place-d'Armes métro,* ☎*842-2925*), built between 1824 and 1829, is a true North American masterpiece of Gothic Revival architecture. It should be seen not as a replica of a European cathedral, but rather as a fundamentally neoclassical structure characteristic of the Industrial Revolution, complemented by a medieval-style decor which foreshadowed the historicism of the Victorian era. These elements make the building remarkable.

Exploring

O'Donnell was so pleased with his work that he converted to Catholicism before dying, so that he could be buried under the church. Between 1874 and 1880, the original interior, considered too austere, was replaced by the fabulous polychromatic decorations found today. Executed by Victor Bourgeau, then the leading architect of religious buildings in the Montréal region, along with about 50 artists, it is made entirely of wood, painted and gilded with gold leaf. Particularly noteworthy features include the baptistery, decorated with frescoes by Ozias Leduc, and the powerful electropneumatic Casavant organ with its 5,772 pipes, often used during the numerous concerts given at the basilica. Lastly, there are the stained-glass windows by Francis Chigot, a master glass artist from France, which depict various episodes in the history of Montréal. They were installed in honour of the church's 100th anniversary.

To the right of the chancel, a passage leads to the Chapelle du Sacré-Cœur (Sacred Heart Chapel), added to the back of the church in 1888. Nicknamed the Chapelle des Mariages (Wedding Chapel) because of the countless nuptials held there every year, it was seriously damaged by fire in 1978. The spiral staircases and the side galleries are all that remain of the exuberant, Spanish-style Gothic-Revival decor of the original. The architects Jodoin, Lamarre and Pratte decided to tie these vestiges in with a modern design, completed in 1981, and included a lovely sectioned vault with skylights, a large bronze reredos by Charles Daudelin and a Guilbault-Thérien mechanical organ. To the right, on the way out of the chapel, visitors will find the small **Musée de la Basilique**, a museum displaying various treasures, including embroidered liturgical clothing as well as the episcopal throne and personal effects of Monseigneur de Pontbriand, the last bishop of New France.

The **Vieux Séminaire** ★ (*116 Rue Notre-Dame Ouest, Place-d'Armes métro*), or old seminary, was built in 1683 in the style of a Parisian *hôtel particulier*, with a courtyard in front and a garden in back. It is the oldest building in the city. For more than three centuries, it has been occupied by Sulpician priests, who, under the French Regime, used it as a manor from which they managed their vast seigneury. At the time of the building's construction, Montréal had barely 500 inhabitants, and was constantly being terrorized by Iroquois attacks. Under those circumstances, the seminary, albeit modest in appearance, represented a precious haven of European civilization in the middle of a wild, isolated land. The public clock at the top of the façade was installed in 1701, and may be the oldest one of its kind in the Americas.

Take Rue Saint-Sulpice, which runs alongside the basilica.

The immense warehouses of the **Cours Le Royer** ★ (*Rue Saint-Sulpice, Place-d'Armes métro*) belonged to the *religieuses hospitalières* of Saint-Joseph. These nursing sisters of Saint-Joseph rented them out to importers. Designed between 1860 and 1871 by Michel Laurent and Victor Bourgeau, who seldom worked on commercial structures, they are located on the site of Montréal's first Hôtel-Dieu (hospital), founded by Jeanne Mance in 1643. The warehouses, covering a total of 43,000m², were converted into apartments and offices between 1977 and 1986. The small Rue Le Royer was excavated to make room for an underground parking lot, now covered by a pleasant pedestrian mall.

Turn right on Rue Saint-Paul, towards Place Royale, which lies on the left-hand side of the street.

Old Montréal contains a large number of 19th-century warehouses with stone frames used to store the goods unloaded from ships at the nearby port. Certain elements of their design – their large glass surfaces, intended to reduce the need for artificial gas lighting and consequently the risk of fire; their wide open interior spaces; the austere style of their Victorian façades – make these buildings the natural precursors of modern architecture.

Montréal's oldest public square, **Place Royale** dates back to 1657. Originally a market square, it later became a pretty Victorian garden surrounded by a cast-iron fence. In 1991, it was raised in order to make room for an archaeological observation site. It now links the Musée d'Archéologie de la Pointe-à-Callière to the **Vieille Douane**, the old customs house, on the north side. The latter is a lovely example of British neoclassical architecture transplanted into a Canadian setting. The building's austere lines, accentuated by the facing, made of local grey stone, are offset by the appropriate proportions and simplified references to antiquity. The old customs house was

Exploring

built in 1836 according to drawings by John Ostell, who had just arrived in Montréal.

The **iSci** *($9.95, IMAX and exhibitions $16.95; every day 10am to 6pm, IMAX every hour from 10:15am to 9:15pm, IMMERSION every 30min from 10am to 8pm; Old Port of Montreal, on King Edward Pier, at the corner of Blvd. St-Laurent and Rue de la Commune, Place d'Armes metro, ☎496-ISCI, 877-496-ISCI, www.isci.ca)* centre, a brand-new interactive science-and-entertainment complex set up in a building of modern architecture, invites you to fathom the secrets of the world of science and technology while having a great time. The centre features three interactive exhibition halls where participants can take part in science experiments, games of skill and several

Pointe-à-Callière, Montréal Museum of Archaeology and History

cultural and educational activities. The iSci Centre also boasts a 2-D and 3-D **IMAX** theatre, the IMMERSION Interactive Cinema, with three giant screens, as well as restaurants and shops. A vast parking lot is also located on site.

The **Musée d'Archéologie et d'Histoire de la Pointe-à-Callière / Pointe-à-Callière, Montréal Museum of Archaeology and History★★** *($9.50; Sep to Jun, Tue to Fri 10am to 5pm, Sat and Sun 11am to 5pm; Jul and Aug, Tue to Fri 10am to 6pm, Sat and Sun 11am to 6pm; 350 Place Royale, Pointe-à-Callière, Place-d'Armes métro, ☎872-9150)*. This archaeology and history museum lies on the exact site where Montréal was founded on May 18, 1642. The Rivière Saint-Pierre used to flow alongside the area now occupied by Place d'You-ville, while the muddy banks of the St. Lawrence reached almost as far as the present-day Rue de la Commune. The first colonists built Fort Ville-Marie out of earth and wooden posts on the isolated point of land created by these two bodies of water. Threatened by Iroquois flotillas and flooding, the leaders of the colony soon decided to establish the town on Coteau Saint-Louis, the hill now bisected by Rue Notre-Dame. The site of the fort was then occupied by a cemetery and the château of Governor de Callière, hence the name.

The museum uses the most advanced techniques available to provide visitors with a survey of the city's history. Attractions include a multimedia presentation, a visit to the vestiges discovered on the site, excellent models showing the different stages of Place Royale's development, holograms and thematic exhibitions. Designed by architect Dan Hanganu, the museum was erected for the celebrations of the city's 350th anniversary in 1992.

Head towards Place d'Youville, to the right of the museum.

Stretching from Place Royale to Rue McGill, **Place d'Youville** owes its elongated shape to its location on top of the bed of the Rivière Saint-Pierre, which was canalled in 1832. In the

middle of the square stands the **Centre d'Histoire de Montréal** (*$6.25; Tue to Sun 10am to 5pm, closed Dec to Jul; 335 Place d'Youville, Square-Victoria métro, renovations until june 30, 2001* ☎872-3207, ╺872-9645), a small, unpretentious historical museum presenting temporary exhibitions on various themes related to life in Montréal. The building itself is the former fire station number 3, one of only a few examples of Flemish-style architecture in Québec. The Marché Sainte-Anne once lay to the west of Rue Saint-Pierre and was, from 1840 to 1849, the seat of the Parliament of United Canada. In 1849, the Orangemen burned the building after a law intended to compensate both French and English victims of the rebellion of 1837-38 was adopted. The event marked the end of Montréal's political vocation.

Turn left on Rue Saint-Pierre.

The Sœurs de la Charité (Sisters of Charity) are better known as the Sœurs Grises (Grey Nuns), a nickname given these nuns falsely accused of selling alcohol to the natives and thus getting them tipsy (in French, *gris* means both grey and tipsy). In 1747, the founder of the community, Saint Marguerite d'Youville, took charge of the former

Lachine Canal

Hôpital des Frères Charon, established in 1693, and transformed it into the **Hôpital Général des Sœurs Grises** ★ (*138 Rue Saint-Pierre, Square-Victoria métro*), a shelter for the city's homeless children. The west wing and the ruins of the chapel are all that remain of this complex built during the 17th and 18th centuries in the shape of an *H*. The other part, which made up another of the old city's classical perspectives, was torn open when Rue Saint-Pierre was extended through the middle of the chapel. The right transept and part of the apse, visible on the right, have been reinforced in order to accommodate a work of art representing the text of the congregation's letters patent.

The small **Musée Marc-Aurèle-Fortin** (*$4; Tue to Sun 11am to 5pm; 118 Rue Saint-Pierre, Square-Victoria métro, ☎845-6108, ≈845-6100, mafortin@globetrotter.net*), which has only a few rooms, is entirely dedicated to the work of Marc-Aurèle Fortin. Using his own unique style, Fortin painted picturesque Québec scenes. Paintings executed on a black background and majestic trees are just a couple of his trademarks. The museum has some lovely pieces.

Head across Rue de la Commune to the Promenade du Vieux-Port, which runs alongside the St. Lawrence.

On the right, directly in line with Rue McGill, visitors

will find the mouth of the **Canal de Lachine / Lachine Canal**, inaugurated in 1825. This waterway made it possible to bypass the formidable rapids known as the Rapides de Lachine upriver from Montréal, thus providing access to the Great Lakes and the American Midwest. The canal also became the cradle of the industrial revolution in Canada, since the spinning and flour-mills were able to harness its power, as well as a direct means of taking in supplies and sending out shipments (from the boat to the factory and vice versa). Closed in 1959 when the seaway was opened, the canal was turned over to the Canadian Parks Services.

A bicycle path now runs alongside it, continuing on to the vieux-port or old port.

The locks, restored in 1991, lie adjacent to a park and a boldly-designed lock-keeper's house. Behind the locks stands the last of the old port's towering **grain silos**. Erected in 1905, this reinforced concrete structure excited the admiration of Walter Gropius and Le Corbusier when they came here on a study trip. It is now illuminated as if it were a monument. In front, visitors will see the strange pile of cubes that form Hab-

itat '67 (see p 196) on the right, and the **Gare Maritime Iberville** (☎496-7678), the harbour station for liners cruising the St. Lawrence, on the left.

The Port of Montréal is the largest inland port on the continent. It stretches 25km along the St. Lawrence, from Cité du Havre to the refineries in the east end. The **Vieux-Port de Montréal / Old Port ★★** (*Place-d'Armes or Champs-de-Mars métros*), or old port, corresponds to the historic portion of the port, located in front of the old city. Abandoned because of its obsolescence, it was revamped between 1983 and 1992, following the example of various other centrally located North American ports.

The old port encompasses a pleasant park, laid out on the embankments and coupled with a promenade, which runs alongside the piers or *quai*, offering a "window" on the river and the few shipping activities that have fortunately been maintained.

The layout accents the view of the water, the downtown area and Rue de la Commune, whose wall of neoclassical, grey stone warehouses stands before the city, one of the only examples of so-called "waterfront planning" in North

Exploring

America. From the port, visitors can set off on an excursion on the river and the Lachine canal aboard **Le Bateau Mouche** (*$20; mid-May to mid-Oct, departures every day at 10am, noon, 2pm, 4pm; Quai Jacques-Cartier; ☎849-9952*), whose glass roof enables passengers to fully appreciate the beauty of the surroundings. These guided tours last 1.5hrs. At night, you can also enjoy a supper and a dance on the boat (*3.5 hrs; $68-$100, mid-Jun to mid-Oct*).

The ***navettes fluviales***, or river shuttles, (☎*281-8000*) ferry passengers to Île Sainte-Hélène (*$3*) and Longueuil (*$3.50*), offering a spectacular view of the old port and Old Montréal along the way.

Walk along the promenade to **Boulevard Saint-Laurent**, one of the city's main arteries, which serves as the dividing line between east and west not only as far as place names and addresses are concerned, but also from an ethnic point of view. Traditionally, there has always been a higher concentration of English-speakers in the western part of the city, and French-speakers in the eastern part, while ethnic minorities of all different origins are concentrated along Boulevard Saint-Laurent.

Head up Boulevard Saint-Laurent to Rue Saint-Paul. Turn right, then left on to a narrow street named Rue Saint-Gabriel.

It was on this street that Richard Dulong opened an inn in 1754. Today, the **Auberge Saint-Gabriel** (*426 Rue Saint-Gabriel, Place-d'Armes, ☎878-3561*), the oldest Canadian inn still open, operates only as a restaurant (see p 286). It occupies a group of 18th-century buildings with sturdy fieldstone walls.

Turn right on Rue Notre-Dame.

Having passed through the financial and warehouse districts, visitors now enter an area dominated by civic and legal institutions; no less than three courthouses lie clustered along Rue Notre-Dame. Inaugurated in 1971, the massive **Palais de Justice** (*1 Rue Notre-Dame Est, Champs-de-Mars métro*), or courthouse, dwarfs the surroundings. A sculpture by Charles Daudelin entitled *Allegro-cube* lies on its steps. A mechanism makes it possible to open and close this stylized "hand of justice."

From the time it was inaugurated in 1926 until it closed in 1970, the **Édifice Ernest-Cormier** ★ (*100 Rue Notre-Dame Est, Champs-de-*

Mars métro) was used for criminal proceedings. The former courthouse was converted into a conservatory and was named after its architect, the illustrious Ernest Cormier, who also designed the main pavilion of the Université de Montréal and the doors of the United Nations Headquarters in New York City. The Courthouse is graced with outstanding bronze sconces, cast in Paris at the workshops of Edgar Brandt. Their installation in 1925 ushered in the Art Deco style in Canada. The main hall, faced with travertine and topped by three dome-shaped skylights, is worth a quick visit.

The **Vieux Palais de Justice** ★ (*155 Rue Notre-Dame Est, Champs-de-Mars métro*), the oldest courthouse in Montréal, was built between 1849 and 1856, according to a design by John Ostell and Henri-Maurice Perrault, on the site of the first courthouse, which was erected in 1800. It is another fine example of Canadian neo-classical architecture. After the courts were divided in 1926, the old Palais was used for civil cases, judged according to the Napoleonic Code. Since the opening of the new Palais to its left, the old Palais has been converted into an annex of the city hall, located to the right.

Place Jacques-Cartier ★ (*Champs-de-Mars métro*) was laid out on the site once occupied by the Château de Vaudreuil, which burned down in 1803. The former Montréal residence of the governor of New France was without question the most elegant private home in the city. Designed by engineer Gaspard Chaussegros de Léry in 1723, it had a horseshoe-shaped staircase, leading up to a handsome cut-stone portal, two projecting pavilions (one on each side of the main part of the building), and a formal garden that extended as far as Rue Notre-Dame. After the fire, the property was purchased by local merchants, who decided to give the government a small strip of land, on the condition that a public market be established there, thus increasing the value of the adjacent property, which remained in private hands. This explains Place Jacques-Cartier's oblong shape.

Merchants of British descent sought various means of ensuring their visibility and publicly expressing their patriotism in Montréal. They quickly formed a much larger community in Montréal than in Québec City, where the government and military headquarters were located. In 1809, they were the first in the world to erect a monument to Ad

Exploring

Montréal's city hall

miral Horatio Nelson, who defeated the combined French and Spanish fleets in the Battle of Trafalgar. Supposedly, they even got the French-Canadian merchants drunk in order to extort a financial contribution from them for the project. The base of the **Colonne Nelson**, or the Nelson Column, was designed and executed in London, according to plans by architect Robert Mitchell. It is decorated with bas-reliefs depicting the exploits of the famous Admiral at Abukir, Copenhagen, and of course Trafalgar. The statue of Nelson at the top was originally made of an artificial type of stone, but after being damaged time and time again by protestors, it was finally replaced by a fibre-glass replica in 1981. The column is the

oldest extant monument in Montréal. At the other end of Place Jacques-Cartier, visitors will see the **Quai Jacques-Cartier** and the river, while **Rue Saint-Amable** lies tucked away on the right, at the halfway mark. During summer, artists and artisans gather on this little street, selling jewellery, drawings, etchings and caricatures.

Under the French Regime, Montréal, following the example of Québec City and Trois-Rivières, had its own governor, not to be confused with the governor of New France as a whole. The situation was the same under the English Regime. It wasn't until 1833 that the first elected mayor, Jacques Viger, took control of the city. This man, who was passionately interested in history, gave Montréal its motto (*Concordia Salus*) and coat of arms, composed of the four symbols of the "founding" peoples, namely the *fleur-de-lys*, the Irish clover, the Scottish thistle and the English rose, all linked together by the Canadian beaver.

After occupying a number of inadequate buildings for decades (a notable example was the Hayes aqueduct, an edifice containing an immense reservoir of water, which cracked one day while a meeting was being held in the council chamber immediately below; it's easy to imagine what happened next), the municipal administration finally moved into its present home in 1878. The **hôtel de ville** ★ (*275 Rue Notre-Dame Est, Champs-de-Mars métro*), or city hall, a fine example of the Second Empire, or Napoleon III, style, is the work of Henri-Maurice Perrault, who also designed the neighbouring courthouse. In 1922, a fire (yet another!) destroyed the interior and roof of the building, later restored in 1926, after the model of the city hall in Tours, France. Exhibitions are occasionally presented in the main hall, which is accessible via the main entrance. Visitors may also be interested to know that it was from the balcony of City Hall that France's General de Gaulle cried out

his famous "*Vive le Québec libre!*" ("Freedom for Québec!") in 1967, to the great delight of the crowd gathered in front of the building.

*Head to the rear of the Hôtel de Ville, by way of the pretty **Place Vauquelin**, the continuation of Place Jacques-Cartier.*

The statue of Admiral Jean Vauquelin, defender of Louisbourg at the end of the French Regime, was probably put here to counterbalance the monument to Nelson, a symbol of British control over Canada. Go down the staircase leading to the **Champ-de-Mars**, modified in 1991 in order to reveal some vestiges of the fortifications that once surrounded Montréal. Gaspard Chaussegros de Léry designed Montréal's ramparts, erected between 1717 and 1745, as well as those of Québec City. The walls of Montréal, however, never saw war, as the city's commercial calling and its location ruled out such rash acts. The large, tree-lined lawns are reminders of the Champ-de-Mars' former vocation as a parade ground for military manoeuvres up until 1924. A view of the downtown area's skyscrapers opens up through the clearing.

Head back to Rue Notre-Dame.

Exploring

The humblest of all the "châteaux" built in Montréal, the **Château Ramezay** ★★ (*$6; summer, every day 10am to 6pm; rest of the year, Tue to Sun 10am to 4:30pm; schedule subject to change; 280 Rue Notre-Dame Est, Champs-de-Mars métro, ☎861-3708*) is the only one still standing. It was built in 1705 for the governor of Montréal, Claude de Ramezay, and his family. In 1745, it fell into the hands of the Compagnie des Indes Occidentales (The French West Indies Company), which made it its North American headquarters. Precious Canadian furs were stored in its vaults awaiting shipment to France. After the conquest (1760), the British occupied the house, before being temporarily removed by American insurgents who wanted Québec to join the nascent United States. Benjamin Franklin even came to stay at the château for a few months in 1775, in an attempt to convince Montrealers to become American citizens.

In 1896, after serving as the first building of the Montréal branch of the Université Laval in Québec City, the château was converted into a museum, under the patronage of the Société d'Histoire et de Numismatique de Montréal (Montréal Numismatic and Antiquarian Society), founded by Jacques Viger. Visitors will still find a rich collection of furniture, clothing and everyday objects from the 18th and 19th centuries here, as well as many Aboriginal artefacts. The Salle de Nantes is decorated with beautiful Louis XV-style mahogany panelling, designed by Germain Boffrand and imported from the Nantes office of the Compagnie des Indes (circa 1750).

Walk along Rue Notre-Dame to Rue Berri.

At the corner of Rue Berri lies the **Sir George-Étienne-Cartier National Historic Site** ★ (*$3.25; early Sep to late Dec and early Apr to late May, Wed to Sun 10am to noon and 1pm to 5pm; Jun, Mon to Fri 10am to 5pm, Sat and Sun, 10am to 6pm; Jul and Aug, every day 10am to 6pm; closed Jan to Mar; 458 Rue Notre-Dame Est, Champs-de-Mars métro ☎283-2282*), composed of twin houses inhabited successively by George-Étienne Cartier, one of the Fathers of Canadian Confederation. Inside, visitors will find a reconstructed mid-19th-century French-Canadian bourgeois home, complete with sound effects. Temporary exhibitions top off a tour of the premises. The neighbouring building, at number 452, is the former **Cathédrale**

Schismatique Grecque Saint-Nicolas, built around 1910 in the Romanesque-Byzantine Revival style.

Rue Berri marks the eastern border of Old Montréal, and thus the fortified city of the French Regime, beyond which extended the Faubourg Québec, excavated in the 19th century to make way for railroad lines, which explains the sharp difference in height between the hill known as Coteau Saint-Louis and the Viger and Dalhousie stations. **Gare Viger**, visible on the left, was inaugurated by Canadian Pacific in 1895 in order to serve the eastern part of the country. Its resemblance to the Château Frontenac in Québec City is not merely coincidental; both buildings were designed for the same railroad company and by the same architect, an American named Bruce Price. The Château-style station, closed in 1935, also included a prestigious hotel and large stained-glass train shed that has been destroyed.

Smaller **Gare Dalhousie**, located near the Maison Cartier (*514 Rue Notre-Dame, Champs-de-Mars métro*) was the first railway station built by Canadian Pacific, a company established for the purpose of building a Canadian transcontinental railroad.

The station was the starting point of the first transcontinental train headed for Vancouver on June 28, 1886. Canadian Pacific seems to have had a weakness for foreign architects, since it was Thomas C. Sorby, Director of Public Works in England, who drew up the plans for this humble structure.

Today, it is used by the École Nationale du Cirque (the National Circus School). From the top of Rue Notre-Dame, the port's former refrigerated warehouse, made of brown brick, is visible, as well as Île Sainte-Hélène, in the middle of the river. This island, along with Île Notre-Dame, was the site of the Expo '67.

Turn right on Rue Berri, and right again on Rue Saint-Paul, which offers a lovely view of the dome of the Marché Bonsecours. Continue straight ahead to Chapelle Notre-Dame-de-Bonsecours.

This site was originally occupied by another chapel, built in 1657 upon the recommendation of Saint Marguerite Bourgeoys, founder of the congregation of Notre-Dame. The present **Chapelle Notre-Dame-de-Bonsecours ★** (*400 Rue Saint-Paul Est, Champs-de-Mars métro*) dates back to 1771, when the Sulpicians wanted

Exploring

to establish a branch of the main parish in the eastern part of the fortified city. In 1890, the chapel was modified to suit contemporary tastes, and the present stone façade was added, along with the "aerial" chapel looking out on the port. Parishioners asked God's blessing on ships and their crews bound for Europe from this chapel.

The interior, redone at the same time, contains a large number of votive offerings from sailors saved from shipwrecks. Some are in the form of model ships, hung from the ceiling of the nave. At the back of the chapel, the little **Musée Marguerite-Bourgeoys** (*$5; summer, 10am to 5pm; Nov 1 to May 1, Tue to Sun 11am to 3:30pm, closed mid-Jan to mid-Mar*, ☎282-8670) displays mementos of the saint. From there, visitors can reach a platform adjoining the "aerial" chapel, which offers an interesting view of the old port.

The **Maison Pierre-du-Calvet**, at the corner of Rue Bonsecours (*number 401*), is representative of 18th-century, French urban architecture adapted to the local setting, with thick walls made of fieldstone embedded in mortar, storm windows doubling the casement windows with their little squares of glass imported from France, and high firebreak walls, then required by local regulations as a means of limiting the spread of fire from one building to the next.

A little higher on Rue Bonsecours, visitors will find the **Maison Papineau** (*440 Rue Bonsecours, Champs-de-Mars métro*) inhabited long ago by Louis-Joseph Papineau (1786-1871), lawyer, politician and head of the French-Canadian nationalist movement up until the insurrection of 1837. Built in 1785 and covered with a wooden facing made to look like cut stone, it was one of the first buildings in Old Montréal to be restored (1962).

Chapelle Notre-Dame-de-Bonsecours

The **Marché Bonsecours** ★★ (*350 Rue Saint-Paul Est,* ☎872-7730) was erected between 1845 and 1850. The lovely grey stone neoclassical edifice with sash windows, is on **Rue Saint-Paul**, for many years Montréal's main commercial artery. The building is adorned with a portico supported by cast iron columns moulded in England, and topped by a silvery dome, which for many years served as the symbol of the city at the entrance to the port. The public market, closed since the early 1960s following the advent of the supermarket, was transformed into municipal offices, then an exhibition hall before finally reopening partially in 1996.

It now presents an exhibition and is host to arts and crafts shops. The building originally housed both the city hall and a concert hall upstairs. The market's old storehouses, recently renovated, can be seen on Rue Saint-Paul. From the large balcony on Rue de la Commune you can see the partially reconstructed Bonsecours dock, where paddle-wheelers, full of farmers who came to the city to sell their produce, used to moor.

Walk to Place Jacques-Cartier, then turn left, toward the old port.

At the southern end of Place Jacques-Cartier rise the multiple metallic points of the **Pavillon Jacques-Cartier**. Inside you'll find a cafeteria and terrace-bar, as well as a promenade extending all the way to the southeastern edge of the pier upon which the pavilion stands.

The **Tour de l'Horloge** ★ (*at the end of the Quai de l'Horloge; May to Oct*) is visible to the east from the end of Quai Jacques-Cartier. Painted a pale yellow, the structure is actually a monument erected in 1922 in memory of merchant marine sailors who died during WWI. It was inaugurated by the Prince of Wales (who became Edward VIII) during one of his many visits to Montréal. An observatory at the top of the tower provides a clear view of Île Sainte-Hélène, the Jacques-Cartier bridge and the eastern part of Old Montréal. Standing on Place Belvédère at the base of the tower, one has the impression of standing on the deck of ship as it glides slowly down the St. Lawrence and out to the Atlantic Ocean.

To return to the métro, walk back up Place Jacques-Cartier, cross Rue Notre-Dame, Place Vauquelin and lastly Champ-de-Mars, to the station of the same name.

Exploring

Tour B: Downtown

The downtown skyscrapers give Montréal a typically North American look. Nevertheless, unlike most other cities on the continent, there is a certain Latin spirit here, which seeps in between the towering buildings, livening up this part of Montréal both day and night. Bars, cafés, department stores, shops and head offices, along with two universities and numerous colleges, all lie clustered within a limited area at the foot of Mont Royal.

At the beginning of the 20th century, Montréal's central business district gradually shifted from the old city to what was up until then a posh residential neighbourhood known as The Golden Square Mile, inhabited by upper-class Canadians. Wide arterial streets such as Boulevard René-Lévesque were then lined with palatial residences surrounded by shady gardens. The city centre underwent a radical transformation in a very short time (1960-1967), marked by the construction of Place Ville-Marie, the métro, the underground city, Place des Arts, and various other infrastructures which still exert an influence on the area's development.

Walk up on Rue Guy from the exit of the Guy-Concordia métro station, then turn right on Rue Sherbrooke.

In addition to being invaded by the business world, the Golden Square Mile also underwent profound social changes that altered its character – the exodus of the Scottish population, the shortage of servants, income taxes, World War I, during which the sons of many of these families were killed, and above all the stock market crash of 1929, which ruined many businessmen. Consequently, numerous mansions were demolished and the remaining population had to adjust to more modest living conditions. **The Linton ★** (*1509 Rue Sherbrooke Ouest, Guy-Concordia métro*), a prestigious apartment building erected in 1907, provided an interesting alternative. It was built on the grounds of the house of the same name still visible in the back, on little Rue Simpson. The façade of the Linton is adorned with lavish Beaux-Arts details made of terracotta and a beautiful cast-iron marquee.

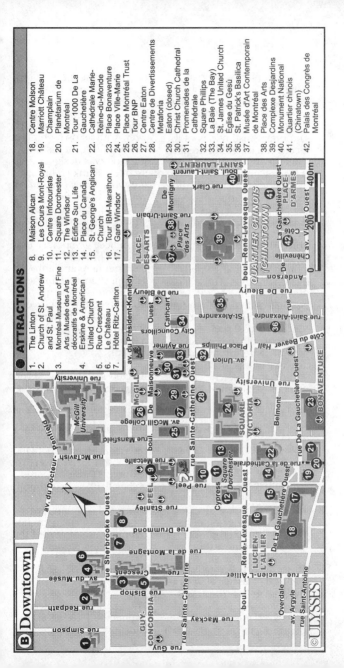

B Downtown

● ATTRACTIONS

1. The Linton
2. Church of St. Andrew and St. Paul
3. Montréal / Musée des Beaux Arts / Musée des Arts décoratifs de Montréal
4. Erskine & American United Church
5. Rue Crescent
6. Le Château
7. Hôtel Ritz-Carlton
8. Maison Alcan
9. Les Cours Mont-Royal
10. Centre Infotouriste
11. Square Dorchester
12. The Windsor
13. Édifice Sun Life
14. Place du Canada
15. St. George's Anglican Church
16. Tour IBM-Marathon
17. Gare Windsor
18. Centre Molson
19. Marriott Château Champlain
20. Planétarium de Montréal
21. Tour 1000 De La Gauchetière
22. Cathédrale Marie-Reine-du-Monde
23. Place Bonaventure
24. Place Ville-Marie
25. Place Montréal Trust
26. Tour BNP
27. Centre Eaton
28. Centre de Divertissements Metaforia
29. Eaton (closed)
30. Christ Church Cathedral
31. Promenades de la Cathédrale
32. Square Phillips
33. La Baie (The Bay)
34. St. James United Church
35. Église du Gesù
36. St. Patrick's Basilica
37. Musée d'Art Contemporain de Montréal
38. Place des Arts
39. Complexe Desjardins
40. Monument National
41. Quartier chinois (Chinatown)
42. Palais des Congrès de Montréal

© ULYSSES

The lovely presbyterian **Church of St. Andrew and St. Paul** ★★ (*at the corner of Rue Redpath, Guy-Concordia métro*) was one of the most important institutions of the Scottish elite in Montréal. Built in 1932 according to plans by architect Harold Lea Fetherstonaugh as the community's third place of worship, it illustrates the endurance of the medieval style in religious architecture. The stone interior is graced with magnificent commemorative stained-glass windows. Those along the aisles came from the second church and are for the most part significant British pieces, such as the windows of Andrew Allan and his wife, produced by the workshop of William Morris after sketches by the famous English Pre-Raphaelite painter, Edward Burne-Jones. The Scottish-Canadian Black Watch Regiment has been affiliated with the church ever since it was created in 1862.

The **Musée des Beaux-Arts de Montréal / Montreal Museum of Fine Arts** ★★★, located in two buildings on either side of Rue Sherbrooke Ouest, is the next tour (see p 128). The small **Musée des Arts Décoratifs de Montréal / Museum of Decorative Arts** ★ (*$4; Tue to Sun 11am to 6pm, Wed 11am to 9pm; 2200 Rue Crescent, Guy-Concordia métro, ☎285-2000*) moved to the the Pavillon Jean-Noël-Desmarais of the Montreal Museum of Fine Arts in May 1997. This is an independent museum, however, with its own entrance on Rue Crescent. Its new location was designed by architect Frank Gehry, and the white walls combined with the wood floor make the place seem more spacious, fully accentuating the works on display. The museum hosts temporary exhibitions of pieces by designers from here and abroad. The museum's permanent collection is made up of furniture and decorative objects in the International Style (from 1935 on) donated by Liliane and David Stewart.

Erected in 1892, the **Erskine & American United Church** ★ (*at the corner of Avenue du Musée*) is an excellent example of the Romanesque Revival style as interpreted by American architect Henry Hobson Richardson. The textured sandstone, large arches flanked by either squat or disproportionately elongated columns, and sequences of small, arched openings are typical of the style. The auditorium-shaped interior was remodelled in the style of the Chicago School in 1937.

The lower chapel (along Avenue du Musée), contains lovely, brilliantly coloured, Tiffany stained-glass windows.

Rue Crescent ★ (*Guy-Concordia métro*), located immediately east of the museum, has a split personality. To the north of Boulevard de Maisonneuve, the street is lined with old row houses, which now accommodate antique shops and luxury boutiques, while to the south, it is crowded with night clubs, restaurants and bars, most with sunny terraces lining the sidewalks. For many years, Rue Crescent was known as the English counterpart of Rue Saint-Denis. Though it is still a favourite among American visitors, its clientele is more diversified now.

A symbol of its era, **Le Château** ★ (*1321 Rue Sherbrooke Ouest, Guy-Concordia métro*), a handsome Château-style building, was erected in 1925 for a French-Canadian businessman by the name of Pamphile du Tremblay, owner of the French-language newspaper *La Presse*. Architects Ross and Macdonald designed what was at the time the largest apartment building in Canada. The Royal Institute awarded these architects a prize for the design of the fashionable **Holt Renfrew** (*1300 Rue Sherbrooke Ouest*) store which stands across the

street in 1937. With its rounded, horizontal lines, the store is a fine example of the streamline Deco.

The last of Montréal's old hotels, the **Ritz-Carlton Kempinski** ★ (*1228 Rue Sherbrooke Ouest, Guy-Concordia or Peel métros*) was inaugurated in 1911 by César Ritz himself. For many years, it was the favourite gathering place of the Montréal bourgeoisie. Some people even stayed here year-round, living a life of luxury among the drawing rooms, garden and ballroom. The building was designed by Warren and Wetmore of New York City, the well-known architects of Grand Central Station on New York's Park Avenue. Many celebrities have stayed at this sophisticated luxury hotel over the years, including Richard Burton and Elizabeth Taylor, who were married here in 1964.

Continue along Rue Sherbrooke to the entrance of Maison Alcan. Three noteworthy buildings lie across the street. **Maison Baxter** (*1201 Rue Sherbrooke Ouest, Peel métro*), on the left, boasts a beautiful stairway. **Maison Forget** (*1195 Rue Sherbrooke Ouest, Peel métro*), in the centre, was built in 1882 for Louis-Joseph Forget, one of the only French-Canadian magnates to live in this neighbourhood dur-

Exploring

ing the 19th century. The building on the right is the **Mount Royal Club**, a private club frequented essentially by business people. Built in 1905, it is the work of Stanford White of the famous New York firm McKim, Mead and White, architects of the head office of the Bank of Montréal on Place d'Armes (see p 83).

Maison Alcan ★ (*1188 Rue Sherbrooke Ouest, Peel métro*), head office of the Alcan aluminum company, is a fine example of historical preservation and inventive urban restructuring. Five buildings along Rue Sherbrooke, including the lovely **Maison Atholstan** (*1172 Rue Sherbrooke Ouest*), the first Beaux-Arts-style structure erected in Montréal (1894), have been carefully restored and joined in the back to an atrium, which is linked to a modern aluminum building. The garden running along the south wall of the modern part provides a little-known passageway between Rue Drummond and Rue Stanley.

Enter the atrium through the Sherbrooke entrance, which used to lead into the lobby of the Berkeley Hotel. Exit through the garden, go to the left and head south on Rue Stanley. Turn left on Boulevard de Maisonneuve, then right on Rue Peel.

Montréal has the most extensive **underground city** in the world (see p 117). Greatly appreciated in bad weather, it provides access to over 2,000 shops and restaurants, as well as movie theatres, apartment and office buildings, hotels, parking lots, the train station, the bus station, Place des Arts and even the Université du Québec à Montréal (UQAM) via tunnels, atriums and indoor plazas. Les **Cours Mont-Royal ★★** (*1455 Rue Peel, Peel métro*) are duly linked to this sprawling network, which centres around the various métro stations. A multi-purpose complex, Les Cours consist of four levels of stores, offices and apartments laid out inside the former Mount Royal Hotel. With its 1,100 rooms, this Jazz Age palace, inaugurated in 1922, was the largest hotel in the British Empire. Aside from the exterior, all that was preserved during the 1987 remodelling was a portion of the ceiling of the lobby, from which the former chandelier of the Monte Carlo casino is suspended. The four 10-story *cours* (inner courts) are definitely worth a visit, as is a stroll through what may be the most well-designed shopping centre in the downtown area. The building that looks like a small Scottish manor across the street is in fact the head office of the Seagram Company (Barton & Guestier wines).

Head south on Rue Peel to Square Dorchester.

At Montreal's tourist office, the **Centre Infotouriste** (*1001 Rue du Square-Dorchester, Peel métro*), visitors will find representatives from a number of tourist-related enterprises, such as tourist offices, Tours Royal Bus Lines, the Le Réseau hotel-reservation service and Ulysses Travel Bookshop.

From 1799 to 1854, **Square Dorchester** ★ (*Peel métro*) was occupied by Montréal's Catholic cemetery, which was then moved to Mont Royal, where it is still located. In 1872, the city turned the free space into two squares, one on either side of Dorchester Street (now Boulevard René-Lévesque). The northern portion is called Square Dorchester, while the southern part was renamed Place du Canada to commemorate the 100th anniversary of Confederation (1967).

A number of monuments adorn Square Dorchester. In the centre, there is an equestrian statue dedicated to Canadian soldiers who died during the Boer War in South Africa, while a handsome statue of Scottish poet Robert Burns styled after Bartholdi's Roaring Lion, donated by the Sun Life insurance company, and Émile Brunet's monument to Sir Wilfrid Laurier, Prime Minister of Canada from 1896 to 1911, stand around the perimeter. The square also serves as the starting point for guided bus tours.

The **Windsor** ★ (*1170 Rue Peel, Peel métro*), the hotel where members of the royal family used to stay during their visits to Canada, no longer exists. The prestigious Second-Empire-style edifice, built in 1878 by architect W. W. Boyinton of Chicago, was claimed by fire in 1957. All that remains of it is an annex erected in 1906, which was converted into an office building in 1986. The ballrooms and lovely Peacock Alley have, however, been preserved. An impressive atrium, visible from the upper floors, has been constructed for the building's tenants. The handsome **Tour CIBC**, designed by Peter Dickinson (1962), stands on the site of the old hotel. Its walls are faced with green slate, which blends harmoniously with the dominant colours of the buildings around the square, namely the greyish beige of stone and the green of oxidized copper.

Exploring

The **Édifice Sun Life** ★★ (*1155 Rue Metcalfe, Peel métro*), erected between 1913 and 1933 for the powerful Sun Life insurance company, was for many years the largest building in the British Empire. It was in this "fortress" of the Anglo-Saxon establishment, with its colonnades reminiscent of ancient mythology, that the British Crown Jewels were hidden during World War II. In 1977, the company's head office was moved to Toronto, in protest against provincial language laws excluding English. Fortunately, the chimes that ring at 5pm every day are still in place and remain an integral part of the neighbourhood's spirit.

Place du Canada ★ (*Bonaventure métro*), the southern portion of Square Dorchester, is the setting for the annual Remembrance Day ceremony (November 11th), which honours Canadian soldiers killed in the two World Wars and in the Korean War. Veterans reunite around the War Memorial, which occupies the place of honour in the centre of the square. A more imposing monument to Sir John A. Macdonald, Canada's first Prime Minister, elected in 1867, stands alongside Boulevard René-Lévesque.

A number of churches clustered around Square Dorchester before it was even laid out in 1872. Unfortunately, only two of the eight churches built in the area between 1865 and 1875 have survived. One of these is the beautiful Gothic-Revival-style **St. George's Anglican Church** ★★ (*at the corner of Rue de la Gauchetière and Rue Peel, Bonaventure métro*). Its delicately sculpted sandstone exterior conceals an interior covered with lovely, dark woodwork. Particularly noteworthy are the remarkable ceiling, with its exposed framework, the woodwork in the chancel, and the tapestry from Westminster Abbey, used during the coronation of Elizabeth II.

The elegant 47-storey **Tour IBM-Marathon** ★ (*1250 Boulevard René-Lévesque Ouest, Bonaventure métro*), forming part of the backdrop of St. George's, was completed in 1991 according to a design by the famous New York architects Kohn, Pedersen and Fox. Its winter bamboo garden is open to the public.

In 1887, the head of Canadian Pacific, William Cornelius Van Horne, asked his New York friend Bruce Price (1845-1903) to draw up the plans for **Gare Windsor** ★ (*at the corner of Rue de* *la Gauchetière and Rue Peel, Bonaventure métro*), a modern train station, which would serve as the terminus of the transcontinental railroad, completed the previous year. At the time, Price was one of the most prominent architects in the eastern United States, where he worked on residential projects for high-society clients, as well as skyscrapers like the American Surety Building in Manhattan. Later, he was put in charge of building the Château Frontenac in Québec City, thus establishing the Château style in Canada.

Massive-looking Gare Windsor, with its corner buttresses, Roman arches outlined in the stone, and series of arcades, is Montréal's best example of the Romanesque Revival style as interpreted by American architect Henry Hobson Richardson. Its construction established the city as the country's railway centre and initiated the shift of commercial and financial activity from the old town to the Golden Square Mile. Abandoned in favour of the Gare Centrale after World War II, Windsor Station was used only for commuter trains up until 1993.

The **Centre Molson / Molson Centre** (*1250 Rue de la Gauchetière, Bonaventure métro*), built on the platforms of Windsor Station, now blocks all train access to the venerable old station. Opened in March 1996, this immense building with its odd shape succeeds the Forum on Sainte-Catherine as the home ice of the National Hockey League's Montréal Canadiens, which are owned by the Molson Brewery. The amphitheatre can seat 21,247 people and boasts 138 glassed-in private boxes sold to Montréal companies for hefty sums. The National Hockey League's regular season runs from October to April, and the play-offs can carry on into June.

Popular music concerts are also often held at the Centre. **Guided tours** (*$8; English tour at 11:15am and 2:45pm, 75 min;* ☎*989-2841*) of the centre are available. These include, when possible, a visit to the Canadiens' dressing room and a chance to see the team practise.

Built in 1966, the **Marriott Château Champlain ★** (*1 Place du Canada, Bonaventure métro*), nicknamed the "cheese grater" by Montrealers due to its many arched, convex openings, was designed by Québec architects Jean-Paul

Exploring

Pothier and Roger D'Astou. The latter is a disciple of American architect Frank Lloyd Wright, with whom he studied for several years. The hotel is not unlike some of the master's late works, characterized by rounded, fluid lines.

Cathédrale Marie-Reine-du-Monde

The **Planétarium de Montréal** ★ (*$6; summer, every day 2:30pm and 7:15pm; winter, Thu to Sun 2:30pm and 7:15pm; presentations last 50 min; 1000 Rue Saint-Jacques Ouest, Bonaventure métro, ☎872-4530*) projects astronomy films onto a 20m hemispheric dome. The universe and its mysteries are explained in a way that makes this marvellous, often poorly understood world accessible to all. Guest lecturers provide commentaries on the presentations.

Tour 1000 de la Gauchetière (*1000 Rue de la Gauchetière, Bonaventure métro*), a 50-story skyscraper, was com-

pleted in 1992. It houses the terminus for buses linking Montréal to the South Shore, as well as the **Amphithéâtre Bell** an indoor skating rink open year-round (*$5, skate rentals $4.50; schedule changes frequently, call ☎395-0555*). The architects wanted to set the building apart from its neighbours by crowning it with a copper-covered point. Its total height is the maximum allowed by the city, namely the height of Mont Royal. The ultimate symbol of Montréal, the mountain may be not surpassed under any circumstances.

Cathédrale Marie-Reine-du-Monde ★★ (*Boulevard René-Lévesque Ouest at the corner of Mansfield, Bonaventure métro*) is the seat of the archdiocese of Montréal and a reminder of the tremendous power wielded by the clergy up until the Quiet Revolution. It is exactly one third the size of St. Peter's in Rome. In 1852, a terrible fire destroyed the Catholic cathedral on Rue Saint-Denis. The ambitious Monseigneur Ignace Bourget (1799-1885), who

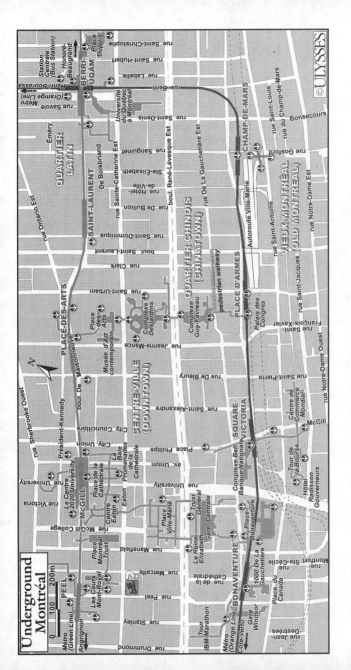

was bishop of Montréal at the time, seized the opportunity to work out a grandiose scheme to outshine the Sulpicians' Basilique Notre-Dame and ensure the supremacy of the Catholic Church in Montréal. What could accomplish these goals better than a replica of Rome's St. Peter's, right in the middle of the Protestant neighbourhood?

Despite reservations on the part of architect Victor Bourgeau, the plan was carried out. The bishop even made Bourgeau go to Rome to measure the venerable building. Construction began in 1870 and was finally completed in 1894. Copper statues of the 13 patron saints of Montréal's parishes were installed in 1900.

Modernized during the 1950s, the interior of the cathedral is no longer as harmonious as it once was. Nevertheless, there is a lovely replica of Bernini's baldaquin, executed by sculptor Victor Vincent. The bishops and archbishops of Montréal are interred in the mortuary chapel on the left, where the place of honour is occupied by the recumbent statue of Monseigneur Bourget.

A monument outside reminds visitors yet again of this individual, who did so much to strengthen the bonds between France and Canada.

An immense, grooved concrete block with no façade, **Place Bonaventure** ★ (*1 Place Bonaventure, Bonaventure métro*), which was completed in 1966, is one of the most revolutionary works of modern architecture of its time. Designed by Montrealer Raymond Affleck, it is a multi-purpose complex built on top of the railway lines leading into the Gare Centrale. It contains a parking area, a two-level shopping centre linked to the métro and the underground city, two large exhibition halls, wholesalers, offices, and an intimate 400-room hotel laid out around a charming hanging garden, worth a short visit.

Place Bonaventure is linked to the métro station of the same name, designed by architect Victor Prus (1964). With its brown-brick facing and bare concrete vaults, the station looks like an early Christian basilica. The **Montréal métro** system has a total of 65 stations divided up among four lines used by trains running on rubber wheels (see map of métro, at the beginning of this guide). Each station has a different design, some very elaborate.

A railway tunnel leading under Mont Royal to the downtown area was built in 1913. The tracks ran under Avenue McGill College, then multiplied at the bottom of a deep trench, which stretched between Rue Mansfield and Rue University. In 1938, the subterranean **Gare Centrale** was built, marking the true starting point of the underground city. Camouflaged since 1957 by the **Hôtel Reine-Elizabeth**, the Queen Elizabeth Hotel, it has an interesting, Streamlined-Deco waiting hall.

Place Ville-Marie ★★★
(*1 Place Ville-Marie, Bonaventure métro*), was erected above the northern part of the formerly open-air trench in 1959. The famous Chinese-American architect Ieoh Ming Pei (Louvre Pyramid, Paris; East Building of the National Gallery, Washington, D.C.) designed the multipurpose complex built over the railway tracks and containing vast shopping arcades now linked to most of the surrounding edifices. It also encompasses a number of office buildings, including the famous cruciform aluminum tower, whose unusual shape enables natural light to penetrate all the way into the centre of the structure, while at the same time symbolizing Montréal, a Catho-lic city dedicated to the Virgin Mary.

In the middle of the public area, a granite compass card indicates true north, while **Avenue McGill College**, which leads straight toward the mountain, indicates "north" as perceived by Montrealers in their everyday life. This artery, lined with multicoloured skyscrapers, was still a narrow residential street in 1950. It now offers a wide view of Mont Royal, crowned by a metallic cross erected in 1927 to commemorate the gesture of Paul Chomedey de Maisonneuve, founder of Montréal, who climbed the mountain in January 1643 and placed a wooden cross at its summit to thank the Virgin Mary for having spared Fort Ville-Marie from a devastating flood.

Cross Place Ville-Marie and take Avenue McGill College.

Avenue McGill College was widened and entirely redesigned during the 1980s. Walking along it, visitors will see several examples of eclectic, polychromatic postmodern architecture composed largely of granite and reflective glass. **Place Montréal Trust** (*at the corner of Rue Sainte-Catherine, McGill métro*) is one of a number of Montréal shopping centres topped by an office building and linked

Exploring

to the underground city and the métro by corridors and private plazas. Children often visualize huge robots from outer space in the building's pink and green façade.

The **Tour BNP** ★ (*1981 Avenue McGill College, McGill métro*), certainly the best designed building on Avenue McGill College, was built for the Banque Nationale de Paris in 1981, by the architectural firm Webb, Zerafa, Menkès, Housden Partnership (Tour Elf-Aquitaine, Paris; Royal Bank, Toronto). Its bluish glass walls set off a sculpture entitled *La Foule Illuminée* (The Illuminated Crowd), by the Franco-British artist Raymond Mason.

Return to Rue Sainte-Catherine Ouest.

Rue Sainte-Catherine is Montréal's main commercial artery. It stretches 15km, changing in appearance several times along the way. Around 1870, it was still lined with row houses; by 1920, however, it had already become an integral part of life in Montréal. Since the 1960s, a number of shopping centres linking the street to the adjacent métro lines have sprouted up among the local businesses. The **Centre Eaton** (*Rue Sainte-Catherine Ouest, McGill métro*) is the most

recent of these. It is composed of a long, old-fashioned gallery lined with five levels of shops, restaurants and movie theatres, and is it's now linked to Place Ville-Marie by a pedestrian tunnel.

The **Centre de Divertissements Metaforia** (*$16 Mon to Fri before 4pm, $20 Thu and Fri after 4pm; 698 Rue Ste-Catherine O., McGill metro, ☎878-6382 or 888-808-META*) presents an imaginative and entertaining show for the whole family in the heart of downtown Montreal. The entertainment centre offers a fantastic 30min voyage through different virtual worlds, creating captivating scenarios with the help of state-of-the-art special effects, including synthetic 3-D images, sound effects, vibrating seats, odour diffusers, sensory devices and a high-fidelity sound system. The Oceania Experience, for example, takes visitors on a one-of-a-kind virtual underwater adventure. The centre also features about 60 innovative, non-violent interactive games, simulators, a climbing wall, children's area, restaurant, two bars and a souvenir shop.

The **Eaton** ★★ department store (*677 Rue Sainte-Catherine Ouest, McGill métro*), one of the largest department stores on Ste-Catherine and an institution across Canada, went bankrupt and had to close its doors in November 1999. The imposing nine-storey building has already been sold, so it will most likely re-open one way or another with new occupants. Its magnificent Art Deco dining room on the 9th floor, designed by Jacques Carlu, should also re-open with the same décor it has had since 1931.

The first Anglican cathedral in Montréal stood on Rue Notre-Dame, not far from Place d'Armes. After a fire in 1856, **Christ Church Cathedral** ★★ (*at the corner of Rue University, McGill métro*) was relocated nearer the community it served, in the heart of the nascent Golden Square Mile. Using the cathedral of his hometown, Salisbury, as his model, architect Frank Wills designed a flamboyant structure, with a single steeple rising above the transepts. The soberness of the interior contrasts with the rich ornamentation of the Catholic churches included in this walking tour. A few beautiful stained-glass windows from the workshops

of William Morris provide the only bit of colour.

The steeple's stone spire was destroyed in 1927 and replaced by an aluminum replica; otherwise, it would have eventually caused the building to sink. The problem, linked to the instability of the foundation, was not resolved, however, until a shopping centre, the **Promenades de la Cathédrale** ★★, was constructed under the building in 1987. Christ Church Anglican Cathedral thus rests on the roof of a shopping mall. On the same occasion, a postmodern glass skyscraper topped by a "crown of thorns" was erected behind the cathedral. There is a pleasant little garden at its base.

Christ Church Cathedral

It was around **Square Phillips** ★ (*at the corner of Rue Union, on either side of Rue Sainte-Catherine, McGill métro*) that the first stores appeared along Rue Sainte-Catherine, which was once strictly residential.

Henry Morgan moved Morgan's Colonial House, now

Exploring

La Baie, the Bay, (*McGill métro*) here after the floods of 1886 in the old city. Henry Birks, descendant of a long line of English jewellers, arrived soon after, establishing his famous shop in a handsome beige sandstone building on the west side of the square. In 1914, a monument to King Edward VII, sculpted by Philippe Hébert, was erected in the centre of Square Phillips. Downtown shoppers and employees alike enjoy relaxing here.

A former Methodist church designed in the shape of an auditorium, **St. James United Church** (*463 Rue Sainte-Catherine Ouest, McGill métro*) originally had a complete façade looking out onto a garden. In 1926, in an effort to counter the decrease in its revenue, the community built a group of stores and offices along the front of the building on Rue Sainte-Catherine, leaving only a narrow passageway into the church. Visitors can still see the two Gothic Revival–style steeples set back from Rue Sainte-Catherine.

Turn right on Rue de Bleury.

After a 40-year absence, the Jesuits returned to Montréal in 1842 at Monseigneur Ignace Bourget's invitation. Six years later, they founded Collège Sainte-Marie, where several generations

of boys would receive an outstanding education.

Église du Gesù ★★ (*1202 Rue de Bleury, Place-des-Arts métro*) was originally designed as the college chapel. The grandiose project begun in 1864 according to plans drawn up by architect Patrick C. Keely of Brooklyn, New York, was never completed, due to lack of funds. Consequently, the church's Renaissance Revival–style towers remain unfinished. The *trompe-l'œil* decor inside was executed by artist Damien Müller. Of particular interest are the seven main altars and surrounding parquetry, all fine examples of cabinet work. The large paintings hanging from the walls were commissioned from the Gagliardi brothers of Rome. The Jesuit college, erected to the south of the church, was demolished in 1975, but the church was fortunately saved, and then restored in 1983.

Visitors can take a short side-trip to St. Patrick's Basilica. To do so, head south on Rue de Bleury. Turn right on Boulevard René-Lévesque, then left on little Rue Saint-Alexandre. Go into the church through one of the side entrances.

Fleeing misery and potato blight, a large number of Irish immigrants came to Montréal between 1820 and 1860, and helped construct the Lachine canal and the Victoria bridge. **St. Patrick's Basilica ★★** (*Rue Saint-Alexandre, Place-des-Arts métro*), was thus built to meet a pressing new demand for a church to serve the Irish Catholic community. When it was inaugurated in 1847, St. Patrick's dominated the city below. Today, it is well hidden by the skyscrapers of the business centre. Architect Pierre-Louis Morin and Père Félix Martin, the Jesuit superior, designed the plans for the edifice, built in the Gothic Revival style favoured by the Sulpicians, who financed the project. One of the many paradoxes surrounding St. Patrick's is that it is more representative of French than Anglo-Saxon Gothic architecture. The high, newly restored interior is spectacular in pale green, pink and gold. Each of the pine columns that divide the nave into three sections is a whole tree trunk, carved in one piece. The entire roof was redone last year and its brilliant copper has not yet dulled to green. Even a brief visit will leave you speechless.

Head back to Rue Sainte-Catherine Ouest.

Formerly located at Cité du Havre, the **Musée d'Art Contemporain de Montréal ★★** (*$6; Tue to Sun 11am to 6pm, half-price on Wed 6pm to 9pm; 185 Rue Sainte-Catherine Ouest, at the corner of Rue Jeanne-Mance, Place-des-Arts métro, ☎847-6226, info@macm.org*), Montréal's modern art museum, was moved to this site in 1992. The long, low building, erected on top of the Place des Arts parking lot, contains eight rooms, where post-1940 works of art from both Québec and abroad are exhibited. The interior, which has a decidedly better design than the exterior, is laid out around a circular hall. On the lower level, an amusing metal sculpture by Pierre Granche entitled *Comme si le temps... de la rue* (As if time... from the street), shows Montréal's network of streets crowded with helmeted birds, in a sort of semicircular theatre.

During the rush of the Quiet Revolution, the government of Québec, inspired by cultural complexes like New York's Lincoln Center, built **Place des Arts ★** (*260 Boulevard de Maisonneuve Ouest, through to Rue Sainte-Catherine Ouest, Place-des-Arts métro*), a collection of five halls for the performing arts. Salle Wilfrid Pelletier, in the centre, was inaugurated in 1963 (2,982 seats). It accommodates both the Montreal Symphony Orchestra and the Opéra de Montréal. The

Exploring

cube-shaped Théâtre Maisonneuve, on the right, contains three theatres, Théâtre Maisonneuve (1,460 seats), Théâtre Jean-Duceppe (755 seats) and the intimate little Café de la Place (138 seats). The Cinquième Salle (350 seats) was built in 1992 in the course of the construction of the Musée d'Art Contemporain. Place des Arts is linked to the governmental section of the underground city, which stretches from the Palais des Congrès convention centre to Avenue du Président-Kennedy. Developed by the various levels of government, this portion of the underground network distinguishes itself from the private section, centred around Place Ville-Marie, farther west.

Since 1976, the head office of the Fédération des Caisses Populaires Desjardins, the credit union, has been located in the vast **Complexe Desjardins** ★ (*Rue Sainte-Catherine Ouest, Place-des-Arts métro*), which houses a large number of government offices as well. The building's large atrium, surrounded by shops and movie theatres, is very popular during the winter months. A variety of shows are presented in this space, also used for recording television programmes.

The tour now leaves the former Golden Square Mile and enters the area around **Boulevard Saint-Laurent**. At the end of the 18th century, the Faubourg Saint-Laurent grew up along the street of the same name, which led inland from the river. In 1792, the city was officially divided into east and west sections, with this artery marking the boundary. Then, in the early 20th century, the addresses of east-west streets were re-assigned so that they all began at Boulevard Saint-Laurent. Meanwhile, around 1880, French-Canadian high society came up with the idea of turning the boulevard into the "Champs-Élysées" of Montréal.

The west side was destroyed in order to make the street wider and to reconstruct new buildings in Richardson's Romanesque Revival style, which was in fashion at the end of the 19th century. Populated by the successive waves of immigrants, who arrived at the port, Boulevard Saint-Laurent never attained the heights of glory anticipated by its developers. The section between Boulevard René-Lévesque and Boulevard de Maisonneuve did, however, become the hub of Montréal nightlife in the early 20th century. The city's big theatres, like the Français, where Sarah

Chinatown

Bernhardt performed, were located around here. During the Prohibition era (1919-1930), the area became run-down. Every week, thousands of Americans came here to frequent the cabarets and brothels, which abounded in this neighbourhood up until the end of the 1950s.

Turn right on Boulevard Saint-Laurent.

Erected in 1893 for the Société Saint-Jean-Baptiste, which is devoted to protecting the rights of French-speakers, the **Monument National ★** (*1182 Boulevard Saint-Laurent, Saint-Laurent métro*) was intended to be a cultural centre dedicated to the French-Canadian cause. It offered business courses, became the favourite platform of political orators and presented shows of a religious nature. However, during the 1940s, it also hosted cabaret shows and plays, launching the careers of a number of Québec performers, including Olivier Guimond Senior and Junior. The building was sold to the National Theatre School of Canada in 1971. As Canada's oldest theatre, it was artfully restored on its 100th anniversary.

Cross Boulevard René-Lévesque, then turn right on Rue de la Gauchetière.

Montréal's **Chinatown ★** (*Rue de la Gauchetière, Place-d'Armes métro*) may be rather small, but it is nonetheless a pleasant place to walk around. A large number of the Chinese who came to Canada to help build the transcontinental railroad, completed in 1886, settled here at the end of the 19th century. Though they no longer live in the neighbourhood, they still come here on weekends to stroll about and stock up on traditional products. Rue de la Gauchetière has been converted into a pedestrian street lined with restaurants and framed by lovely Chinese-style gates.

To the west of Rue Saint-Urbain lies Montreal's convention centre, the **Palais des Congrès de Montréal** (*201 Rue Viger Ouest, Place-d'Armes métro*, ☎871-3170,), a forbidding mass of concrete erected over the Autoroute Ville-Marie highway, which contributes to the isolation of the old city from down-town. A small entrance on Rue de La Gauchetière leads into the long, windowed main hall in the centre. The conference rooms (16,700m²) can hold up to 5000 convention-goers at a time.

To return to the starting point of the tour, walk back up Boulevard Saint-Laurent to the Saint-Laurent métro station (at the corner of Boulevard de Maisonneuve). Take the subway west to the Guy-Concordia station.

Tour C: Montreal Museum of Fine Arts

The **Musée des Beaux-Arts de Montréal / Montreal Museum of Fine Arts** (*free admission for the permanent collection; adults $10, students $5 for temporary exhibitions; half-price Wed 5:30pm to 9pm; open Wed to Sun 11am to 6pm, Wed until 9pm; 1380 Sherbrooke O, Guy-Concordia métro*, ☎285-2000), located in the heart of the down-town area, is the oldest and largest museum in Québec. It houses a variety of collections, which illustrate the evolution of the fine arts from antiquity up until the present day. The museum occupies two separate

Montreal Museum of Fine Arts

buildings on either side of Rue Sherbrooke Ouest: the Benaiah Gibb Pavilion at no. 1379 and the Jean-Noël Desmarais Pavilion at no. 1380. Only 10% of the permanent collection, which contains over 25,000 pieces in all, is on display. Furthermore, as many as three world-class temporary exhibitions can be presented at the museum simultaneously, thus accounting for a significant portion of the institution's activity.

The museum, known up until 1949 as the Art Association of Montreal, was founded in 1860, when the city was at the height of its glory, by a group of affluent, art-loving, Anglo-Saxon Montrealers. The core of the permanent collection still reflects the tastes of these wealthy families of English and Scottish descent, who donated many works to the museum. It wasn't until nearly 20 years later, however, that the museum was set up in a permanent exhibition space. With funds donated by local patron of the arts Benaiah Gibb, a modest gallery, which no longer exists, was built on the southeast corner of Square Phillips and Rue Saint-Catherine Ouest in 1879.

A subscription campaign was launched in 1909 to finance the construction of a more prestigious home for the museum, which would be erected on Rue Sherbrooke Ouest, in the heart of the Golden Square Mile, the upper-class residential neighbourhood that has since become the downtown core of modern-day Montréal. This building, the present Benaiah Gibb Pavil-

Exploring

ion, was inaugurated in 1912. The architects, brothers Edward and William Sutherland Maxwell, graced it with an elegant white, Vermont marble façade in the Classical Revival style, with lines reminiscent of ancient Rome. Expanded twice towards the back, in 1939 and in 1976, the building nonetheless proved to be too small.

Since demolishing the neighbouring buildings to the north and to the west was out of the question, the museum's directors turned their attention to the property across the street, thus proposing an original solution and offering quite a challenge to their architect, Moshe Safdie, already well-known for designing Habitat '67 (see p 196) and the National Gallery (Ottawa). The new wing, named after Jean-Noël Desmarais, father of arts patron Paul Desmarais, was inaugurated in 1991. On the left, it has a white marble façade that echoes the Maxwell brothers' museum, while incorporated into its right side is the red brick façade of a former apartment building (1905). A series of underground passageways running beneath Rue Sherbrooke Ouest makes it possible to walk from the Jean-Noël Desmarais Pavilion to the Benaiah Gibb Pavilion without ever stepping outside.

In addition to the usual exhibitions, the Museum of Fine Arts offers visitors the following services and facilities: a bookstore specializing in literature on art and architecture (*Jean-Noel Desmarais Pavilion, level 1*); a gift shop (*Jean-Noel Desmarais Pavilion, level 1*); a cafeteria (*Jean-Noel Desmarais Pavilion, level 2*); a library containing over 75,000 volumes on art (*Benaiah Gibb Pavilion, level S1, by appointment only*); guided tours for groups of 10 or more (*for reservations, call ☎285-1600, ext. 135*); an educational and cultural service that organizes conferences, concerts and film screenings in the Maxwell-Cummings Auditorium (*Benaiah Gibb Pavilion, level S1*), as well as art workshops for children and adults in the "Carrefour" (*Jean-Noël Desmarais Pavilion, level 1*).

There are a number of ways to visit the Musée des Beaux-Arts de Montréal. We have outlined a whirlwind tour of the permanent collection, starting at the main entrance of the museum (*Jean-Noël Desmarais Pavilion*). Those who prefer to start out with the Canadian Art, Inuit or pre-Columbian collections, can enter the museum through the big

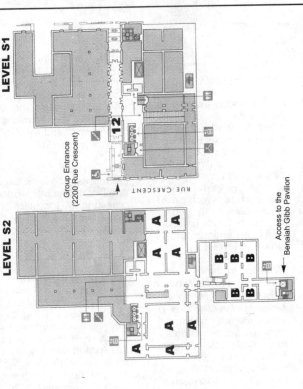

C Montreal Museum of Fine Arts
Jean-Noël Desmarais Pavilion

LEVEL S2

LEVEL S1

Group Entrance
(2200 Rue Crescent)

RUE CRESCENT

Access to the
Benaiah Gibb Pavilion

Permanent Collection

A Contemporary Arts

B Galleries of Ancient African, Oceanic,
Asian and Arab Cultures, Asian Art
Japanese Art, Etruscan and Roman
Art, Ancient Glass, Islamic Art,
Ancient-Middle-Eastern art and Great
Art

Other Areas and Services

12 Cultural Corridor

▓ Restricted Areas

oak doors of the Benaiah Gibb Pavilion (*1379 Rue Sherbrooke Ouest*).

Do not bother lingering in the museum's sober lobby, located in the Jean-Noël Desmarais Pavilion. Instead, make your way quickly to the extremely inconvenient ramp-like staircase, or to the elevators, each of which provides access to the museum's six levels (two of which are underground). Go up to level 4.

Head left to the galleries containing the **Old Masters collection** ★★ (*Jean-Noël Desmarais Pavilion, level 4*), which includes paintings, furniture and sculptures from the Middle Ages, the Renaissance and the baroque and classical periods, thus offering a vast panorama of the history of European art from 1000 A.D. up to the end of the 18th century. The medieval art on display includes fragments of stained-glass windows from the Abbaye de Saint-Germain-des-Prés (circa 1245) and a lovely *Crowning of the Virgin* by Nicolò di Pietro Gerini (circa 1390).

Among the most significant works from the Renaissance are *Portrait of a Man* by Hans Memling (1490), *The Return from the Inn* by Bruegel the Younger (1620), *Portrait of a Man from the House* of Leiva by El Greco (1580) and a superb triptych attributed to Jan de Beer and depicting the *Annunciation*, the *Adoration of the Shepherds* and the *Flight to Egypt* (circa 1510).

The 17th and 18th centuries are represented by a large number of Flemish works, reflecting the fondness of the affluent residents of the Golden Square Mile for these paintings, with their complex light effects. Of note is the *Portrait of a Young Woman* by Rembrandt (circa 1665) and the *Adoration of the Shepherds* by Nicolaes Maes (1658). English painters figure prominently in the last room of this section, in works like *Rustic Courtship* (circa 1755-58) and the *Portrait of Mrs. George Drummond* (1779-83), both by Thomas Gainsborough. Paintings by Canaletto and Tiepolo also adorn the walls of this gallery.

Head to the **Belvedere**, a sort of aerial promenade over the lobby, where you can admire Mont Royal and the buildings along Sherbrooke. It leads to the museum's collection of **European Decorative Arts** ★ (*Jean-Noël Desmarais Pavilion, level 4*), which consists mainly of small objects in display cases. You'll find some

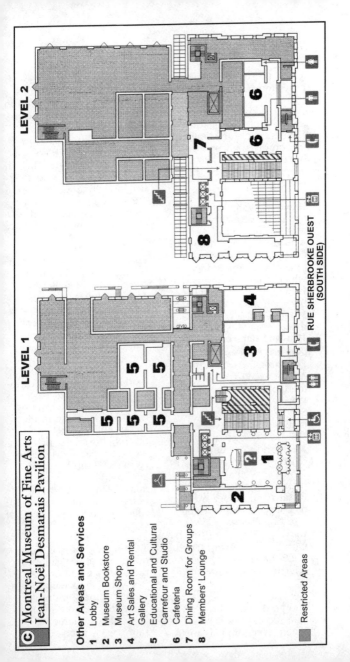

Montreal Museum of Fine Arts
Jean-Noël Desmarais Pavilion

LEVEL 1

LEVEL 2

RUE SHERBROOKE OUEST
(SOUTH SIDE)

Other Areas and Services

1 Lobby
2 Museum Bookstore
3 Museum Shop
4 Art Sales and Rental Gallery
5 Educational and Cultural Carrefour and Studio
6 Cafeteria
7 Dining Room for Groups
8 Members' Lounge

Restricted Areas

lovely pieces of English porcelain (Chelsea, Worcester, Derby and Wedgwood), silver, glassware, crystal, and part of Georges Clemenceau's amazing collection of Japanese incense boxes (there are 3,000 in all), now owned by the museum.

Leave the galleries through the doors near the elevators. Go down to level 3, where you'll find the **Glass Court**, the space used for temporary exhibitions, which offers an impressive view of the urban chaos of the rooftops of downtown Montréal, along with the museum's collection of **19th- and 20th-century European Art** ★ (*Jean-Noël Desmarais Pavilion, level 3*). As the wealthy residents of the Golden Square Mile were fond of the Barbizon School, the collection includes a number of works by Corot (*l'Île heureuse*, 1868) and Daumier (*Nymphes Pursued* by Satyrs, 1850), as well as a few impressionist pieces by Sisley, Pissaro and Monet. More recent works include the arresting *Portrait of the Lawyer* Hugo Simons (1925) by Otto Dix and *Seated Woman, Back Turned to the Open Window* by Matisse (1921-23).

Get back on the elevator and go down to level S2 (the second lower level), where you'll find six-metre-high galleries that look as if they were made for giants. These are perfectly suited to the large pieces in the **Contemporary Art collection** ★ (*Jean-Noël Desmarais Pavilion, level S2*), which consists chiefly of works by Canadian artists. The museum occasionally uses some of the space on level S2 for temporary international exhibitions of contemporary art.

Follow the passageway that runs alongside the ramp/staircase to the **Galleries of Ancient Cultures** ★ (*Jean-Noël-Desmarais Pavilion, level S2*), which stretch under Rue Sherbrooke and contain collections of decorative arts from Africa, Oceania, Asia, the Arab world and the ancient civilizations of the Near East, Greece and Rome. Among the many items on display are an interesting Assyrian bas-relief from the palace of Assurnasirpal II, a lead sarcophagus found in Tyre and a large basin, originally inlaid with silver, which belonged to the Sultan of Aleppo and Damascus (13th century).

Take the elevator at the north end of the galleries to the entrance hall of the Benaiah Gibb Pavilion. Designed in the spirit of the École des Beaux-Arts, it leads to a monumental staircase, which you must

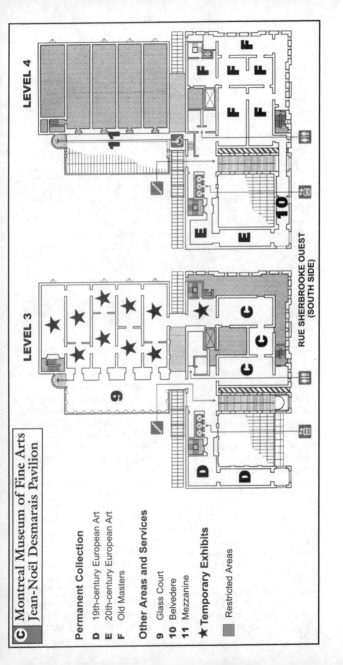

Montreal Museum of Fine Arts
Jean-Noël Desmarais Pavilion

LEVEL 4

LEVEL 3

Permanent Collection

D 19th-century European Art
E 20th-century European Art
F Old Masters

Other Areas and Services

9 Glass Court
10 Belvedere
11 Mezzanine

★ **Temporary Exhibits**

■ Restricted Areas

RUE SHERBROOKE OUEST
(SOUTH SIDE)

Paul-Émile Borduas

The Montreal Museum of Fine Arts inaugurated an exhibition hall dedicated to the work of Québécois painter Paul-Émile Borduas in January 1998. In the same year, Québec celebrated the 50th anniversary of the *Refus Global*, the revolutionary manifesto that marked the beginning of the great transformation of Québec society, written by Paul-Émile Borduas and signed by many other artists. The museum, which owns about 50 of the painter's canvases, will exhibit these works on an alternating basis to introduce the public to one of the most important painters in Québec's history.

climb in order to reach the temporary exhibition galleries and the **collection of Canadian Art** ★★★ (*Benaiah Gibb Pavilion, levels 1 and 2*), the true highlight of the museum. Presented in chronological order, this collection enables viewers to relive Canadian history through paintings, sculptures, furniture and ecclesiastical silver.

In the first gallery, visitors learn about everyday life in the Canada of yesteryear, through lovely paintings by Paul Kane (*Mah Min* and *Caw Wacham*, circa 1848), Cornelius Kreighoff (*Montmorency Falls*, 1853) and many others (*View of Quebec City* by Fred Holloway,

1853). Portrait painters Théophile Hamel (1817-1870) and Antoine Plamondon (1804-1895), for their part, depicted the aristocracy of their era. To round it all off, there are various pieces of furniture, some dating back to the French Regime. Tucked away in a small gallery on the right is a treasure trove of ecclesiastical silver, including pieces by François Ranvoyzé (late 18th century) and Laurent Amiot.

In the gallery devoted to the Victorian era, visitors can admire the academic style of Paul Peel's *The Spinner* (1881) and the shimmering January light in William Brymner's *Champ-de-*

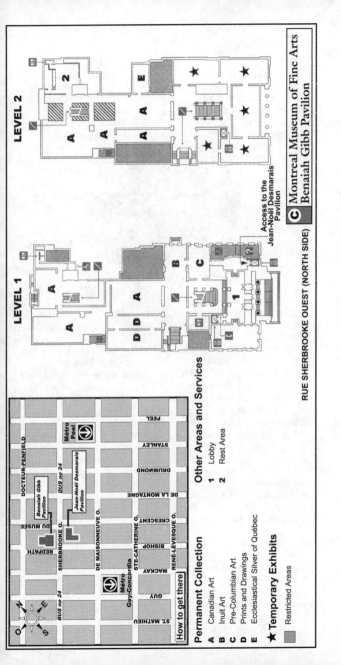

LEVEL 1

LEVEL 2

How to get there

Other Areas and Services

1 Lobby
2 Rest Area

Permanent Collection

A Canadian Art
B Inuit Art
C Pre-Columbian Art
D Prints and Drawings
E Ecclesiastical Silver of Québec

★ **Temporary Exhibits**

Restricted Areas

Access to the
Jean-Noël Desmarais
Pavilion

C Montreal Museum of Fine Arts
Benaiah Gibb Pavilion

RUE SHERBROOKE OUEST (NORTH SIDE)

Mars, Winter (1892). In Canada, the first 30 years of the 20th century were marked by a veritable explosion of colour, as evidenced by Emily Carr's *Indian War Canoe* (1912) and Tom Thomson's *In the Northland* (1915). This section also contains paintings by the Group of Seven, including *Cathedral Mountain* by Arthur Lismer (1928).

Inuit art

A large staircase with a glass railing leads down to the lower floor, which displays works influenced by the Art Deco style, such as Adrien Hébert's *Montreal Harbour* (circa 1924) and Edwin Holgate's *The Bathers* (1937). You'll also learn about the history of the École du Meuble de Montréal, founded in 1935 by Jean-Marie Gauvreau. Two of the most noteworthy sculptures on level 1 are Robert Tait Mackenzie's *The Plunger* (1923) and Sylvia Daoust's *My Brother* (1931).

A ramp leads down to a gallery devoted primary to the work of Paul-Émile Borduas. You will also see the colourful paintings of Jean-Paul Riopelle (*Crosswind*, 1952) and Alfred Pellan (*The Green Jug*, 1942).

The adjacent gallery is used to display the museum's collection of **Prints and Drawings** ★★ (*Benaiah Gibb Pavilion, level 1*), which includes works by Rembrandt, Hendrick Goltzius, Ferdinand Hodler, Pietro Bracci, Honoré Daumier, Manet, Paul Klee and Salvador Dali, among others. Exit the cabinet into the secondary lobby of the Benaiah Gibb Pavilion, which serves as the exhibition space for the museum's **Inuit Art collection** ★ (*Benaiah Gibb Pavilion, level 1*), most of which is recent. Two of the more notable pieces are a stone carving entitled *Two Hunters Cutting up a Walrus* by Levi Alashuak (1951) and *The Migration* by Joe Talirunili (1964), which will enlighten visitors on the customs of this northern people.

Near the exit, there is one last gallery, which is devoted to **Pre-Columbian Art** ★ (*Benaiah Gibb Pavilion, level 1*) from Central and South America. Here, you can admire a piece of Peruvian tapestry dating back 2,000 years. Among the ceramic objects, you'll find a *Standing Warrior* (Jalisco, AD 300-500) and a handsome *Stirrup-Spout Vessel with Portrait Head* (Mochica, AD 200-600).

You can exit the museum through the front doors of the Benaiah Gibb Pavilion. If you need to return to the main lobby of the Jean-Noël Desmarais Pavilion, take the elevator down to level S2 and follow the passageway to the other elevators. Go up to level 1, where the cloakroom, bookstore and boutique are located (the cafeteria is on level 2).

Tour D:
The Golden Square
Mile

The Golden Square Mile was the residential neighbourhood of the Canadian upper class between 1850 and 1930. Since the early 20th century, the shady streets lined with sumptuous Victorian houses have gradually given way to the city's modern business centre. At its apogee, around 1900, the Golden Square Mile was bounded by Avenue Atwater to the west, Rue de Bleury to the east, Rue de la Gauchetière to the south and the mountain, Mont Royal, to the north. In

those years, an estimated 70% of the country's wealth lay in the hands of local residents, the majority of whom were of Scottish descent. Only a few houses from this era remain, most of which are clustered north of Rue Sherbrooke, the Golden Square Mile's luxurious main street.

From the McGill métro station, head north on Avenue McGill College toward the campus of McGill University. The tour starts on Rue Sherbrooke.

The **Maison William Alexander Molson** (*888 Rue Sherbrooke Ouest, McGill métro*) provides a good idea of Rue Sherbrooke's modest scale and residential character back in the early 20th century. It was built in 1906 according to a design by Robert Findlay, favourite architect of the famous Molsons, a name associated with the brewing of beer for two centuries. William Alexander Molson chose a different path, however, becoming an eminent doctor. After his death in 1920, this Neo-Elizabethan-style house served first as the head office of the Anglin-Norcross construction company and was then used by McGill University's Institute of Space Research. The Banque Commerciale Italienne du Canada took over the building in 1993.

Exploring

The **Musée McCord d'Histoire Canadienne / McCord Museum of Canadian History** ★★ (*$7, free on Sat 10am to noon; Tue to Fri 10am to 6pm, Sat and Sun 10am to 5pm; 690 Rue Sherbrooke Ouest, McGill métro, ☎398-7100, info@ mccord.lan.mcgill.ca*), the McCord Museum of Canadian History, occupies a building formerly used by the McGill University Students' Association. Designed by architect Percy Nobbs (1906), this handsome building of English baroque inspiration was enlarged toward the back in 1991. Along Rue Victoria, visitors can see an interesting sculpture by Pierre Granche entitled *Totem Urbain/Histoire en Dentelle* (Urban totem/History in lace). For anyone interested in the First Nations and daily life in Canada in the 18th and 19th centuries, this is *the* museum to see in Montréal. It houses a large ethnographic collection, as well as collections of costumes, decorative arts, paintings, prints and photographs, including the famous Notman collection, composed of 700,000 glass plates and constituting a veritable portrait of Canada at the end of the 19th century.

McGill University ★★ (*805 Rue Sherbrooke Ouest, McGill métro*) was founded in 1821, thanks to a donation by fur-trader James McGill. It is the oldest of Montréal's four universities. Throughout the 19th century, the institution was one of the finest jewels of the Golden Square Mile's Scottish bourgeoisie. The university's main campus lies nestled in greenery at the foot of Mont Royal. The entrance is located at the northernmost end of Avenue McGill College, at the Roddick Gates, which contain the university's clock and chimes. On the right are two Romanesque-Revival-style buildings, designed by Sir Andrew Taylor to house the physics (1893) and chemistry (1896) departments. The Faculty of Architecture now occupies the second building. A little farther along, visitors will see the Macdonald Engineering Building, a fine example of the English baroque-revival style, with a broken pediment adorning its rusticated portal (Percy Nobbs, 1908). At the end of the drive stands the oldest building on campus, the Arts Building (1839). For three decades, this austere neoclassical structure by architect John Ostell was McGill University's only building. It houses Moyse Hall, a lovely theatre dating back to 1926, with a design inspired by antiquity (Harold Lea Fetherstonaugh, architect).

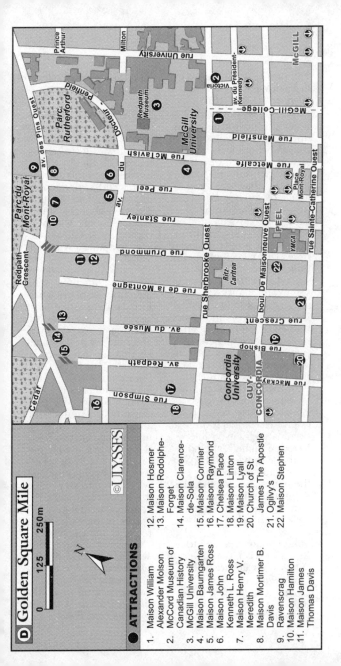

Golden Square Mile

0 125 250m

N

© ULYSSES

● ATTRACTIONS

1. Maison William Alexander Molson
2. McCord Museum of Canadian History
3. McGill University
4. Maison Baumgarten
5. Maison James Ross
6. Maison John Kenneth L. Ross
7. Maison Henry V. Meredith
8. Maison Mortimer B. Davis
9. Ravenscrag
10. Maison Hamilton
11. Maison James Thomas Davis
12. Maison Hosmer
13. Maison Rodolphe-Forget
14. Maison Clarence-de-Sola
15. Maison Cormier
16. Maison Raymond
17. Chelsea Place
18. Maison Linton
19. Maison Lyall
20. Church of St. James The Apostle
21. Ogilvy's
22. Maison Stephen

The profile of the unusual **Redpath Museum** (*815 Rue Sherbrooke Ouest, McGill métro*) stands out to the left. It is a protorationalist openwork building concealed behind a composite façade, the work of architects Hutchison and Steele. Precious objects relating to archaeology, botany, geology and palaeontology, accumulated by the university's researchers and professors, have been collected here. This was the first building in Québec designed specifically as a museum, and it also serves as a rare example of a building with an iron and stone framework, not intended for industrial or commercial purposes. South of the museum, visitors will see the library and Redpath Hall, equipped with a French-style mechanical organ. Baroque music concerts are often held in this lovely hall dominated by its visible wooden frame. Take note of the gargoyles and lavishly sculpted columns of the library, among the most sophisticated examples of the Romanesque Revival style in Canada.

Take the lane leading to Rue McTavish. On the north side stands **Morrice Hall** (*3485 Rue McTavish*), a Gothic-Revival-style building erected in 1881, which once housed the Presbyterian Theological College of Montréal.

The **Maison Baumgarten** (*3450 Rue McTavish, McGill métro*), located a little lower on Rue McTavish, serves as the McGill Faculty Club. It houses a restaurant, reading rooms and a room containing pool tables from the former residences of the Golden Square Mile now owned by McGill University. The house was built in stages between 1887 and 1902 for Alfred Friedrich Moritz Baumgarten, son of the personal physician of King Frédéric-Auguste of Saxony, chemist, inspector of German sugar refineries and founder of the Saint-Laurent sugar refinery in Montréal. His house stands out from the other bourgeois residences in the Golden Square Mile because of its exterior sobriety and three levels of reception rooms. On the first floor of the stairwell, the privileged individuals offered access into the club will see a bird's-eye view of the Battle of Arras (17th century), brought back from France by Sir Arthur Currie, rector of the University.

Walk uphill on Rue McTavish. Visitors can enjoy a view of Ravenscrag (see p 136) on the hillside before turning left on Avenue Docteur-Penfield, then right onto Rue Peel.

The **Maison James Ross** ★ (*3644 Rue Peel, Peel métro*) was constructed in 1890 according to a design by American architect Bruce Price (Windsor Station, Château Frontenac in Québec City) for the head engineer of Canadian Pacific. Enlarged on several occasions, it was once the scene of glittering receptions. With its resemblance to a medieval castle, it contributes to the charm of the Golden Square Mile. Particularly noteworthy is the combination of colours of its exterior, made up of a mixture of buff-coloured sandstone, pink granite and red slate. James Ross owned an exceptional collection of paintings, including works by Rembrandt, Rubens, Reynolds, Courbet, Corot, Millet, Rossetti and Edward Burne-Jones. In 1948, the house became the McGill University Faculty of Law. It lost a considerable portion of its large garden when Avenue Docteur-Penfield was laid out in 1957.

The **Maison John Kenneth L. Ross** (*3647 Rue Peel, Peel métro*) was originally the residence of James Ross's son, who lived in grand style for several years, accumulating yachts and race horses and travelling extensively. Once his father's fortune was exhausted, he had to sell the precious family collection of paintings at Christie's in London, a useless sacrifice in the end, since the crash of 1929 ruined him anyway. His house (1909), a fine example of the Beaux-Arts style, is the work of brothers Edward and William Sutherland Maxwell, the favourite architects of Montréal's Scottish bourgeoisie. It is now an annex of the McGill University Faculty of Law.

Go up Rue Peel to Avenue des Pins. In another era, children used to toboggan down Rue Peel, which, like all of the city's streets during the long winter months, was covered with a thick layer of snow.

The **Maison Henry V. Meredith** ★ (*1110 Avenue des Pins Ouest*) is perhaps Montréal's best example of the trend toward eclecticism, polychromy and the picturesque that swept through North America in the last two decades of the 19th century. In fact, visitors will discover on its façades a mixture of styles ranging from the Romanesque to the late 18th century, as well as strong hues and a marvellous jumble of towers, inlays, bay windows and chimneys. The house was built in 1894 for Henry Vincent Meredith, who was president of the Bank of Montreal at the time.

Exploring

Growing up English in Montreal

Montreal is my home, not Montréal, and when I think of this city and its sights I think of the Olympic Stadium, the Botanical Gardens, the Montreal Museum of Fine Arts, Old Montreal, Mount Royal, Beaver Lake and St. Joseph's Oratory. I know the names of these places should technically be in French, but as an anglophone they have different names because they are part of my city.

As a Montrealer of Anglo-Saxon descent, I grew up in the Anglo stronghold of Montreal and by extension of Québec, that former cottage-country we affectionately call the West Island. I was at an English elementary school when Bill 101 was announced, and thought he was a newscaster! My parents had the good sense to enroll me in French immersion, yet my existence was decidedly anglophile. After English high school, I moved downtown; this time we made our home in Westmount, another of the few anglophone enclaves. I attended an English CÉGEP, and then went on to McGill University for a degree in English Literature.

Ironically it was during these years that I began to make francophone friends. Initially, I realized how different we were when they insisted on greeting me with kisses all the time (called *la bise*, by the way). Then I tried to get them to explain Bill 101. Why was it necessary to deny me what I thought was a basic right and why did I detect fear amongst them? They explained that they were here before us, so naturally they felt justified in wanting to preserve their distinct culture, and surrounded by a sea of English, measures had to be taken. Yet my anglophone heritage has been greatly enhanced by its location within a francophone environment, and I also intend to preserve the distinct culture that has resulted. To me Montreal is a unique city because we are both here, and I do not wish that either group be forced out.

Visitors to Montréal always wonder what I am doing here. Why do I choose to live in a city where signs in my language used to be illegal, where the locals refer to me as a *tête-carrée* (square head), where the spots I cherish no longer have names I recognize? Well, I live here because I was born and raised here. I choose to live here because, although I am not francophone, I understand those signs and at least some of the politics behind them, and because I understand why they call me a *tête-carrée*; it is the same reason I call them frogs and peppers. I cannot say we do not have our differences, so naturally we have our silly names for each other. Fundamentally we are all Quebecers and we are defined by these differences. I am a Canadian, yet I cannot imagine having to live in any other province or to identify with any other provincial mind set. I relish the warm welcome of shopkeepers when my accent betrays me and they think I am a tourist. I am proud when people cannot detect my English accent, or when I return to the West Island and see that I could still exist exclusively in English. It is then that I know I fit in, that I am at home in both English and French. You see, I love Schwartz's Deli just as much as I love the Binerie Mont Royal! I eat both *tourtière* and plum pudding at Christmas! I paint *fleurs de lys* on my cheeks on June 24th and maple leaves on July 1st!

Jennifer McMorran

Exploring

The **Maison Mortimer B. Davis** ★ (*1020 Avenue des Pins Ouest*) was once the residence of the founder of the Imperial Tobacco Company, Mortimer Barnett Davis. It was later occupied by Sir Arthus Purvis, and then sold to McGill University. Purvis was responsible for the secret shipment of North American-made arms to Europe during World War II, enabling Great Britain to avoid a Nazi invasion. The Davis house was designed in the Beaux-Arts style, recognizable by the balustrade along the top, the wrought-iron balconies supported by brackets and the grandiose, symmetrical design.

Ravenscrag ★★ (*1025 Avenue des Pins Ouest*). Montréal is not a political capital. It is above all a commercial city endowed with an important port. Its castle is not that of a king, but rather that of a financial and commercial magnate. Ravenscrag could indeed be labelled the castle of Montréal, due to its prominent location overlooking the city, its exceptional size (originally over 60 rooms) and its history, which is rich in memorable receptions and prestigious hosts. This immense residence was built in 1861-1864 for the extremely wealthy Sir Hugh Allan, who at the time had a near monopoly on sea transport between Europe and Canada. From the central tower of his house, this "monarch" could keep a close eye on the comings and goings of his ships in and out of the port.

Sir Hugh Allan's house is one of the best North American examples of the Renaissance Revival style, inspired by Tuscan villas and characterized, notably, by an irregular plan and an observation tower. The interior, almost entirely destroyed when the building was converted into a psychiatric institute (1943),

used to include a Second Empire-style ballroom that was able to accommodate 200 polka dancers. Interesting aspects around the building include a cast-iron entry gate, a gate house and luxurious stables now used as offices.

Head west on Avenue de Pins.

The **Maison Hamilton** (*1132 Avenue des Pins Ouest*) has a unique and personal design by the Maxwell brothers, who had developed their own style, characterized by a gradual widening of their structures toward the base and whimsical little openings distributed in a carefully studied disorder. The Hamilton house (1903) has Arts & Crafts elements, as well as features foreshadowing the Art Deco style, such as the zigzag pattern of the bricks on the first floor.

Go down the stairway leading to Rue Drummond.

The **Maison James Thomas Davis ★** (*3654 Rue Drummond*) originally belonged to a building contractor, who reinforced his house with a reinforced concrete structure. The design for this Elizabethan "manor" was also drawn up by the Maxwells (1908). Those who enter the house will find the lovely original tapestries still in place, in addition to remounted paintings by Canadian artist Maurice Cullen. Like so many old residences in the neighbourhood, the Davis house now belongs to McGill University.

The **Maison Hosmer** ★ (*3630 Rue Drummond*) is without question the most exuberant Beaux-Arts style house in Montréal. Thick mouldings, twin columns and cartouches, all carved in red sandstone imported from Scotland, were sure to impress both visitors and business rivals. Edward Maxwell drew up the plans while his brother William was studying at the École des Beaux-Arts in Paris. The sketches sent from across the Atlantic clearly had a great influence on the design of this house, erected in 1900 for Charles Hosmer, who had ties with Canadian Pacific and 26 other Canadian companies. Each room was designed in a different style, in order to serve as a showcase for the Hosmer family's diverse collection of antiques. The family lived here until 1968, at which time the house became part of McGill University's Faculty of Medicine.

Turn right on Avenue Docteur-Penfield, then right again on Avenue du Musée.

The **Maison Rodolphe-Forget** ★ (*3685 Avenue du Musée*). Few residences in the Golden Square Mile were built for members of the French-Canadian elite. These individuals, generally less affluent than their Anglo-Saxon colleagues, preferred the area around Square Saint-Louis. Rodolphe Forget (1861-1919) was thus regarded as an exception. This distinguished Francophile founded the Banque Internationale du Canada, was a member of the council of the Société Générale and took part in the founding of the Franco-Canadian Crédit Foncier. His house, inspired by Parisian *hôtels particuliers* of the Louis XV era, was designed in 1912 by Jean Omer Marchand, the first French-Canadian graduate of Paris' École des Beaux-Arts. The famous Québec suffragette Thérèse Casgrain, daughter of Rodolphe Forget, spent her early childhood here. The building is now part of the Russian consulate.

Climb the Avenue du Musée stairs. There is a lovely view of the downtown area and the river at the top.

The **Maison Clarence-de-Sola** ★ (*1374 Avenue des Pins Ouest*) is an extremely exotic Hispano-Moorish style residence, which stands out clearly against the urban

Exploring

landscape of Montréal. The contrast is even more amusing the day after a snowstorm. The house was erected in 1913 for Clarence de Sola, son of a rabbi of Portuguese-Jewish descent.

Head west on Avenue des Pins.

The **Maison Cormier** ★★ (*1418 Avenue des Pins Ouest*) was designed in 1930 for his personal use by Ernest Cormier, architect of the Université de Montréal (see p 174) and the Supreme Court in Ottawa. He experimented with the house, giving each side a different look – Art Deco for the façade, monumental for the east side and distinctly modern for the back. The interior was planned in minute detail. Cormier created most of the furniture, while the remaining pieces were acquired at the 1925 Exposition des Arts Décoratifs in Paris. Though the façade on Avenue des Pins appears quite small, the house actually has four above-ground floors on the other side, due to the steep incline of the terrain south of the avenue. The entire building, now listed as a historic monument, has been carefully restored by its present owner.

Go down the stairs on the left, which lead to Avenue Redpath. Turn right on Avenue Docteur-Penfield.

The **Maison Raymond** (*1507 Avenue Docteur-Penfield, Guy-Concordia métro*) was one of the last single-family residences to be erected in the Golden Square Mile (1930), and it is still lived in today. It belongs to the family of businessman Aldéric Raymond, who owned the Montréal Forum in the 1950s, as well as several big hotels in Montréal. It is another excellent example of the French Beaux-Arts style.

Go down Rue Simpson toward Rue Sherbrooke Ouest.

Chelsea Place ★ (*on the east side of Rue Simpson, Guy-Concordia Métro*) is a subtle grouping of Neo-Georgian-style residences built on a more modest scale than the homes seen thus far. It was erected in 1926 according to plans by architect Ernest Isbell Barott, in the years when Montréal's Scottish bourgeoisie was starting to decline. Decimated by the Great War, burdened by taxes (which were practically nonexistent before 1914) and suffering from a shortage of servants, many businessmen were forced to sell their "palaces" and move into more practical dwellings. Of particular interest is the lovely central garden, giving Chelsea Place a unique style, both communal and refined. Summerhill Terrace, located on the west side of Rue

Simpson, is a similar grouping built by the same architect.

The **Maison Linton** (*3424 Rue Simpson, Guy-Concordia métro*) is one of the most well-executed examples of the Second Empire style in Montréal. Do not be fooled by the exterior; the façade on Rue Simpson is in fact the east side of the house, whose main façade originally looked south out onto a vast lawn stretching all the way to Rue Sherbrooke. The portico and staircase were dismantled, then reconstructed facing Rue Simpson when the Linton apartment building was erected in 1907 (see p 100). The little cartouches, the openings with segmented arches and above all the mansard roof are all characteristic of the Second Empire, or Napoleon III, style. The house was erected in 1867 according to a design by Cyrus P. Thomas. An underground garage was built all around it in 1990, but its interior remains just as it was at the end of the 19th century, from the fireplaces to the embossed wall paper and lavish mouldings on the ceilings.

Turn left on Rue Sherbrooke, then right on Rue Bishop, which runs alongside the main campus of **Concordia University**, *Montréal's second English-language university*

and the most recently founded of the city's four universities (1974). The Maison Lyall lies south of Boulevard de Maisonneuve.

The **Maison Lyall** (*1445 Rue Bishop, Guy-Concordia métro*). Throughout the 19th century, a large number of Scots emigrated to the British colonies. The market in their own land was controlled by the London upper class, who prevented the Scots from expanding their modest businesses. In those years, Montréal was the primary destination of these merchants, industrialists and inventors from Glasgow and Inverness. They were anxious to open stores or factories in this new country, which, with its rapidly growing population, needed everything. Peter Lyall was one of these immigrants. Immediately after his arrival from Castletown in 1870, he founded a construction company that prospered and he was even commissioned to reconstruct the Canadian Parliament after the fire in 1916. His eclectic, polychrome, delightfully picturesque residence looks like a big gingerbread house. It has been converted into business and office space. The entrance hall, graced with a lovely fireplace inlaid with various types of marble, is open to the public.

Exploring

The **Church of St. James The Apostle** (*1439 Rue Sainte-Catherine Ouest, Guy-Concordia métro*) was built in 1864. At the time, it was located in the middle of a field, not far from where local cricket games were played, thus earning it the nickname "St. Cricket in the Fields". Before long, Rue Sainte-Catherine was lined with row houses. These have since made way for commercial buildings.

Turn left on Rue Sainte-Catherine; 15km long, it is Montréal's main commercial artery.

Ogilvy's department store (*1307 Rue Sainte-Catherine Ouest, Peel métro*), the most elegant of Montréal's department stores, was purchased several years ago by a group of French-Canadian businessmen. The new owners have striven to preserve the original character of this Scottish Montréal institution, whose atmosphere is enlivened each day at noon by a bagpipe player. The Tudor room on the top floor is often used for concerts and receptions. Across the street is a group of neoclassical houses dating back to 1864 (groupings such as these are known as terraces), among the last houses on the street that have survived to the present day.

Turn left on Rue Drummond.

The Maison Stephen ★★ (*1440 Rue Drummond, Peel métro*). Lord Mount Stephen, born in Stephen Croft, Scotland, was a determined man. Co-founder and first president of Canadian Pacific, he realized the construction of a transcontinental railroad stretching over 5,000 kilometres from New Brunswick to British Columbia. His house is a veritable monument to Montréal's Scottish bourgeoisie.

It was built in 1883 according to plans by William Tutin Thomas at a cost of $600,000, an astronomical sum at the time. Stephen called upon the best artisans in the entire world, who covered the interior walls with marble, onyx and woodwork made of such rare materials as English walnut, Cuban mahogany and Sri Lankan satinwood. The ceilings are so high that the house seems to have been built for giants. Since 1925, it has been owned by the Mount Stephen Club, a private club for businesspeople.

Tours of the house are occasionally organized during the summer.

To return to the starting point of the tour, head east on Boulevard de Maisonneuve or Rue Sainte-Catherine, the more pleasant of the two. The entrance to the McGill métro station is located near the corner of Avenue McGill College.

Tour E: Shaughnessy Village

When the Sulpicians took possession of the island of Montréal in 1663, they kept a portion of the best land for themselves, then set up a farm and a native village there in 1676. Following a fire, the native village was relocated several times before being permanently established in Oka. A part of the farm, corresponding to the area now known as Westmount, was then granted to French settlers. The Sulpicians planted an orchard and a vineyard on the remaining portion. Starting around 1870, the land was separated into lots. Part of it was used for the construction of mansions, while large plots were awarded to Catholic communities allied with the Sulpicians. It was at this time that Shaughnessy House was built – hence the name of the neighbourhood. During the 1970s, the number of local inhabitants increased considerably, making Shaughnessy Village the most densely populated area in Québec.

From Rue Guy (Guy-Concordia métro) turn left on Rue Sherbrooke.

Masonic lodges, which had already existed in New France, increased in scale with British immigration. These associations of free-thinkers were not favoured by the Canadian clergy, who denounced their liberal views. Ironically, the **Masonic Temple ★** (*1850 Rue Sherbrooke Ouest, Guy-Concordia métro*), one of Montréal's Scottish lodges, stands opposite the Grand Séminaire, where Catholic priests are trained. The edifice, built in 1928, enhances the secret, mystical character of Freemasonry with its impenetrable, windowless façade, equipped with antique vessels and double-headed lamps.

The Sulpicians' farmhouse was surrounded by a wall linked to four stone corner towers, earning it the name Fort des Messieurs. The house was destroyed when the **Grand Séminaire ★★** (1854-1860) (*2065 Rue Sherbrooke Ouest, Guy-Concordia métro*) was built, but two towers, erected in the 17th century according to plans by François Vachon de Belmont, superior of the Montréal Sulpicians, can still be found in the institution's shady gardens. It was in one of these that Saint Marguerite Bourgeoys

Exploring

taught young native girls. Around 1880, the long neoclassical buildings of the Grand Séminaire, designed by architect John Ostell, were topped by a mansard roof by Henri-Maurice Perrault. Information panels, set up on Rue Sherbrooke, directly in line with Rue du Fort, provide precise details about the farm buildings.

It is well worth entering the Seminary to see the lovely Romanesque Revival–style chapel, designed by Jean Omer Marchand in 1905. The ceiling beams are made of cedar from British Columbia, while the walls are covered with stones from Caen. The 80m-wide nave is lined with 300 hand-carved oak pews. Sulpicians who have died in Montréal since the 18th century are interred beneath it. The Sulpician order was founded in Paris by Jean-Jacques Olier in 1641, and its main church is the Saint-Sulpice in Paris, which stands on the square of the same name.

The Congrégation de Notre-Dame, founded by Saint Marguerite Bourgeoys in 1671, owned a convent and a school in Old Montréal. Reconstructed in the 18th century, these buildings were expropriated by the city at the beginning of the 20th century as part of a plan to extend Boulevard Saint-Laurent all the way to the port. The nuns had to leave the premises and settle into a new convent. The congregation thus arranged for a convent to be built on Rue Sherbrooke, according to a design by Jean Omer Marchand (1873-1936), the first French-Canadian architect to graduate from the École des Beaux-Arts in Paris. The immense complex now bears witness to the vitality of religious communities in Québec before the Quiet Revolution of 1960.

The decline of religious practices and lack of new vocations forced the community to move into more modest buildings. **Dawson College ★** (*3040 Rue Sherbrooke Ouest, Atwater métro*), an English-language CÉGEP (*collège d'enseignement général et professionnel*, a post-secondary college), has been located in the original convent since 1987.

The yellow-brick building, set on luxuriant grounds, is probably the most beautiful CÉGEP in Québec. It is now directly linked to the subway and underground city. The Romanesque Revival–style chapel in the centre has an elongated copper dome reminiscent of Byzantine architecture. It now serves as a library and has been barely altered.

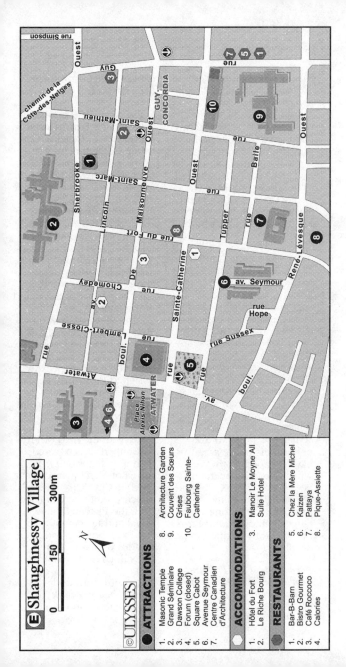

Shaughnessy Village

0   150   300m

N

© ULYSSES

ATTRACTIONS

1. Masonic Temple
2. Grand Séminaire
3. Dawson College
4. Forum (closed)
5. Square Cabot
6. Avenue Seymour
7. Centre Canadien d'Architecture
8. Architecture Garden
9. Couvent des Sœurs Grises
10. Faubourg Sainte-Catherine

ACCOMMODATIONS

1. Hôtel du Fort
2. Le Riche Bourg
3. Manoir Le Moyne All Suite Hotel

RESTAURANTS

1. Bar-B-Barn
2. Bistro Gourmet
3. Café Roccoco
4. Calories
5. Chez La Mère Michel
6. Kaizen
7. Pattaya
8. Pique-Assiette

Head south on Avenue Atwater, then turn left on Rue Sainte-Catherine Ouest.

On Avenue Atwater, stands **Place Alexis-Nihon**, a multi-purpose complex containing a shopping mall, offices and apartments. It is linked to the underground city. **Square Cabot** used to be the terminal for all buses serving the western part of the city.

Turn right on Rue Lambert-Closse, then left on Rue Tupper.

Between 1965 and 1975, Shaughnessy Village witnessed a massive wave of demolition. A great many Victorian row houses were replaced by high-rises, whose rudimentary designs, characterized by an endless repetition of identical glass or concrete balconies, are often referred to as "chicken coops." **Avenue Seymour** ★ is one of the only streets in the area to have escaped this wave, which has now been curbed. Here, visitors will find charming houses made of brick and grey stone, with Queen Anne, Second Empire or Romanesque Revival details.

Turn right on Rue Fort and then left on small Rue Baile (watch out for the fast-moving traffic heading to the highway on-ramp). Follow the path east alongside the CCA to reach René-Lévesque.

Founded in 1979 by Phyllis Lambert, the **Centre Canadien d'Architecture / Canadian Centre for Architecture** ★★★ (*$6, free Thu 5:30pm to 8pm; Oct to Jun, Wed and Fri 11am to 6pm, Thu 11am to 8pm; Sat and Sun 11am to 5pm; 1920 Rue Baile, Guy-Concordia métro, ☎939-7026*), is both a museum and a centre for the study of world architecture. Its collections of plans, drawings, models, books and photographs are the most important of their kind in the entire world. The Centre, erected between 1985 and 1989, has six exhibition rooms, a bookstore, a library, a 217-seat auditorium and a wing specially designed for researchers, as well as vaults and restoration laboratories. The main building, shaped like a "U," was designed by Peter Rose, with the help of Phyllis Lambert. It is covered with grey limestone from the Saint-Marc quarries near Québec City. This material, which used to be extracted from the Plateau Mont-Royal and Rosemont quarries in Montréal, adorns the façades of many of the city's houses.

The centre surrounds the **Maison Shaughnessy** ★, whose façade looks out onto Boulevard René-Lévesque Ouest. This house is in fact a pair of residences, built in 1874 according to a design by architect William Tutin Thomas. It is representative of the mansions that once lined Boulevard René-Lévesque (formerly Boulevard Dorchester). In 1974, it was at the centre of an effort to salvage the neighbourhood, which had been torn down in a number of places. The house, itself threatened with demolition, was purchased at the last moment by Phyllis Lambert. She set up the offices and reception rooms of the Canadian Centre for Architecture inside. The building was named after Sir Thomas Shaughnessy, a former president of the Canadian Pacific Railway Company, who lived in the house for several decades. The inhabitants of the neighbourhood, grouped together in an association, subsequently chose to name the entire area after him.

The amusing **architecture garden**, by artist Melvin Charney, lies across from Shaughnessy House between two highway on-ramps. It illustrates the different stages of the neighbourhood's development using a portion of the Sulpicians' orchard on the left, stone lines to indicate borders of 19th-century properties and rose bushes reminiscent of the gardens of those houses. A promenade along the cliff that once separated the wealthy neighbourhood from the working-class sector below offers a view of the lower part of the city (Little Burgundy, Saint-Henri, Verdun) and the St. Lawrence River. Some of the highlights of this panorama are represented in a stylized manner, atop concrete posts.

Walk along Boulevard René-Lévesque and turn left on Rue Saint-Mathieu.

Like the Congrégation de Notre-Dame, the Sœurs Grises had to relocate their convent and hospital, which used to be situated on Rue Saint-Pierre in Old Montréal (see p 90). They obtained part the Sulpicians' farm, where a vast convent, designed by Victor Bourgeau, was erected between 1869 and 1874. The **Couvent des Sœurs Grises** ★★ (*1185 Rue Saint-Mathieu, Guy-Concordia métro*) located in the Centre Marguerite d'Youville is the product of an architectural tradition developed over the centuries in Québec. The chapel alone reveals a foreign influence, namely the Romanesque revival style favoured by the Sulpicians, as opposed to the Renaissance and baroque Revival styles preferred by the church. The

Exploring

centre also presents exhibitions (*free admission; Tue to Sun 1:30am to 4pm*)

In the northwest wing, visitors will find the **Musée Marguerite-d'Youville** (*free admission; Wed to Sun 1:30 pm to 4:30 pm;* ☎937-9501), named after the founder of the community, which displays objects relating to the daily life of the nuns, as well as paintings, furniture, First Nations and missionary art, and some beautiful liturgical clothing. Upon request, it is possible to enter the Chapelle de l'Invention- de-la--Sainte-Croix, in the centre of the convent. Its stained-glass windows come from the Maison Champigneule in Bar-le-Duc, France. In 1974, the convent was supposed to be demolished and replaced by high-rises. Fortunately, Montrealers protested, and the buildings were saved. Today, the convent is listed as a historic monument.

Turn right on Rue Sainte-Catherine Ouest.

At the **Faubourg Sainte-Catherine** ★ (*1616 Rue Sainte-Catherine Ouest, Guy-Concordia métro*), a large converted, glass-roofed garage, visitors will find movie theatres, a market made up of small specialty shops selling local and foreign products, and a fast-food area.

To return to the Guy-Concordia métro station, head north on Rue Guy.

Tour F: Around the Hôtel-Dieu

In 1860, the *religieuses hospitalières* of Saint-Joseph, or nuns who were nurses, left the Hôtel-Dieu (hospital) founded by Jeanne Mance in 1643 in Old Montréal and moved to Avenue des Pins. Victor Bourgeau designed the new hospital, located in what was then open country. In the following years, the nuns gradually sold off the remaining property in lots, laying out streets soon to be lined with Victorian row houses. A number of these row houses were threatened with demolition after the unveiling of a gigantic real-estate development project in 1973. However, neighbourhood residents fought against the developers, who in the end only succeeded in tearing down a few of the coveted buildings. The houses that were saved are now part of the Milton Park project, the largest housing co-operative in Canada.

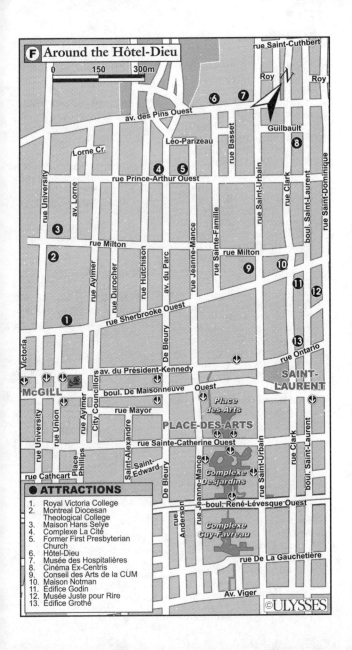

F Around the Hôtel-Dieu

0   150   300m

● ATTRACTIONS

1. Royal Victoria College
2. Montreal Diocesan Theological College
3. Maison Hans Selye
4. Complexe La Cité
5. Former First Presbyterian Church
6. Hôtel-Dieu
7. Musée des Hospitalières
8. Cinéma Ex-Centris
9. Conseil des Arts de la CUM
10. Maison Notman
11. Edifice Godin
12. Musée Juste pour Rire
13. Edifice Grothé

©ULYSSES

For this guide, the Hôtel-Dieu area tour also covers the McGill ghetto, a neighbourhood inhabited by many students from that English-language university, whose main campus lies to the west of Rue University (see p 130). The students who attend McGill in large numbers have converted some of the ghetto's houses into fraternities typical of those depicted in U.S. movies. These are identifiable by the large letters of the Greek alphabet that adorn their exteriors.

The tour starts at the exit of the McGill métro station. Head north on Rue University. The former Royal Victoria College, affiliated with McGill University, is located at the corner of Rue Sherbrooke Ouest and Rue University.

Royal Victoria College (*555 Rue Sherbrooke Ouest, McGill Métro*) was once a professional school for young women from good families. Today, it houses McGill University's Faculty of Music, as well as the 300-seat Pollack Hall, a perfect place for chamber music. On the front steps of the building, designed by American architect Bruce Price (1899), is a lovely bronze statue of Queen Victoria, executed by her daughter, the talented Princess Louise. Walking up Rue University, visitors will see **Montreal**

High School, a pale yellow brick building.

The **Montreal Diocesan Theological College ★** (*3473 Rue University, McGill métro*) is dedicated to the training of Anglican priests. With its densely ornamented walls of beige sandstone and red brick, the 1896 Gothic-Revival-style building is representative of the picturesque, polychrome period of the end of the Victorian era.

Turn right on Rue Milton.

The **Maison Hans Selye** (*659 Rue Milton, McGill métro*) is at the corner of Rue University and Milton.

The famous Dr. Hans Selye, a stress specialist, lived and worked here during the 1940s and 1950s.

Turn left on Avenue Lorne. Continue up beyond Rue Prince-Arthur to Lorne Crescent, a residential street little known even to Montrealers.

On this street, visitors will find some interesting semi-detached Victorian houses (circa 1875). During the Vietnam War, American protesters dodging the U.S. draft took refuge in this neighbourhood. Turn right on Rue Aylmer, then left on Rue Prince-Arthur.

Complexe La Cité (*at the corner of Avenue du Parc*) was renamed "Place du Parc" a few years ago. Spread over four blocks on either side of Rue Prince-Arthur, it is the only completed portion of an extensive urban renewal project involving the destruction of most of the Victorian buildings on Rue Hutchison, Rue Jeanne-Mance and Rue Sainte-Famille. La Cité, erected between 1974 and 1976, is one of the only complexes of this size in the world to have been designed by a woman, architect Eva Vecsei. It includes high-rise apartment buildings, a hotel, a shopping centre, a movie theatre and a large health club.

Cross Avenue du Parc, which links Rue de Bleury to downtown Montréal and the Mile End ethnic neighbourhood, located north of Parc Jeanne-Mance.

The former **First Presbyterian Church** (*3666 Rue Jeanne-Mance*), at the corner of Rue Prince-Arthur was erected in 1910 for American Presbyterians. It underwent a radical transformation in 1986 when apartments were laid out under the nave and all the way to the top of its steeple. Behind the church lies the former Strathearn School, now occupied by local community organizations, while the little German Lutheran **Église Saint-Jean** stands across the street. East of Rue Jeanne-Mance, there is an opening offering a view of an alley that was given a complete face-lift in 1982. After the creation of a residential cooperative, the numerous sheet-metal sheds and wooden walkways were replaced by small grassy yards enclosed by fences.

Turn left on Rue Sainte-Famille, which offers two interesting perspectives, one on the chapel of the Hôtel-Dieu on Avenue des Pins to the north and the other on the UQAM School of Design on Rue Sherbrooke to the south. The street is thus reminiscent of classical French town-planning, several examples of which could once be found in Old Montréal. Celebrated physicist Ernest Rutherford lived at 3702 Rue Sainte-Famille while he was teaching at McGill. A little farther up the street, visitors will find six residential buildings with vaguely Art Nouveau-style details. These were erected by the sisters in 1910 to house the doctors working at the Hôtel-Dieu (*3705 to 3739 Rue Sainte-Famille*).

The **Hôtel-Dieu** ★ (*215 Avenue des Pins Ouest, Place-des-Arts métro and bus no.80*) is still one of Montréal's main hospitals. The institution

Exploring

and the city were founded almost simultaneously, as part of a project initiated by a group of devout Parisians led by Jérôme Le Royer de La Dauversière. Thanks to the wealth of Angélique Faure de Bullion, wife of the superintendent of finances under Louis XIV, and the devotion of Jeanne Mance, from Langres, the institution grew rapidly on Rue Saint-Paul in Old Montréal. However, the lack of space, polluted air and noise in the old city forced the nuns to move the hospital to their farm in Mont-Sainte-Famille in the mid-19th century. The complex has been enlarged many times and is centred around a lovely neoclassical chapel with a dome and a façade reminiscent of urban churches in Québec under the French Regime. The interior, simplified in 1967, has, however, been divested of several interesting remounted paintings.

The **Musée des Hospitalières ★** (*$5; mid-Jun to mid-Oct, Tue to Fri 10am to 5pm, Sat and Sun 1pm to 5pm; mid-Oct to mid-Jun, Wed to Sun 1pm to 5pm; 21 Avenue des Pins Ouest, Place-des-Arts métro and bus no.80, ☎849-2919*) is located in the former chaplain's lodgings, next door to the chapel of the hospital. It provides a detailed account of both the history of the Filles Hospitalières de Saint-Joseph, a community founded at the Hôtel-Dieu de La Flèche (Anjou, France) in 1636, and the evolution of medicine over the last three centuries. Visitors can see the former wooden stairway of the Hôtel-Dieu de La Flèche (1634), given to the City of Montréal by the French region Sarthe in 1963. The piece was skilfully restored by the Compagnons du Devoir and incorporated into the museum's beautiful entrance hall, the work of Anjou architects, Bernard and Mercier (1992).

Head east on Avenue des Pins to Boulevard Saint-Laurent. Turn right on this long street, which divides the city between east and west. Montréal's multi-ethnic businesses are concentrated here. The portion of the boulevard located within the limits of the Hôtel-Dieu area is lined with an assortment of specialty food shops selling products from Eastern Europe, bookstores, second-hand shops, and fashionable restaurants and cafés.

Cinéma Ex-Centris / Ex-Centris Cinema (*3536 Boulevard Saint-Laurent, Saint-Laurent métro and bus no.55; ☎847-3536*) is a new stone building that blends in well with the older buildings next to it. A movie and new-media complex, Ex-Centris was officially opened on June 1,

1999 by its founder Daniel Langlois, who financed the entire construction from beginning to end. The complex plays the best independent films, produced either locally or internationally, in three magnificent rooms of different sizes. See also p 346.

The next street down is **Rue Prince-Arthur**, a pedestrian street east of Boulevard Saint-Laurent. Here, visitors will find a cluster of family restaurants, with terraces stretching all the way to the middle of the street. On summer evenings, a dense crowd gathers between the buildings to applaud street performers. Rue Prince-Arthur also provides access to Square Saint-Louis and Rue Saint-Denis (*Sherbrooke métro*).

Turn right on Rue Milton. Continue past the corner of Rue Clark then turn left on Rue Saint-Urbain.

The **Conseil des Arts de la CUM** (*3460 Rue Saint-Urbain, Place-des-Arts métro*), the city's arts council, occupies the former École d'Architecture de Montréal, erected in 1922. Ernest Cormier's former studio (1923), a small red-brick building with stained glass, stands on the grounds of the school. The Conseil rents it to Québec artists wishing to withdraw from the world for a certain period of time in order to create a specific work. At the corner of Rue Sherbrooke stands the former École des Beaux-Arts, now used by the department of maps of the archives of the Bibliothèque Nationale du Québec, the national library.

Turn left on Rue Sherbrooke.

Montréal photographer William Notman, known for his Canadian scenes and portraits of the 19th-century bourgeoisie, lived in the **Maison Notman** ★ (*51 Rue Sherbrooke Ouest, Place-des-Arts Métro*) from 1876 to 1891. The inexhaustible Notman photographic archives may be viewed at the Musée McCord (see p 130). The house, erected in 1844 according to a design by John Wells, is a fine example of the Greek Revival style as it was interpreted in Scotland in those years. Its extreme austerity is broken only by some small, decorative touches, such as the palmettes and rosettes of the portico. From 1894 to 1990, the residence served as a hospital, St. Margaret's Home for the Incurables, which provided extended care for the elderly.

The neighbouring service station has a prime location at the corner of two of the city's main streets, Boule-

Exploring

vard Saint-Laurent and Rue Sherbrooke. The residence of the Molson family, famous brewers and bankers, once stood here. Unfortunately, none of the plans to build libraries, opera houses and concert halls on this prestigious site have been realized.

Head south on Boulevard Saint-Laurent.

The **Édifice Godin** ★ (*2112 Boulevard Saint-Laurent, Saint-Laurent métro*), located at the corner of Rue Sherbrooke, is quite certainly the most daring example of early 20th-century modern architecture in Canada (1914). With its visible reinforced concrete structure, the building is evidence of the experiments of Auguste Perret and Paul Guadet, while the addition of a few subtle Art Nouveau curves gives it a very Parisian appearance. The building, designed by architect Joseph-Arthur Godin, to whom we also owe the Saint-Jacques (see p 156), was originally intended to be residential, but its novelty frightened off potential renters – so much so that it remained empty for a number of years after being completed, and was finally converted into a clothing factory.

Set up inside the former buildings of the Ekers brewery, the **Musée Juste Pour Rire / Just for Laughs Museum** (*$11; every day 11am to 8pm; 2111 Boulevard Saint-Laurent, Saint-Laurent métro, ☎845-4000, www.hahaha.com*), opened in 1993. This museum, the only one of its kind in the world, explores the different facets of humour, using a variety of film clips and sets. Visitors are equipped with infrared headphones, which enable them to follow the presentation. The building itself was renovated and redesigned by architect Luc Laporte and has some 3,000m² of exhibition space.

Édifice Grothé (*2000 Boulevard Saint-Laurent, Saint-Laurent métro*). Boulevard Saint-Laurent changes appearance several times from one end to the other. For a brief while, it takes on an industrial air and then regains its busy commercial look. Located at the corner of Rue Ontario, the former Grothé cigar factory is an austere red-brick edifice dating back to 1906, which has been converted into residences. In the early 20th century, when transportation, energy and the big banks were controlled by Anglo-Saxon magnates, French-Canadian strength, as the Grothé company proves, lay in the food and tobacco industries.

The tour of the Hôtel-Dieu neighbourhood ends at the Saint-Laurent métro station, at the corner of Boulevard de Maisonneuve.

Tour G: Quartier Latin

People come to this university neighbourhood, centred around Rue Saint-Denis, for its theatres, cinemas and countless outdoor cafés, which offer a glimpse of its heterogeneous crowd of students and revellers. The area's origins date back to 1823, when Montréal's first Catholic cathedral, Église Saint-Jacques, was inaugurated on Rue Saint-Denis. This prestigious edifice quickly attracted the cream of French-Canadian society – mainly old noble families who had remained in Canada after the conquest – to the area.

In 1852, a fire ravaged the neighbourhood, destroying the cathedral and Monseigneur Bourget's bishop's palace in the process. Painfully reconstructed in the second half of the 19th century, the area remained residential until the Université de Montréal was established here in 1893, marking the beginning of a period of cultural turmoil that would eventually lead

to the Quiet Revolution of the 1960s. The Université du Québec, founded in 1974, has since taken over from the Université de Montréal, now located on the north side of Mont Royal. The presence of the university has ensured the quarter's prosperity.

This tour starts at the west exit of the Sherbrooke Métro station.

The **Institut de Tourisme et d'Hôtellerie du Québec** (*3535 Rue Saint-Denis, Sherbrooke métro*), a school devoted to the tourism and hotel industries, ironically occupies what many people consider the ugliest building in Montréal. Set on the east side of Square Saint-Louis, on Rue Saint-Denis, it is part of an uninspiring group of buildings designed between 1972 and 1976, on the eve of the Olympics. The institute's courses in cooking, tourism and hotel management are nevertheless excellent.

Go across Rue Saint-Denis to Square Saint-Louis.

After the great fire of 1852, a reservoir was built at the top of the hill known as Côte-à-Barron. In 1879, it was dismantled and the site was converted into a park by the name of **Square Saint-Louis** ★★ (*Sherbrooke métro*). Developers built

Exploring

● ATTRACTIONS

1. Institut de Tourisme et d'Hôtellerie du Québec (ITHQ)
2. Square Saint-Louis
3. Mont-Saint-Louis
4. Maison Fréchette
5. Le Saint-Jacques
6. Bibliothèque Nationale
7. Théâtre Saint-Denis
8. Université du Québec à Montréal (UQÀM)
9. Chapelle Notre-Dame-de-Lourdes
10. Place Émilie-Gamelin
11. Former École des Hautes Études Commerciales
12. Square Viger
13. Union Française
14. Église Saint-Sauveur

○ ACCOMMODATIONS

1. Auberge de l'Hôtel de Paris (Hôtel de Paris)
2. Auberge des Glycines
3. Crowne Plaza Métro Centre
4. Days Inn Montréal Centre-Ville
5. Hôtel de l'Institut
6. Hôtel des Gouverneurs Place Dupuis
7. Jardin d'Antoine
8. Le Chasseur Bed and Breakfast
9. Lord Berri
10. Manoir Sherbrooke
11. Pierre et Dominique
12. UQÀM Residences

● RESTAURANTS

1. La Brioche Lyonnaise
2. La Brûlerie Saint-Denis
3. La Paryse
4. La Sila
5. Le Commensal
6. Le Pèlerin
7. Le Piémontais
8. Les Gâteries
9. Mikado
10. Zyng

beautiful Second Empire–style residences around the square, making it the nucleus of the French-Canadian bourgeois neighbourhood. These groups of houses give the area a certain harmonious quality rarely found in Montréal's urban landscape. **Rue Prince-Arthur** extends west from the square. In the 1960s, this pedestrian street (between Boulevard Saint-Laurent and Avenue Laval) was the centre of the counterculture and the hippie movement in Montréal. Today, it is lined with numerous restaurants and terraces. On summer evenings, street performers liven up the atmosphere.

Turn left onto **Avenue Laval**, one of the only streets in the city where the Belle Époque atmosphere is still

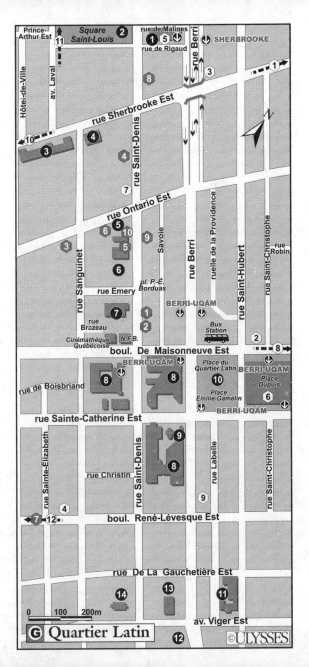

G Quartier Latin

© ULYSSES

0 100 200m

very tangible. Abandoned by the French-Canadian bourgeoisie from 1920 on, the houses were converted into rooming houses before attracting the attention of local artists, who began restoring them one by one. Poet Émile Nelligan (1879-1941) lived at number 3688 with his family at the turn of the century. The Union des Écrivains Québécois (Québec Writers' Association) occupies number 3492, the former home of film-maker Claude Jutra, who directed such films as *Mon Oncle Antoine* (Uncle Antoine). A number of other artists, including singer Pauline Julien, writers Michel Tremblay and Yves Navarre and pianist André Gagnon, live or have lived in the area around Square Saint-Louis and Avenue Laval.

Mont-Saint-Louis ★ (*244 Rue Sherbrooke Est, Sherbrooke métro*), a former boys' school run by the brothers of the Écoles Chrétiennes, was built facing straight up Avenue Laval in 1887. The long façade punctuated with pavilions, grey stone walls, openings with segmental arches and mansard roof make this building one of the most characteristic examples of the Second Empire style as adapted to suit Montréal's big institutions. The school closed its doors in 1970, and the edifice was converted into an apartment building in 1987, at which time an unobtrusive parking lot was built under the garden.

Maison Fréchette (*306 Rue Sherbrooke Est, Sherbrooke métro*). Journalist, poet and Member of Parliament Louis Fréchette (1839-1908) lived in this Second-Empire-style house. Sarah Bernhardt stayed here on several occasions during her North American tours.

Turn right on Rue Saint-Denis and walk down "Côte-à-Barron" toward the Université du Québec à Montréal.

Montée du Zouave, the hill on the right known today as *Terrasse Saint-Denis*, was the favourite meeting place of Québec's poets and writers at the turn of the century. The group of houses was built on the site of the home of Sieur de Montigny, a proud papal Zouave.

Montréal architect Joseph-Arthur Godin was one of the precursors of modern architecture in North America. In 1914, he began construction on three apartment buildings with visible reinforced concrete frames in the Quartier Latin area. One of these is the **Saint-Jacques** ★ (*1704 Rue Saint-Denis, Berri-UQÀM métro*). Godin blended this avant-garde concept with subtle Art-Nouveau curves, giving the buildings a light, graceful appearance. The venture was a commercial failure, however, leading Godin to bankruptcy and ending his career as an architect.

The Bibliothèque Nationale ★ (*1700 Rue Saint-Denis, Berri-UQÀM métro*), the national library, was originally built for the Sulpicians, who looked unfavourably upon the construction of a public library on Rue Sherbrooke. Even though many works were still on the *Index*, and thus forbidden reading for the clergy, the new library was seen as unfair competition. Known in the past as Bibliothèque Saint-Sulpice, this branch of the Bibliothèque Nationale du Québec was designed in the Beaux-Arts style by architect Eugène Payette in 1914. This style, a synthesis of classicism and French Renaissance architecture, was taught at Paris' École des Beaux-Arts, hence its name in North America. The interior is graced with lovely stained-glass windows created by Henri Perdriau in 1915.

The Théâtre Saint-Denis (*1594 Rue Saint-Denis, Berri-*

UQÀM métro, ☎ *790-1111*) is made up of two theatres, among the most popular in the city. During summer, the Festival Juste pour Rire, also known as the Just for Laughs Festival, is presented here. The theatre opened in 1914, and has since welcomed big names in show business from the world over. Modernized several times over the years, it was completely renovated yet again in 1989. As visitors can see, the top of the original theatre is higher than the recently added pink-granite façade.

The screening room and rental service of the **Office National du Film du Canada**

Exploring

(ONF) / National Film Board of Canada (NFB) are located at the corner of Boulevard de Maisonneuve. The ONF-NFB has the world's only **cinérobothèque** (*$5 for two hours; Tue to Sun noon to 9pm;* ☎496-6887), enabling about 100 people to watch different films at once. The complex also has a movie theatre (*$5 for two hours, $3 for one hour; every day, monthly schedule*) where various documentaries and NFB films are screened. Movie lovers can also visit the **Cinémathèque Québécoise** (*exhibits $5, films and exhibits $7.50, Wed free admission from 6pm to 8.30pm; Wed 3pm to 8.30pm, Thu to Sun 3pm to 6pm; 335 Boulevard de Maisonneuve Est;* ☎842-9768), a little further west, which has a collection of 25,000 Canadian, Québec and foreign films, as well as hundreds of pieces of equipment dating back to the early history of film. The Cinémathèque recently re-opened after extensive renovations. UQÀM's new concert hall, **Salle Pierre-Mercure**, is across the street.

Unlike most North American universities, with buildings contained within a specific campus, the campus of the **Université du Québec à Montréal (UQÀM)** ★ (*405 Rue Sainte-Catherine Est, at the corner of rue Saint-Denis, Berri-UQÀM métro*) is integrated into the city fabric like French and German universities built during the Renaissance. It is also linked to the underground city and the Métro. The university is located on the site once occupied by the buildings of the Université de Montréal and the Église Saint-Jacques, which was reconstructed after the fire of 1852. Only the wall of the right transept and the Gothic Revival steeple were integrated into Pavillon Judith-Jasmin (1979), and these elements have since become the symbol of the university. UQÀM is part of the Université du Québec, founded in 1969 and established in different cities across the province. Every year, over 40,000 students attend this flourishing institution of higher learning.

Turn left on Rue Sainte-Catherine Est.

Artist Napoléon Bourassa lived in a large house on Rue Saint-Denis. **Chapelle Notre-Dame-de-Lourdes** ★ (*430 Rue Sainte-Catherine Est, Berri-UQÀM métro*), erected in 1876, was his greatest achievement. It was commissioned by the Sulpicians, who wanted to secure their presence in this part of the city. Its Roman-Byzantine style is in some way a summary of its author's travels. The little chapel's recently restored interior, adorned with Bourassa's vibrantly coloured frescoes, is a must-see.

Place Émilie-Gamelin ★ (*at the corner of Rue Berri and Rue Sainte-Catherine, Berri-UQÀM métro*), laid out in 1992 for Montréal's 350th anniversary, is the city's newest large public space. In 1994, the area along Rue Sainte-Catherine was renamed **Esplanade Émilie-Gamelin**, while the northern section was renamed **Place du Quartier Latin**. At the far end, visitors will find some curious metal sculptures by Melvin Charney, who also designed the garden of the Centre Canadien d'Architecture (see p 144). Across the street lies the bus terminal (Terminus Voyageur), built on top of the Berri-UQAM Métro station, where three of the city's four metro lines converge. To the east, the Galeries Dupuis and the Atriums, two shopping centres containing a total of about 100 stores, are located on the site of the former Dupuis Frères department store. A few businesses dear to Montrealers, such as the Archambault record shop, still grace Rue Sainte-Catherine Est. The part of this street between Rue Saint-Hubert and Avenue Papineau is regarded as Montréal's Gay Village (see p 204) because it is lined with a large number of

bars, danceclubs and specialty shops frequented mainly by gay men and women.

Turn right on Rue Saint-Hubert, then right again on Avenue Viger.

A symbol of the social ascent of a certain class of French-Canadian businessmen in the early 20th century, the former business school, the **École des Hautes Études Commerciales ★** (*535 Avenue Viger, Berri-UQÀM or Champs-de-Mars métro*), profoundly altered Montréal's managerial and financial circles. Prior to the school's existence, these circles were dominated by Canadians of British extraction. This imposing building's very Parisian Beaux-Arts architecture (1908), characterized by twin columns, balustrades, a monumental staircase and sculptures, bears witness to the Francophile leaning of those who built it. In 1970, this business school, known as HEC, joined the campus of the Université de Montréal on the north side of Mont Royal.

Before moving to the Square Saint-Louis area around 1880, members of the French-Canadian bourgeoisie settled around **Square Viger** (*Avenue Viger, Berri-UQÀM or Champs-de-Mars métros*) during the

1850's. Marred by the underground construction of Autoroute Ville-Marie (1977-79), the square was redesigned in three sections by as many artists, who opted for an elaborate design, as opposed to the sober style of the original 19th-century square. In the background, visitors will see the castle-like former Gare Viger (see p 97).

The Union Française (*429 Avenue Viger Est, Berri-UQÀM or Champs-de-Mars métro*), Montréal's French cultural association, has occupied this old, aristocratic residence since 1909. Lectures and exhibitions on France and its various regions are held here. Every year, Bastille Day (July 14) is celebrated in Square Viger, across the street. The house, attributed to architect Henri-Maurice Perrault, was built in 1867 for shipowner Jacques-Félix Sincennes, founder of the Richelieu and Ontario Navigation Company. It is one of the oldest examples of Second Empire architecture in Montréal.

At the corner of Rue Saint-Denis is the **Église Saint-Sauveur** (*329 Avenue Viger, Berri-UQÀM or Champs-de-Mars métro*), a Gothic Revival church built in 1865, according to a design by architects Lawford and Nelson. From 1922 to 1995, it was the seat of Montréal's Syrian Catholic community. The church has a semicircular chancel, adorned with lovely stained-glass windows by artist Guido Nincheri.

Tour H: Plateau Mont-Royal

If there is one neighbourhood typical of Montréal, it is definitely this one. Thrown into the spotlight by writer Michel Tremblay, one of its illustrious sons, the "Plateau," as its inhabitants refer to it, is a neighbourhood of penniless intellectuals, young professionals and old Francophone working-class families. Its long streets are lined with duplexes and triplexes adorned with amusingly contorted exterior staircases leading up to the long, narrow apartments that are so typical of Montréal.

Flower-decked balconies made of wood or wrought iron provide box-seats for the spectacle on the street below. The Plateau is bounded by the mountain to the west, the Canadian Pacific railway tracks to the north and east, and Rue Sherbrooke to the south. It is traversed by a few major streets lined with cafés and theatres, such as Rue

Saint-Denis and Avenue Papineau, but is a tranquil area on the whole. A visit to Montréal would not be complete without a stroll through this area to truly grasp the spirit of Montréal.

This tour starts at the exit of the Mont-Royal Métro station. Turn right on Avenue du Mont-Royal, the neighbourhood's main commercial artery.

The **Monastère des Pères du Très-Saint-Sacrement ★** (*500 Avenue du Mont-Royal Est, Mont-Royal métro*) and its church, Église Notre-Dame-du-Très-Saint-Sacrement, were built at the end of the 19th century for the community of priests (*Père* is the French word for Father) of the same name. The somewhat austere façade of the church conceals an extremely colourful interior with an Italian-style decor designed by Jean-Zéphirin Resther. This sanctuary, dedicated to the "eternal Exhibition and Adoration of the Eucharist," is open for prayer and contemplation every day of the week. Baroque music concerts are occasionally presented here.

Continue heading east on Avenue du Mont-Royal Est, blending in with the neighbourhood's widely varied inhabitants on their way in and out of an assortment of businesses, ranging from the chic Pâtisserie Bruxelloise (a Belgian pastry shop) to shops selling knick-knacks for a dollar and used records.

Turn right on Rue Fabre for some good examples of Montréal-style housing. Built between 1900 and 1925, the houses contain between two and five apartments, all with private entrances from outside. Decorative details vary from one building to the next. Visitors will see Art Nouveau stained glass, parapets, cornices made of brick or sheet metal, balconies with Tuscan columns, and ornamental ironwork shaped in ringlets and cables.

Turn left on Rue Rachel Est.

At the end of Rue Fabre, visitors will find **Parc Lafontaine** (*Sherbrooke métro*), the Plateau's main green space, laid out in 1908 on the site of an old military shooting range. Monuments to Sir Louis-Hippolyte Lafontaine, Félix Leclerc and Dollard des Ormeaux have been erected here. The park covers an area of 40ha and is embellished with two artificial lakes and shady paths for pedestrians and bicyclists. There are tennis courts and bowling greens for summer sports enthusiasts, and in the winter the frozen lakes form a large rink, which is illumi-

Exploring

nated at night. The Théâtre de Verdure (outdoor theatre) is also located here. Every weekend, the park is crowded with people from the neighbourhood, who come here to make the most of beautiful sunny or snowy days.

The parish churches on Plateau Mont-Royal, designed to accommodate large French-Canadian working-class families, are enormous. The Romanesque Revival **Église de l'Immaculée-Conception** (*at the corner of Avenue Papineau, Sherbrooke or Mont-Royal métro*), designed by Émile Tanguay, was built in 1895.

The interior, decorated with plaster statues and remounted paintings, is typical of that period. The stained-glass windows come from the Maison Vermont in France.

Turn right on Avenue Papineau, and right again on Rue Sherbrooke Est.

An obelisk dedicated to General de Gaulle, by French artist Olivier Debré, towers over the long **Place Charles-de-Gaulle** (*at the corner of Avenue Émile-Duployé, Sherbrooke métro*), located alongside Rue Sherbrooke. The monument, made of blue granite from the quar-

● ATTRACTIONS

1. Monastère des Pères du Très-Saint-Sacrement
2. Parc Lafontaine
3. Église de l'Immaculée-Conception
4. Place Charles-de-Gaulle
5. Hôpital Notre-Dame
6. École Le Plateau
7. Bibliothèque Municipale de Montréal
8. Agora de la Danse
9. Former Institut des Sourdes-Muettes
10. Église Saint-Jean-Baptiste
11. Collège Rachel
12. Former Hospice Auclair

○ ACCOMMODATIONS

1. Auberge de la Fontaine
2. B & B Bienvenue
3. Gîte du Parc Lafontaine
4. Gîte Sympathique
5. Vacances Canada 4 Saisons

● RESTAURANTS

1. 917
2. Ambala
3. Anubis
4. Aux Baisers Volés
5. Aux Entretiens
6. Baie du Bengale
7. Bières & Compagnie
8. Byblos
9. Cactus
10. Café Cherrier
11. Café El Dorado
12. Café Rico
13. Casa Tapas
14. Chez Claudette
15. Chu Chai
16. Continental
17. Côté Soleil
18. Crêperie Bretonne Ty-Breiz
19. Dali & Matice
20. El Zaziummm
21. Fondue Mentale
22. Frite Alors
23. Fruit Folie
24. Il Piatto della Nonna
25. L'Académie
26. L'Anecdote
27. L'Avenue
28. L'Express
29. L'Harmonie d'Asie
30. La Binerie Mont-Royal
31. La Boulange du Commensal
32. La Brûlerie Saint-Denis
33. La Chilenita
34. La Colombe
35. La Gaudriole
36. La Petite Marche
37. La Piazzetta
38. La Prunelle
39. La Psarotaverna du Symposium
40. La Raclette
41. La Selva
42. Laloux
43. Le Flambard
44. Le Goût de la Thaïlande
45. Le Jardin de Panos
46. Le Persil Fou
47. Le Toasteur
48. Lélé da Cuca
49. Misto
50. Modigliani
51. Nil Bleu
52. Ouzeri
53. P'tit Plateau
54. Pistou
55. Pizzédélic
56. Poco Piu
57. Porté Disparu
58. Restorante-Trattoria Carrissima
59. Soy
60. Tampopo
61. Toqué
62. Un Monde Sauté

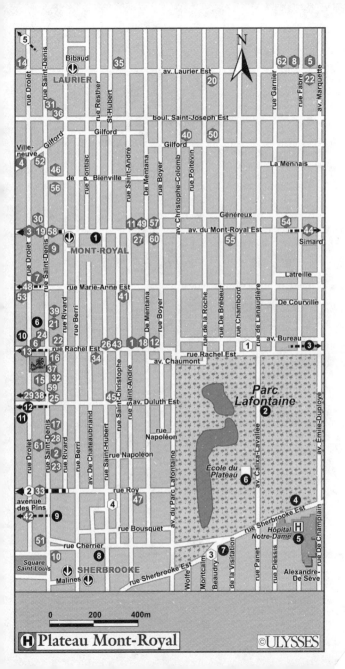

Plateau Mont-Royal
©ULYSSES

The Pull of Montréal

I arrived here from Calgary, didn't know a soul, and ran into my best friend from kindergarten on Saint-Laurent four days later. What can I say? Montréal is a magnetic city.

I have no statistics, but Montréal's vibrant reputation moves a huge crowd of young people from across the country to come and soak up their own part of the ethnic mix. Though the prospect of learning and re-learning French puts some people off, a surprising number of English Canadians seek out Montréal, eager to experience another culture and language. The good thing about the city is you can do both — spend the day putting the accents on your e's, and the evening watching movies made in Toronto. This co-habitation survives, running along the usual love-hate roller coaster, sending out sparks from Vancouver to Halifax.

We all unpack our bags here, but after that, similarities are difficult to define. I would say Anglos who choose Montréal have a penchant for diversity, and a love of things exotic. We are travellers at heart, but need to feel at home — many of us are clustered in the Plateau. We are willing to accept a small English-speaking community, in exchange for a city with soul. We are glad political, linguistic and cultural debates are part of everyday conversation — life would be so boring without them!

Something about Montréal fascinates those of us from the more homogeneous parts of Canada, makes us want to try living in a city where everyone from symphony conductors to grocery store clerks must speak a few words in at least two languages. Something about the kaleidoscope of equally adamant points of view being expressed simultaneously on any given day brings curious minds pouring on to the island. And then sometimes, not always, something about the contradictions and quirks of our adopted home makes us stay.

Carol Wood

ries of Saint-Michel-de-Montjoie in Normandy, stands 17m high. It was given to the City of Montréal by the City of Paris in 1992, on the occasion of Montréal's 350th anniversary.

Hôpital Notre-Dame, one of the city's major hospitals, lies across the street. The attractive **École Le Plateau** (1930) is located a little further west, at 3700 Avenue Calixa-Lavallée. This Art-Deco building, designed by architects Perrault and Gadbois, also houses the hall used by the Montréal Symphony Orchestra in its early days. A trail to the north of the school provides access to the lakes in Parc Lafontaine. Back on Rue Sherbrooke Est, visitors will find the **Bibliothèque Municipale de Montréal** (*1210 Rue Sherbrooke Est*), the city's public library, inaugurated in 1917 by Maréchal Joffre. Even back in the early 20th century, the edifice was of modest size, given the number of people it was intended to serve, a result of the clergy's reservations about a non-religious library being opened in Montréal. Today, fortunately, the library has a network of 27 neighbourhood branches. Inside, an entire room is devoted to the genealogy of French-Canadian families (Salle Gagnon, in the basement).

The monument to Sir Louis-Hippolyte Lafontaine (1807-1864), after whom the park was named, is located on the other side of the street. Regarded as the father of responsible government in Canada, Lafontaine was also one of the main defenders of the French language in the country's institutions. Take **Rue Cherrier**, which branches off from Rue Sherbrooke Est across from the monument. This street, along with Square Saint-Louis, located at its west end, once formed the nucleus of the French Canadian bourgeois neighbourhood. At number 840, visitors will find the **Agora de la Danse**, where the studios of a variety of dance companies are located. The red-brick building, completed in 1919, originally served as the Palestre Nationale, a sports centre for the neighbourhood youth and the scene of many tumultuous public gatherings during the 1930s.

Turn right on Rue Saint-Hubert, lined with fine examples of vernacular architecture. Turn left on Rue Roy to see **Église Saint-Louis-de- France**, *built in 1936 as a replacement for the original church, destroyed by fire in 1933.*

At the corner of **Rue Saint-Denis** stands the former **Institut des Sourdes-**

Muettes (*3725 Rue Saint-Denis, Sherbrooke métro*), a large, grey stone building made up of numerous wings and erected in stages between 1881 and 1900. Built in the Second Empire style, it covers an entire block and is typical of institutional architecture of that period in Québec. It once took in the region's deaf-mutes. The strange chapel with cast-iron columns, as well as the sacristy, with its tall wardrobes and surprising spiral staircase, may be visited upon request from the entrance on Rue Berri.

Head north on Rue Saint-Denis.

Between Rue Sainte-Catherine, to the south, and Boulevard Saint-Joseph, to the north, this long artery is lined with numerous outdoor cafés and beautiful shops, established inside Second-Empire-style former residences built during the second half of the 19th century. Visitors will also find many bookstores, tea rooms and restaurants, that have become veritable Montréal institutions over the years.

Take a brief detour left onto Rue Rachel Est in order to see Église Saint-Jean-Baptiste and the institutional buildings around it.

Église Saint-Jean-Baptiste ★★ (*309 Rue Rachel Est, Mont-Royal métro*), dedicated to the patron saint of French Canadians, is a gigantic symbol of the solid faith of the Catholic working-class inhabitants of the Plateau Mont-Royal at the turn of the 20th century, who, despite their poverty and large families, managed to amass considerable amounts of money for the construction of sumptuous churches. The exterior was built in 1901, according to a design by architect Émile Vanier. The interior was redone after a fire, and is now a veritable Baroque Revival masterpiece designed by Casimir Saint-Jean that is not to be missed. The pink-marble and gilded wood baldaquin in the chancel (1915) shelters the altar, which is made of white Italian marble and faces the large Casavant organs – among the most powerful in the city – in the jube. Concerts are frequently given at this church. It can seat up to 3,000 people.

Collège Rachel, built in 1876 in the Second Empire style, stands across the street from the church. Finally, west of Avenue Henri-Julien, visitors will find the former **Hospice Auclair** (1894), with its semi-circular entrance on Rue Rachel. On Rue Drolet, south of Rue Rachel, there are several good examples of the working-class architecture of the 1870s and

1880s on the Plateau, before the advent of vernacular housing, namely duplexes and triplexes with exterior staircases like those found on Rue Fabre.

Go back to Rue Saint-Denis and continue walking up it to Avenue du Mont-Royal. Turn right in order to return to the Mont-Royal métro station.

Tour I: Mont Royal, Westmount and Western Montréal

Montréal's central neighbourhoods were built around Mont Royal, an important landmark in the cityscape. Known simply as "the mountain" by Montrealers, this squat mass, measuring 234m at its highest point, is composed of intrusive rock. It is in fact one of the seven hills of the St. Lawrence plain in the Montérégie region. A "green lung" rising up at the far end of downtown streets, it exerts a positive influence on Montrealers, who, as a result, never lose touch with nature. The mountain actually has three summits; the first is occupied by Parc du Mont-Royal, the second by the Université de Montréal, and the third by Westmount, an independent city with lovely English-style homes. In addition to these areas, there are the Catholic, Protestant and Jewish cemeteries, which, considered as a whole, form the largest necropolis in North America.

To reach the starting point of the tour, take bus no.11 from the Mont-Royal métro station, located on the Plateau Mont-Royal, and get off at the Belvédère Camilien-Houde.

From the **Belvédère Camilien-Houde ★★** (*Voie Camilien-Houde*), a lovely scenic lookout, visitors can look out over the entire eastern portion of Montréal. The Plateau Mont-Royal lies in the foreground, a uniform mass of duplexes and triplexes, pierced in a few places by the oxidized copper bell towers of parish churches, while the Rosemont and Maisonneuve quarters lie in the background, with the Olympic Stadium towering over them. In clear weather, the oil refineries in the east end can be seen in the distance.

The St. Lawrence River, visible on the right, is only 1.5km wide at its narrowest point. The Belvédère Camilien-Houde is Montréal's version of Inspiration Point and a favourite gathering place of sweethearts with cars.

Exploring

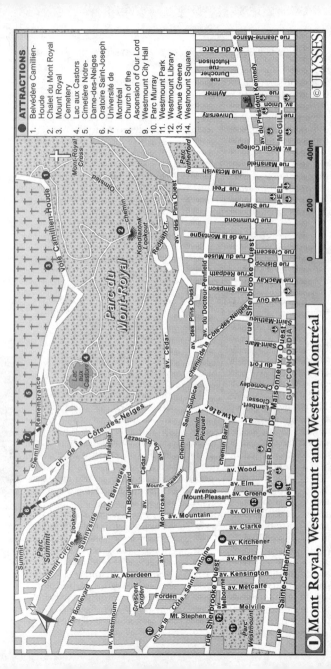

ATTRACTIONS

1. Belvédère Camillien-Houde
2. Chalet du Mont Royal
3. Mount Royal Cemetery
4. Lac aux Castors
5. Cimetière Notre-Dame-des-Neiges
6. Oratoire Saint-Joseph
7. Université de Montréal
8. Church of the Ascension of Our Lord
9. Westmount City Hall
10. Parc Murray
11. Westmount Park
12. Westmount Library
13. Avenue Greene
14. Westmount Square

Mont Royal, Westmount and Western Montréal

© ULYSSES

Climb the staircase at the south end of the parking lot, and follow Chemin Olmsted on the left, which leads to the chalet and main lookout. You will pass the mountain's cross on the way.

Pressured by the residents of the Golden Square Mile (see tour p 129), who saw their favourite playground being deforested by various firewood companies, the City of Montréal created **Parc du Mont-Royal / Mount Royal Park**★★★ in 1870. Frederick Law Olmsted (1822-1903), the celebrated designer of New York's Central Park, was commissioned to design the park. He decided to preserve the site's natural character, limiting himself to a few lookout points linked by winding paths. Inaugurated in 1876, the park, which covers 101ha on the southern part of the mountain, is cherished by Montrealers as a place to enjoy the fresh air (see also p 247).

The **Chalet du Mont Royal** ★★★ *(every day 8:30am to 9pm; Parc du Mont-Royal, ☎872-3911)*, located in the centre of the park, was designed by Aristide Beaugrand-Champagne in 1932 as a replacement for the original structure, which was about to collapse. During the 1930s and 1940s, big bands gave moonlit concerts on the steps of the building. The interior is decorated with remounted paintings depicting scenes from Canadian history.

These were commis sioned from some of Québec's great painters, such as Marc- Aurèle Fortin and Paul-Émile Borduas. Nevertheless, people go to the chalet mainly to stroll along the lookout and take in the exceptional view of downtown, best in the late afternoon and in the evening, when the skyscrapers light up the darkening sky.

Take the gravel road leading to the parking lot of the chalet and Voie Camilien-Houde. One of the entrances to the Mount Royal Cemetery lies on the right.

The **Mount Royal Cemetery** ★★ (*Voie Camilien Houde*) is a Protestant cemetery that ranks among the most beautiful parks in the city. Designed as an Eden for the living visiting the deceased, it is laid out like a landscape garden in an isolated valley, giving visitors the impression that they are a thousand miles from the city, though they are in fact right in the centre of it. The wide variety of hardwood and fruit trees attract species of birds found nowhere else in Québec. Founded by the Anglican, Presbyterian, Unitar-

Cimetière Notre-Dame-des-Neiges

In 1855, Cimetière Notre-Dame-des-Neiges (Notre Dame des Neiges Cemetery) was inaugurated. It stretches on land that was once the north shore of a lost island in the ancient Champlain Sea (the site of present-day Mont Royal) following the thaw of the Inlandsis Laurentidien (a 3km thick continental glacier) 10,000 years ago. Non-fossilized seashells were discovered in the sandy sediment of this ancient post-glacial beach when the site was temporarily used as a dump.

On May 29, 1855, Mrs. Jane Gilroy, wife of Thomas McCready, then a Montréal municipal councilor, was the first person to be buried in the new cemetery. Standing on lot *F56*, her granite monument's epitaph is surprisingly still legible, unlike other historic gravestones, which often eroded because of the poor quality of the material they were made of, mostly limestone, which is soluble.

Since the burial of Mrs. Gilroy, almost one million people have been laid to rest here, making Cimetière Notre-Dame-des-Neiges the second-largest cemetery in North America after Arlington Cemetery in Washington. A walk through the 55 km of trails that crisscross the site proves that this cemetery is a unique treasure, as much for its architectural, cultural and historical facets as for its natural setting.

Not only do people come to Cimetière Notre-Dame-des-Neiges for its tranquillity, greenery and birds, but also to admire the often magnificently carved gravestones. To better plan your walk, pick up a detailed map of the cemetery at the reception area across from Chapelle de la Résurrection. Sumptuously detailed monuments attest to a dominant upper class, and many sections of the cemetery are recommended for the sheer beauty of these memorials.

One area you should not miss is section *T*, with its majestic monuments and dozens of crypts that are something out of a classic horror film. The Veterans section, with hundreds of small, grey tombstones lined up in perfect rows, is also worth seeing. As well, the ethnic sections are often worth a detour for a glimpse of other funerary traditions; for example, the Chinese section *(U598-604)*, where every monument bears an image of the deceased; the orthodox section is full of gravestones decorated with multi-coloured beds of flowers, and most of these have epitaphs in gold letters.

Aside from rich families proudly displaying their wealth in sculpted granite, the lower classes are equally represented in section *FT* (*fosse temporaire*, "temporary grave"), where, as the name sug-gests, families can rent lots for a period of 10 years. Some of these fami-lies could not afford ex-pensive monuments, which explains the pre-sence of several little wooden crosses scattered about this section.

A visit to the Cimetière Notre-Dame-des-Neiges would not be complete without a look at the many commemorative monuments scattered about the cemetery. Among the most eye-catching is the one belonging to the Société Saint-Jean-Baptiste *(lot C24)*, which stands on the grave of its founder, Ludger Duvernay. There is also a magnificent black granite monument for the Union des Artistes *(O203)*, honouring actors who left their mark on Québec theatre. Finally, the most impressive of all is a tribute to the many Patriots of 183738 *(lot B261)*, who fell in battle against the English, were hanged, or were exiled.

Of the hundreds of thousands of people buried here, a significant number are historic figures including politicians Robert Bourassa *(secteur E)*, former prime minister of Québec, and Georges-Étienne Cartier *(lot O1)*, who was one of the Founding Fathers of Canada.

Exploring

Many artists have also been laid to rest here including Philippe Aubert-de-Gaspé (*lot G26*), author of the first French Canadian novel, Olivier Guimond and his father Ti-Zoune (*lot GA1341*), famous actors of Québec theatre, Émile Nelligan (*lot N588*), one of Québec's most admired poets, and Marie Travers, a popular singer of the 1930s better known as La Bolduc (*TROIE1912*).

Admiring the many interesting gravestones along the paths is like a walk back into the past. Who knows? Perhaps you will come across a familiar name, or read an epitaph that will remind you of something, a pleasant déjà-vu. Even if it has never occurred to you to visit a cemetery, Notre-Dame-des-Neiges is a moving experience that you will not regret for an instant.

ian and Baptist churches, the cemetery opened in 1852. Some of its monuments are true works of art, executed by celebrated artists.

The families and eminent personalities buried here include the Molson brewers, who have the most impressive and imposing mausoleum, shipowner Sir Hugh Allan, and numerous other figures from the footnotes and headlines of history, such as Anna Leonowens, governess of the King of Siam in the 19th century and inspiration for the play *The King and I*. On the left, on the way to Lac aux Castors, visitors will see the last of the mountain's former farmhouses.

Continue along Voie Camilien Houde, then head west on Chemin Remembrance. Take the road leading to Lac aux Castors (see map).

Small **Lac aux Castors / Beaver Lake** (*alongside Chemin Remembrance*), was created in 1958 in what used to be a swamp. In winter, it becomes a pleasant skating rink. This part of the park also has grassy areas and a sculpture garden. It is laid out in a more conventional manner than the rest, violating Olmsted's purist directives.

The **Cimetière Notre-Dame-des-Neiges**, Montréal's largest cemetery, is a veritable city of the dead, as more than a million people have been buried here since its inauguration in 1854. It replaced the cemetery in Square Dominion, which was deemed too close to the neighbouring houses. Unlike the Protestant cemetery, it has a conspicuously religious character, clearly identifying it with the Catholic faith. Accordingly, two heavenly angels flanking a crucifix greet visitors at the main entrance on Chemin de la Côte-des-Neiges. The "two solitudes" (Canadians of French Catholic and Anglo-Saxon Protestant extraction) thus remain separated even in death. The tombstones read like a who's-who in the fields of business, arts, politics and science in Québec. An obelisk dedicated to the Patriotes of the rebellion of 1837-38 and numerous monuments executed by renowned sculptors lie scattered alongside the 55km of roads and paths that crisscross the cemetery.

Oratoire Saint-Joseph

Both the cemetery and the roads leading to it offer a number of views of the **Oratoire Saint-Joseph ★★** (*free admission; every day 6:30am to 9:30pm; 3800 Chemin Queen Mary, ☎ 733-8211 for information*). The enormous building topped by a copper dome, the second largest dome in the world after that of St. Peter's in Rome, stands on a hillside, accentuating its mystical aura. From the gate at the entrance, there are over 300 steps to climb to reach the oratory. Small buses are also available for worshippers who do not want to climb the steps. The Oratoire was built between 1924 and 1956, thanks to the efforts of the blessed Frère André, porter of Collège Notre-Dame (across the street), to whom many miracles are attributed. A veritable religious complex, the oratory is dedicated to both Saint Joseph and its humble creator. It includes the lower and upper basilicas, the crypt of Frère André and two museums, one dedi-

Exploring

cated to Frère André's life, the other to sacred art.

Visitors will also find the porter's first cha pel, built in 1910, a cafeteria, a hostelry and a store selling devotional articles. The oratory is one of the most important centres of worship and pilgrimage in North America. Each year, it attracts some 2,000,000 visitors. The building's neoclassical exterior was designed by Dalbé Viau and Alphonse Venne, while the essentially modern interior is the work of Lucien Parent and French Benedictine monk Dom Paul Bellot, the author from Saint-Benoît-du-Lac in the Cantons de l'Est, or Eastern Townships. It is well worth visiting the upper basilica to see the stained-glass windows by Marius Plamondon, the altar and crucifix by Henri Charlier, and the astonishing gilded chapel at the back. The oratory has an imposing Beckerath-style organ, which can be heard on Wednesday evenings during the summer. Outside, visitors can also see the chimes, made by Paccard et Frères and originally intended for the Eiffel Tower, as well as the beautiful Chemin de Croix (Way of the Cross) by Louis Parent and Ercolo Barbieri, in the gardens on the side of the mountain. Measuring 263m, the Oratory's obser-vatory, which commands a sweeping view of the entire city, is the highest point on the island.

After many attempts, Québec City's Université Laval, aiming to preserve its monopoly on French-language university education in Québec, finally opened a branch of its institution in the Château Ramezay (see p 106). A few years later, it moved to Rue Saint-Denis, giving birth to the Quartier Latin (see p 151). The **Université de Montréal** ★ (*2900 Boulevard Édouard-Montpetit*) finally became autonomous in 1920, enabling its directors to develop grandiose plans. Ernest Cormier (1885-1980) was approached about designing a campus on the north side of Mont Royal. The architect, a graduate of the École des Beaux-Arts in Paris, was one of the first to acquaint North Americans with the Art Deco style.

The plans for the main building evolved into a refined, symmetrical Art Deco structure faced with pale yellow bricks and topped by a central tower, visible from Chemin Remembrance and Cimetière Notre-Dame-des-Neiges. Begun in 1929, construction on the building was interrupted by the Stock Market Crash, and it wasn't until 1943 that the first students entered the main building on the mountain. Since then, a whole host of pavilions has been added, making the Université de Montréal the second-largest French-language university in the world, with a student body of over 58,000. Since the entrance to the university is somewhat removed from the present route, a visit to the campus constitutes an additional excursion that takes about an hour.

The École Polytechnique of the Université de Montréal, which is also located on Mont Royal, was the scene of a tragedy that marked the city and all of Canada. On December 6, 1989, 14 female students were murdered in cold blood inside the École Polytechnique by a crazed women-hating man who targeted the women at the school. To keep the memory of these women and that of all female victims of violence alive, the **Place du 6-décembre-1989** (*corner Decelles and Queen-Mary*) was erected on December 6, 1999, to commemorate the 10th anniversary of the massacre. There, artist Rose-Marie Goulet erected her *Nef pour quatorze reines* (Nave for Fourteen Queens), inscribed with the names of the victims of the Polytechnique massacre.

Back on the mountain, follow the trails through Parc du Mont-Royal to the exit leading to Westmount (see map).

This wealthy residential city of 20,239 inhabitants enclosed within the city of Montréal, has long been regarded as the bastion of the Anglo-Saxon elite in Québec. After the Golden Square Mile was invaded by the business centre, Westmount assumed its role. Its shady, winding roads, on the southwest side of the mountain are lined with Neo-Tudor and Neo-Georgian residences, most of which were built between 1910 and 1930. The heights of Westmount offer some lovely views of the city below.

Take The Boulevard to Avenue Clarke (near the small triangular park), then turn left to reach Rue Sherbrooke Ouest.

Erected in 1928, Westmount's English Catholic church, The **Church of the Ascension of Our Lord** ★ (*at the corner of Avenue Kitchener, Atwater métro*) is evidence of the staying power of the Gothic Revival style in North American architecture and the historical accuracy, ever more apparent in the 20th century, of buildings patterned after ancient models. With its rough stone facing, elongated lines and delicate sculp-

Exploring

tures, it looks like an authentic church from a 14th-century English village.

Westmount is like a piece of Great Britain in North America. Its **City Hall ★** (*4333 Rue Sherbrooke Ouest*) was built in the Neo-Tudor style, inspired by the architecture of the age of Henry VIII and Elizabeth I, which was regarded during the 1920s as the national style of England because it originated from the British Isles. The style is characterized in part by horizontal openings with multiple stone transoms, bay windows and flattened arches. The impeccable green of a lawn-bowling club lies at the back, frequented by members wearing their regulation whites.

Take Chemin de la Côte-Saint-Antoine to Parc Murray.

In Québec, the term *côte*, which translates literally as "hill," usually has nothing to do with the slope of the land, but is a leftover division of the seigneurial system of New France. The roads linking one farm to the next ran along the tops of the long rectangles of land distributed to colonists. As a result, these plots of land gradually became known as *côtes*, from the French word for "side," *côté*. Côte Saint-Antoine is one of the oldest roads on the island of Montréal. Laid out in 1684 by the Sulpicians on a former native trail, it is lined with some of Westmount's oldest houses. At the corner of Avenue Forden is a **milestone** dating back to the 17th century, discreetly identified by the pattern of the sidewalk, which radiates out from it. This is all that remains of the system of road signs developed by the Sulpicians for their seigneury on the island of Montréal.

For those who would like to immerse themselves in a Mid-Atlantic atmosphere, a blend of England and America, **Parc Murray** (*north of Avenue Mount Stephen*) offers the perfect combination – a football field and tennis courts in a country setting. Here, visitors will find the remains of a natural grouping of acacias, an extremely rare species at this latitude, due to the harsh climate. The trees' presence is an indication that this area has the mildest climate in Québec. This mildness is a result of both the southwest slant of the land and the warm air coming from the nearby Lachine rapids.

Go down Avenue Mount Stephen to return to Rue Sherbrooke Ouest.

Westmount Park and the
Westmount Library ★
(*4575 Rue Sherbrooke Ouest*).
Westmount Park was laid
out on swampy land in
1895. Four years later, Québec's first public library was
erected on the same site.
Up until then, religious
communities had been the
only ones to develop this
type of cultural facility, and
the province was therefore
somewhat behind in this
area. The red-brick building
is the product of the trends
toward eclecticism, pictur-
esqueness and polychromy
that characterized the last
two decades of the
19th century.

*From the park, head east on
Avenue Melbourne, where
there are some fine examples of
Queen-Anne-style houses.
Turn right on Avenue
Metcalfe, then left on Boule-
vard de Maisonneuve Ouest.*

At the corner of Avenue
Clarke stands **Église
Saint-Léon** ★, the only
French-language Catholic
parish in Westmount. The
sober, elegant Romanesque
Revival façade conceals an
exceptionally rich interior
décor begun in 1928 by
artist Guido Nincheri, who
also painted the frescoes in
Château Dufresne (see
p 217). Nincheri was pro-
vided with a large sum of
money to decorate the
church using no substitutes
and no tricks. Accordingly,

the floor and the base of
the walls are covered with
the most beautiful Italian
and French marble avail-
able, while the upper portion of the nave is made of
Savonnières stone and the
chancel, of the most pre-
cious Honduran walnut,
hand-carved by Alviero
Marchi. The complex
stained-glass windows de-
pict various scenes from the
life of Jesus Christ, including a few personages from
the time of the church's
construction, whom visitors
will be amused to discover
among the Biblical figures.
Finally, the entire Christian
pantheon is represented in
the chancel and on the
vault in vibrantly coloured
frescoes, executed in the
traditional manner using an
egg-wash. This technique
(used, notably, by Michel-
angelo) consists of making
pigment stick to a wet surface with a coating made of
egg, which becomes very
hard and resistant when
dry.

*Continue along Boulevard de
Maisonneuve, which leads
through the former French
section of Westmount before
intersecting with Avenue
Greene.*
On **Avenue Greene**, a small
street with a typically
English-Canadian character,
visitors will find several of
Westmount's fashionable
shops. In addition to

Exploring

service-oriented businesses, there are art galleries, antique shops and bookstores filled with lovely things.

Architect Ludwig Mies van der Rohe (1886-1969), one of the leading masters of the modernist movement and the head of Bauhaus in Germany, designed **Westmount Square** ★★ (*at the corner of Avenue Wood and Boulevard de Maisonneuve Ouest, Atwater métro*) in 1964. The complex is typical of the architect's North American work, characterized by the use of black metal and tinted glass. It includes an underground shopping centre, topped by three towers containing offices and apartments. The public areas were originally covered with veined white travertine, one of Mies's favourite materials, which was replaced by a layer of granite, more resistant to the harsh climatic effects of freezing and thawing.

An underground corridor leads from Westmount Square to the Atwater métro station.

Tour J: Outremont

On the other side of Mont Royal (*outremont*) is the

municipality of Outremont, which, like Westmount (its anglophone counterpart on the south side), clings to the side of the mountain and has, over the course of its development, welcomed a fairly well-off population, including many influential Quebecers.

Outremont has long been a sought-after residential area. In fact, recent research suggests that the mysterious native village of Hochelaga, which disappeared between the voyages of Jacques Cartier and De Maisonneuve (16th and 17th centuries), was probably situated in this region. Furthermore, Chemin de la Côte-Sainte-Catherine, the main road around which Outremont developed, supposedly attests to native activity in the area and follows a former communication route cleared by natives to enable them to skirt the mountain.

The Europeans first used the territory known today as Outremont for market gardening during the 17th and 18th centuries. It was later used for horticultural purposes and, being a rural area close to the city, as a

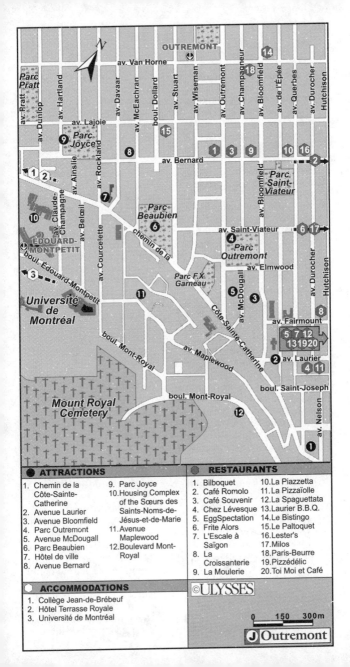

OUTREMONT

● ATTRACTIONS

1. Chemin de la Côte-Sainte-Catherine
2. Avenue Laurier
3. Avenue Bloomfield
4. Parc Outremont
5. Avenue McDougall
6. Parc Beaubien
7. Hôtel de ville
8. Avenue Bernard
9. Parc Joyce
10. Housing Complex of the Sœurs des Saints-Noms-de-Jésus-et-de-Marie
11. Avenue Maplewood
12. Boulevard Mont-Royal

● RESTAURANTS

1. Bilboquet
2. Café Romolo
3. Café Souvenir
4. Chez Lévesque
5. EggSpectation
6. Frite Alors
7. L'Escale à Saïgon
8. La Croissanterie
9. La Moulerie
10. La Piazzetta
11. La Pizzaïolle
12. La Spaguettata
13. Laurier B.B.Q.
14. Le Bistingo
15. Le Paltoquet
16. Lester's
17. Milos
18. Paris-Beurre
19. Pizzédélic
20. Toi Moi et Café

○ ACCOMMODATIONS

1. Collège Jean-de-Brébeuf
2. Hôtel Terrasse Royale
3. Université de Montréal

0   150   300m

J Outremont

vacation spot for middle-class Montrealers in the 19th century. Agricultural goods produced here at the time were popular and served at important tables throughout the American Northeast. Montréal's urban expansion brought an end to Outremont's agricultural vocation near the close of the 19th century and led to the development of the essentially residential municipality found today.

Our suggested tour of Outremont runs along Chemin de la Côte-Sainte-Catherine, beginning at the corner of Avenue Mont-Royal.

A means of circling the mountain, **Chemin de la Côte-Sainte-Catherine** curves for a good part of its length, at an angle to the grid network of local streets. The *côte*, or slope, serves as the border between two types of terrain, while at the same time separating what has come to be known as "Outremont-en-haut" (Upper Outremont), perched atop the mountain, from the rest of the municipality. Initially, many imposing residences were built along this large boulevard in order to take advantage of the sharp incline of the south side (*homes of the heirs of the famous cigar manufacturer Grothé at numbers 96 and 98*). Accordingly, the land all along the road has been

laid out in accordance with this slope. For example, some entrances and façades face Avenue Maplewood, located in the back, yards are terraced, wooded areas are left intact to prevent erosion and low retaining walls have been constructed. For the past 20 years, however, the sporadic and controversial development of prestigious high-rises on the north side has somewhat altered the general appearance of the street, or at least the section between Boulevard Mont-Royal and Avenue Laurier. Relatively unoriginal in style, these high-rises, which the municipality hoped would make the street look something like New York's Fifth Avenue, have often replaced older, more interesting residences, such as those of the Berthiaume-Du Tremblay group, owner of the French-language newspaper *La Presse*, which stood at the corner of Avenue Bloomfield (*replaced by Le Tournesol, at number 205*).

Walk to the corner of Bloomfield and Laurier.

Avenue Laurier ★ is one of the three trendy shopping streets in the municipality and are popular among well-off Outremontais and Montrealers. Over the past few years, the avenue has been given a face-lift, contributing a certain stylishness to the local specialty shops. At the corner of Laurier and Bloomfield visitors will find **Église Saint-Viateur**, which dates back to the second decade of the 20th. Its remarkable interior, inspired by the Gothic Revival style, was decorated by artists renowned in the fields of painting (Guido Nincheri), glass-working (Henri Perdriau), cabinet-making (Philibert Lemay) and sculpting (Médard Bourgault and Olindo Gratton). The ceiling vaults, covered with paintings depicting the life of St. Viateur are quite exceptional.

Walk alongside the church on Avenue Bloomfield.

Avenue Bloomfield (*Outremont Métro*) is believed to have been named after a farm once located here, where the harvest would have been typical of the market gardening and fruit growing of the time. Today, the avenue serves as a reminder of the first urban-style lots that would eventually line the city streets from east to west. The overall lay-out of this winding street is very pleasant, with large trees, spacious front yards and distinctive architecture. Several buildings are worth a look. The **Académie Querbes**, at numbers 215 to 235 was built in 1915-1916. The architectural detail – monu-

mental entrance and stone galleries reaching all the way up to the third floor – is quite original for the period. Furthermore, the facilities were ahead of their time, including a swimming pool, bowling alley and gymnasium. The canopy-shaped balconies over the entrances of numbers 249 and 253 have been unusually styled as loggias. The building at number 261 was designed by the same architect as the latter two houses. It was once lived in by Canon Lionel Groulx, a priest, writer, history professor and prominent Québec nationalist. The building now houses a foundation bearing his name. Number 262 stands out for its façade, made of alternating red brick and grey stone. A little farther, in front of Parc Outremont, at number 345, is a house built in 1922 by and for architect Aristide Beaugrand-Champagne, which is distinguished by its cathedral roof and white stucco.

Turn left on Avenue Elmwood.

Parc Outremont (*Outremont métro*) is one of the municipality's many much-appreciated parks, used for both sports and leisure activities. Laid out at the beginning of the century on swamplands supplied with water by a stream flowing from the neighbouring hills, it gives

Exploring

the area a serene beauty. Occupying the place of honour in the middle of the Bassin McDougall is a fountain resembling the *Groupes d'Enfants*, which adorns the grounds of the Château de Versailles in Paris. A monument to the citizens of Outremont who died during World War I faces the street.

Turn left on Avenue McDougall.

Avenue McDougall (*Outremont métro*) is particularly interesting, in part for the house at numbers 221 and 223 that occupies a very important place in the history of Outremont: the "**Ferme Outre-Mont**," built for L.-T. Bouthillier between 1833 and 1838. From 1856 to 1887, the farm was the family residence of a financier named McDougall. It later became a horticultural school for deaf-mutes run by the clergymen of Saint-Viateur. This was the scene of the first Mass ever celebrated in Outremont, on April 21, 1887. The house is believed to be the third oldest residence in the city. Henri Bourassa, founder of the newspaper *Le Devoir*, was supposedly once a tenant here. The white section (now divided into two dwellings) still has most of its original characteristics, namely the large

porch topped with a gallery, the dormer window wedged between the two chimneys and the small windows. Number 268, designed by a Toronto architect named Ralston for an architecture competition, is a good example of the international Bauhaus style. This influential school of thought from the 1920s emphasized functionalism, and greatly affected the art and science of architecture.

Turn right on Chemin de la Côte-Sainte-Catherine.

Chemin de la Côte-Sainte-Catherine once again becomes lined with residences, some of undeniable architectural interest in this area. This is especially the case with number 325, which has a very large gallery and numerous ornamental details, and number 356, home of architect Roger d'Astous, who added an aviary. D'Astous, a student of celebrated architect Frank Lloyd Wright, conceived the idea for Montréal's Olympic Village. **Parc Beaubien** (*Outremont*

Métro or Édouard-Montpetit métro) is located on the site of a farming estate once owned by the important Beaubien family of Outremont, the members of which included several prominent figures on the Québec scene. The members of the Beaubien clan lived right near each other on the side of the hill, overlooking their land (part of which is now occupied by the Terrasses Les Hautvilliers). Among the family members were Madame Justine Lacoste Beaubien, founder of the renowned Hôpital Sainte-Justine for children; Louis Beaubien, federal and provincial deputy and his wife, Lauretta Stuart. Louis Riel, the Métis chief from Manitoba whose trial and execution became famous throughout North America, apparently worked on the Beaubiens' land between 1859 and 1864.

Walk to Avenue Davaar and turn right.

The municipal administration apparently occupies one of the oldest buildings in Outremont (1817). The **hôtel de ville** (*Édouard-Montpetit métro*) alternately served as a warehouse for the Hudson's Bay Company, a school and a prison. A tollbooth used to stand here on Chemin de la Côte-Sainte-Catherine to collect a fee to finance the upkeep of the road, which, like many others in those years, was administered by a private company.

Go down Avenue Davaar to Avenue Bernard.

Avenue Bernard ★ (*Outremont métro*) is lined with shops, offices, apartment buildings and houses. This wide avenue with large, grassy medians, curbside landscaping and stately buildings, appears quite imposing and reflects the will of an era to clearly affirm the growing municipality's prestige. The **Théâtre Outremont** (*numbers 1234-1248*), once a very popular repertory theatre, whose future use presently remains uncertain, is located on the street. Its interior was designed by Emmanuel Briffa. The former post office at number 1145 and the **Clos Saint-Bernard**, a large garage now converted into condominiums at numbers 1167 to 1175, are also interesting. Another highlight on this street is the first large-scale grocery store opened by the Steinberg family, who later came to own more than 190 such stores across Québec, but nevertheless went bankrupt in 1992. Several residential buildings along Avenue Bernard are architecturally beautiful as well, including the **Montcalm** (*numbers 1040 to 1050*), the **Gar-**

Exploring

den Court (*numbers 1058 to 1066*), the **Royal York** (*numbers 1100 to 1144*) and the **Parkland** (*number 1360*).

Head west on Avenue Bernard to Avenue Rockland to reach the park located along this avenue.

Parc Joyce (*Outremont Métro or Édouard-Montpetit métro*) was laid out on a vast piece of property formerly owned by James Joyce, a Canadian of British descent, who was a confectioner by profession. The buildings, which were of great architectural interest, were demolished because no one could find a use for them after the land was transferred to the City in 1926. The resulting park has gentle hills and mature vegetation dating back to the time of the estate.

It is worth taking the time to see three residences on Avenue Ainslie, which ends at the park. Numbers 18 and 22 are especially impressive, as much for the size of the lots of land upon which they were built as for the dimensions of the buildings and the majesty of their Victorian-inspired design. Number 7 was built in 1936 and represents one of the first attempts at modernism in this country.

Back on Chemin de la Côte-Sainte-Catherine, take a moment to walk along Avenue Claude-Champagne. On the north side of the street are three residences whose architectural and patrimonial value is obvious: number 637, the country-style **Maison J.B. Aimbault**, built around 1820, is an extremely rare legacy of a bygone era in Outremont; number 645, the neighbouring house, has a sharply pitched roof, the trademark of architect Beaugrand-Champagne and, finally, number 661, built at the very end of the last century, whose design, relatively unique for the neighbourhood, is inspired by the New England Georgian style.

Turn onto Avenue Claude-Champagne.

The housing complex of the **Sœurs des Saints-Noms-de-Jésus-et-de-Marie** (*Édouard-Montpetit Métro*) is a string of big institutional buildings that extends along Avenue Claude-Champagne, and beyond, onto the mountain and along Boulevard Mont-Royal. It once belonged to a single community of nuns, the Sœurs des Saints-Noms-de-Jésus-et-de-Marie. These women came to Outremont in the last century with an essentially educational mission, which they managed to fulfill while this large area was developing. Walking along Avenue Claude-

Champagne, visitors will first see the **Pensionnat du Saint-Nom-de-Marie** (boarding school), built in 1903. It stands out on Chemin de la Côte-Sainte-Catherine thanks to its architecture, which includes a Renaissance-style portico, silvery roof and dome crowned with a cupola, its massive size and its location on higher ground. Farther up, immediately behind the boarding school, lies the much more modern the **Pavillon Marie-Victorin**, which was originally used as a college by the nuns before being purchased by the Université de Montréal for its Faculty of Education. Even higher, this time right on the mountain, stands **Pavillon Vincent d'Indy**, which has also become part of the Université de Montréal and its Faculty of Music. The building's concert hall, **Salle Claude-Champagne**, has exceptionally good acoustics, and is used for recordings on a regular basis. The grounds offer a remarkable view of the municipality, as well as the entire northern part of the island of Montréal. Finally, east of and a little below this building, on Boulevard Mont-Royal (*numbers 1360 to 1430*), the nuns' mother house, built in the 1920s, completes the tableau.

Avenue Claude-Champagne, as part of "Outremont-en-

haut," is also graced with residential buildings befitting the reputation of this section of the city. The imposing **"Villa" Préfontaine**, located at number 22, epitomizes the style many local residents wanted to give their property. Higher up, from number 36 to 76, visitors will notice a very well-executed series of twin houses, successfully differentiated from one another by certain ornamental and architectural details.

At the end of Avenue Claude-Champagne, turn left on Boulevard Mont-Royal and continue straight ahead to the traffic lights to Avenue Maplewood.

Also known as the "avenue of power," **Avenue Maplewood ★** (*Édouard Montpetit Métro*) forms the central axis of the area referred to as "Outremont-en-haut," where various opulent-looking houses with distinctive architecture lie perched in a very hilly landscape, occupied both past and presently by influential Quebecers.

On Place Duchastel, numbers 161, 159 and 6 are remarkable for their architecture, inspired by the Tudor and Elizabethan period. The massive structure at number 153, built by architect Randolph C. Betts, is impressive. The different

Exploring

coloured materials used for the facing and the roof, as well as the organized diversity of the architectural components used in the design, help tone down the building's impact on the landscape. The lovely residences at numbers 118 and 114, from a different period, hem in a lovely little stream, which adds to the beauty of the avenue. This stream once supplied a watering place for horses on Côte-Sainte-Catherine before forming the swamp where Parc Outremont is now located. Today, it disappears into the pipes located below the avenue, and under the property of the Religieuses de l'Imaculée-Conception (Sisters of the Immaculate Conception).

Beyond Avenue McCulloch (where former Prime Minister of Canada, Pierre Elliott Trudeau, lived for a certain period of time, at number 84), Avenue Maplewood becomes even more picturesque. Its slight slope and gentle twists and turns, combined with the beauty of the residences and careful landscaping of the yards, are examples of how appealing "Outremont-en-haut" has always been for the Québec intelligentsia. Many houses here are worth a quick look: number 77 is a fine example of the Colonial American style;

numbers 71 and 69 resemble 1920s-style suburban houses; numbers 49 and 47, twin houses dating back to 1906, have a country look about them (they are the oldest houses on the street), and finally number 41, where the architectural style and large front yard bring to mind the great French manors of the Renaissance.

Take the footpath between numbers 54 and 52, which leads to Boulevard Mont-Royal via the lane of the same name.

Boulevard Mont-Royal is the second major artery of "Outremont-en-haut." It was thus named because the first section of the road led to the Cimetière Mont-Royal. Although strictly residential, the road now tends to be quite busy with motorists en route to the Université de Montréal. It is also used as a jogging path by neighbourhood residents.

The section of the boulevard included in this tour is an example of the quality of the local architecture and landscaping. Lovely period residences have been built here, some of which were designed while bearing in mind their double access to the boulevard and Avenue Maplewood. This is especially the case with number 1151, which has two well-balanced façades, one facing each street. Number 1139 is typically Art Deco in style. The vast wooded area that has been preserved south of the boulevard adds to the beauty of the neighbourhood. Once threatened with over-development along the lines of the large residential high-rises found on Chemin de la Côte-Sainte-Catherine, the area is now part of Parc du Mont-Royal.

From the end of the street (at the bend in the road), there is a beautiful view of the eastern part of Montréal (Plateau Mont-Royal), which also reveals the radical difference between this part of Outremont and the city at its feet. After the turn, at the end of this tour, visitors will see the **Couvent des Sœurs de Marie-Réparatrice** on the left. This convent, with its buff-coloured brick, was considered very modern for its time in 1911.

Tour K: Little Italy

Montréal has a large Italian community. By the beginning of the 19th century, many of the best hotels in town were owned by Italians. At the end of the same century, the first group of immigrants from the poorer regions of southern Italy and Sicily settled in the area around Rue Sainte-Christophe, north of Rue Ontario. The largest wave, however, arrived at the end of World War II, when thousands of Italian peasants and workers disembarked at the port of Montréal. Many of these settled around Marché Jean-Talon and Église Madonna Della Difesa, thereby creating Little Italy, where visitors will now find cafés, trattorias, specialty food shops, etc. Since the 1960s, many of Montréal's Italians have moved to Saint-Léonard, a separate municipality located in the northeast, though they still return to Little Italy to do their shopping.

From the Jean-Talon métro station, head east to Rue Saint-Hubert, and turn right. The Jean-Talon station is named after the man who served as intendant (administrator) of New France from 1665 to 1668 and 1670 to 1672. During his two short mandates, Jean Talon was responsible for reorganizing the colony's finances and diversifying its economy.

The **Casa d'Italia** (*505 Rue Jean-Talon Est, Jean-Talon Métro*) is the Italian community centre. It was built in 1936 in the Art Moderne style, a variation on Art Deco characterized by rounded, horizontal lines inspired by the streamlined designs of steamships and

Exploring

locomotives. A fascist group took up residence here briefly before the Second World War.

Plaza Saint-Hubert (*Rue Saint-Hubert between Rue de Bellechasse Est and Jean-Talon Est, Jean-Talon métro or Beaubien métro*) is one of Montréal's main shopping streets. Here, visitors will find a great many clothing and shoe stores, as well as restaurants serving North American cuisine. It was also on this street that the first Rôtisserie Saint-Hubert, now famous throughout Québec for its roast chicken, opened in 1951. The glass awnings were put up over the sidewalks in 1986.

Turn right on Rue Bélanger.

The former **Rivoli and Château Cinemas** (*6906 and 6956 Rue Saint-Denis, Jean-Talon métro*), located on both sides of Rue Bélanger, are two examples of neighbourhood movie theatres that have been converted for other uses. The Cinéma Château was built in 1931 according to plans by architect René Charbonneau. The original decor, executed in an exotic Art Deco style by Emmanuel Briffa, has been preserved. The Cinéma Rivoli, however, was not so lucky – only the

Adamesque façade dating back to 1926 remains; the interior was transformed into a pharmacy. This part of Rue Saint-Denis is lined with typical Montréal apartment buildings and their traditional exterior metal and wood staircases. Notice the many finely worked cornices and balconies, as well as the Art-Nouveau-style stained glass in the upper part of the windows and doors.

Continue heading west on Rue Bélanger, then turn left on Rue Drolet.

École Sainte-Julienne-Falconieri (*6839 Rue Drolet, Jean-Talon métro*) was designed in 1924 by Ernest Cormier, architect of the Université of Montréal's main building (see p 174). The school was clearly influenced by the buildings of American architect Frank Lloyd Wright, erected about 10 years earlier.

Go back to Rue Bélanger and turn left. Take another left on Avenue Henri-Julien.

The design of **Église Madonna Della Difesa ★** (*6810 Avenue Henri-Julien, Jean-Talon métro*), or Our Lady of the

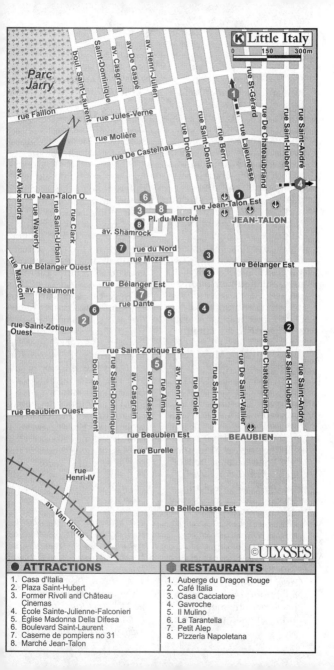

K Little Italy

0   150   300m

Parc Jarry

av. De Gaspé
av. Henri-Julien
Saint-Dominique
av. Casgrain
boul. Saint-Laurent

rue Faillon

rue Jules-Verne

rue Molière

rue De Castelnau

rue Saint-Denis
rue Drolet
rue Berri
rue Lajeunesse
rue St-Gérard
rue De Chateaubriand
rue Saint-Hubert
rue Saint-André

1

4

av. Alexandra
rue Jean-Talon O.
rue Waverly
rue Saint-Urbain
rue Clark

6
3 **8**
8
Pl. du Marché
av. Shamrock
7 rue du Nord
rue Mozart

rue Jean-Talon Est
1
JEAN-TALON

rue Marconi
rue Bélanger Ouest
av. Beaumont

6
2
rue Saint-Zotique Ouest

rue Bélanger Est
7
rue Dante

3
3
rue Bélanger Est

4
5

2

rue Saint-Zotique Est

boul. Saint-Laurent
av. Saint-Dominique
av. Casgrain
av. De Gaspé
rue Alma
av. Henri-Julien
rue Drolet
rue Saint-Denis
rue De Saint-Vallier
rue De Chateaubriand
rue Saint-Hubert
rue Saint-André

5

rue Beaubien Ouest

rue Beaubien Est
rue Burelle

BEAUBIEN

rue Henri-IV

av. Van Horne

De Bellechasse Est

©ULYSSES

● **ATTRACTIONS**
1. Casa d'Italia
2. Plaza Saint-Hubert
3. Former Rivoli and Château Cinemas
4. École Sainte-Julienne-Falconieri
5. Église Madonna Della Difesa
6. Boulevard Saint-Laurent
7. Caserne de pompiers no 31
8. Marché Jean-Talon

⬟ **RESTAURANTS**
1. Auberge du Dragon Rouge
2. Café Italia
3. Casa Cacciatore
4. Gavroche
5. Il Mulino
6. La Tarantella
7. Petit Alep
8. Pizzeria Napoletana

Defense Church, is of Roman-Byzantine inspiration, characterized by small arched openings and varied treatment of the surfaces, arranged in horizontal bands. A basilica-style plan such as this is unusual in Montréal. The church was designed in 1910 by painter, master glass-worker and decorator Guido Nincheri, who spent over 30 years working on it, finishing every last detail of the décor himself. Nincheri was in the habit of depicting contemporary figures in his stained-glass windows and in his vibrantly coloured frescoes, made with an egg-wash, a technique he had mastered. One of these, showing Mussolini on his horse, was a source of controversy for many years. To erase or not to erase? It can still be seen above the high altar.

At number 6841, visitors will find the Art Moderne-style **École Madonna Della Difesa** (*Jean-Talon métro*). The bas-reliefs depicting school children are particularly noteworthy. Parc Dante stretches west of the church, with the place of honour in its centre occupied by a modest bust of the Italian poet, sculpted by Carlo Balboni in 1924. Neighbourhood chess and checkers buffs meet here during the summer months.

Take Rue Dante west to Boulevard Saint-Laurent, turn right.

Boulevard Saint-Laurent (*Jean-Talon métro*) could be described as Montréal's "immigration corridor." Since 1880, immigrants to the city have been settling along different segments of the boulevard, depending on their ethnic background. After several decades, they leave the area, then scatter throughout the city or re-group in another neighbourhood. Some communities leave few traces of their passage on Boulevard Saint-Laurent, while others have opened shopping areas where descendants of these first arrivals still come with their families. Between Rue de Bellechasse to the south and Rue Jean-Talon to the north, the boulevard is lined with numerous Italian restaurants and cafés, as well as food stores, swarmed by Montrealers of all origins on weekends. Some of the recently erected buildings along the street have interesting modern façades.

Turn right on Avenue Shamrock, whose name serves as a reminder that the neighbourhood was Irish before it was Italian.

The **Caserne de Pompiers no 31** (*7041 Rue Saint-Dominique, Jean-Talon métro*), or Fire Station no.

31, was built as part of a job creation project initiated after the economic crisis of 1929. The building, which dates back to 1931, was designed by architect E.A. Doucet in the Art Deco style. At the intersection of Avenue Shamrock and Avenue Casgrain, a small, Art Moderne brick building with a rounded corner once served as the Clinique Jean-Talon, where many new arrivals came for care and comfort.

Marché Jean-Talon ★ (*Avenue Casgrain, Jean-Talon métro*) was built in 1934 on the site of the Irish lacrosse field known as Shamrock Stadium. The space was originally intended for a bus station, which explains the platforms with concrete shelters over them. Despite its less than attractive appearance, the market is a pleasant place to shop because of the constant buzz of activity. It is surrounded by specialty food shops, often set up right in the back yards of buildings facing the neighbouring streets.

Passing through the neighbourhood, visitors will see vegetable gardens laid out in whatever meagre space is available, Madonnas in their niches and grape-laden vines climbing up trellises on balconies, all of which lend this part of Montréal a Mediterranean feel.

★

Tour L: Sault-au-Récollet

Around 1950, the Sault-au-Récollet neighbourhood was still a farming village isolated from the city on the banks of Rivière des Prairies. Today, it is easy to reach on the Métro, at Henri-Bourassa, the north-east terminal station. The history of the "Sault" dates back a long way. In 1610, Monsieur des Prairies headed up the river that now bears his name, thinking it was the St. Lawrence. Then, in 1625, Récollet Nicolas Viel and his native guide Ahuntsic drowned in the river's rapids, hence the name of the area *Sault*, means rapids. In 1696, the Sulpicians established the Fort Lorette Huron mission here. In the 19th century, Sault-au-Récollet became a popular resort area among Montrealers looking for a spot close to the city during the

Exploring

summer months, which explains the existence of the handful of summer cottages that have survived the recent development of the area.

From the exit of the Henri-Bourassa Métro station, head east on the boulevard of the same name. Turn left on Rue Saint-Hubert, then right on Boulevard Gouin Est.

Collège Sophie-Barat (*1105 et 1239 Boulevard Gouin Est, Henri-Bourassa*). Monseigneur Ignace Bourget, Montréal's second bishop, courted a number of French religious communities during the 1840s, in an attempt to get them to establish schools in the Montréal region. The Dames du Sacré-Cœur were among those who accepted to make the long voyage. In 1856, they settled on the banks of Rivière des Prairies, where they built a convent school for girls. The former day school (1858) at 1105 Boulevard Gouin Est is all that remains of the original complex. After a fire, the convent was rebuilt in stages. The building resembling an austere English manor is the most interesting of the new facilities (1929). The school now bears the name of the founder of the Dames du Sacré-Cœur community, Sophie Barat.

Before reaching Église de la Visitation, visitors will see a few ancestral homes, such as the **Maison David-Dumouchel**, at number 1737, built in 1839 for a carpenter from Sault-au-Récollet. It has high firebreak walls even though there are no buildings adjoining it, showing that this architectural element, once strictly utilitarian, had become a decorative feature and a symbol of prestige and urbanity.

Église de la Visitation ★★ (*1847 Boulevard Gouin Est*) is the oldest church still in use on the island of Montréal. It was built between 1749 and 1752, but was considerably modified afterwards. Its beautiful Palladian façade, added in 1850, is the work of Englishman John Ostell, who designed the Vieille Douane (old customs house) on Place Royale and the Vieux Palais de Justice (old courthouse) on Rue Notre-Dame. The degree of refinement reached here is a tribute to the fierce competition between the parishioners of Sault-au-Récollet and those of Sainte-Geneviève, further west, who had just built themselves a church in the same style.

Viewed as a whole, the interior of Église de la Visitation is one of the most remarkable works of

This sculpture by artist Raymond Mason, entitled *The Illuminated Crowd*, is beautifully reflected in the stunning BNP tower.
- *Philippe Renault*

Those who are looking for fun and excitement should definitely not miss the Quartier Latin.
- *Philippe Renault*

In the Village, even the Beaudry métro station displays the colours of the rainbow, a symbol of gay pride, proving that tolerance is a serious matter here.
- *Philippe Renault*

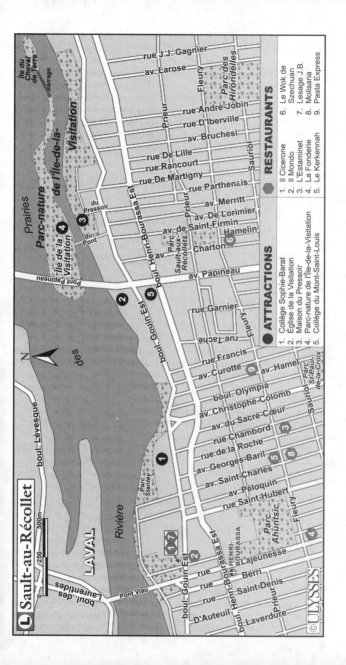

Sault-au-Récollet

ATTRACTIONS

1. Collège Sophie-Barat
2. Église de la Visitation
3. Maison du Pressoir
4. Parc-nature de l'île-de-la-Visitation
5. Collège du Mont-Saint-Louis

RESTAURANTS

1. Il Cicerone
2. Il Mondo
3. L'Estaminet
4. La Fonderie
5. Le Kerkennah
6. Le Wok de Szechuan
7. Lesage J.B.
8. Molisana
9. Pasta Express

© ULYSSE

woodcarving in Québec. The decor, begun in 1764, was not completed until 1837. Philippe Liébert, born in Nemours, France, executed the first decorative elements, including the sculpted doors of the reredos, which are precious Louis-XV-style pieces. It was David-Fleury David, however, who completed the bulk of the work, namely the cornice, Louis-XVI pilasters and finely chiselled vault. The church is adorned with beautiful paintings, such as *La Visitation de la Vierge* (The Visitation of the Virgin), purchased by Curé Chambon in 1756 and painted by Mignard.

At the end of Rue Lambert, visitors will find the former Noviciat Saint-Joseph (*1700 Boulevard Henri-Bourassa Est*), now **Collège du Mont-Saint-Louis**. The neoclassical building, erected in 1853, was enlarged by the addition of a Second-Empire-style pavilion in 1872. The heart of the village of Sault-au-Récollet lies along Boulevard Gouin Est, east of Avenue Papineau. There are some noteworthy buildings here, including number 1947, the Maison Boudreau, built around 1750; number 2010, the former general store, which is a small Second-Empire building of urban design, transposed in a rural set-

ting, and finally, number 2086, the proud Maison Persillier-Lachapelle, former residence of a prosperous miller and bridge-builder, erected around 1830.

Turn left on Rue du Pressoir.

The **Maison du Pressoir** ★ (*free admission; Apr-Oct every day 11am to 5pm; 10865 Rue du Pressoir, ☎280-6783*). Around 1810, Didier Joubert built a cider press on his property in Sault-au-Récollet. Researchers believe that this is Montréal's only surviving example of half-timbering architecture. Restored in 1982, it houses an exhibition on cider-making and the historical background of the press and the Sulpician mission.

Backtrack along Boulevard Gouin, heading west. Turn right on Rue du Pont in order to reach Île de la Visitation.

The **Parc-nature de l'Île-de-la-Visitation** encompasses a vast area alongside Rivière des Prairies, as well as the island itself, a long strip of land hemmed in at each end by dykes used to control the level and flow of the river, thus eliminating the famous *sault* or rapids, for which the area was named. On the way to the island, visitors will cross over the Rue du Pont dyke. Under the French Regime, the Sulpicians built powerful mills along here; unfortunately, however, very little remains of these structures.

The dyke located at the east end of the island supports Rivière-des-Prairies's hydroelectric power station, built in 1928 by Montreal Island Power. The dam includes a fish trap, which makes it a favourite spot for fishing for shad, one of the river's most abundant species.

★★

Tour M:
Île Sainte-Hélène
and Île Notre-Dame

When Samuel de Champlain reached the island of Montréal in 1611, he found a small rocky archipelago located in front of it. He named the largest of these islands in the channel after his wife, Hélène Boulé. Île Sainte-Hélène later became part of the seigneury of Longueuil. Around 1720, the Baroness of Longueuil chose the island as the site for a country house surrounded by a garden. It is also worth noting that in 1760, the island was the last foothold of French troops in New France, commanded by Chevalier François de Lévis. Recognizing Île Saint-Hélène's strategic importance, the British army built a fort on the eastern part of the island at the beginning of the 19th century. The threat of armed conflict with the United States having diminished, the Canadian government rented Île Sainte-Hélène to the City of Montréal in 1874, at which time the island was turned into a park and linked to Old Montréal by ferry and, from 1930 on, by the Jacques-Cartier bridge.

In the early 1960s, Montréal was chosen as the location of the 1967 World's Fair (Expo '67). The city wanted to set up the event on a large, attractive site near the downtown area; a site such as this, however, did not exist. It was thus necessary to build one: using earth excavated during the construction of the Métro tunnel, Île Notre-Dame was created, doubling the area of Île Sainte-Hélène. From April to November 1967, 45 million visitors passed through Cité du Havre, the gateway to the fairground, and crisscrossed both islands. Expo, as Montrealers still refer to it, was more than a jumble of assorted objects; it was Montréal's awakening, during which the city opened itself to the world, and visitors from all over discovered a new art of living, including miniskirts, colour television, hippies, flower power and protest rock.

Exploring

It is not easy to reach Cité du Havre from downtown. The best way is to take Rue Mill, then Chemin des Moulins, which runs under Autoroute Bonaventure to Avenue Pierre-Dupuy. This last road leads to Pont de la Concorde and then over the St. Lawrence to the islands. It is also possible to take bus number 168 from the McGill métro station, or the taxi-boat from Quai Jacques-Cartier, in the old port.

The **Tropique Nord**, **Habitat '67** and the **Parc de la Cité du Havre ★★** were all built on a spit of land created to protect the port of Montréal from ice and currents. This point of land also offers some lovely views of the city and the water. The administrative offices of the port are located at the entrance to the area, along with a group of buildings that once housed the Expo-Théâtre and Musée d'Art Contemporain (see p 115). A little further on, visitors will spot the large glass wall of the Tropique Nord, a residential complex composed of apartments with a view of the outdoors on one side, and an interior tropical garden on the other.

L'Homme

Next, visitors will see Habitat '67, an experimental housing development built for Expo '67 in order to illustrate construction techniques using prefabricated concrete slabs, and to herald a new art of living. The architect, Moshe Safdie, was only 23 years old when he drew up the plans. Habitat '67 looks like a gigantic cluster of cubes, each containing one or two rooms. The apartments are as highly prized as ever and are lived in by a number of notable Quebecers.

At the Parc de la Cité du Havre, visitors will find 12 panels containing a brief description of the history of the St. Lawrence River. A section of the bicycle path leading to Île Notre-Dame and Île Sainte-Hélène passes through the park.

Cross Pont de la Concorde.

Parc Hélène-de- Champlain ★★ (*Île-Sainte-Hélène métro*) lies on Île Sainte-Hélène, which originally covered an area of 50ha but was enlarged to over 120ha for Expo '67. The original portion corresponds to the raised area studded with

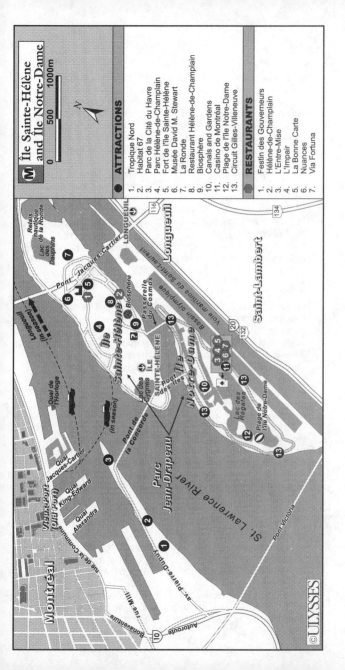

Île Sainte-Hélène and Île Notre-Dame

0 500 1000m

ATTRACTIONS

1. Tropique Nord
2. Habitat 67
3. Parc de la Cité du Havre
4. Fort de l'île Sainte-Hélène
5. Parc Hélène-de-Champlain
6. Musée David M. Stewart
7. La Ronde
8. Restaurant Hélène-de-Champlain
9. Biosphère
10. Canals and Gardens
11. Casino de Montréal
12. Plage de l'île Notre-Dame
13. Circuit Gilles-Villeneuve

RESTAURANTS

1. Festin des Gouverneurs
2. Hélène-de-Champlain
3. L'Entre-Mise
4. L'Impair
5. La Bonne Carte
6. Nuances
7. Via Fortuna

boulders made of breccia. Peculiar to the island, breccia is a very hard, ferrous stone that takes on an orange colour when exposed to air for a long time. In 1992, the western part of the island was transformed into a vast open-air amphitheatre, where large-scale shows are presented. In this lovely park bordering the river, visitors will find *L'Homme* ("Humankind"), a large metal sculpture by Alexandre Calder, created for Expo '67.

A little further, close to the entrance to the Île-Sainte-Hélène Métro station, is a work by the Mexican artist Sebastian entitled *La porte de l'amitié* (The Door to Friendship). This sculpture was given to the City of Montréal by Mexico City in 1992 and erected on this site three years later to commemorate the signing of the free-trade agreement between Canada, the United States and Mexico (NAFTA).

Follow the trails leading toward the heart of the island.

The pool house, faced with breccia stone, and outdoor swimming pools, built during the Great Depression of the 1930s, lie at the edge of the original park. This island, with its varied contours, is dominated by the **Tour Lévis**, a simple water tower built in 1936, which

looks like a dungeon, and by the blockhouse, a wooden observation post erected in 1849.

Follow the signs for the Fort de l'Île Sainte-Hélène.

After the War of 1812 between the United States and Great Britain, the **Fort de l'Île Sainte-Hélène** ★★ (*Île-Sainte-Hélène métro*) was built so that Montréal could be properly defended if ever a new conflict were to erupt. The construction, supervised by military engineer Elias Walker Durnford, was completed in 1825. Built of breccia stone, the fort is in the shape of a jagged "U," surrounding a drill ground, used today by the Compagnie Franche de la Marine and the 78th Regiment of the Fraser Highlanders as a parade ground. These two costumed mock regiments delight visitors by reviving Canada's French and Scottish military traditions. The drill ground also offers a lovely view of both the port and **Pont Jacques-Cartier**, inaugurated in 1930, which straddles the island, separating the park from La Ronde.

The arsenal is now occupied by the **Musée David M. Stewart** ★★ (*$6; May to Labour Day, every day 10am to 6pm; Labour Day to May, Wed to Mon 10am to 5pm;* ☎861-6701), which exhibits a collection of objects from the 17th and 18th centuries, including interesting collections of maps, firearms, and scientific and navigational instruments put together by Montréal industrialist David Stewart and his wife Liliane. The latter heads both the museum and the Macdonald-Stewart Foundation, which also manages the Château Ramezay (see p 106) and the Château Dufresne (see p 217) (the former Musée des Arts Décoratifs).

The vaults of the former barracks now house **Le Festin des Gouverneurs**, a restaurant geared mainly toward large groups. Each evening, it recreates the atmosphere of a New France feast (see p 332).

La Ronde ★ (*adults $25.25, children 3 to 11 years old $13.50; Jun to mid-Jun every day 10am to 9pm mid-Jun to late Aug, every day 10:30am to 11pm, Île-Sainte-Hélène métro,; ☎872-4537 or 800-797-4537*), an amusement park set up for Expo '67 on the former Île Ronde, opens its doors to both the young and the not so young every summer. For Montrealers, an annual trip to La Ronde has almost become a pilgrimage. An international fireworks competition is held here twice a week during the months of June and July.

Head toward the Biosphere on the road that runs along the south shore of the island.

Built in 1938 as a sports pavilion, the **Restaurant Hélène-de-Champlain** ★ was inspired by the architecture of New France and is thus reminiscent of the summer house of the Baroness of Longueuil, once located in the area. Behind the restaurant is a lovely rose garden planted for Expo '67, which embellishes the view from the dining room. The **former military cemetery** of the British garrison stationed on Île Sainte-Hélène from 1828 to 1870 lies in front of the building. Most of the original tombstones have disappeared. A commemorative monument, erected in 1937, stands in their place.

Very few of the pavilions built for Expo '67 have survived the destructive effects of the weather and the changes in the islands' roles. One that has is the former American pavilion, a veritable monument to modern architecture. The first complete geodesic dome to be taken beyond the stage of a model, it was created by the celebrated engineer Richard Buckminster Fuller (1895-1983). **The Biosphere** ★★ (9) (*$6.50; late Jun to early Sep every day 10am to 6pm; early Sep to late Jun, Tue to Sun, 10am to 5pm; Île-Sainte-*

Hélène métro, ☎283-5000,),
built of tubular aluminum
and measuring 80m in di-
ameter, unfortunately lost
its translucent acrylic skin in
a fire back in 1978. An environmental interpretive centre on the St. Lawrence
River, the Great Lakes and
the different Canadian ecosystems is now located in
the dome. The permanent
exhibit aims to sensitize the
public on issues of sustain-
able development and the
conservation of water as a
precious resource. There
are four interactive galleries
with giant screens and
hands-on displays to ex-
plore and delight in. A terrace restaurant with a panoramic view of the islands
completes the museum.

*Cross over to Île Notre-Dame
on the Passerelle du Cosmos.*

Île Notre-Dame emerged
from the waters of the St.
Lawrence in no less than

10 months, with the help of
15 million tons of rock and
soil transported here from
the Métro construction site.
Because it is an artificial
island, its creators were
able to give it a fanciful
shape by playing with both
soil and water. The island is
therefore traversed by
pleasant **canals and
gardens** ★★ *(Île-Sainte-
Hélène métro and bus
no.167)*, laid out for the
1980 Floralies Interna-
tionales, an international
flower show. Boats are
available for rent, enabling
visitors to ply the canals
and admire the flowers
mirrored in their waters.

Casino de Montréal ★ *(free
admission, parking and coat
check; every day 24hrs; Île-
Sainte-Hélène métro, bus
no.167;* ☎392-2746*)* occupies
the former French and Québec pavilions of Expo '67.
The main building corre-
sponds to the old **French**

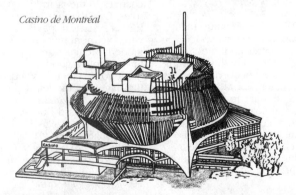

Casino de Montréal

Pavilion ★, an aluminum structure designed by architect Jean Faugeron. It was renovated in 1993 at a cost of $92.4 million in order to accommodate the Casino. The upper galleries offer some lovely views of downtown Montréal and the St. Lawrence Seaway.

Immediately to the west of the former French pavilion, the building shaped like a truncated pyramid is the former **Québec pavilion ★** (*every day 9am to 3am*). It was incorporated into the Casino after being raised and recovered with gold-tinted glass in 1996.

Visitors will find all sorts of things to do at the Casino, and all this in a very festive atmosphere among some of the 15,000 people that visit the casino each day. With 2,700 slot machines and 107 gaming tables, this is one of the 10 largest casinos in the world. This is also a popular spot thanks to its bars and cabaret (see p 353), along with its four restaurants, including Nuances (see p 332), which is rated as one of the best in Canada. Entrance is reserved for 18 and over.

Nearby, visitors will find the entrance to the **Plage de l'Île Notre-Dame**, a beach enabling Montrealers to lounge on real sand right in the middle of the St. Lawrence.

A natural filtering system keeps the water in the small lake clean, with no need for chemical additives. The number of swimmers allowed on the beach is strictly regulated, however, so as not to disrupt the balance of the system.

There are other recreational facilities here as well, namely the Olympic Basin created for the rowing competitions of the 1976 Olympics and the **Circuit Gilles-Villeneuve** (*Île-Sainte-Hélène métro and bus no.167*), where Formula One drivers compete every year in the Grand Prix Player's du Canada, part of the international racing circuit.

To return to downtown Montréal, take the Métro from the Île-Sainte-Hélène station.

Tour N: The Village

This neighbourhood, located on the edge of the downtown area, developed in the late 18th century when Old Montréal extended eastward. Originally known as "Faubourg Québec" because it ran alongside the road leading to Québec City, it was renamed "Quartier Sainte-Marie" after becoming industrialized, then nicknamed "Faubourg à

M'lasse" around 1880, when hundreds of barrels of sweet-smelling molasses began to be unloaded every day onto the wharves of the nearby port (*mélasse* is the French word for molasses). In the mid-1960s, civil servants affixed the somewhat unromantic name "Centre-Sud" to the neighbourhood. This was before the homosexual community took it over in 1980 and made it the "Gay Village". Despite its many names, The Village is a place with a profound soul, which has always been marked by poverty and life on the fringe. Occasionally ugly and in poor taste, it is full of activity and can be fascinating if given a chance.

The Village is divided into three zones of varying sizes from north to south: the port and industrial area, almost impassable on foot as it is blocked by Autoroute Ville-Marie, which was built between 1974 and 1977; the Cité des Ondes or on-air city, home to Radio-Canada, whose 1970 construction led to the demolition of a third of the neighbourhood, and finally, Rue Sainte-Catherine, where visitors will find a large concentration of cafés, nightclubs, restaurants and bars.

From the Berri-UQAM métro station, head east on Rue Sainte-Catherine.

The numbers following the names of attractions refer to the map of The Village.

In 1979, **Place Dupuis** (*in front of Place du Quartier Latin, Berri-UQÀM métro*) replaced the Dupuis Frères department store, the French-Canadian counterpart of stores like Eaton and Ogilvy's in downtown and the western end of Montréal. The section of Rue Sainte-Catherine around Rue Saint-Hubert was, moreover, considered the commercial hub of French-Canadian Montrealers up until the mid-20th century. The complex of shops at the Galeries Dupuis also includes Les Atriums, a multi-level shopping mall laid out around a hotel, an office building and classrooms belonging to UQAM.

A little farther east, visitors will find the former **Pilon Clothing Store** (*915 Rue Sainte-Catherine Est*). Its protorationalist, stone-frame structure dates back to 1878, making it the oldest commercial building in the neighbourhood. The lovely Art-Deco façade at number 916 once belonged to the **Pharmacie Montréal** (1934), the first institution of its type in Québec to make home-deliveries and stay open both day and night.

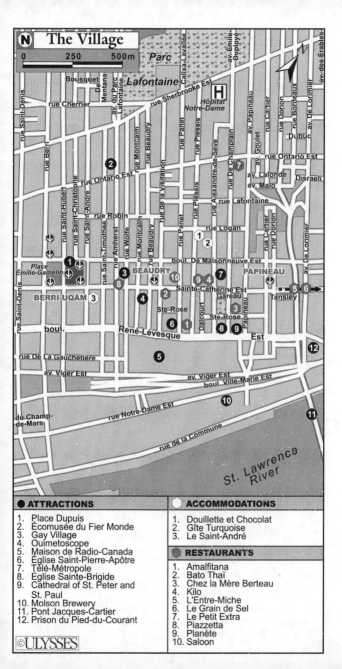

The Village

N

0   250   500m

Parc Lafontaine

St. Lawrence River

● **ATTRACTIONS**

1. Place Dupuis
2. Écomusée du Fier Monde
3. Gay Village
4. Ouimetoscope
5. Maison de Radio-Canada
6. Église Saint-Pierre-Apôtre
7. Télé-Métropole
8. Église Sainte-Brigide
9. Cathedral of St. Peter and St. Paul
10. Molson Brewery
11. Pont Jacques-Cartier
12. Prison du Pied-du-Courant

○ **ACCOMMODATIONS**

1. Douillette et Chocolat
2. Gîte Turquoise
3. Le Saint-André

⬡ **RESTAURANTS**

1. Amalfitana
2. Bato Thaï
3. Chez la Mère Berteau
4. Kilo
5. L'Entre-Miche
6. Le Grain de Sel
7. Le Petit Extra
8. Piazzetta
9. Planète
10. Saloon

©ULYSSES

Walk up Amherst to number 2050.

Those interested in industrial and worker culture won't want to miss the **Écomusée du Fier Monde ★** (*$5; Tue 11am to 8pm, Thu to Sun 10:30am to 5pm; 2050 Rue Amherst, Berri-UQÀM métro*, ☎528-8444). The museum is located to the north of Rue Ontario, in an old bathhouse known as the Bain Généreux, built in 1927 and modelled after the Butte-aux-Cailles pool in Paris. The social and economic history of this south-central neighbourhood is presented in a wonderfully rehabilitated interior.

Montréal's Gay Village starts east of Rue Amherst.

The **Gay Village** (*Rue Sainte-Catherine Est, between Rue Amherst and Avenue Papineau, Berri-UQÀM métro*). Originally clustered in the "West," along Rue Stanley and Rue Drummond, the gay bars were considered too conspicuous by some local real-estate developers and town councillors. The continual badgering and periodic attempts to "clean house" led bar owners, then renters in the downtown area, to purchase inexpensive buildings in the Centre-Sud in hopes of running their businesses as they pleased. Thus was born the Gay Village, a concentration of establishments catering to a homosexual clientele (saunas, bars, restaurants, clothing stores and hotels). Far from being hidden or mysterious, many of these establishments open onto the street with terraces and gardens during the warm summer months.

The **Ouimetoscope** (*1206 Rue Sainte-Catherine Est, Beaudry métro*). Film-maker, distributor and theatre-owner Ernest Ouimet (1877-1973) pioneered Montréal's film industry. In 1907, he built the Ouimetoscope, the first theatre designed for and devoted exclusively to film in all of Canada. Moved, modernized and recently closed, the Ouimetoscope is nothing but a memory now. Immediately east lies the former **Théâtre National** (*1220 Rue Sainte-Catherine Est*), whose pretty little Renaissance-Revival-style theatre, inaugurated in 1900, is still intact. As indicated on a plaque outside the entrance, this theatre, which once specialized in burlesque and vaudeville, was run for many years by the hilarious Rose Ouellette, known as "La Poune." A few other old theatres dot Rue Saint-Catherine on the way to the Jacques-Cartier bridge.

Turn right on Rue Beaudry, then left on Boulevard René-Lévesque Est.

From the end of small Rue Beaudry, an oversized structure set like an island in the middle of a vast parking lot is visible. This is the **Maison de Radio-Canada** (*1400 Boulevard René-Lévesque Est, Beaudry métro*), built between 1970 and 1973 according to a design by Scandinavian architect Tore Bjornstad and to accommodate the province's French-language and the local English-language programming of the CBC, or Canadian Broadcasting Corporation (Société Radio-Canada in French), the national radio and television network. When it was built, the traditional urban fabric of the neighbourhood was completely erased. Six hundred and seventy-eight families, nearly 5,000 people, had to be relocated. Even 20 years before Radio Canada was built, the width of Boulevard René-Lévesque (formerly Dorchester) had been tripled, separating the south part of the neighbourhood from the north.

Église Saint-Pierre-Apôtre ★ ★ (*1323 Boulevard René-Lévesque Est, Beaudry métro*) is part of the monastery of the Oblate fathers, who settled in Montréal in 1848, thanks to the assistance of Monseigneur Ignace Bourget. The building, completed in 1853, is a major work of Québec Gothic Revival architecture, as well as prolific architect Victor Bourgeau's first project in this style. Notable elements include the flying buttresses, exterior supports for the walls of the nave, rarely used in Montréal, and the spire, which measures 70m at its tallest point, an exceptional height for the time. The finely decorated interior reveals a number of other uncommon elements, such as the limestone pillars separating the nave from the side aisles, here in a land where church structures were usually made entirely of wood. Some of the stained-glass windows from the Maison Champigneule in Bar-le-Duc, France, merit careful examination, including the 9m tall St. Peter in the Choir.

Walk up Rue de la Visitation, then turn right on little **Rue Sainte-Rose**. On the way, you will pass alongside the neoclassical presbytery of Saint-Pierre-Apôtre and the former buildings of the Maîtrise Saint-Pierre, a choir school and priests' residence, which has been converted into a community centre. Rue Sainte-Rose is a picturesque street, lined to the north with a series of working-class homes with mansard roofs. It has preserved part of its appearance of days gone by. Since 1975, a number of neighbourhood houses have been restored by executives

Exploring

and artists working at nearby Radio-Canada.

Turn left on Rue Panet, then right on Rue Sainte-Catherine. Cross small **Rue Dalcourt**, a secondary street between two main arteries patterned after London's mews. It is lined with cramped housing, intended in the past for the poorest workers. In 1982, Rue Dalcourt was redesigned by the City of Montréal as part of its Place au Soleil (Place in the Sun) program.

Télé-Métropole (*at the corner of Rue Alexandre-de-Sève, Papineau métro*) occupies an entire block of the neighbourhood. Founded in 1961 by Alexandre de Sève, this private television network out-rated Radio Canada among working-class viewers for many years. Some of the network's studios are located inside the former Théâtre Arcade and the **Pharmacie Gauvin** (*1425 Rue Alexandre-de-Sève*) (1911), a handsome four-storey building made of glazed white terracotta. Télé-Métropole, along with Sonolab, Radio-Canada, Télé-Québec and Téléglobe, forms a veritable Cité des Ondes (on-air city) in eastern Montréal.

Turn right on Rue Alexandre-de-Sève. The red-brick building on the left, preceded by a neighbourhood park, is the for-

mer **École Sainte-Brigide** (*1125 Rue Alexandre-de-Sève, Papineau métro*), opened by the Frères des Écoles Chrétiennes in 1895. It was converted into a retirement home in 1989.

Église Sainte-Brigide ★ (*1153 Rue Alexandre-de-Sève, Papineau métro*). The high concentration of Catholic workers in the Faubourg à M'lasse at the end of the 19th century, combined with the competition still being waged between the bishopric and the Sulpicians at that time, justified the 1878 construction of a second church only a few hundred metres from Église Saint-Pierre-Apôtre, described above. Église Sainte-Brigide was designed by architect Louis-Gustave Martin (Poitras et Martin) in the Romanesque Revival style then advocated by the Sulpicians. The interior of the church, which belongs to a deteriorating parish, has undergone few changes since its construction and contains lovely lamps dating back to the end of the 19th century, as well as a jumble of dingy plaster statues serving as eloquent witnesses of better days.

Walk east on Boulevard René-Lévesque.

The Cathedral of St. Peter and St. Paul ★ (*1151 Rue de Champlain, Papineau métro*)

is Montréal's Russian Orthodox Cathedral. The build-
ing, a former Episcopal
church, was erected in
1853. Those who attend the
Sunday Mass can see a
lovely collection of icons
and treasures from Russia,
as well as listen to the spell-
binding chants of the choir.

The Molson Brewery is
visible from Boulevard
René-Lévesque Est. Those
who want a closer look
should be very careful
crossing the busy streets of
the area. The brewery's
entrance hall contains en-
largements of photographs
from the company archives,
as well as a souvenir shop.
Across the street, a monument commemorates the
Accommodation, the first
steamship launched on the
St. Lawrence by the Molson
family (1815).

The **Molson Brewery** (*1650
Rue Notre-Dame Est;
☎521-1786, no organized
tours available*) was opened
back in 1786 in the Fau-
bourg Québec by an Eng-
lishman named John
Molson (1763-1836). It
would later become one of
the most successful busi-
nesses in Canada. This
brewery, reconstructed and
enlarged many times, still
stands alongside the port.
The Molsons, for their part,
remain one of the pillars of
Montréal's upper class. Involved in banking (see

p 82), construction, rail
transport and shipping, the
family has never deviated
from its first rule of con-
duct, which is to innovate
constantly. At the beginning
of the 19th century, a bourgeois neighbourhood with
an Anglican church and
market square (Avenue
Papineau) surrounded the
brewery. The last signs of
those years disappeared
when Autoroute Ville-Marie
was built in 1974.

*Continue eastward on Boule-
vard René-Lévesque. Go under
the Jacques-Cartier bridge,
then turn right onto Avenue de
Lorimier. Cross Lorimier Avenue Viger to reach the head
office of the Québec liquor
commission, the Société des
Alcools du Québec, located
inside Montréal's former peni-
tentiary, better known by its
former name, Pied-du-Cou-
rant.*

Pont Jacques-Cartier was inaugurated in 1930. Up until
then, the Pont Victoria,
completed in 1860, was the
only means of reaching the
Rive-Sud (South Shore)
apart from taking a ferry.
The Jacques Cartier bridge
also made it possible to link
Parc de l'Île Sainte-Hélène
(see p 76) directly to the
central neighbourhoods of
Montréal. It was a true nui-
sance to build because the
city councillors couldn't
agree on a plan that would
make it possible to avoid

Exploring

demolishing all sorts of buildings. It was finally decided that the bridge should be curved on its way into Montréal, earning it the nickname *le pont croche* (the crooked bridge). Even today, this curve is the source of a great many headaches for the thousands of motorists who take the bridge every day to and from work.

Prison du Pied-du-Courant ★★ (*2125 Place des Patriotes, Papineau métro*) is thus named (literally, "Foot-of-the-Current") because it is located in front of the river, at the foot of the Sainte-Marie current, which used to offer a certain amount of resistance to ships entering the port. Built between 1830 and 1836 according to plans by George Blaiklock, it is a long, neoclassical cut-stone building with a gate made of the same material. It is the oldest public building still standing in Montréal. In 1894, a house for the prison warden was added at the corner of Avenue de Lorimier. In 1912, the last prisoners left Pied-du-Courant, which became the head office of the Commission des Liqueurs, the liquor commission, in 1922. Over the years, annexes and warehouses were added to the old forgotten prison. Between 1986 and 1990, however, the Québec

government proceeded to demolish the additions and restore the prison, rekindling old memories of tragic events that took place shortly after it was opened.

It was within these walls that 12 of the Patriotes who participated in the armed rebellion of 1837-38, an attempt to emancipate Québec, were executed. One of these was the Chevalier de Lorimier, after whom the neighbouring street was named. Five hundred others were imprisoned here before being deported to the penal colonies of Australia and Tasmania in the South Pacific. A handsome **Monument to the Patriotes** by Alfred Laliberté stands on the grounds of the former prison. The Gothic-Revival-style warden's residence now houses the reception roomsof the Societé des Alcools du Québec (S.A.Q.).

To return to Rue Sainte-Catherine, head north on Avenue de Lorimier, then turn left toward the Papineau métro station.

Tour O: Maisonneuve

In 1883, the city of Maisonneuve was founded in the east part of Montréal by farmers and French-Canadian merchants; port facilities expanded into the area and the city's development picked up. Then, in 1918, the formerly autonomous city was annexed to Montréal, becoming one of its major working-class neighbourhoods, with a 90% francophone population. In the course of its history, Maisonneuve has been profoundly influenced by men with grand ideas, who wanted to make this part of the province a place where people could thrive together.

Upon taking office at the Maisonneuve town hall in 1910, brothers Marius and Oscar Dufresne instituted a rather ambitious policy of building prestigious Beaux-Arts-style public buildings intended to make "their" city a model of development for French Québec. Then, in 1931, Frère Marie-Victorin founded Montréal's Jardin Botanique (botanical garden) in Maisonneuve; today, it is the second largest in the world. The last major episode in the area's history was in 1971, when Mayor Jean Drapeau initiated construc-

tion on the immense sports complex used for the 1976 Olympic Games.

From the Pie-IX Métro station, climb the hill leading to the corner of Rue Sherbrooke Est.

The **Jardin Botanique, Maison de l'Arbre** and **Insectarium** ★★★ (*admission to the greenhouses and Insectarium, $9.50 in the high season, $7 in the low season, combined ticket for the Biôdome and the Tour Olympique (Olympic Tower) $22.50 valid for 2 days; May to Sep, every day 9am to 7pm; Sep to May 9am to 5pm; 4101 Rue Sherbrooke Est, métro Pie-IX, ☎872-1400).* The Jardin Botanique, covering an area of 73ha, was begun during the economic crisis of the 1930s on the site of Mont-de-La-Salle, home base of the brothers of the Écoles Chrétiennes. Behind the Art Deco building occupied by the Université de Montréal's institute of biology, visitors will find a stretch of 10 connected greenhouses, which shelter, most notably, a precious collection of orchids and the largest grouping of bonsais and *penjings* outside of Asia. The latter includes the famous Wu collection,

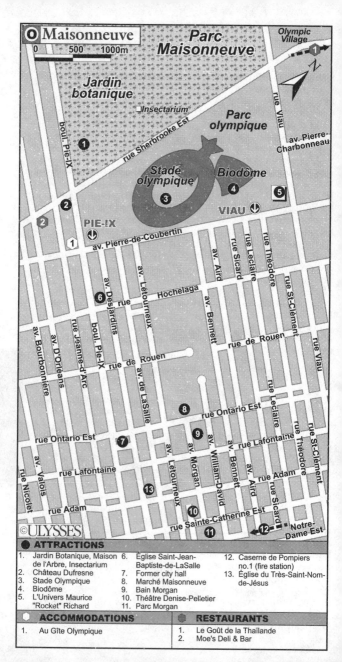

O Maisonneuve

0   500   1000m

Parc Maisonneuve

Jardin botanique

Insectarium

Parc olympique

Olympic Village

rue Sherbrooke Est

Stade olympique ③

Biodôme ④

⑤

VIAU ⊕

av. Pierre-Charbonneau

boul. Pie-IX

① ②

② PIE-IX ⊕

① av. Pierre-de-Coubertin

av. Aird

rue Sicard

rue Leclaire

rue Théodore

rue St-Clément

⑥ rue Hochelaga

av. Desjardins

av. Létourneux

boul. Pie-IX

av. Jeanne-d'Arc

rue D'Orléans

av. Bourbonnière

rue Jeanne-d'Arc

av. Bennett

rue de Rouen

rue de Rouen

av. de LaSalle

rue Viau

⑧ rue Ontario Est

⑨ av. Aird

av. Bennett

rue Lafontaine

av. William-David

rue Leclaire

rue Théodore

rue St-Clément

⑦ rue Ontario Est

rue Lafontaine

av. Valois

rue Nicolet

⑬

av. Morgan

av. Létourneux

rue Adam

⑩

⑪ rue Sainte-Catherine Est

rue Adam

rue Sicard

⑫ ← Notre-Dame-Est

© ULYSSES

● ATTRACTIONS

1. Jardin Botanique, Maison de l'Arbre, Insectarium
2. Château Dufresne
3. Stade Olympique
4. Biodôme
5. L'Univers Maurice "Rocket" Richard
6. Église Saint-Jean-Baptiste-de-LaSalle
7. Former city hall
8. Marché Maisonneuve
9. Bain Morgan
10. Théâtre Denise-Pelletier
11. Parc Morgan
12. Caserne de Pompiers no.1 (fire station)
13. Église du Très-Saint-Nom-de-Jésus

● ACCOMMODATIONS

1. Au Gîte Olympique

● RESTAURANTS

1. Le Goût de la Thaïlande
2. Moe's Deli & Bar

given to the garden by master Wu Yee-Sun of Hong Kong in 1984.

Thirty outdoor gardens, open from spring through autumn, and designed to educate and amaze visitors, stretch to the north and west of the greenhouses. Particularly noteworthy are the symmetrical display gardens around the restaurant, the Japanese garden and its *sukiya*-style tea pavilion, as well as the very beautiful Chinese Lac de Rêve, or Dream Lake, garden, whose pavilions were designed by artisans who came here from China specifically for the task. Since Montréal is twinned with Shanghai, it was deemed appropriate that it should have the largest such garden outside of Asia.

The northern part of the botanical garden is occupied by an arboretum. The **Maison de l'Arbre**, literally the "tree house", was established in this area to educate people about the life of a tree. The interactive, permanent exhibit is actually set up in an old tree trunk. There are displays on the yellow birch, Québec's emblematic tree since 1993. The building's structure, consisting of different types of wooden beams, reminds us how leafy forests really are. Note the play of light and shade from the frame

onto the large white wall, meant to resemble trunks and branches. The terrace in the back is an ideal spot from which to contemplate the arboretum's pond; it also leads to a charming little bonsai garden. To reach the Maison de l'Arbre, climb on board the *Balade*, the shuttle that regularly tours the garden, or use the garden's northern entrance located on Boulevard Rosemont.

The complementary **Insectarium** (*same schedule as the gardens;* ☎872-8753) is located to the east of the greenhouses. This innovative, living museum invites visitors to discover the fascinating world of insects.

There is a combination ticket that provides access to the Jardin Botanique, Insectarium, Maison de l'Arbre and Biodome and can be used on two consecutive days.

Return to Boulevard Pie-IX.

The **Château Dufresne ★★** (*2929 Rue Jeanne-d'Arc, Pie-IX Métro*) is in fact two 22-room private mansions behind the same façade, built in 1916 for brothers Marius and Oscar Dufresne, shoe-manufacturers and authors of a grandiose plan to develop Maisonneuve. The plan was abandoned after the onset of World War I,

Exploring

causing the municipality to go bankrupt. Their home, designed by Marius Dufresne and Parisian architect Jules Renard, was supposed to be the nucleus of a residential upper-class neighbourhood, which never materialized. It is one of the best examples of Beaux-Arts architecture in Montréal.

Go back downhill on Boulevard Pie-IX, then turn left on Avenue Pierre-de-Coubertin.

Stade Olympique ★★★
(*$5.25, package with tour and funicular $10.25; guided tours in French at 11am and 2pm, and in English at 12:40pm and 3:40pm; 4141 Avenue Pierre-de-Coubertin, ☎252 8687*) is also known as the Olympic Stadium and the "Big O." Jean Drapeau was mayor of Montréal from 1954 to 1957, and from 1960 to 1986. He dreamed of great things for "his" city. Endowed with exceptional powers of persuasion and unfailing determination, he saw a number of important projects through to a successful conclusion, including the construction of Place des Arts, the Métro, Expo '67

Stade Olympique

and, of course, the 1976 Summer Olympics.

For this last international event, however, it was necessary to equip the city with the appropriate facilities. In spite of the controversy this caused, the city sought out a Parisian visionary to design something completely original. A billion dollars later, the major work of architect Roger Taillibert, who also designed the stadium of the Parc des Princes in Paris, stunned everyone with its curving, organic concrete shapes. The 56,000-seat oval stadium is covered with a kevlar roof supported by cables stretching from the 190m leaning tower. In the distance, visitors will see the two pyramid shaped towers of the **Olympic Village**, where the athletes were housed in 1976. Each year, the stadium hosts different events, such as the Salon de l'Auto (Car Show) and the Salon National de l'Habitation (National Home Show). From April to September, Montréal's National League baseball team, the Expos, plays its home games here.

The Top Montréal Attractions for Children

If you read French and want to better enjoy Montréal with your kids, pick up the *Montréal pour enfants* guide by Ulysses Travel Publications, 1999.

Vieux-Montréal

At the **old port**, there is a whole range of activities for children, including SOS Labyrinthe, Expotec, quadricycles and shows where the performers make sure everyone is entertained (see p 91).

At the **Château Ramezay**, children can participate in thematic tours specially designed for them. They learn about various facets of daily life in the time of New France, such as weaving. These educational tours are offered to groups. Reservations required (see p 96).

The **Musée d'Archéologie et d'Histoire de la Pointe-à-Callière** *(adults $7, children free)* offers guided tours adapted for a young audience, and available only to groups. Furthermore, families visiting the museum on Sundays *(from 1pm to 5pm)* can participate in an activity known as *Jeune Découvreur* (Young Discoverer), intended to introduce the public to an archaeologist's work (see p 88).

Downtown

During summer, the **Musée des Beaux-Arts** or **Museum of Fine Arts** organizes day camps *(1 day, $140)* aiming to awaken children's creativity. Accompanied by counsellors, the children visit the temporary summer exhibition on comic strips and then participate in a workshop, where they can create their own artwork, inspired by the tour (see p 118).

During Sunday workshops *(from 1pm to 5pm)* at the **Musée d'Art Contemporain** *(adults $4.75, children free)*, children have the opportunity to learn various techniques used in painting and the crafts (see p 115).

In order to introduce the very young to the marvellous world of astronomy, the **Planétarium de Montréal** *(adults $4.50, children $2.50)* has a visual presentation entitled *Le Royaume du Soleil* (The Kingdom of the Sun), which deals with subjects such as the solar system and the seasons. This presentation is offered to groups, and reservations are required; when there are extra seats available, the public is welcome to attend (see p 108).

Exploring

The stadium's tower, which is the tallest leaning tower in the world, was rebaptised the **Tour de Montréal**. A funicular (*$7.25; every day 10am to 5pm; ☎252-8687*) climbs the structure to an interior observation deck which commands a view of the eastern part of Montreal. Exhibits on the Olympics are presented on the upper levels and there is also a rest area with a bar. The foot of the tower houses the swimming pools of the Olympic Complex, while the former cycling track, known as the Vélodrome, located nearby, has been converted into an artificial habitat for plants and animals called the **Biodôme** ★★★ (*$9.50; every day 9am to 5pm; 4777 Avenue Pierre de Coubertin, Viau métro, ☎868-3000*). This new type of museum, associated with the Jardin Botanique, contains four very different ecosystems – the Tropical Rainforest, the Laurentian Forest, the St. Lawrence Marine Ecosystem and the Polar World – within a space of 10,000m². These are complete micro- climates, including vegetation, mammals and free-flying birds, and close to real climatic conditions. Be careful not to catch a cold!

Ice hockey holds a special place in the hearts of Quebecers. Many consider Maurice "the Rocket" Rich-

ard as the greatest hockey player of all time. **L'Univers Maurice "Rocket" Richard** (*free admission; Tue to Sun noon to 8pm; 2800 Rue Viau, ☎251-9930, Viau métro*) is a small museum in his honour. Located in the arena that carries his name next to the Olympic facilities, the museum contains equipment, trophies and other significant memorabilia that once belonged to this hero of hockey who played for the Canadiens from 1942 to 1960. The museum also has a small boutique with hockey paraphernalia, as well as a skate-sharpening service.

As for the **Aréna Maurice-Richard** (*2800 Rue Viau, ☎872-6666, Viau métro*), it precedes the Olympic Village by 20 years, with which it is now affiliated. Its rink is the only one in Eastern Canada whose area respects international norms. Canada's Olympic speed-skating team practises here, as do several figure-skating champions. A statue of Maurice Richard has stood in front of the entrance to the arena since 1998. Measuring 2.5m in height and cast at the Atelier du Bronze Inverness, it is the work of sculptors Annick Bourgeau and Jules Lasalle.

Return to Boulevard Pie-IX and head south.

Église Saint-Jean-Baptiste-de-LaSalle (*at the corner of Rue Hochelaga, Pie-IX métro*) was built in 1964 within the context of the Vatican II liturgical revival. In an effort to maintain its following, members of the Catholic clergy cast aside traditions and introduced an audacious style of architecture, which still, however, did not enable them to accomplish their goal. The evocative mitre-like exterior conceals a depressing interior made of bare concrete, which looks like it is falling onto the congregation.

Continue south on Boulevard Pie-IX, then turn left on Rue Ontario.

The **former hôtel de ville ★** (*4120 Rue Ontario Est*). In 1911, the Dufresne administration kicked off its policy of grandeur by building a city hall, designed by architect Cajetan Dufort. From 1926 to 1967, the building was occupied by the Institut du Radium, which specialized in cancer research. Since 1981, the edifice has served as the Maison de la Culture Maisonneuve, one of the City of Montréal's neighbourhood cultural centres. On the second floor, a 1915 bird's-eye view drawing of Maisonneuve shows the prestigious buildings as they stood back then, as well as those that remained only on paper.

Built directly in line with Avenue Morgan in 1914, the **Marché Maisonneuve ★** (*Place du Marché*) is in keeping with a concept of urban design inherited from the teachings of the École des Beaux-Arts in Paris, known as the City Beautiful movement in North America. It is a mixture of parks, classical perspectives and civic and sanitary facilities. Designed by Cajetan Dufort, the market was the most ambitious of Dufresne's projects to be completed. The centre of Place du Marché is adorned with an important work by sculptor Alfred Laliberté, entitled *La Fermière* (The Woman Farmer). The market closed in 1962, then partially reopened in 1980.

Follow Avenue Morgan.

Although it is small, the **Bain Morgan ★** (*1875 Avenue Morgan*), a bath house, has an imposing appearance due to its Beaux-Arts elements – a monumental staircase, twin columns, a balustrade on the top and sculptures by Maurice Dubert from France. A bronze entitled *Les Petits Baigneurs* (The Little Bathers) is another piece by Alfred Laliberté. Originally, people came to the public baths not only to relax and enjoy the water, but also to wash, since not all houses in working-class neighbourhoods such as this were equipped with bathrooms.

In 1977, the former Cinéma Granada was converted into a theatre and renamed **Théâtre Denise Pelletier** (*4353 Rue Sainte-Catherine Est*) after one of the great actresses of the Quiet Revolution, who died prematurely. The terra cotta façade is decorated in the Italian Renaissance style. The original interior (1928), designed by Emmanuel Briffa, is of the atmospheric type, and has been partially preserved. Above the colonnade of the mythical palace encircling the room is a black vault that used to be studded with thousands of stars, making the audience feel as if they were attending an outdoor presentation. A projector was used to create images of moving clouds and even airplanes flying through the night.

Parc Morgan (*at the southernmost end of Avenue Morgan*) was laid out in 1933 on the site of the country house of Henry Morgan, owner of the stores of the same name. From the cottage in the centre there is an interesting perspective on the Marché Maisonneuve silhouetted by the enormous Olympic Stadium.

Follow Rue Sainte-Catherine Est west to Avenue Létourneux, and turn left.

Maisonneuve boasted two firehouses, one of which had an altogether original design by Marius Dufresne. He was trained as an engineer and businessman, but he also took a great interest in architecture. Impressed by the work of Frank Lloyd Wright, he designed the **Caserne de Pompiers no 1** ★ (*on the south side of Rue Notre-Dame*), or fire station, as an adaptation of the Unity Temple (1906) in Oak Park, on the outskirts of Chicago. The building was therefore one of the first works of modern architecture erected in Canada.

Turn right on Avenue Desjardins. Due to the unstable ground in this part of the city, some of the houses tilt to an alarming degree.

Behind the somewhat drab Romanesque Revival façade of the **Église du Très-Saint-Nom-de-Jésus** ★ (*at the corner of Rue Adam*), built in 1906, visitors will discover a rich, polychromatic decor, created in part by artist Guido Nincheri, whose studio was located in Maisonneuve. Particularly noteworthy are the large organs built by the Casavant brothers, divided up between the rear jube and the chancel, very unusual in a Catholic church. Because this building stands on the same shifting ground as the neighbouring

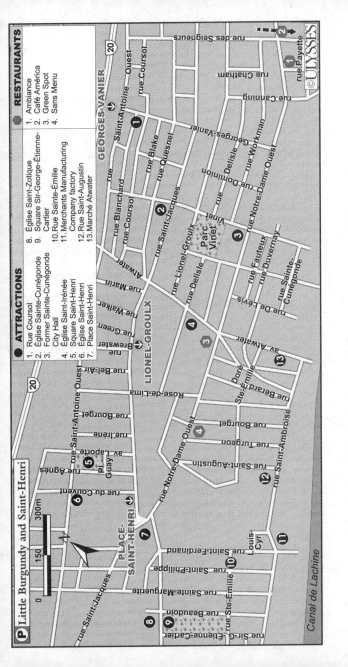

Little Burgundy and Saint-Henri

ATTRACTIONS

1. Rue Coursol
2. Église Sainte-Cunégonde
3. Former Sainte-Cunégonde City Hall
4. Église Saint-Irénée
5. Square Saint-Henri
6. Église Saint-Henri
7. Place Saint-Henri
8. Église Saint-Zotique
9. Square Sir-George-Étienne-Cartier
10. Rue Sainte-Émilie
11. Merchants Manufacturing Company factory
12. Rue Saint-Augustin
13. Marché Atwater

RESTAURANTS

1. Ambiance
2. Café América
3. Green Spot
4. Sans Menu

© ULYSSES

houses, its vault is supported by metal shafts.

Tour P:
Little Burgundy and Saint-Henri

These two working-class neighbourhoods of Montréal were both autonomous municipalities in the past. In 1905, however, the cities of Saint-Henri-des-Tanneries and Petite Bourgogne or Little Burgundy, then officially known as the City of Sainte-Cunégonde, were annexed by Montréal. Saint-Henri was founded at the end of the 18th century around the Rolland family's tannery, which no longer exists (it was located at the corner of Chemin Glen and Rue Saint-Antoine). After the opening of the Lachine canal in 1825, the little town grew significantly, with industries clustering in its southern portion, around the canal.

Little Burgundy's prosperity was also ensured by the industries along the canal, as well as by rail transport, since the town was crossed by a series of railroad tracks leading up to the Gare Bonaventure on Rue Peel (destroyed in 1952). The tracks were dismantled during the 1970s to make way

for housing, the suburban appearance of which does not at all fit in with the rest of the neighbourhood.

From the Georges-Vanier métro station, head to the boulevard of the same name. Both honour the memory of General Georges-Philias Vanier (1888-1971), governor general of Canada from 1959 to 1967. His son Jean founded "L'Arche", an organization providing assistance to the mentally challenged in Trosly-Breuil, in northern France. Turn right onto little Rue Coursol.

Rue Coursol is lined with charming single-family row houses, built around 1875 for the foremen and semi-skilled workers at the factories in Sainte-Cunégonde. The Second-Empire-style stone residences on Rue Saint-Antoine Ouest, farther north, were occupied by local notable residents and certain shop owners. Since Sainte-Cunégonde was located near the downtown train stations (Bonaventure and Windsor), a number of houses on these two streets later became boarding houses for railway employees, mainly those who worked on the trains (waiters, packers, cooks, etc.). Before 1960, most of these employees were black. Little Burgundy was thus identified with this community from the late 19th century on, although there was never a black majority in the neighbourhood. These individuals, who came here from the United States between 1880 and 1900 in hopes of a better future, contributed greatly to the history of music in Montréal.

In fact, Little Burgundy was the birthplace of celebrated jazz pianist Oscar Peterson, as well as the location of a famous cabaret, Rockhead's Paradise, which opened in 1928 at the corner of Rue Saint-Antoine and Rue de la Montagne, and where Louis Armstrong and Cab Calloway played and sang regularly (closed in 1984). On the corner of Rue Vinet lies the former **St. Jude's Church** (*2390 Rue Coursol*), now the Bible-Way Pentecostal Church (1878, Goodwin and Mann, architects).

Turn left on Rue Vinet.

Église Sainte-Cunégonde ★ (*2641 Rue Saint-Jacques*), at the corner of Rue Saint-Jacques, is a large Catholic Beaux-Arts-style church, designed by architect Jean-Omer Marchand in 1906. The building has a remarkable rounded chevet, as well as an ingenious roof with a single-span steel framework that makes it possible to open up the spacious interior, which is completely free of columns and pillars. Decorated with lovely woodwork and vibrantly coloured remounted paintings, shown off to advantage by the natural light coming through the large windows, the interior was damaged when the church was closed in 1971. The building was slated for demolished, but was fortunately saved at the last minute, and is now used, notably, for traditional Catholic services, given in Latin.

Take Rue Vinet to Rue Notre-Dame Ouest.

The former **Sainte-Cunégonde city hall** (*in front of Parc Vinet*), erected at the end of the 19th century, also served as a post office, a firehouse and a police station. Famous strong man Louis Cyr was a member of the local police force for several years.

Turn right on Rue Notre-Dame Ouest. The part of the street between Rue Guy to the east and Rue Atwater to the west is nicknamed the **rue des antiquaires** (antique-dealers row), due to the presence of about 30 shops dealing in second-hand goods and, in some cases, local antiques (especially Victorian and Art Deco-style furniture). These shops, where all sorts of treasures lay hidden, are set up inside handsome 19th-century commercial build-

Exploring

ings, all located on the south side of the street. Behind these sprawl the dilapidated factories along the Lachine canal. Some of these were converted into housing complexes during the 1980s. At number 2490 Rue Notre-Dame Ouest, visitors can see the façade of the former **Cinéma Corona** (1912), whose interior is still intact (*closed to the public*).

Turn right on Avenue Atwater.

Église Saint-Irénée (*3030 Rue Delisle*) is one of those churches whose copper, verdigris-coated bell towers pierce through the low skyline of Montréal's working-class neighbourhoods. It was built in 1912, incorporating a portion of the walls of an earlier church, built in 1904 and burned down in 1911. Its cramped interior is the work of architects MacDuff and Lemieux. Particularly noteworthy are the exaggerated curves of the arches and the typical Belle Époque motifs used in the décor.

Saint-Henri starts on the west side of Avenue Atwater. Head west on Rue Delisle. The Union United Church, dating back to 1899, stands on the corner. Turn right on Rue Rose-de-Lima, left on Rue Saint-Jacques and, finally, right on Avenue Laporte.

Square Saint-Henri ★ (*between Avenue Laporte, Place Guay, Rue Agnès and Rue Saint-Antoine*). As in Sainte-Cunégonde, Saint-Henri's upper-class neighbourhood lies along Rue Saint-Antoine. The beautiful Square Saint-Henri, adorned with a cast-iron fountain topped with a statue of Jacques Cartier (1896), was a gathering point for the municipality's affluent residents. Mayor Eugène Guay, who was responsible for laying out these areas, also had a residence built for himself in front of the square, at number 846 Rue Agnès, in 1902. The house was recently converted into a pleasant bed and breakfast.

Turn left on Rue Saint-Antoine, then left again on Rue du Couvent.

Église Saint-Henri (*872 Rue du Couvent*). When the venerable Église Saint-Henri was demolished in 1969, the French-Canadian Catholic parish of Saint-Henri was relocated to this little church on Rue du Couvent, originally used by the St. Thomas Aquinas English Catholic community. Erected in 1923, it is an Italianized Baroque-Revival-style building by architect Joseph-Albert Karch. The stained glass inside is particularly lovely.

Continue southward on Rue du Couvent, then turn right on Rue Saint-Jacques to reach Place Saint-Henri, which is centred around the Métro station of the same name.

The once remarkable **Place Saint-Henri** has been altered beyond recognition. In an unbridled attempt at modernization, the college, school, convent and church, whose Renaissance-Revival-style façade fronted on the north side of the square, were torn down in 1969-70 and replaced by a high school and a public pool, concealed behind a blind brick wall. This grouping faces away from the square, which grew up naturally at the railroad crossing of Rue Saint-Jacques and Rue Notre-Dame (the train station was located nearby); at the end of the 18th century, this was the main route to the west part of the island of Montréal.

Only a few buildings have survived the wave of changes that took place in the 1960s. These include the Art Deco **fire station**, built in 1931 on the site of the former town hall of Saint-Henri; the **Caisse Populaire** (*4038 Rue Saint-Jacques Ouest*), or credit union, which occupies the former post office and the **Banque Laurentienne** (*4080 Rue Saint-Jacques Ouest*). The latter building used to be-

long to the City and District Savings Bank of Montréal, whose branches across Montréal display a quality of architecture worthy of special mention.

Cross the square to return to Rue Notre-Dame-Ouest. Turn right on this street and continue walking to Église Saint-Zotique.

Église Saint-Zotique (*4565 Rue Notre-Dame Ouest*) was erected in stages between 1910 and 1927 for the least affluent parish in Saint-Henri. This explains the brick facing on the church, a less expensive material than stone. The Baroque-Revival-style steeples rise up from a structure not unlike the industrial buildings along the nearby Lachine canal. The neighbouring credit union oddly resembles some sort of futuristic spaceship.

Square Sir-Georges-Étienne-Cartier ★ (*Rue Notre-Dame Ouest, in front of Église Saint-Zotique*) honours the memory of one of the Fathers of Canadian Confederation. It was among the measures approved by the city of Montréal to clean up the neighbourhood and improve the area's reputation, as we shall see a little further on. In 1912, this green space surrounded by typical Montréal triplexes replaced the Saint-Henri slaughter-

Exploring

houses, whose putrid stench had permeated the entire area. The pretty cast-iron fountain in the middle of the square is particularly interesting.

Cross the square and head east on Rue Sainte-Émilie. Turn right on Rue Saint-Ferdinand.

Rue Sainte-Émilie is lined with typical 19th-century working-class houses. Saint-Henri, like Sainte-Cunégonde and Pointe-Saint-Charles, corresponds to the lower town of Montréal, which, before 1910, was among the poorest areas in North America. Infant mortality was four times higher here than elsewhere on the continent. The workers lived in poverty, steeped in pollution and at the mercy of destructive fires and infectious diseases. In 1897, local reformist Herbert Browne Ames published *The City Below the Hill*, a work that stands out in the history of urban renewal movements. It revealed to the world the decrepit state of Montréal's working-class neighbourhoods at the end of the 19th century. Today, renovation and social assistance programs have put some order back into the local streets, but Saint-Henri's future nevertheless remains uncertain, since its aging industrial facilities have led

to the closing down of a number of the factories that provided local families with a living. As if to exaggerate the contrast between the upper and lower city, the hill of Westmount, surrounded by large, luxurious residences shrouded in greenery, is visible to the north if you look straight up most of the streets intersecting with Rue Sainte-Émilie.

Turn left on Rue Saint-Ambroise, which runs along-side the Lachine canal.

For many years, the **Merchants Manufacturing Company** (*4000 Rue Saint-Ambroise*) was the main employer in Saint-Henri. Purchased by Dominion Textile in the early 20th century, the factory was used to manufacture fabric, blankets, sheets and clothing. Many women worked in the factory, which, in 1891, was the scene of the first textile strike in Montréal. The long low building erected in 1880, is a good example of late 19th-century industrial architecture, characterized by large glass windows and staircase towers crowned with brick cornices.

On **Rue Saint-Augustin** (*immediately east of the railroad tracks serving the factories along the Canal de Lachine*), visitors will find some of

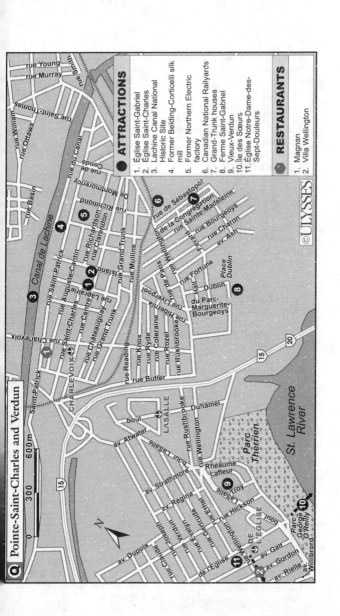

Q Pointe-Saint-Charles and Verdun

ATTRACTIONS

1. Église Saint-Gabriel
2. Église Saint-Charles
3. Lachine Canal National Historic Site
4. Former Belding-Corticelli silk mill
5. Former Northern Electric factory
6. Canadian National Railyards
7. Grand-Trunk houses
8. Ferme Saint-Gabriel
9. Vieux-Verdun
10. Île des Sœurs
11. Église Notre-Dame-des-Sept-Douleurs

RESTAURANTS

1. Magnan
2. Villa Wellington

© ULYSSES

Saint-Henri's oldest houses, lived in for many years by the poorest local families. Of modest size, they are made of wood (some were recently covered with aluminum siding). The **Maison Clermont** (*110 Rue Saint-Augustin*), dating back to 1870, was admirably restored in 1982, and provides a good idea of what this type of working-class dwelling looked like when it was new. It was from these houses with their backs against the railroad tracks that Canadian novelist Gabrielle Roy drew inspiration for her famous novel **Bonheur d'Occasion** (*The Tin Flute, 1945*).

Take Rue Saint-Ambroise to Marché Atwater.

Marché Atwater ★ (*110 Avenue Atwater, Lionel-Groulx métro*) is one of the only two public markets in Montréal still open year-round, the other being Marché Jean-Talon (see p 191). Farm-fresh fruits and vegetables are sold outside during summer and fall, while the interior specialty shops selling meat, cheese and fish are open all year long. The market was built in 1932 as part of job-creation programs initiated during the Great Depression. Designed by architect Ludger Lemieux, it is an elegant Art-Deco-style building.

Head north on Avenue Atwater to reach the Lionel-Groulx métro station, erected on the Sainte-Cunégonde railroad tracks.

Tour Q: Pointe-Saint-Charles and Verdun

The actual point of Pointe-Saint-Charles was named by fur traders Charles LeMoyne and Jacques LeBer, to whom the piece of land was first granted. They sold it to Marguerite Bourgeoys, who built the Ferme Saint-Gabriel for the Sœurs de la Congrégation de Notre-Dame here in 1668. The location's pastoral nature was greatly disrupted by the construction of the Lachine canal between 1821 and 1825, which attracted various types of mills to the area, turning it into the cradle of the Canadian Industrial Revolution.

The village of Saint-Gabriel grew up on Saint Charles point, south of the factories. With the construction of the Victoria bridge, between 1854 and 1860, and the laying-out of various railroad installations near the St. Lawrence, Saint-Gabriel developed into a veritable little city.

The Irish, omnipresent on the construction sites of these two major projects, settled in large numbers in Saint-Gabriel and other villages farther east (Griffintown, Sainte-Anne and Victoriatown), of which, unfortunately, only a few traces remain. The village of Saint-Gabriel was annexed by Montréal in 1887 and renamed Pointe-Saint-Charles. Though it is located near the downtown area, it is separated from it by the canal and a number of highways, and bisected by railroad tracks. It nevertheless boasts a rich heritage from the Industrial Revolution.

Today, Pointe-Saint-Charles resembles a working-class area whose aging production facilities can barely generate any more jobs. A few factories have been converted into housing complexes, while the area along the Lachine canal, closed in 1959, has been transformed into a linear park with a pleasant bicycle path. Verdun, located to the west, has a more recent history. Many descendants of Irish Catholic immigrants, along with French Canadians, took up residence there in the period between the two World Wars.

Head east on Rue Centre from the Charlevoix Métro station. This tour can also easily be completed by bicycle, starting from the bike path alongside the Lachine canal.

Église Saint-Gabriel (*2157 Rue Centre, Charlevoix métro*). Victims of a dreadful famine caused by potato blight in the mid-19th century, the Irish fled their island in large numbers to seek refuge in Canada. The sick and very weak, however, did not make it past Grosse Île, downriver from Québec City. Those able to overcome illness went to work on the colonial building sites, forming an inexpensive, unskilled workforce. These people lived in poverty for many years. Their first medieval-looking wooden houses, built in Victoriatown (also known as Village aux Oies), have been torn down and replaced in the name of progress.

Saint-Gabriel church was built in 1893 by the Irish Catholic community of Pointe-Saint-Charles. At the same time, a French-Canadian Catholic church was being constructed on the neighbouring piece of land. In fact, the two imposing buildings were built side by side according to designs by the same architects (Perrault and Mesnard), thus creating an unusual sight that makes Montréal truly worthy of the nickname "city of a hundred

Exploring

steeples." The original interior decoration of Saint Gabriel church was destroyed by fire in 1959. It was replaced by a minimalist décor that highlights the building's thick rubble stone walls. Next to the church is a lovely Romanesque-Revival-style presbytery with Queen Anne details.

Église Saint-Charles ★ (*2125 Rue Centre, Charlevoix métro*), by architects Perrault and Mesnard, was consumed by flames in 1913. The following year, it was rebuilt according to the plans of architects MacDuff and Lemieux, who recreated its Romanesque-Revival-style appearance. The interior, with its columns painted with imitation marble patterns, is worth a short visit. The presbytery of the parish of Saint-Charles is, unlike that of Saint-Gabriel, a symmetrical building with a Beaux-Arts-inspired design.

Turn left on Rue Island. Cross Rue Saint-Patrick to reach the Parc du Canal de Lachine. Be very careful crossing the bike path, where cycling enthusiasts sometimes ride at high speeds; this is not a pedestrian trail so do not stop here.

The Lachine Canal National Historic Site ★ (*on the southwest part of the island of Montréal, between Vieux-Montréal and Lachine, Charlevoix métro*). In the 17th century, a farm owned by the Messieurs de Saint-Sulpice, then seigneurs of the island of Montréal, occupied the entire northern part of Pointe-Saint-Charles. In 1689, the Sulpicians, anxious to develop their island, began digging a canal next to Rivière Saint-Pierre, which bordered their property. Their goal was to bypass the famous Lachine rapids, a hindrance to navigation on the St. Lawrence upriver from Montréal. These visionary priests, perhaps too ambitious for their time, launched the project before even asking permission from their order or obtaining funds from the king, both of which they were later denied. The enterprise was thus suspended until 1821, when work had begun on the present canal. Enlarged twice afterward, it was used until the opening of the seaway in 1959. The Canadian Parks Service purchased the canal and its banks in 1979.

Walk eastward along the canal and enjoy the view of the industrial buildings and the skyscrapers in the business centre.

The water in the canal was used not only for navigation but also as a source of power. The former **Belding Corticelli silk mill ★** (*1790 Rue du Canal, Charlevoix métro*) was one of the establishments that ran its machines on hydraulic energy. The red-brick building has a cast-iron structure. It was erected in 1884 and has since been renovated to make room for apartment lofts. The abandoned former buildings of the Redpath sugar refinery, founded by John Redpath in 1854, stand a little farther along. Redpath, a native of Berwickshire, Scotland, had 17 children and was one of McGill University's principal donors.

Head back to Rue Saint-Patrick by walking through the residential complex at the former Belding-Corticelli mill, and cross over one of the few arms of the canal that have not been filled in. Turn left on Rue Saint-Patrick, then right on Rue Richmond, which runs alongside the former Northern Electric factory.

The former **Northern Electric factory** (*Rue Richmond and Rue Richardson, Charlevoix métro*) houses the Nordelec business "incubator." Dozens of little clothing and contemporary furniture manufacturers share the same secretarial services, as well as the advice of marketing specialists, thereby reducing the start-up expenses and making it possible to avoid costly errors while manufacturing their goods or placing them on the market. The huge,

monolithic edifice was built between 1913 and 1926 for the Northern Electric Company, which manufactured everyday electrical appliances here. The company is now known as Nortel. Across the street is the Société des Alcools du Québec's (Québec liquor commission's) distribution centre for restaurants and bars, as well as the old **Caserne de Pompiers no 15** (*72 Rue Richardson*), a fire station erected in 1903 in a vaguely Romanesque Revival style.

Continue south on Rue Richmond. In the area around Rue Mullins, there are some good examples of the residential working-class architecture of Pointe-Saint-Charles. Some houses have even retained their original fenestration. Turn right on Rue Wellington, which passes under the viaduct for the railroad tracks leading up to the Canadian National railyards. Turn left on small Rue de Sébastopol and continue alongside the marshalling yard. The street was laid in 1855, when the Crimean War, marked by the siege of Sebastopol (Ukraine), was raging in Europe.

The **Canadian National Railyards** (*east of Rue de Sébastopol, Charlevoix métro*) used to belong to the Grand Trunk Railway, a company founded in London in 1852 with the aim of developing railroads in

Canada. It merged with Canadian Northern Railway in 1923 to form Canadian National. The Grand Trunk Railway was behind the construction of the Victoria bridge, and built its repair shops near the exit of the bridge in 1856.

The **Grand Trunk houses** (*422 to 444 Rue de Sébastopol, Charlevoix métro*) are among the earliest examples of North American housing specially designed by a company for its workers. These "company houses," inspired by British models, were built in 1857 according to plans by Robert Stephenson (1803-1859), engineer and designer of the Victoria bridge and son of the inventor of the steam engine. Of the seven houses designed by Stephenson, each containing four apartments, only about half remain, while the others are in a sad state of disrepair.

From Rue de Sébastopol, take Rue Favard. Like the neighbouring streets, Rue Favard is lined with various examples of residential working-class architecture. Particularly interesting are the patterns of the brick, the woodwork and the terra cotta inlays. The names of the streets indicate that this area was once owned by the Sœurs de la Congrégation de Notre Dame. The nuns' land was gradually sold off in lots, which explains why the neighbourhood seems newer as you approach the Saint-Gabriel farmhouse.

Turn left at Place Dublin.

Ferme Saint-Gabriel ★★ (*2146 Place Dublin, Charlevoix or LaSalle métro*) offers precious evidence of what daily life was like in New France. The farmhouse and nearby barn, now surrounded by the city, were built between 1662 and 1698. Marguerite Bourgeoys purchased the entire property from the Le Ber family in 1668 as a place of residence for the Dames de la Congrégation de Notre-Dame, a religious community founded by her in 1653. The house later served as a school for young native girls and as accommodations for the *Filles du Roy*. The latter were young women with no families, whom Louis XIV sent from Paris to Montréal to find husbands amongst the men here. In 1964, the house was restored and opened to the public. Since then, it has housed displays of 17th- and 18th-century objects belonging to the community. The building itself is of great interest, as it has, most notably, one of the only authentic 17th-century roof frames in North

America, as well as rare sinks made of black stone.

Head north on Place Dublin, and then along the street of the same name. Turn left onto Rue Wellington.

Here, visitors will find two Gothic-Revival-style brick churches dating back to the end of the 19th century (*625 Rue Fortune and 2183 Rue Wellington*), Art-Deco-style public baths, built during the economic crisis of the 1930s (*2188 Rue Wellington*), and a row of Victorian houses designed around 1875 by the architect of Montréal's City Hall, Henri-Maurice Perrault.

It takes about 10min to reach Verdun on foot. Walk along Rue Wellington to Boulevard La Salle. Take a left on Avenue Lafleur, where there are some rare examples of exterior staircases that wind all the way up to the third floor of several triplexes and quadruplexes.

Vieux-Verdun (*east of Avenue Willibrord, De l'Église métro*). Verdun is an autonomous municipality with about 60,000 inhabitants. Its history began in 1665, when eight militiamen settled alongside the river, west of the Ferme Saint-Gabriel. These armed colonists, nicknamed "*les Argoulets*," were ultimately massacred by the Iroquois. In 1671, the territory was granted to

Zacharie Dupuys, a native of Saverdun, near Carcassonne France, who named it Verdun in memory of his former village. Between 1852 and 1865, the channel of the aqueduct of Montréal was dug in the northern portion of Verdun. A village emerged south of the aqueduct, but its development was slowed by frequent spring floods. Once a dyke was built along the river (1895), its growth accelerated. Today, 97% of Verdun is urbanized. The city contains a large number of buildings typical of Montréal, as well as an astonishing variety of charming loggias.

Avenue Lafleur runs into Avenue Troy. In the 1930s and 1940s, many families from the Îles de la Madeleine were attracted to this area by the jobs offered at the nearby hospital, the Hôpital du Christ-Roi. In those years, nurses were required to be fully bilingual since the hospital served a population that was half anglophone and half francophone. At the time, the Madelinots, as natives of the Îles de la Madeleine are known, were among the few Quebecers capable of expressing themselves easily in both of Canada's official languages. One of the entrances to Parc Therrien, which runs alongside the St. Lawrence,

Exploring

is located at the end of Rue Troy. From inside the park, visitors can enjoy a lovely view of the skyscrapers of downtown Montréal to the east and the residential high-rises of Île des Sœurs to the south. Île des Sœurs is extremely interesting for contemporary architecture buffs. Anyone wishing to go there should, however, make a separate trip, as the island is difficult to reach from Verdun, even though it is part of the municipality. (*To go there by car, head east on Rue Wellington, then take Highway 20 toward the Champlain bridge until the Île des Sœurs Exit*).

Île des Sœurs ★ (*in the St. Lawrence River*), literally Nun's Island, was purchased by the Dames de la Congrégation de Notre-Dame in 1676, who named it Île Saint-Paul. Around 1720, a large stone manor and various farm buildings were erected on the northern part of the island. After the nuns left in 1956, the buildings were destroyed by fire. The island passed into the hands of an important developer, who laid out the first streets and built three residential high-rises (*on Boulevard de l'Île des Sœurs, southwest of Rue Corot*). These were designed in 1967 by the celebrated German architect Ludwig Mies van der Rohe, who also drew up the plans for the elegant service station near Rue Berlioz (1968). The more recent projects carried out on Île des Sœurs have been more or less successful. The best include the yellow-brick houses on Rue Corot, designed in 1982 by architect Dan Hanganu, and the housing in the "L'Isle" development project (*Chemin du Golf and Chemin Marie-LeBer*), the work of architect and professor Aurèle Cardinal.

Still in Verdun, walk westward along Parc Therrien to the Auditorium de Verdun, then take Avenue de l'Église to Rue Wellington.

Église Notre-Dame-des-Sept-Douleurs ★ (*4155 Rue Wellington, De l'Église métro*) is one of the largest parish churches on the island of Montréal. It was built between 1907 and 1914 according to plans by Joseph Venne. The Baroque-Revival-style interior is particularly interesting. A handsome Art-Deco-style bank (1931) stands across the street.

The nearby De L'Église métro station is on the same line as the Charlevoix station, the starting point of this tour.

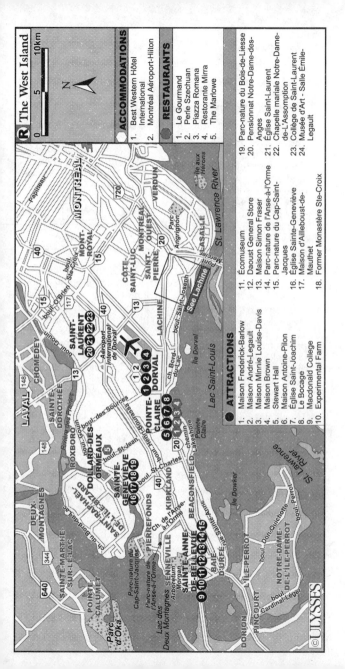

R The West Island

N

0   5   10km

ACCOMMODATIONS

1. Best Western Hôtel
   International
2. Montréal Aéroport-Hilton

RESTAURANTS

1. Le Gourmand
2. Perle Szechuan
3. Piazza Romana
4. Restorante Mirra
5. The Marlowe

● ATTRACTIONS

1. Maison Frederick-Barlow
2. Maison André-Legault
3. Maison Minnie Louise-Davis
4. Maison Brown
5. Stewart Hall
6. Maison Antoine-Pilon
7. Église Saint-Joachim
8. Le Bocage
9. Macdonald College
10. Experimental Farm
11. Écomuseum
12. Daoust General Store
13. Maison Simon Fraser
14. Parc-nature de l'Anse-à-l'Orme
15. Parc-nature du Cap-Saint-
    Jacques
16. Église Sainte-Geneviève
17. Maison d'Aillleboust-de-
    Mauthet
18. Former Monastère Ste-Croix
19. Parc-nature du Bois-de-Liesse
20. Pensionnat Notre-Dame-des-
    Anges
21. Église Saint-Laurent
22. Chapelle mariale Notre-Dame-
    de-L'Assomption
23. Collège de Saint-Laurent
24. Musée d'Art - Salle Émile-
    Legault

© ULYSSES

Tour R: West Island

The only real riverside tour on the island of Montréal, this visit to the "West Island", as the western part of this island is known, will allow visitors to discover old villages and the loveliest panoramic views of the St. Lawrence, Lac Saint-Louis and Lac des Deux-Montagnes. Although a number of the towns that make up the West Island were founded by French colonists, many now have an anglophone majority. Therefore, do not be surprised to hear the language of Shakespeare more often than that of Molière in the shops and along the residential streets.

This is not considered an urban walking tour, since it covers nearly 50km. It can, however, be enjoyed on bicycle, because a good part of the excursion runs along either a well laid-out bike path or streets with low speed limits. It is possible to reach the starting point of the tour by following the Lachine canal bike path from Old Montréal. Drivers coming from downtown should take Autoroute 20 Ouest, then

the 138 briefly towards the Mercier Bridge.

Take the exit for Rue Clément in LaSalle. Turn right on Rue Clément, left on Rue Saint-Patrick, then immediately left on Avenue Stirling to reach the river. Turn right on Chemin LaSalle.

Lachine

In 1667, the Messieurs de Saint-Sulpice granted some land on the west part of the island of Montréal to explorer Robert Cavelier de La Salle, who, obsessed with the idea of finding a passage to China, later discovered Louisiana at the mouth of the Mississippi. Montrealers mockingly referred to his land as *La Chine* (China), a name that later became official. In 1689, the inhabitants of Lachine were victims of the worst Iroquois massacre of the French Regime. However, instead of leaving the area, the population grew. Two forts were built to protect Lachine, strategically located upriver from the rapids of the same name, which at the time still hindered shipping on the St. Lawrence. Consequently, the precious furs from the hinterland destined for the European market had to be unloaded at Lachine and transported by land to

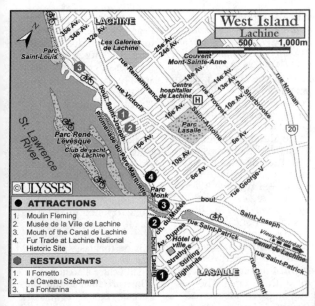

West Island
Lachine

©ULYSSES

ATTRACTIONS

1. Moulin Fleming
2. Musée de la Ville de Lachine
3. Mouth of the Canal de Lachine
4. Fur Trade at Lachine National Historic Site

RESTAURANTS

1. Il Fornetto
2. Le Caveau Szechwan
3. La Fontanina

Montréal, located downriver from the rapids. In the years following the opening of the Lachine canal in 1825, many industries set up shop in Lachine, leading to an important period of urbanization. Today, its aging industry is fortunately counterbalanced by an enchanting location that still charms and attracts enthusiastic residents.

The **Moulin Fleming** (*free admission; Jun, every day noon to 6pm; Jul and Aug, Wed noon to 6pm; in Parc Stinson, ☎367-6489*). Although located within the limits of the city of LaSalle, this mill is closely linked to the development of Lachine, to which it used to belong. Built in 1816 for a Scottish merchant, it is cone-shaped like mills in the United States. An exhibition relates its history.

Fort Rémy, one of the two fortified enclosures in Lachine, stood nearby. The former factory of the Burrows-Wellcome pharmaceutical company, visible to the west, now serves as La-Salle's city hall.

Take Boulevard LaSalle to Chemin du Musée. Turn left to reach the parking lot of the Musée de Lachine, which faces Chemin LaSalle.

Exploring

Musée de Lachine ★ (*free admission; mid-Mar to mid-Dec, Wed to Sun 11:30am to 4:30pm; 110 Chemin LaSalle, ☎634-3471 ext. 346*). Erected in 1670, this former trading post and its fur warehouse, perforated with loopholes for its defence, are the oldest extant structures in the entire Montréal region. At the time of their construction, Lachine was the last inhabited area in the valley of the St. Lawrence before the wild regions to the west. It was also the final destination of cargoes of fur, for many years Canada's main natural resource and the true *raison d'être* of the French colonies in North America. The building was erected for Jacques LeBer and Charles LeMoyne, two wealthy Montréal merchants. Since 1948, it has served as a historical museum, as well as an art gallery, where contemporary works by local artists are exhibited.

Take Chemin LaSalle, in front of the museum. Turn right on Chemin du Canal, then left on Chemin du Musée, which turns into Boulevard Saint-Joseph.

Three narrow, man-made spits of land make up the mouth of the **Canal de Lachine ★★** (*Parc Monk*), which resembles a sprawling estuary widening at the end. Majestic Lac Saint-Louis extends beyond **Parc René-Lévesque**, accessible from Chemin du Canal. The park is scattered with a number of contemporary sculptures, including *Les Forces Vives* by Georges Dyens, in homage to the former premier of Québec after whom the park is named. The Lachine Yacht Club occupies the second strip of land, while the **Promenade du Père Marquette** and **Parc Monk** lie between the original entrance of the canal, opened in 1825, and the 1848 widening.

It is on this last spit of land that visitors will find the small **Centre d'Accueil et d'Interprétation du Canal de Lachine** (*admission included with fur trade site, see below; mid-May to early Sep, Tue to Sun 10am to noon and 1pm to 6pm, ☎283-6054*). The information and interpretative centre recounts the history of the canal, which enabled ships to bypass the Lachine rapids on their way to the Great Lakes and the middle of the continent (see p 226). The canal, now replaced by the St. Lawrence Seaway, on the south shore of the river, is closed to ships. The other end of this artificial waterway is in the old port, opposite Old Montréal.

By following the Promenade du Père Marquette, visitors

can reach the Fur Trade at Lachine National Historic Site.

The **Fur Trade at Lachine National Historic Site ★** (*$2.50; mid-Apr to mid-Oct, Mon 1pm to 6pm; Tue to Sun 10am to 12:30pm and 1pm to 6pm; mid-Oct to early Dec, Wed to Sun 9:30am to 12:30pm and 1pm to 5pm; closed mid-Dec to end of Mar; 1255 Boulevard Saint-Joseph, ☎637-7433*). For nearly two centuries, the fur trade was the main economic activity in the Montréal region. Lachine played a crucial role in the transport of pelts to the European market – so much so that the Hudson's Bay Company made it the centre of its operations. The National Historic Site occupies the company's former warehouse, erected in 1803. Various objects and examples of furs and clothing made with these pelts are on display. Temporary exhibits also explore the lives of the trappers or *voyageurs*; the native tribes who, in the 17th century, caught most of the animals; as well as the heads of powerful French and English companies, who were engaged in a bitter struggle for a monopoly on this lucrative trade.

Continue heading west on Boulevard Saint-Joseph.

The **Couvent de Lachine ★** (*1250 Boulevard Saint-Joseph*). In 1861, the sisters of Sainte-Anne purchased a house built in 1833 for Sir George Simpson, then head of the Hudson's Bay Company. They built their mother house, and then a convent school for young girls, around the original building. This house was later demolished and replaced in 1889 with an imposing, Russian-style chapel topped with a silvery dome, designed by architects Maurice Perrault and Albert Mesnard. The interior of the chapel, reminiscent of a Victorian concert hall, is worth a short visit.

Behind the convent, visitors will find **St. Stephen's Anglican Church** (*25 12e Avenue*), built in 1831 to serve the executive personnel of the Hudson's Bay Company. The humble, vaguely Gothic-Revival-style building, made of rubble stone, contrasts with the immense Catholic church located nearby.

Up until 1865, the Catholic church of Lachine was located farther east, in the enclosure at Fort Rémy. That year, a French Gothic-Revival-style church was inaugurated on the present site, in the centre of the town. Unfortunately, a huge fire destroyed the church in 1915. The present **Église des Saints-Anges Gardiens** (*1400 Boulevard Saint-Joseph*) was erected on the ruins of the

Exploring

former church in 1919, according to plans by architects Dalbé Viau and Alphonse Venne. The Romanesque Revival – style edifice is one of the largest parish churches located outside the city of Montréal.

St. Andrew's United Church, once Presbyterian, is located near the Catholic church, west of 15e Avenue. It was built in the Gothic Revival style in 1832, according to a design by John Wells. Its bell tower was damaged by fire a few years ago. At 1560 Boulevard Saint-Joseph, visitors will see the lovely residence of the church's pastor, the Reverend Doctor, whose openings are framed by small, neoclassical columns (1845). The municipal library nearby was recently renamed Saul Bellow Library in honour of this famous writer, a Lachine native.

The **former Brasserie Dawes** ★ (*2801 Boulevard Saint-Joseph*) (not to be confused with the Dow Brewery) opened in Lachine in 1811 to provide beer for trappers and traders passing through. The company closed in 1922 after the merger of several small regional breweries. The facilities, among the oldest of their kind in North America, can nevertheless still be found on either side of Boulevard Saint-Joseph. On the lake side, visitors will see the brewery (two rubble-stone buildings erected around 1850), as well as the home of Thomas Amos Dawes, son of the company founder, built in 1862 (*2901 Boulevard Saint-Joseph*). This lovely Victorian residence now serves as Lachine's cultural centre. The great ice house, converted into apartments (1878), and the old warehouse (circa 1820), located at the end of 21e Avenue, lie on the city side. The remains of the working-class neighbourhood centred around the brewery completes this grouping, which is of exceptional anthropological value.

Continue westward on Boulevard Saint-Joseph.

A monument reminds visitors that **Fort Rolland** (*west of 34e Avenue*), the main trading post in Lachine in the 17th century, was once located on this site. Military troops were stationed here to ensure the protection of local inhabitants and supervise the transshipment of precious cargoes of fur. On their way past, visitors can see some lovely houses dating back to the French Regime, including the **Maison Quesnel** (*5010 Boulevard Saint-Joseph*), built around 1750, and the **Maison Picard**

(*5430 Boulevard Saint-Joseph*), erected in 1719.

*Once in the city of Dorval,
Boulevard Saint-Joseph is
known as Lakeshore Drive,
sometimes awkwardly translated as Chemin du Bord-du-
Lac, though it is essentially the
same road.*

Dorval

In 1691, Sieur d'Orval purchased La Présentation, a
fort established by the
Sulpicians in 1667, from the
estate of Pierre Le Gardeur
of Repentigny, and named
it after himself. Later, from
1790 to 1821, small Dorval
Island, located opposite the
city, became the point of
departure of the Northwest
Company's *coureurs des bois*
and *voyageurs*, who travelled to the Outaouais and
Great Lakes regions in
search of beaver pelts each
year. Nowadays, Dorval is a
comfortable Montréal sub-
urb, known mainly for its
airport. It is still possible to
find old farmhouses here
that have been carefully
restored by their residents,
who clearly appreciate the
decorative elements of Québec's French heritage.

The stone walls at the base
of the **Maison Frederick
Barlow** (*900 Chemin du Bord-
du-Lac*) are supposedly
those of the Sulpicians' Fort
de La Présentation, erected
in the 17th century.

At number 940, visitors can
see the **Maison André Legault**,
dit Deslauriers, with its decorative firebreak walls
(1817). Before being carefully restored by architect
Galt Durnford in 1934, it
was the summer home of
Lord Strathcona, one of the
Canadian Pacific's principal
shareholders.

The **Maison Minnie Louise
Davis** (*1240 Chemin du Bord-
du-Lac*), built in 1922, reveals the interest certain
architects of British descent
and their clients took in
traditional Québec architecture between the two World
Wars. These individuals
even went so far as to build
new homes in the style of
the 18th century. Percy
Nobbs, a professor of architecture at McGill University,
drew up the plans for the
Davis house, which its
owner called "Le Canayen"
(*Le Canadien*, or The Canadian, as pronounced with a
heavy Québec accent).

The **Maison Brown** (*1800
Chemin du Bord-du-Lac*). A
number of sporting clubs
once favoured by Mont-
réal's Anglo-Saxon bour-
geoisie are located in
Dorval, including the Royal
Montreal Golf Club, the
oldest golf club in North
America (it was founded in
1873), and the Royal St.

Exploring

Lawrence Yacht Club, founded in 1888, whose facilities may still be seen alongside Lac Saint-Louis.

The strangest of these clubs, however, is without question the Forest and Stream Club, which occupies the former villa of Alfred Brown, erected in 1872. Though still in existence, the organization has seen better days. Back in the 1920s, tea was served to dozens of people in its gardens on Saturday and Sunday summer afternoons.

Continue to Pointe-Claire.

Pointe-Claire

One of the first missions established by the Sulpicians along the periphery of the island of Montréal, Pointe-Claire has become a comfortable suburb that has nevertheless preserved the core of its original village. Up until 1940, Chemin du Bord-du-Lac, which leads through the municipalities on the West Island, from Lachine to Sainte-Anne-de-Bellevue, passing through Pointe-Claire on the way, was the only route for motorists travelling from Montréal to Toronto.

Stewart Hall *(free admission, Mon and Wed 2pm to 4pm and 7pm to 9pm, Tue, Thu and Fri 2pm to 4pm, Sept to May Sat and Sun 1pm to 5pm; concerts every Sun at 3pm; 176 Chemin du Bord-du-lac, ☎630-1220)* is a rather long house, built in 1915 for industrialist Charles Wesley MacLean, according to a design by Robert Findlay. Since 1963, it has served as Pointe-Claire's cultural centre, and is therefore open to the public, offering visitors a chance to see its interior and enjoy unobstructed views of Lac Saint-Louis from its back porch, a pleasure previously reserved for its owner alone.

Built back in 1710, the small **Maison Antoine-Pilon** *(258 Chemin du Bord-du-Lac)* is the oldest house in Pointe-Claire. A recent restoration has given it back its former appearance.

Turn left on Rue Sainte-Anne to reach Pointe Claire (the actual point), extending into Lac Saint-Louis. The institutional buildings of the traditional village are clustered here.

Église Saint-Joachim, the mill and the convent ★ *(1 Rue Saint-Joachim)*. The Gothic-Revival-style church (1882) has an extremely original steeple that dominates the entire institutional grouping. It is one of the last buildings designed by Victor Bourgeau, architect of dozens of churches in the Montréal area. Its flamboyant, polychrome wooden interior, decorated with numerous statues, is worth a short visit. The convent of the Sœurs de la Congrégation de Notre-Dame was built in 1867 on the southern portion of the windswept point. The mill, which could not have been built in a better spot, was erected in 1709 by the Messieurs de Saint-Sulpice.

Return to Chemin du Bord-du-Lac and head toward Beaconsfield and Baie d'Urfé. These two municipalities form the heart of the English-speaking West Island. They also, however, include a number of old properties once owned by great French-Canadian families.

Jean-Baptiste de Valois, a direct descendant of the French royal family, settled in Canada in 1723. His son, Paul Urgèle Gabriel, built **Le Bocage ★** (*26 Lakeshore Drive, Beaconsfield*) in 1810. Houses with cut-stone façades were extremely rare in rural areas in the early 19th century, therefore this one thus indicated the special status of its owner. In 1874, Le Bocage was sold to Henri Menzies, who converted the property into a vineyard. The experiment was a pitiful failure due to the unproductive soil and, above all, the location's

exposure to both warm and cold winds. Menzies was more successful naming the estate Beaconsfield, in honour of British Prime Minister Disraeli, annointed Lord Beaconsfield by Queen Victoria. From 1888 to 1966, the house was used by a private club, before becoming the lodge of the Beaconsfield Yacht Club.

Sainte-Anne-de-Bellevue

Just like Lachine, Sainte-Anne-de-Bellevue has a more or less compact centre, compressed along the lakeside panoramic road that now takes on the name Rue Sainte-Anne. Here, visitors will find numerous boutiques and a number of restaurants, most of which have pleasant terraces looking out on the water behind the buildings. The houses on Île Perrot are visible across the water. The village owes its existence to the lock, today used by pleasure crafts to pass from Lac Saint-Louis to the very beautiful Lac des Deux-Montagnes, into which the Rivière des Outaouais (Ottawa River) flows. Just east of the old village, visitors will find a comfortable suburb and institutions such as the

Exploring

veterans' hospital, Macdonald College and John Abbott College, an anglophone CÉGEP (post-secondary college).

Macdonald College ★ (*21111 Chemin du Bord-du-Lac*). Arriving in Sainte-Anne-de-Bellevue, visitors will be surprised to see a whole series of English Baroque-Revival-style buildings faced with orange-coloured brick, surrounding a vast, closely trimmed lawn. Erected between 1905 and 1908, they are part of the Macdonald Campus of McGill University's Department of Agriculture. Some of the buildings belong to John Abbott College, the only English CEGEP west of Vanier College in Ville St-Laurent. At the **Experimental Farm** (*$3, guided tours from May to Aug; 9am to 3:30pm; from Montréal, take Autoroutw 40 Ouest, Sortie 41, and follow the signs for Chemin Sainte-Marie, turn left at the first stop, then left again at the second stop;* ☎*398-7701*), visitors can see a number of animals bred on the farm. The gardens and Morgan Arboretum (see p 78), complete the facilities and are open to the public.

The goal of the **Ecomuseum** (*$6; every day 9am to 5pm, arrive before 4pm; from Montréal, take Autoroute 40 Ouest, Sortie 41, and follow Chemin Sainte-Marie; 21125 Chemin Sainte-Marie;* ☎*457-9449*) is to educate the public about the flora and fauna of the St. Lawrence plain. In a large, well-laid out park, visitors can see several different animal species, including the fox and the black bear. There is also an aviary for aquatic birds.

In the centre of the village is the **Daoust General Store** (*73 Rue Sainte-Anne,* ☎*457-5333*). This once common type of family business has now practically disappeared in Québec. Founded in 1902, the Daoust store sold everything from flour to boots, wool blankets and snuff. These days they mostly sell knick-knacks and clothing. The best reason to stop in, however, is to see the Lamson money conveyor in action. The system of cables, pulleys and suspended rails, one of few still in use in Canada, links the various departments of the store to a central cash register. It was installed in 1924.

Around 1960, the **Maison Simon Fraser** (*153 Rue Sainte-Anne*) was scheduled for demolition in order to make way for the ramp of the bridge on Autoroute 20. It was saved by a historical society, but the bridge, built a few years later, passes less than 5m from the house, occupied sporadically by Simon Fraser in the early 19th century. This

Montréal merchant was one of the heads of the Northwest Company, which specialized in fur trading. It was here that Irish poet Thomas Moore (1779-1852) stayed during his trip to North America in 1804, and composed his famous *Canadian Boat Song*, in memory of the *voyageurs* who passed through Sainte-Anne-de-Bellevue on their way to the forests of the Canadian shield. The house now serves as a non-profit café run by the Victorian Order of Nurses, a charitable organization founded in the 19th century to provide assistance and home care to sick people.

This is the western tip of the island of Montréal, 32km from the eastern extremity at Pointe-aux-Trembles, and about 16km from downtown Montréal. Running alongside the **lock** (*mid-May to mid-Oct; 170 Rue Sainte-Anne ☎457-5546*) is a pleasant boardwalk where visitors can observe the doors of the lock opening and closing and the chambers filling with water and crowded with the boats of *marins d'eau douce* (literally, fresh-water sailors, a French term for amateurs) and other Sunday afternoon captains. A tiny beach and a picnic area lie nearby. **Église Sainte-Anne** (1853-1875) and the convent face the lock north of the bridges.

Follow the curve of Rue Sainte-Anne, then turn left on **Chemin Senneville ★★**. This road passes through Senneville, the most rural of all of the municipalities on the island of Montréal. As a matter of fact, it is here that visitors will find the last farms on the island, as well as a number of large properties on the shores of Lac des Deux-Montagnes. The country setting lends itself marvellously well to cycling excursions. The road then leads through Pierrefonds, where two important regional parks are located.

Parc-Nature de L'Anse-à-l'Orme, see "Outdoors," p 249.

Parc-Nature du Cap-Saint-Jacques, see "Outdoors," p 249.

At Pierrefonds, Chemin Senneville becomes Boulevard Gouin, and keeps this name across the entire Montréal territory.

Sainte-Geneviève

The old village of Sainte-Geneviève is a francophone enclave in the city of Pierrefonds. Its origins date back to 1730, when a small fort was built here to defend the portage of the Rapides du Cheval-Blanc on

Exploring

Rivière des Prairies, which ran alongside the village. In the 19th century, the *cajeux*, robust fellows who floated logs down the river toward Québec, where the largest shipyards were then located, used to stop in Sainte-Geneviève. There they made rafts (called *cages*, hence their name) with the logs, in order to pass through the many rapids along Rivière des Prairies. Starting in 1880, this method of floating logs was gradually replaced by rail transport.

Église Sainte-Geneviève ★★ (*16037 Boulevard Gouin Ouest*) is the only building designed by the Baillargé family in the Montréal region. Thomas Baillargé designed the church in 1836, giving it an imposing neoclassical façade with two bell towers, thereby influencing the architecture of Catholic churches across the entire region during the 1840s and 1850s. The interior was inspired by a since-vanished church in Rotterdam, built by the architect Guidichi. Of particular interest are the tabernacle and the tomb of Ambroise Fournier, as well as the painting in the choir, entitled *Sainte-Geneviève*, by Ozias Leduc. The church is flanked by the convent of Sainte-Anne and the presbytery, and has outdoor Stations of the Cross made of

bronzed cast iron, executed by the *Union Artistique de Vaucouleurs* in France.

Just like the church, the **Maison d'Ailleboust-de-Manthet** (*15886 Boulevard Gouin Ouest*) is neoclassical in style. It was built in 1845 and occupied by the d'Ailleboust de Manthet family, one of the great French-Canadian families of the 18th and 19th centuries, whose members won renown in both military and civilian circles on a number of occasions. (*Closed to the public*).

At the bend in the road, visitors will see the Lombard-style former **Monastère Sainte-Croix** ★ (*15693 Boulevard Gouin Ouest*), which looks like it came straight out of the Middle Ages. It was in fact built for the fathers of Sainte-Croix in 1932, according to plans by talented architect Lucien Parent. The cloister in the centre is a haven of peace and serenity. Since being sold in 1968, the building has been used as an alcohol rehabilitation centre, known as the Centre Dom-Rémy.

Continue on Boulevard Gouin. After crossing the eastern portion of Pierrefonds, the road leads through Roxboro and then on to Montréal. At the meeting point of these two municipalities, there are two regional parks, Parc Régional du Bois-de-Liesse and Parc Régional du Bois-de-Sanaguay.

Parc Nature du Bois-de-Liesse, see "Outdoors" chapter, p 77.

Turn right on Boulevard O'Brien, then take the fork in the road leading to Boulevard Sainte-Croix, the last leg of this tour.

Saint-Laurent

The residential part of Saint-Laurent is concentrated on a fifth of the municipality's territory. All the rest is monopolized by a huge industrial park, making it the second largest industrial city in Québec. Saint-Laurent developed inland after the signing of the peace treaty with the Iroquois tribes in 1701. The arrival of the Fathers, Brothers and Sisters of Sainte-Croix in 1847, encouraged by Monseigneur Ignace Bourget, the second bishop of Montréal, made it possible for the village to grow, dominated by the institutions of this religious community from Le Mans, France.

The former convent school of the Sisters of Sainte-Croix, the **Pensionnat Notre-Dame-des-Anges** (*821 Boulevard Sainte-Croix*), was founded in 1862, while the modern chapel by architect Gaston Brault was added in 1953. A wing of the building was once occupied by Collège Basile-Moreau, one of the only institutions in Québec to offer higher education in French to young women before the Quiet Revolution. In 1970, the convent became Vanier College, an anglophone CÉGEP.

The design of **Église Saint-Laurent ★** (*805 Boulevard Sainte-Croix*), built in 1835, was inspired by Montréal's Église Notre-Dame, inaugurated six years earlier. Unfortunately, both the pinnacles and the decorative battlements of the façade and aisles were removed in 1868. What was the oldest extant Gothic-Revival-style interior décor in a Catholic church, executed by François Dugal and Janvier Archambault between 1836 and 1845, was spoiled during the frenzied wave of religious revival of Vatican II in the early 1960s.

South of the church, visitors will find the **Chapelle Mariale Notre-Dame-de-l'Assomption**, the presbytery and the former grain warehouse (1810), where parishioners could pay their tithe in the form of grain or other food-

Exploring

stuffs. It now serves as the church hall. In front of it is a monument commemorating the visit of Monseigneur de Forbin-Janson, the apostle of temperance, to Saint-Laurent in 1841.

When the Fathers and Brothers of Sainte-Croix arrived in Canada in 1847, they were lodged in the house located at number 696 Boulevard Sainte-Croix. In 1852, they moved across the street to their college. The building has been modified and enlarged on several occasions. Over the course of its history, **Collège de Saint-Laurent** ★ (*625 Boulevard Sainte-Croix, Du Collège Métro station*) has stood out for its avant-garde policies. Accordingly, it trained businessmen at a time when greater importance was given to the priesthood, law, medicine and the notarial profession.

During the 1880s, a biology museum was created here, which was later set up inside an octagonal tower in 1896. That same year, the college built a 300-seat auditorium for the students' theatrical productions. In 1968, as part of the wave of changes of the Quiet Revolution, the college became a CÉGEP, and the priests who had founded the institution and directed it for over a century had only a few days to pack their bags.

The **Musée d'Art** and the **Salle Émile-Legault** ★★ (*$3; free admission on Wed 1pm to 9pm; Tue to Sun 1pm to 5pm; 615 Boulevard Sainte-Croix, Du Collège métro,* ☎747-7367). In 1928, the administration of Collège de Saint-Laurent decided to build a new chapel since the old one was overflowing with students. In the meantime, a graduate of the institution, then president of the executive committee of the City of Montréal, suggested purchasing the Presbyterian Church of St. Andrew and St. Paul (then located on Boulevard René-Lévesque where the Queen Elizabeth Hotel now stands) and reconstructing it in Saint-Laurent. The building, expropriated by the Canadian National railway company in 1926, had to be destroyed to make way for the railroad tracks of the Gare Centrale. The project was approved, despite its unusual character.

In 1930-31, the Protestant church, erected in 1866 according to a design by architect Frederick Lawford, was dismantled stone by stone and reconstructed in Saint-Laurent. Lucien Parent made a few modifications to the structure.

For example, the basement was raised to make space for a modern auditorium. During the 1930s and 1940s, this room played a large role in the evolution of the arts in Québec, thanks, notably, to the Compagnons de Saint-Laurent, a theatre company founded by Père Paul-Émile Legault in 1937, which trained a number of the province's actors. The chapel, meanwhile, was the scene of numerous concerts. In 1968, however, when the college was transformed into a CÉGEP, the building lost its purpose.

The Musée d'Art de Saint-Laurent, founded a few years earlier by Gérard Lavallée, was set up there in 1979. It displays collections of tools, traditional fabrics and Québec furniture, as well as a number of 18th and 19th-century religious *objets d'art*.

To get back on the highway, take Boulevard Sainte-Croix south to the Autoroute 40 junction. To return to the centre of Montréal, head south on Chemin Lucerne, turn left on Rue Jean-Talon and then right on Chemin de la Côte-des-Neiges.

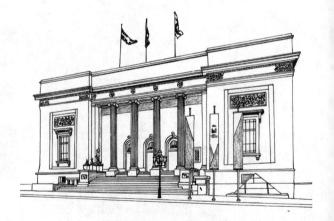

Outdoors

The island of Montréal is strewn with parks where visitors can enjoy all sorts of activities.

Year round, Montrealers take advantage of these small islands of greenery to unwind far from the urban tumult, while remaining in the heart of the city.

Parks

Parc Angrignon *(3400 Boulevard des Trinitaires) (see p 251)*, **Parc Lafontaine**, *(between Rachel and Sherbrooke, and Papineau and Lafontaine) (see p 161)* **Parc Jeanne-Mance** *(Avenue de l'Esplanade, between Avenue du Mont-Royal and rue Duluth)* and **Parc René-Lévesque** *(at the west end of the Lachine canal) (see p 234)* are all very pleasant places to relax in a peaceful atmosphere away from the bustle of the city.

All year-round, Montrealers flock to **Parc du Mont-Royal**, a huge green expanse in the middle of the city, to enjoy a wide range of athletic

activities. During summer, footpaths and mountain bike trails are open. Bird feeders have been set up along one trail for bird-watchers. During winter, the paths serve as cross-country ski trails, leading across the snowy slopes of the mountain, and Lac aux Castors becomes a big, beautiful skating rink, where people of all ages come to enjoy themselves.

Parc des Îles (☎ 872-4537) encompasses both Île Sainte-Hélène and Île Notre-Dame. In summer, Montrealers flock here on sunny days to enjoy the beach and the swimming pools. Footpaths and bicycle trails crisscross the park. During the winter, the islands make a pleasant outing, particularly during the Fête des Neiges (see p 359).

Parc Maisonneuve (4601 Rue Sherbrooke Est., ☎872-6211) occupies what was once an extensive 18-hole golf course. The vast expanse of green is now a pleasant spot for a leisurely stroll or a relaxing picnic. There is a nine-hole golf course right next to the park (see p 256).

Parc Jarry (Boulevard Saint-Laurent, Métro De Castelneau or Jarry) was laid out where the farm of the clerics of Saint-Viateur once lay; their former Institut des Sourds-Muets (Deaf-Mute Institute) is still visible south of Rue Faillon. Originally known for its stadium, which was home to the Expos baseball team from 1968 to 1976, the park is now home to the **Centre de Tennis du Parc Jarry** (see p 256). It also encloses various playing fields big and small (football, soccer, baseball). There is also a sculpture celebrating peace in the world.

The **Morgan Arboretum** extends over 245ha, making it the largest arboretum in Canada. An arboretum is an area planted with different tree species for use in experiments on cultivation methods. A network of managed walking trails criss-crosses the arboretum. Trails used for forest management penetrate 3km into the woods and are lined with signs explaining the different methods of forest management and the ecosystems found within the forest. The ecological trail, 1km long, is marked by 11 stations illustrating the relationships between organisms and their environment.

Another trail stretches over 2km and is reserved for people wanting to walk their dogs without a leash. Take note that only members have access to the Morgan Arboretum on the weekends in January and February. There are over 20km of trails in all. A visit to the Arboretum would not be complete without a stop at the **Ecomuseum** ($6; ☎457-9449), where you can see and gain an appreciation of the flora and fauna of the St. Lawrence valley (birds of prey, wolves, lynx, bears, caribou, etc.).

Since the beginning of the 1980s, **Parcs-Nature** *(2580 Boulevard St-Joseph Est, H1Y 2A2, ☎280-7272, ≠280-6787, www.cum.qc.ca/parcs-nature)* has been operating a network of well-maintained nature parks throughout the island. These parks are open year-round from early morning until nightfall and have picnic tables, hiking and cross-country skiing trails, bike paths and summer pavilions. Some parks rent skis, canoes and bikes. Here is a short description of the six major ones:

Parc-Nature du Cap Saint-Jacques *(20099 Boulevard Gouin Ouest, ☎280-6784 or 280-6781)* is located on the north shore of the island of Montréal on a point measuring 288ha that extends out into Lac des Deux-Montagnes. Its shores are lined with relaxing beaches. Trails and an interpretation centre have been organized to highlight the diversity of the plant and wildlife. An outdoor centre, open year-round, offers accommodation and various ecological activities. The park is also home to the **Ferme Écologique du Cap Saint-Jacques** *(free admission for self-guided tours, admission fee for groups and guided tours; ☎280-6743)*, where children can get close to some friendly farm animals.

Parc-Nature du Bois-de-Liesse *(9432 Boulevard Gouin Ouest, Pierrefonds, ☎280-8517 or 280-6784)* offers an exceptional variety of wildlife for visitors to admire. It is ideally located amidst hardwood forests and fields of wildflowers. Hiking trails, bike paths and cross-country ski trails help visitors discover the winged and aquatic wildlife that call this park home. Bicycles and cross-country skis can be rented. There is also a tobogganing hill.

Parc-Nature de l'Anse-à-l'Orme *(Autoroute 40 Ouest, Exit Chemin Sainte-Marie Nord, then follow chemin de l'Anse-à-l'Orme to Boulevard Gouin Ouest, ☎280-6784)* is intended exclusively for windsurfers, as it is swept by exceptional westerly winds. There is also a picnic area.

Covering 178ha, the **Parc-Nature du Bois-de-l'île-Bizard** *(187 Chemin du Cap-Saint-Jacques, Pierrefonds, ☎280-6784 or 280-8517)* occupies the western extremity of the island of Montréal and offers mostly ecological activities.

Parc-Nature de l'Île-de-la-Visitation *(2425 Boulevard Gouin Est, ☎280-6733 or 872-6555)* attracts crowds of city-dwellers yearning for nature, who come here to enjoy picnics and walks

Outdoors

along the short trails. Set along the Rivière des Prairies, the park has magnificent scenery. There are also two historic houses here, the **Maison du Pressoir** (*☎280-6783*) and the **Maison du Meunier** (*closed Oct 30 2000 to Spring 2001; ☎280-6709 or 850-4222*). During winter, people come here to go cross-country skiing and tobogganing.

With an area of 247ha, the **Parc-Nature de la Pointe-aux-Prairies** (*12980 Boulevard Gouin Est, ☎280-6767*) offers 13.5km of hiking trails, 12km of bicycle trails and 19km of cross-country skiing trails. All of these run through wooded areas and open fields bordering marshlands; observation points are set up beside the latter, which are inhabited by many species of birds.

Outdoor Activities

Hiking

Montréal is a city that is easy to explore on foot. However, those who would like to roam about magnificent green spaces that have yet to be taken over by asphalt and concrete will find that Montréal also has hundreds of kilometres of trails, which offer a delightful means of soaking up the beauty of these vast, rolling expanses of land.

To learn more about the city's hiking trails, pick up a copy of *Hiking in Quebec*, which has a chapter about hiking in and around Montréal, by Ulysses Travel Guides.

The Morgan Arboretum (*see p 248*) offers wonderful walks.

Parc-Nature du Bois-de-Liesse has 12km of walking trails, some of which are nature-interpretation trails (see p 249). This 159ha park is home to the superb **Pitfield House** (1954), as well as a magnificent Japanese footbridge with an unusual design.

Parc-Nature du Cap Saint-Jacques offers 20km of hiking trails through mature maple forests, as well as beech, hickory, birch and poplar trees, and vast expanses of varied aquatic and riverside plant life (see p 249).

Parc-Nature de l'Île-de-la-Visitation has 7.6km of ecological walking paths (see p 249). Hikers can explore hilly areas, small patches of undergrowth, the banks of the Rivière des Prairies and the very pretty island after which the park is named. There are guided hikes as well (☎280-6733).

Right next to downtown, **Parc du Mont-Royal** (☎844-4928) is an oasis of greenery ideal for hiking and walking. The park has about 15km of trails, including numerous little secondary paths, the magnificent **Olmsted Trail** and the loop at the top (see p 169).

Parc-Nature de la Pointe-aux-Prairies covers a variety of different ecosystems crisscrossed by 13.5km of hiking trails (see p 250). This 247ha park shelters the only mature woods east of Mont Royal. Stretching along Rivière des Prairies to the St. Lawrence, it also contains fields and marshes.

Parc-Nature du Bois-de-l'Ile-Bizard covers 178ha and has 10km of hiking trails. It is divided into two sections, Pointe-aux-Carrières and the woods, and boasts a pretty sandy beach and a superb 406m footbridge over a swamp (see p 249).

Parc Maisonneuve (4601 Rue Sherbrooke Est., ☎872-6555) has 5km of trails, which crisscross what was once an 18-hole golf course (see p 248).

The **Jardin Botanique** (☎872-1400) has a very large network of paths (over 5km in all), which crisscross the 30 or so outdoor gardens (see p 209).

There are nearly 10km of trails running through **Parc Lafontaine** (☎872-2644), where Montrealers come to relax beneath the big trees or near one of the two little lakes (see p 161).

Parc des Îles, which covers an area of 268ha, has about a dozen kilometres of trails. There are scores of little paths, as well as a number of more carefully cleared trails and small roads (see p 248).

Parc Angrignon (3400 Boulevard des Trinitaires, ☎872-3816), which covers 107ha, was originally supposed to contain a large zoo. It has about 10km of trails, including a number of little paths, as well as the small main road.

The path that runs alongside the **Canal de Lachine** (☎283-6054), a favourite with cyclists, can also be enjoyed by pedestrians. It links the old port to Parc René-Lévesque in Lachine, passing through the municipalities of Montréal, Ville Saint-Pierre, Ville La Salle and Lachine along the way.

Outdoors

The Canal de Sainte-Anne-de-Bellevue (☎457-5546) is located at the west end of the island of Montreal. There are 2km of trails here, including the Sainte-Anne-de-Bellevue boardwalk.

Cycling

Cyclists will be thrilled to discover nearly 400km of interesting bicycle paths that traverse the island of Montréal. A map of the paths is available at tourist information offices, or visitors can purchase the *Great Montréal Bike Path-Guide Map* in travel bookstores. Except during rush hour, bicycles can be taken on the metro.

Those interested in participating in the **Tour de l'Île** (see p 360), which takes place in June must sign up well in advance. Registration generally begins in early April and is done through the **Maison des Cyclistes** (see below)

Below are some of the more picturesque excursions. For more information visit the **Maison des Cyclistes**. A counter that is open year-round, every day of the week, offers all sorts of information for cyclists.

Maps and guides are also sold here.

Maison des Cyclistes
1251 Rue Rachel Est
Montréal H2J 2J9
☎*(514) 521-8356,*
≠*(514) 521-5711*

There is another association called **Le Monde à Bicyclette** (The World by Bike), whose horizons stretch a little farther. It publishes a small French-language newsletter of the same name, free of charge.

Le Monde à Bicyclette
911 Rue Jean-Talon Est
Bureau 270
Montréal H2W 2R3
☎*270-4884*

The area around the **Canal de Lachine** has been redesigned in an effort to highlight this communication route, so important during the 19th and early 20th centuries (see p 91). A pleasant bike path was laid out alongside the canal. Very popular with Montrealers, especially on Sundays, the path leads out to **Parc René-Lévesque**, a narrow strip of land jutting out into Lac Saint-Louis that offers splendid views of the lake and surroundings. There are benches and picnic tables in the park and plenty of seagulls to keep you company. The path leads around the park, returning beside the river and the

Lachine rapids. Many birds frequent this side of the park, and if you are lucky you might see some great herons.

To the north of the island *(accessible via the bicycle path that crosses the island north-south, or by Métro to the Henri-Bourassa station)*, a bicycle path follows **Boulevard Gouin** and Rivière des Prairies. It leads to **Parc-Nature de l'Île-de-la-Visitation**. Continuing alongside the river, the trail then leads to a very peaceful part of Montréal. It is possible to ride all the way to **Parc-Nature de la Pointe-aux-Prairies**, and from there follow the path to **Vieux-Montréal**, through the southeast part of the city (a good half-day).

Île Notre-Dame and **Île Sainte-Hélène** are accessible from Old Montreal. The path runs through an industrial area, then through the Cité du Havre before reaching the islands (cyclists can cross the river on the Pont de la Concorde). It is easy to ride from one island to the other. The islands are well maintained and are a great place to relax, stroll and admire Montréal's skyline.

Parc-Nature du Bois-de-Liesse is crisscrossed by 8km of bicycle paths through a hardwood forest (see p 249).

Bicycle Rentals

Many bicycle shops also rent out bicycles. We have suggested five. For others (and there are a lot), check with Vélo-Québec or with regional tourist offices. You could also look in the Yellow Pages under *"Bicyclettes-Location"* or under "Bicycle-Rental." Purchasing insurance is a good idea. Some places include the insurance in the rental price. Be sure to check when renting.

Bicycletterie J.R.
151 Rue Rachel Est
☎843-6989
$22 per day; a cash or credit-card deposit is required ($150 for a road bike and $300 for a mountain bike or hybrid).

La Cordée
2159 Rue Sainte-Catherine Est, Métro Papineau
☎524-1515
$18 to $35 for a full day (a $250 to $300 deposit is required).

Ça Roule Montréal
27 Rue de la Commune Est
☎866-0633
www.caroulemontreal.com
$20 for a full day, Mar to Oct

Montréal EN-LIGNE
117 Rue de la Commune Ouest
☎849-5211
$25 for half a day.

VÉLOCITÉ
99 Rue de la Commune Est
☎*876-3660*
20$ for 4 hours

Bird-Watching

info oiseaux Montréal
☎*648-2400*

Association des Groupes d'Ornithologues (*birdwatching association*)
☎*252-3190*

Bird feeders have been set up along a special trail in **Parc du Mont-Royal** to attract various species, including cardinals and sometimes pheasants (see p 169)

Once a year between the months of October and November, an owl-watching visit to the **Morgan Arboretum**, promising a unique show, is organized. Migrating birds are also commonly seen during this period (see p 248).

Countless species of birds can be observed along the shores of Lac des Deux-Montagnes in the **Parc-Nature du Bois-de-l'Île-Bizard**, particularly American coots and several kinds of ducks (see p 249.)

More than a 100 species of winged creatures can be

observed at the **Parc-Nature du Cap Saint-Jacques**, mostly wading birds, birds of prey, and other types of aquatic birds. Wood ducks, eagle owls and red-tailed hawks, among others, take advantage of these natural surroundings (see p 249).

A good number of birds of over 125 species nest in **Parc-Nature de la Pointe-aux-Prairies** (see p 250).

The Jardin Botanique (*4140 Rue Sherbrooke Est*, ☎*872-6824*) is visited throughout the winter by numerous winged creatures. If you're lucky you might spot a hawfinch, a woodpecker, a coal tit or a red-breasted nuthatch (see Tour O: Maisonneuve, p 209).

Swimming

Neighbourhood swimming pools abound in Montréal. Prices and schedules are subject to change, so it is best to check with the administrative offices before hand.

CÉGEP du Vieux-Montréal
Indoor pool
255 Rue Ontario Est
☎*872-2644*

Centre Claude-Robillard
Indoor pool
1000 Rue Émile-Journault
☎872-6905

Université de Montréal
$5
Indoor pool
2100 Boulevard Édouard-Montpetit
☎343-6150

John-Abbott College
adults $2.50
Indoor pool
21275 Bord du Lac, Sainte-Anne-de-Bellevue
☎457-2737

Parc Olympique
$3.80
Indoor pool
3200 Viau
☎252-4622

Île Sainte-Hélène
Outdoor pool
Île Sainte-Hélène
☎872-6093

The fine sandy beaches bordering Lac des Deux-Montagnes in the **Parc-Nature du Cap Saint-Jacques** are beautiful places to relax and take a dip (see p 249).

All sorts a water activities can be enjoyed at the beautiful beach of the **Parc-Nature du Bois-de-l'Île-Bizard** (see p 249).

The water at **Île Notre-Dame** beach is naturally filtered, allowing beach-goers to swim in clean, chemical-free water (see p 248).

Rafting

**Les Descentes sur
le Saint-Laurent**
beginning of May to end of Oct; C.P. 511
Succursale Champlain, LaSalle
☎767-2230
≠767-6396
Les Descentes sur le Saint-Laurent offer various types of river rides in inflatable boats down the Lachine rapids, and the office is located only minutes from downtown. Along with the river ride, there is a presentation on the history and ecology of the rapids and the bird sanctuary on Île aux Hérons. A shuttle service is offered free of charge from the Centre Infotouriste.

**Expéditions Dans les Rapides
de Lachine**
May to Oct
5 expeditions per day
47 Rue de la Commune Ouest, H2Y 2C7
☎284-9607
≠287-9401
They organizes various excursions on the Lachine rapids.

Outdoors

Sailing

Parc-Nature de l'Anse-à-l'Orme is dedicated exclusively to windsurfing (see p 249).

The École de Voile de Lachine
2105 Boulevard Saint-Joseph, Lachine
☎634-4326
The École de Voile de Lachine rents out windsurfers and small sailboats and offers private and group lessons.

Tennis

Jarry Park Tennis Centre
$28.49 per hour to reserve a court
7am to 11pm
285 Rue Faillon Ouest,
Métro De Castelneau
☎273-1234
With eight indoor and 12 outdoor courts, the Jarry Park Tennis Centre is more than well equipped to satisfy tennis-buffs at any time of the year. Matches of the Davis Cup and Omnium Du Maurier are played here each summer. The facilities are open to everyone; they include showers, changing rooms, lockers, a sports medicine clinic, a boutique, a restaurant and a bar.

Golf

Much of the 18-hole golf course that once extended north of the present site of the Olympic Stadium in **Parc Maisonneuve** was lost with the construction of the Olympic Village. A par-three nine-hole course does remain, however, just east of Rue Viau and it is open to everyone *($20; 4235 Rue Viau, ☎872-GOLF)*.

In-line Skating

The growing popularity of in-line skating is particularly evident in Montréal. Unfortunately, according to the driving code, in-line skating on the streets of Canadian cities is officially prohibited. It is nevertheless tolerated on the city's bicycle paths. In-line skating fans can also flock to the Circuit Gilles-Villeneuve on Île Notre-Dame, where they have the car-free race track all to themselves. The craze over this new activity and mode of transport has lead to the opening of several specialized boutiques which buy and sell skates and all the necessary equipment that

For nearly a century, the silver dome of the Bonsecours market was the city's symbol. Today, you will find many handicraft shops here.
- *Patrick Escudero*

Entirely decorated with painted wood and gilt, the Notre-Dame basilica is one of the most exquisite works of its kind in North America.
- *Philippe Renault*

In addition to an animated Chinatown, Montréal has a unique Chinese garden in its Jardin Botanique. - *Philippe Renault*

goes with them; some even offer lessons. Here are a few addresses of shops that rent and sell in-line skates.

Ça Roule Montréal
27 Rue de la Commune Est
☎*866-0633*
⇌*866-8909*
www.caroulemontreal.com
$20 for a full day, Mar to Oct.

Vélocité
99 Rue de la Commune Est
☎*876-3660*
⇌*876-2803*

Montréal En-Ligne
117 Rue de la Commune Est
☎*849-5211*
⇌*849-2320*

Skating

Ice-skating has not lost any of its popularity in Montréal. This outdoor sport is inexpensive and requires a minimum amount of equipment and technique.

During the winter, a number of public skating rinks are set up. Among the nicest ones are:

Lac aux Castors
Parc du Mont-Royal

Parc Lafontaine
between Sherbrooke and Rachel, and Papineau and Lafontaine

Vieux-Port
333 Rue de la Commune Ouest
☎*496-PORT*

Parc Maisonneuve
4601 Rue Sherbrooke Ouest
☎*872-5558*

Parc des Îles
on the Olympic rowing basin on Île Notre-Dame
This rink is the longest in Montréal at 1.6km.

Amphithéatre Bell
$5
every day 11:30am to 10pm
1000 Rue De La Gauchetière Ouest
☎*395-0555*
The Amphithéatre Bell located in 1000 de la Gauchetière (the tallest office building in Montréal), houses a large skating rink with a surface area of 900m^2. The rink is surrounded by food stands and rest areas, and overlooked by a mezzanine. Above the skating rink is a superb glass dome that lets the sun shine in. Ice skates can be rented at the rink for $4.

Cross-Country Skiing

Montréal is full of places that are easily accessible by bus or Métro and where you can enjoy lovely skiing excursions in settings that often make you forget all about the city. Besides that, standing on your skis at the top of Mont Royal and admiring the downtown office buildings is an unforgettable experience that few cities can rival!

Over 25km of cross-country ski trails running beside groves of various types of trees are maintained throughout the winter season at the **Morgan Arboretum**. Only members have access on weekends in January and February.

In the spring, you can visit the Arboretum's charming *cabane à sucre*, considered the oldest sugar shack still in operation on the island of Montréal.

The 26km of hiking trails in **Parc-Nature du Cap-Saint-Jacques** become beautiful cross-country skiing trails in the winter. They are open to everyone (see p 249). Ski rentals ☎280-6871.

Parc-Nature de la Pointe-aux-Prairies has 19km of cross-country ski trails set amidst beautiful and abundant forest and plantlife (see p 250). Ski rentals ☎280-6691.

The **Parc-Nature de l'Ile-de-la-Visitation** has nearly 8km of cross-country ski trails, enabling skiers to go all the way around both the park and the island after which it is named (see p 249). Ski rentals ☎280-6733.

The **Parc-Nature du Bois-de-Liesse** has 21km of cross-country trails (see p 249). Ski rentals ☎280-6729.

The **Parc-Nature du Bois-de-l'Ile-Bizard** has 20km of cross-country trails divided into three loops (see p 249). Ski rentals ☎280-8517.

There are nearly 6km of trails in the **Jardin Botanique**, offering skiers a chance to familiarize themselves with the many different kinds of trees here (see p 209).

Parc Maisonneuve has about 10km of trails, enabling skiers to go all the way around the park while admiring the tower of the Olympic Stadium (see p 248).

Skiers can explore **Parc du Mont-Royal**, the city's green lung, or perhaps more appropriately called its white lung in the winter, on over 15km of trails, all the while enjoying exceptional views of the city (see p 247).

The **Parc Angrignon** (*Boulevard Des Trinitaires*, ☎872-3066 *or* 872-6211) has two cross-country ski trails, each approximately 12km long. The park can be reached from the Angrignon Métro station.

The **Parc des Îles Sainte-Hélène** *(Île Sainte-Hélène,* ☎872-6093) is crisscrossed by three cross-country ski trails, 1.6, 1.7 and 1.9km long respectively (see p 248).

Adventure Packages

If you are travelling to Montréal and long for the outdoors, why not take part in one of the activities offered by **Globe-Trotteur Aventure Canada** *(4764 Papineau,* ☎849-8768 or 888-598-7688, ≈286-3866, *www.aventurecanada.com)*? This young company offers many winter and summer tour packages, such as horseback riding, canoeing,

camping and snowmobiling in different regions around Montréa!. These packages include transportation and equipment rental, which can be quite useful for travellers. An experienced guide will accompany you during these tours, which can last from half a day to 24 days. In summer, a fixed activity schedule will help you better plan your expeditions.

Another company offering guided tours in the great outdoors, **Excursions Seconde Nature** *(May to Oct; 5067A Marquette,* ☎528-1910) will take you canoeing or hiking around Montréal or in other regions of the province. These packages include transportation from the city as well as lodging, meals and equipment.

Ulysses's Favourite Accommodations

Classic Establishments:

Fairmont La Reine Elizabeth   p 273
Ritz-Carlton Kempinski   p 273

For history buffs:

Auberge du Vieux-Port   p 264
La Maison Pierre-du-Calvet   p 265

For the friendly reception:

Auberge de la Fontaine   p 279

For business people:

Omni Montréal   p 274
Loews Hôtel Vogue   p 274
Bonaventure Hilton   p 273
Hôtel Inter-continental   p 265
Novotel   p 272
Centre Sheraton   p 271
Marriott Château Champlain   p 272

For the swimming pool:

Hôtel de la Montagne   p 270
Bonaventure Hilton   p 273

Accommodations

This chapter suggests several different types of accommodation, listed by tour and by price, from the most economical to the most luxurious.

Travellers will discover a large variety of hotels and inns in all categories in Montréal. Rates vary greatly from one season to the next. They are much higher during the summer, but usually lower on the weekends than during the week. Finally, remember that the weeks of the Grand Prix Player's du Canada Formula 1 in June and of the Jazz Festival, beginning of July, are the busiest of the year; we recommend making reservations well in advance if you plan to be in Montréal during these events. In the off-season, it is often possible to obtain better rates than the ones quoted in this guide. Several establishments also offer discounts to automobile club members and corporate employees. Make sure to

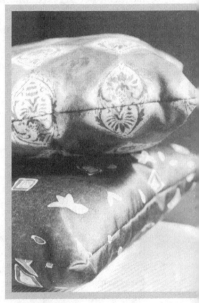

ask about these discounts, as they are easy to obtain.

Depending on your mode of travel, the choice is extensive. Most places are very comfortable and offer a number of extra services. Prices vary according to the type of accommodation, but remember to add the 7% GST (Federal Goods and Services Tax) and the 7.5% QST (Québec Services Tax). These taxes are refundable for non-residents (see p 66). A new tax has been put in place for all accommodations in Montréal. The revenue from this *"Taxe spécifique sur l'hébergement"* is used to maintain the area's tourist infrastructure. The tax is a flat rate of $2 per night (no matter how much the rooms cost), and is non-refundable. When making reservations a credit card is indispensable, as a deposit for the first night is often required in advance.

Unless otherwise indicated, the prices in the guide are for one room for two people in the high season, excluding taxes.

In Montréal's Infotouriste information centre, there is a service which makes hotel reservations free of charge:

Hospitalité Canada
1001 Rue du Square-Dorchester
Montréal H3B 4V4
☎393-9049 or 800-665-1528

Types of Accommodation

Bed and Breakfasts

The Fédération des Agricotours produces an annual guide entitled *Inns and Bed & Breakfasts in Québec*, which lists the names and telephone numbers of all of its members who provide rooms for travellers. The rooms offered have been selected according to the federation's standards of quality. They are also fairly economical. The book is available in bookstores.

Gîte Montréal
$45-$65 bkfst incl.
3458 Avenue Laval, H2X 3C8
☎289-9749 or 800-267-5180
≈287-7386
bbdtown@cam.org
Gîte Montréal is an association of nearly 100 bed and breakfasts (*gîtes*), mostly Victorian houses in the Quartier Latin. In order to make sure that all rooms offered are comfortable, the organization inspects each one. Reservations required. About 30 bed and breakfasts are also registered with the:

Relais Montréal Hospitalité
$50 to $95 bkfst incl.
3977 Avenue Laval, H2W 2H9
☎287-9635 or 800-363-9635
≈287-1007

All have been carefully inspected, and the rooms are clean and comfortable. The establishments are located throughout Montréal, though many are on Rue Laval.

A few choice bed and breakfasts are listed throughout this chapter.

University Residences

Due to certain restrictions, this can be a complicated alternative. Residences are only available during the summer (*mid-May to mid-August*), and making reservations in advance is strongly recommended; this can usually be done by paying the first night with a credit card.

This type of accommodation, however, is less costly than the "traditional" alternatives, making the effort to reserve early worthwhile. Visitors with valid student cards can expect to pay approximately $20 plus tax, while non-students can expect to pay around $33. Bedding is included in the price, and there is usually a cafeteria in the building (*meals are not included in the price*).

Camping

Camping is not possible on the island of Montréal itself, but there are many campgrounds on the south shore and a number of areas for trailer-camping in Laval. The Centre Infotouriste (☎873-2015) can offer guidance to anyone opting for this type of accommodation.

Travellers With Disabilities

Many Montréal hotels are equipped to accommodate disabled visitors, but we have decided only to mention this when the establishment in question is completely wheelchair-accessible. That does not mean that other hotels might not be able to meet the needs of disabled travellers. We recommend contacting Kéroul (see p 73). It publishes a tour guide entitled *Accessible Québec*, which provides a list of wheelchair-accessible hotels all over the province, grouped by tourist region. The guide costs $10 plus tax and postage.

Accommodations

Vieux-Montréal

For the location of the following hotels, please refer to p 81.

Auberge Alternative
$18 per person in the dormitory, $50 for two people in the rooms
◻
358 Rue Saint-Pierre, H2Y 2M1
☎*282-8069*
www.auberge-alternative.qc.ca
Located in Old Montreal, the Auberge Alternative opened in April 1996. Run by a young couple, it is a renovated building dating from 1875. The 34 beds in the rooms and dormitories are rudimentary but comfortable, and the bathrooms are very clean. Brightly coloured walls, lots of space and a large common room and kitchen with stone walls and old wooden floors complete the facilities. A blanket costs $2 per night, and guests have laundry machines at their disposal. Twenty-four hour access.

Gîte du Vieux Montréal
$65 bkfst incl.
K, sb
209 Rue St-Paul O. Suite 500, H2V 2A1
☎*288-1109*
The Gîte du Vieux Montréal occupies the upper floors of a building on Rue Saint-Paul and has nine rooms that are simply decorated, but warm and comfortable

with brick walls or ceiling beams. There is a charming and pleasant reading room on the third floor and a kitchen on the fourth floor where you can have breakfast or prepare your own food. Each floor has two impeccably clean bathrooms with showers. There is also a pleasant rooftop terrace open in warm weather. The hostess will greet you warmly and make you feel right at home.

Passants du Sans-Soucy
$140 bkfst incl.
≡, tv, pb, P, ⊛
171 Rue Saint-Paul Ouest, Métro Place d'Armes
☎*842-2634*
⇆*842-2912*
Even though Old Montreal is visited by thousands of tourists, it has little to offer in the way of accommodation. There is, however, the Passants du Sans-Soucy, an extremely pleasant inn set in the heart of the old city, whose charming rooms are furnished with antiques. Built in 1723, the building was renovated eight years ago. Reservations required.

Auberge du Vieux-Port
$190-$265 bkfst incl.
≡, tv, ℝ, ⊛, P
97 Rue de la Commune E., H2Y 1J1
☎*876-0081 or 888-660-7678*
⇆*876-8923*
www.aubergeduvieuxport.com
The Auberge du Vieux-Port stands right in front of the old Port. Opened in 1996,

this place is a real gem. It occupies an historic building dating from 1882, whose stone walls have been left exposed in the chic, attractively decorated lobby. All the rooms have been decoratedas to pay homage to the past, with outstanding results. Each has a telephone with voice mail. There is a French restaurant in the basement, where you can see a segment of the fortifications of the old city. No smoking in the rooms. Valet service $12.50.

⚓ Maison Pierre du Calvet
$195 bkfst incl.
ℑ, ≡, ℜ
405 Rue Bonsecours
Métro Champ-de-Mars
☎ 282-1725
≈ 282-0456
www.pierreducalvet.ca

This is one of Montréal's oldest homes, discretely tucked away at the intersection of Bonsecours and Saint-Paul streets. It has recently been entirely renovated, as have many other older houses in the neighbourhood. The rooms, each different from the next and each with its own fireplace, exude an irresistible charm, with lovely antique wood panelling accentuated by oriental rugs, stained glass and beautiful antiques; the ancestral yet refined setting gives visitors the illusion of travelling back in time. Moreover, the bathrooms

are immaculately clean and tiled in Italian marble.

A pretty indoor courtyard and day room allow guests to escape from the swarming crowds. Breakfast is served in a lovely Victorian dining room. The service is attentive and meticulous. In short, this inn, located in the heart of the city's historic district, is a real gem that will make your stay absolutely unforgettable.

⚓ Hôtel Inter-Continental
$199-$340
357 rooms
≈, ☉, ℜ, △ for men only, ≡, &
360 Rue Saint-Antoine Ouest,
H2Y 3X4
☎ 987-9900 or 800-327-0200
≈ 847-8525
www.montreal.interconti.com

Except for one of its wings, this hotel, located on the edge of Old Montreal, is a fairly new building (1991) that is linked to the Centre de Commerce Mondial (World Trade Centre) and several shops. The Palais des Congrès (convention centre) is right nearby.The hotel has an original appearance, due to its turret with multiple windows, where the living rooms of the suites are located. The rooms are tastefully decorated with simple furniture. Each one is equipped with a spacious bathroom, among other nice touches.

Guests are courteously and attentively welcomed. Business people will enjoy all the necessary services, such as computer hook-ups, fax machines and photocopiers.

Delta Centre-Ville
$195
710 rooms, 25 suites
≈, ℜ, ⌂, ☉
777 Rue University
☎*879-1370 or 800-333-3333*
www.deltamontreal.com
The Delta is visible when arriving in Montréal via the Autoroute Bonaventure (Highway 10). The rooms are attractive, but small. On the top floor, there is a revolving panoramic restaurant, from which diners enjoy a spectacular view of the city. The hotel is linked to Montréal's underground city.

Downtown and the Golden Square Mile

For the location of the following hotels, please refer to p 267.

Auberge de Jeunesse
$24 to $30 for non-members
1030 Rue Mackay, H3G 2H1
☎*843-3317*
⇄*934-3251*
www.ajmontreal.qc.ca
This youth hostel, located a stone's throw from the downtown area, is one of the least expensive places to sleep in Montréal. Two-

hundred and fifty beds (*sb*) plus a dozen rooms (*pb*). Breakfast is served in the café, which opened in 1996. Guests have the use of a washer and dryer, as well as a kitchen, a luggage check-room and a pool table. Finally, a variety of reasonably priced activities and excursions are organized by the hostel; these can include anything from trips to a sugar-shack or guided tours of the city. This is a non-smoking hostel.

Concordia University Student Residences
$30 per person
sb
7141 Rue Sherbrooke Ouest, H4B 1R6
☎*848-4757*
⇄*848-4780*
Located 15min by bus from the Vendôme métro station, these residences have 144 beds. Open from mid-May to mid-August. Weekly and monthly rentals available.

McGill University residence halls
$40 per person
sb, K
mid-May to mid-Aug
550 Rue Sherbrooke Ouest, West Tower, Suite 490, H3A 1B9
McGill Métro
☎*398-6367*
⇄*398-6770*
www.residences.mcgill.ca/ summer.html
There are 1,100 rooms, each containing one or two

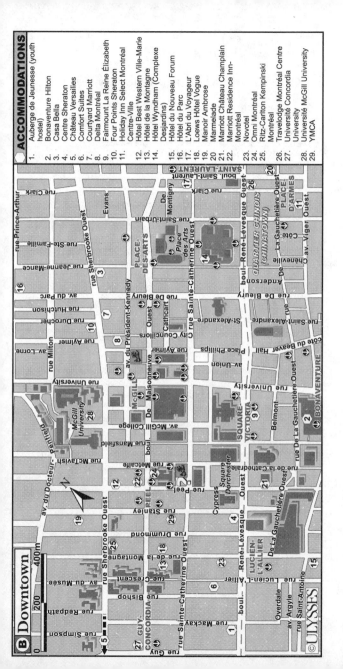

ACCOMMODATIONS

1. Auberge de Jeunesse (youth hostel)
2. Bonaventure Hilton
3. Casa Bella
4. Centre Sheraton
5. Château Versailles
6. Comfort Suites
7. Courtyard Marriott
8. Delta Montréal
9. Fairmont La Reine Élizabeth
10. Four Points Sheraton
11. Holiday Inn Select Montréal Centre-Ville
12. Hôtel Best Western Ville-Marie
13. Hôtel de la Montagne
14. Hôtel Wyndham (Complexe Desjardins)
15. Hôtel du Nouveau Forum
16. Hôtel du Parc
17. L'Abri du Voyageur
18. Loews Hôtel Vogue
19. Manoir Ambrose
20. Marmelade
21. Marriott Château Champlain
22. Marriott Residence Inn-Montréal
23. Novotel
24. Omni Montréal
25. Ritz-Carlton Kempinski Montréal
26. Travelodge Montréal Centre
27. Université Concordia University
28. Université McGill University
29. YMCA

B Downtown

0 200 400m

boul. Saint-Laurent

rue Clark
rue Prince-Arthur
Evans
De Montigny
rue Ste-Famille
rue Saint-Urbain
PLACE-DES-ARTS
Place des Arts
rue Sherbrooke Ouest
rue Jeanne-Mance
av. du Parc
rue Hutchison
rue Durocher
rue Aylmer
av. du Président-Kennedy
rue De Bleury
Cathcart
rue Sainte-Catherine Ouest
QUARTIER CHINOIS (CHINATOWN)
PLACE D'ARMES
Côté
Chenville
av.-Viger Ouest
Anderson
rue De Bleury
St-Alexandre
rue Saint-Alexandre
rue City Councillors
rue Aylmer
Place Phillips
rue Beaver Hall
Côté du Beaver Hall
BONAVENTURE
rue De La Gauchetière Ouest
rue Milton
av.-Lorne
rue University
McGILL
De Maisonneuve
av. McGill College
rue Mansfield
rue Metcalfe
rue Peel
Square Dorchester
Cypress
SQUARE VICTORIA
av.-Union
rue University
Belmont
McGill University
rue McTavish - Penfield
av. du Docteur-Penfield
rue Stanley
rue Drummond
rue de la Montagne
rue Crescent
rue Bishop
rue MacKay
rue Guy
GUY-CONCORDIA
rue Sherbrooke Ouest
av.-du-Musée
rue Redpath
rue Simpson
rue Sainte-Catherine Ouest
René-Lévesque
boul. René-Lévesque Ouest
LUCIEN-L'ALLIER
boul. Lucien-L'Allier
rue de-Cathcart Ouest
rue De La Gauchetière Ouest
Overdale
av. Argyle
rue Saint-Antoine

N

© ULYSSES

beds, in the six residence halls of McGill University. The rooms are small, but each has a large chest of drawers and a desk, and some offer a magnificent view of Mont Royal. Most are equipped with a miniature refrigerator, and all the windows open. There are two kitchenettes and two large bathrooms on each floor. For an additional charge, guests can use the university pool, gym and tennis courts.

YMCA
$40 per person
sb, ≈, ℜ, ☉, △, ☉
1450 Rue Stanley, H3A 2W6, Peel Métro
☎*849-8393*
≈*849-7821*

The downtown YMCA, the oldest in North America, was built in 1851 and has 331 basic but comfortable rooms with one or two beds each. Men, women and children are welcome. Most of the rooms are equipped with telephones and televisions; some have sinks or bathrooms. The cafeteria on the ground floor serves morning and evening meals (*$3-$6*). Guests enjoy free access to the YMCA's swimming pool, fully equipped gym and locker room. The Young Men's Christian Association (YMCA) was founded in London in 1844 to help young English workers.

L'Abri du Voyageur
$50
sb, ⊗, tv
9 Rue Sainte-Catherine Ouest
H2X 1Z5
☎*849-2922*
≈*499-0151*

This is the perfect hotel for young travellers. It is located on bustling Rue Sainte-Catherine, almost at the corner of Boulevard Saint-Laurent, right in the heart of Montréal's nightlife! There are only four bathrooms in the two-storey hotel, but all of the rooms have sinks. The rooms are simple and clean, and the welcome is friendly.

Manoir Ambrose
$65
22 rooms
sb or pb, tv, ☉, P
3422 Rue Stanley, H3A 1R8
☎*288-6922*
≈*288-5757*
www.manoirambrose.com

Manoir Ambrose is set in two big, beautiful Victorian houses made of hewn stone, side by side on a peaceful street. It has several little rooms, scattered all over the house. The outdated décor will amuse some guests, but the rooms are well-kept and the service is friendly. Laundry service for a fee (*$5*).

Hôtel du Nouveau Forum
$70 bkfst incl.
pb or sb, ≡, tv
1320 Rue Saint-Antoine Ouest,
H3C 1C2
☎989-0300
⇌931-3090
bdforum@globale.net

Located right next to the Molson Centre and not far from Old Montreal, the Hôtel du Nouveau Forum opened in June 1996, and has about 40 small, modest but decent rooms. It occupies an historic house, whose stone façade has been restored, and whose interior was completely redone. Fortunately, the friendly staff add a little warmth to the sterile atmosphere of the hallways and the dining room, where you can enjoy a very hearty breakfast. There is a public telephone on each floor, and guests can communicate with the reception desk by intercom. The rooms do not have bathtubs. Parking $7. Patio.

Casa Bella
$75 bkfst incl.
20 rooms
P, pb or sb, ≡, tv
264 Rue Sherbrooke Ouest, H2X 1X9
☎849-2777
⇌849-3650
www.hotelcasabella.com

Located near Place des Arts on Rue Sherbrooke beside an abandoned lot, the Casa Bella is a charming hotel set in a 100-year-old house. The rooms are pretty and reflect the care that has gone into decorating them. There are free laundry service and free parking. The friendly welcome makes guests feel quickly at ease. This hotel offers good value for the money.

Marmelade
$75 bkfst incl.
sb
1074 Rue Saint-Dominique, H2X 2W2
☎876-3960
⇌876-3926

The Marmelade near Chinatown, is a bed and breakfast with five rooms in a beautifully decorated Victorian townhouse. Guests are enthusiastically welcomed by the family dog.

Travelodge Montréal Centre
$109 bkfst incl.
242 rooms
ℜ, tv, ≡, ⅓
50 Boulevard René-Lévesque Ouest
H2Z 1A2
☎874-9090
☎800-365-6535 from Canada only
⇌874-0907

The Travelodge has comfortable rooms with modern though conventional decor. Its location and rates make this place a good deal.

Comfort Suites
$120 bkfst incl.
96 rooms
tv, ☎, ≡
1214 Rue Crescent, H3G 2A9
☎878-2711
⇌878-0030
comfmon1@letcom.ca

Located in a quiet section of Rue Crescent, this hotel is just a few steps from a busy area full of restaurants and boutiques. Each of the rooms is simply yet comfortably decorated and has a small balcony. Parking $12.

Château Versailles
$129-$209
ℜ, ⊛, △, ⊘, ≡
1659 Rue Sherbrooke Ouest, H3H 1E3
☎*933-3611 or 800-361-7199*
⇌*933-6867*
www.versailleshotels.com

This hotel is composed of both the Château Versailles, dating back to the Edwardian era, and the more recent Tour Versailles, on opposite sides of the street, for a total of 176 rooms. All things considered, however, the rooms are disappointing. The furnishings in most of them are too modern, entirely inappropriate for a "château." Furthermore, the insufficient amount of furniture leaves the rooms looking bare. The larger rooms are nevertheless adorned with very pretty mouldings and some rooms have whirlpool baths. Parking $14.50/day.

Courtyard Marriott
$169
180 rooms
≈, △, ⊘, ℜ, ≡, ⊛
410 Sherbrooke Ouest, H3A 1B3
☎*844-8855 or 800-449-6654*
⇌*844-0912*

Located at the edge of the downtown area, the Courtyard Marriott has 180 rooms, but no more than nine per floor, which gives this hotel the feeling of a small inn. Renovations were recently finished. The attractively decorated rooms offer views of either the mountain or the river. Some rooms are equipped with kitchenettes. The hotel also has conference rooms and a fitness centre.

Marriott - Residence Inn Montréal
$149 bkfst incl.
⊘, ≈, P, ≡, K
2045 Rue Peel, H3A 1T6, Peel Métro
☎*982-6064 or 800-999-9494*
⇌*844-8361*

This was completely renovated before re-opening at the beginning of 1997. It has 189 suites, each with a kitchenette complete with stove, microwave oven, refrigerator and dishwasher. These may be rented for a single night or for months at a time. Twenty-four-hour laundry service, a large outdoor terrace and a rooftop swimming pool are all available to guests. Parking $12.50/day.

Hôtel de la Montagne
$165 bkfst incl. on weekends
⊛, ℜ, ≈, ≡, ⚹
1430 Rue de la Montagne, H3G 1Z5
☎*288-5656 or 800-361-6262*
⇌*288-9658*
www.hoteldelamontagne.com

Besides its 134 rooms spread over 19 floors, the Hôtel de la Montagne also has a pool, an excellent restaurant and a bar, as well as friendly and courteous staff. The pool is outside, on the roof, and is only open in the summer. Parking $12/day.

Hôtel du Parc
$169
459 rooms
ℜ, ≈, ☺, ≡
3625 Avenue du Parc, H2X 3P8
☎288-6666 or 800-363-0735
≠288-2469
www.duparc.com
Both tourists and business people stay in these fully equipped rooms. The hotel has a new exercise centre, and guests have access to the pool at the Université de Montréal's athletic centre. There is a coffee maker in each room.

Centre Sheraton
$139-$219
≈, ☺, △, ℜ
1201 Boulevard René-Lévesque H3B 2L7
☎878-2000 or 800-627-7102
≠878-3958
Standing over 30 stories high, this giant has 824 rooms. A number of little extras (coffee makers, hair dryers, irons and ironing boards, non-smoking floors) attest to the meticulous service provided here. Some rooms are equipped for businesspeople with fax machines, modem hook-

ups, voice mailboxes, etc. The rooms are pretty without being too luxurious. Take some time to admire the beautiful lobby, decorated with picture windows and tropical plants. Parking $14/day.

Holiday Inn Select Montréal Centre-Ville
from $169
ℜ, ≈, ⊛, ☺, △, ✪
99 Av. Viger Ouest, H2Z 1E9
☎878-9888 or 888-879-9888
≠878-6341
Built in 1992, the Holiday Inn provides all the comforts of a high-class hotel. Located in the heart of Chinatown, it is easy to spot with its pagoda-style roof. The interior is also decorated in an oriental style. The 235 rooms are spacious and impeccable, and the service is courteous and attentive. Its restaurant, Chez Chine (see p 299), is very good.

Hôtel Best Western Ville-Marie
$169
163 rooms on 19 floors
ℝ, ☺, ℜ
3407 Rue Peel, H3A 1W7
☎288-4141 or 800-361-7791
≠288-2433
www.botelvillemarie.com
Right in the heart of downtown, this hotel offers plainly decorated but comfortable rooms, each with a mini-bar and hair dryer. The exercise room was recently completely revamped. The lobby, however, with its

assortment of little shops, is not very inviting. Sixty-five suites are suited specifically to the needs of business people. Parking $15/day.

Marriott Château Champlain
$219
611 rooms
☼, ⊘, △, ℜ, ⊛
1 Place du Canada, H3B 4C9
☎*878-9000 or 800-200-5909*
⇄*878-6761*
www.marriott.com
The Marriott Château Champlain is a very original-looking white building with semicircular windows, much resembling a cheesegrater. This renowned hotel has small but elegant rooms, and is close to Old Montreal. Guests nevertheless enjoy a slew of services. Direct access to the underground city (see p 361).

Hôtel Wyndham
$199 bkfst incl.
572 rooms
≈, △, ⊘, ℜ, bar, ⅙
4 Complexe Desjardins, H5B 1E5
☎*285-1450 or 800-361-8234*
⇄*285-1243*
The Wyndham is part of Complexe Desjardins. Consequently, on the main floor, there is a series of shops, movie theatres and restaurants. Located a step away from Place des Arts and the Musée d'Art Contemporain, the hotel has a prime downtown location right next to all the action of the Jazz Festival

along Rue Ste-Catherine. The large, comfortable rooms live up to the expectations for a hotel of this category. Parking $19/day.

Delta Montréal
$219
435 rooms
≈, ⊘, ℜ
450 Rue Sherbrooke Ouest, H3A 2T4
☎*286-1986 or 800-463-1133*
⇄*284-4342*
www.deltahotels.com
The Delta has two entrances, one on Rue Sherbrooke and the other on Avenue du Président-Kennedy. Recent renovations included a new décor, new carpeting, new beds, new paint, etc. It has pleasant rooms, which are attractively decorated with dark wooden furniture. Each room has a voice mailbox.

Four Points Sheraton
$199
194 rooms
⊘, ℜ, ⅙
475 Rue Sherbrooke Ouest, H3A 2L9
☎*842-3961 or 800-325-3535*
⇄*842-0945*
www.fourpoints.com
Offers simple but very comfortable rooms. Parking $15/day.

Novotel
$190
⊘, △, ℜ
1180 Rue de la Montagne, H3G 1Z1
☎*861-6000 or 800-668-6835*
⇄*861-0992*
Novotel is a French hotel chain. The pleasant rooms

in its downtown Montréal hotel are equipped with numerous extras, including a large desk and outlets for computers. Special packages are available for guests travelling with children. The emphasis seems to be on security, as there is no access to the upper floors after 10pm without your room key. No-smoking rooms.

Fairmont La Reine Elizabeth
$219
1022 rooms
☉, ≈, ℜ, ☉, △, ⅙
900 Boulevard René-Lévesque Ouest
H3B 4A5
☎*861-3511 or 800-441-1414*
⇌*954-2256*
www.fairmont.com
The Queen Elizabeth is one Montréal hotel that has set itself apart over the years. Its lobby, decorated with fine wood panelling, is magnificent. Visitors will find a number of shops on the main floor. Two of the hotel's floors, designated "Entrée Or," boast luxurious suites and are like a hotel within the hotel. Numerous renovations were completed in 1996. The hotel has the advantage of being located in the heart of downtown, and its underground corridors, furthermore, provide easy access to the train station and the underground city.

Ritz-Carlton Kempinski Montréal
$310
☉, ℜ
1228 Rue Sherbrooke Ouest, H3G 1H6
☎*842-4212 or 800-363-0366*
⇌*842-4907*
www.ritzcarlton.com
The Ritz Carlton was inaugurated in 1912. Renovated over the years in order to continue offering its clientele exceptional comfort, it has managed to preserve its original elegance. The rooms are decorated with superb antique furniture. The marble bathrooms, moreover, add to the charm of this outstanding establishment.

Bonaventure Hilton
$235
367 rooms
≈, ☉, ℜ, ≡, K, ⅙
1 Place Bonaventure, H5A 1E4
☎*878-2332 or 800-267-2575*
⇌*878-3881*
Guests of the Montréal Bonaventure Hilton, located on the boundary between downtown and Old Montreal, enjoy a number of little extras that make this hotel a perfect place to relax. The rooms are decorated in a simple manner, without a hint of extravagance, and the bathrooms are small. The hotel has a heated outdoor swimming pool, where guests can swim all year-round, as well as a lovely garden and access to the underground city (see p 361).

Omni Montréal
$249
300 rooms
☼, ℝ, ≈, ⊘, △, ℜ
1050 Rue Sherbrooke Ouest, H3A 2R6
☎*284-1110 or 800-THE-OMNI*
≈845-3025
www.omnihotels.com
One of the most renowned hotels in Montréal, the Omni Montréal offers comfortable, spacious accommodations. Nevertheless, the standard rooms are decorated in an unoriginal fashion and the bathrooms are small for such a prestigious establishment. The lobby, however, is large and elegant, and the hotel is famous for its restaurants. The outdoor pool is heated and open year-round.

Loews Hôtel Vogue
$339
126 rooms, 16 suites
⊛, ⊘, ℜ
1425 Rue de la Montagne, H3G 1Z3
☎*285-5555 or 800-465-6654*
≈849-8903
www.loewshotels.com
At first sight, the Loews Hôtel Vogue, a glass and concrete building with no ornamentation, looks bare. The lobby, embellished with warm-coloured woodwork, gives a more accurate idea of the luxury and elegance of this establishment. The large rooms, with their elegant furniture, reveal the comfort of this hotel. Each room has a whirlpool bath and two suites have saunas.

Shaughnessy Village

For the location of the following hotels, please refer to p 143.

Riche Bourg
$105
221 suites
≈, K, ⊘, △
2170 Avenue Lincoln, H3H 2N5, Métro Atwater
☎*935-9224 or 800-678-6233*
≈935-5049
www.iber.com
This hotel has spacious rooms, each one equipped with a kitchenette. The hotel is somewhat modest-looking, but its location, on a quiet street on the western edge of the downtown area, makes it an excellent place to stay. Parking $10/day.

Manoir Le Moyne All Suite Hotel
$135
266 suites
⊛, ⊘, △, ℜ, K
2100 Boulevard de Maisonneuve Ouest, H3H 1K6
☎*931-8861 or 800-361-7191*
≈931-7726
Manoir LeMoyne is located on a busy street near downtown. A cold atmosphere pervades the lobby, which is decorated with mirrors and gilded chandeliers. The rooms, equipped with a kitchenette, are nevertheless decent.

Hôtel du Fort
$135
K, ☉
1390 Rue du Fort, H3H 2R7
Atwater or Guy-Concordia Métro
☎*938-8333 or 800-565-6333*
⇌*938-2078*

The Hôtel du Fort offers comfort, security and personalized service. All 127 rooms have kitchenettes equipped with microwave ovens, refrigerators, coffee makers, as well as hair dryers and mini-bars. The deluxe rooms and suites also have modem hook-ups. All the windows in the rooms open.

Quartier Latin

For the location of the following hotels, please refer to p 155.

Auberge de l'Hôtel de Paris
$19 per person (dormitory)
sb, K
901 Rue Sherbrooke Est, H2L 1L3,
Sherbrooke Métro
☎*522-6861 or 800-567-7217*
⇌*522-1387*
www.hotel-montreal.com

In 1995, the Hôtel de Paris (see p 276) opened the Auberge de l'Hôtel de Paris, a house across the street with 10 big rooms and a 40-bed hostel divided into dormitories for four, eight or 14 people. A blanket, sheets and a pillow are provided. The common kitchen is small but has everything you'll need to prepare meals, and there's an outdoor seating area with an attractive view. The place has four showers and toilets, and there's a laundromat right nearby. No curfew.

Manoir Sherbrooke
$58-$109 bkfst incl.
35 rooms
sb or pb, ⊛
157 Rue Sherbrooke Est, H2X 1C7
☎*285-0895 or 800-203-5485*
⇌*284-1126*

The Manoir Sherbrooke is an old stone house. The rooms are modest, while the staff are polite and efficient. ***Parking $5/day.***

Pierre et Dominique
$65 bkfst incl.
sb
271 Square Saint-Louis, H2X 1A3
☎*286-0307*
www.pierdom.qc.ca

Square Saint-Louis (see p 153) is a pleasant park surrounded by beautiful Victorian houses. This private home stands out for its extremely comfortable and tastefully decorated rooms. Non-smoking.

UQÀM Residences
$36 per person in the dormitory (2 to 8 people/room)
$51 for a room with pb
mid-May to mid-Aug
sb
303 Boulevard René-Lévesque E.,
H2X 3Y3, métro Berri-UQÀM
☎*987-6669*
⇌*987-0344*

The residences at UQÀM have comfortable studio-style rooms that can accommodate between two and eight people. All the rooms have a living room, a kitchenette and a complete bathroom. Clean and pleasant, the residences are conveniently located near Old Montreal and downtown.

Auberge des Glycines
$85 bkfst incl.
P, ≡, tv
819 Boulevard de Maisonneuve Est, H2L 1Y7, Berri-UQAM Métro
☎ *526-5511 or 800-361-6896*
⇌ *523-0143*
www.aubergedesglycines.com
The Auberge des Glycines is located in the heart of the Quartier Latin, right near the Université du Québec à Montréal and the Voyageur bus station. This little hotel has 30 comfortable rooms whose décor is outdated and slightly sombre, but nonetheless gives an idea of how beautiful the house was originally. Breakfast is served in the dining room.

Le Chasseur Bed and Breakfast
$89 bkfst incl.
P
1567 Rue St-André, H2L 3T5
☎ *521-2238 or 800-451-2238*
www.lechasseur.com
Not too far from the gay village, this B&B offers tastefully decorated rooms and service with a smile. In the summer, the terrace provides a welcome escape from the bustle of the city and a chance to relax.

Hôtel de Paris
$80
≡, tv
901 Rue Sherbrooke Est, H2L 1L3
Sherbrooke Métro
☎ *522-6861 or 800-567-7217*
⇌ *522-1387*
www.hotel-montreal.com
A lovely house built in 1870, the Hôtel de Paris has 29 rooms. Recently renovated, the house has retained its distinctive character, thanks to the magnificent woodwork in the entryway. The rooms are comfortable. Free outdoor parking; indoors $8/day.

Jardin d'Antoine
$110 bkfst incl.
≡, ⊛
2024 Rue Saint-Denis, H2X 3K7
☎ *843-4506*
⇌ *281-1491*
The three-storey Jardin d'Antoine has about 25 carefully decorated rooms, some with exposed brick walls and hardwood floors. Many comfortable, well-equipped suites are available, as well. The back garden is rather small, but the balconies are adorned with flower baskets and the effect is very attractive.

Days Inn Montréal Centre-Ville
$119
tv, ≡, ℜ
215 Boulevard René-Lévesque Est,
H2X 1N7
☎*393-3388 or 800-668-3872*
⇄*395-9999*
www.daysinn.com

The Days Inn has 72 rooms with one queen-sized or two double beds and 35 mini-suites, each with a king-sized bed, a sofa-bed and a stove. The entire place was renovated in 1997. The rooms are small, and the location, on the edge of the Quartier Latin, is a little dreary. On the other hand, the hotel is relatively close to Old Montreal, where it is often very difficult to find a place to stay. Furthermore, some of the rooms offer lovely views of the city. A number of floors are reserved for non-smokers. The hotel has a French and a Chinese restaurant. Outdoor parking $7.50/day; indoors $10/day.

Lord Berri
$109
154 rooms
≡, ☎, *tv*, ℜ, ♿
1199 Rue Berri, H2L 4C6
☎*845-9236 or 888-363-0363*
⇄*849-9855*

The façade of the Lord Berri conceals a slightly plain decor, a simple lobby and large rooms. Renovations in 1995 added new carpeting, a newly decorated lobby and new colours. Parking $12/day.

Hôtel de l'Institut
$145 bkfst incl.
≡, *P*, ℜ, ♿
3535 Rue Saint-Denis, H2X 3P1,
Sherbrooke Métro
☎*282-5120 or 800-361-5111*
⇄*873-9893*
www.ithq.qc.ca

The Hôtel de l'Institut occupies the upper floors of the Institut de Tourisme et d'Hôtellerie du Québec (ITHQ), a renowned post-secondary college devoted to the hospitality industries. The hotel is run by students enrolled in practical classes at the ITHQ or who are undergoing on-the-job training there. Their work is closely monitored by the professors charged with grooming them for the finest hotels in the world; the result is very comfortable rooms and quality service, including full concierge service. The hotel is located right on Rue Saint-Denis, with its scores of restaurant terraces, shops and cafés, and right near the pedestrian mall on Rue Prince-Arthur, which is packed with good restaurants. Parking $11.50/day.

Crowne Plaza Métro Centre
$159
ℜ, ☉, ≈, ❀, ≡, △, *tv*
505 Rue Sherbrooke Est, H2L 1K2
Sherbrooke Métro
☎*842-8581 or 800-2CROWNE*
⇄*842-8910*
www.crowneplaza-montreal.com

The 320 spacious rooms of the Crowne Plaza Métro

Centre have a modern decor and are all equipped with coffee makers, colour televisions and two telephones. The hotel is located right near the Quartier Latin, steps away from numerous restaurants, bars and shops. It offers a large number of services for businesspeople, including voice mail and a secretarial service. Parking $16.50/day.

Hôtel des Gouverneurs Place Dupuis
$140
352 rooms
≈, *tv*, △, ℜ, *P*, ≡, ☺, ♿
1415 Rue Saint-Hubert, H2L 2Y9
Berri-UQAM Métro
☎ *842-4881 or 800-463-2820*
⇄ *842-1584*

The Hôtel des Gouverneurs Place Dupuis has an elegant lobby and 346 rooms with all the modern comforts. It is located right in the heart of the Quartier Latin, a stone's throw away from the outdoor cafés on Rue Saint-Denis, and is linked to both Place Dupuis, with its many shops, and the Université du Québec à Montréal. Parking lot *($12)* and direct underground access (by way of the Métro) to points all over the city.

Plateau Mont-Royal

For the location of the following hotels, please refer to p 163.

Vacances Canada 4 Saisons
$14.50 per person
550 beds in summer, 220 in winter; sb
Collège Français, 5155 de Gaspé,
H2T 2A1, Laurier Métro
☎ *270-4459*
⇄ *278-7508*

Unlike those in the university residences, the rooms at Vacances Canada 4 Saisons are available year-round. In addition, studios with private baths and kitchenettes may be rented for $300 a month (all included).

Gîte du Parc Lafontaine
$45-$65 bkfst incl.
Jun to late Aug
sb, K
1250 Rue Sherbrooke Est, H2L 1M1
☎ *522-3910 or 877-350-4483*
www.hostelmontreal.com

This is a sort of youth hostel that is also a cosy inn for young travellers. Guests have access to furnished rooms, a kitchen, a living room and a small laundry room. The hostel is ideally located next to Parc Lafontaine and close to Rue Saint-Denis. The owners of this 100-year-old rooming house have built a terrace with a magnificent view of Montréal's central library.

🏕 B & B Bienvenue
$75 sb bkfst incl.
$85 pb bkfst incl.
tv, P
3950 Avenue Laval, H2W 2J2
☎ *844-5897 or 800-227-5897*
⇄ *844-5894*
www.bienvenuebb.com

The B & B Bienvenue is just two steps south of Rue Duluth. Located on a quiet street, this establishment offers eight small but charmingly decorated rooms with large beds. For the last 10 years, the inn has been operating in a pretty, well-maintained house with a peaceful, friendly atmosphere. A very generous breakfast is served in the pleasant dining room.

Gîte Sympathique
$55 bkfst incl.
sb
3728 Rue Saint-Hubert, H2L 4A2
☎843-9740

The Gîte Sympathique has three charming rooms, a large sitting room and a dining room where breakfast is served. The calm and well-kept nature of this bed and breakfast makes it a good address to remember.

Auberge de la Fontaine
$160 bkfst incl.
21 rooms
tv, P, ⊛, Ᏽ
1301 Rue Rachel Est, H2J 2K1
☎597-0166
⇰597-0496
www.aubergedelafontaine.com

The Auberge de la Fontaine lies opposite lovely Parc Lafontaine. Designed with a great deal of care, it has a lot of style. A feeling of calm and relaxation emanates from the rooms, all of which are attractively decorated. Guests are offered a complimentary snack during the day. All these features have made this a popular place – so much so that it is best to make reservations.

Outremont

For the location of the following hotels, please refer to p 179.

Collège Jean-de-Brébeuf
$28 single room or
$44 double room
sb
5625 rue Decelles,
H3T 1W4
Côte-des-Neiges Métro
☎342-1320, ext.358
⇰342-0130

Located in a pretty area where it is otherwise quite difficult to find accommodations, The renowned university rents out 130 single and double rooms containing a total of 190 beds from mid-May to mid-August.

Hôtel Terrasse Royale
$89
K
5225 Côte-des-Neiges, H3T 1Y1,
Côte-des-Neiges Métro
☎739-6391 or 800-567-0804
⇰342-2512

The Hôtel Terrasse Royale is located steps away from the Université de Montréal, in an area full of shops and restaurants. Its 48 rooms are basic and nondescript, but spacious, clean and modern. Parking $7/day.

Université de Montréal
$23 person
mid-May to end of August
sb, ♿
2350 Boulevard Édouard-Montpetit,
H3T 1J4, Édouard-Montpetit Métro
☎ *343-6531*
↪ *343-2353*
residence@sea.umontreal.ca
There are 1,120 single
rooms, each equipped with
a sink, in the student residences of the Université de
Montréal These rooms may
also be rented by the week
or by the month.

The Village

For the location of the following hotels, please refer
to p 203.

Le Saint André
$76.50 bkfst incl.
pb, ≡, tv, P
1285 Rue St-André, H2L 3T1
☎ *849-7070 or 800-265-7071*
↪ *849-8167*
A charming little hotel, Saint
André is conveniently lo-
cated in the Quartier Latin,
near the bars and restau-
rants on Rue Saint-Denis,
Old Montreal and down-
town. In addition to the
warm greeting, there are 62
comfortable, well-decorated
rooms, all of which have air
conditioning, private bathrooms and colour televi-
sions. A continental breakfast is served in the morning. After checking out of
this hotel, you'll want to
stay here again!

Gîte Turquoise
$80 bkfst incl.
5 rooms
sb
1576 Rue Alexandre-de-Sève, H2L 2V7
☎ *523-9943*
Located in the heart of the
gay village, this B&B was
recently completely reno-
vated. This Victorian building (though only the interior is indicative of the period) was enlarged last year,
when the owner trans-
formed an office into a
large four-person suite. The
terrace is also perfect for
having breakfast outdoors
on warm mornings.

Douillette et Chocolat
$72 bkfst incl.
1631 Rue Plessis, H2L 2X6
☎ *523-0162*
↪ *523-6795*
douillette.choco@arobas.net
Douillette et Chocolat
opened in 1996 and is run
by a young Frenchman
(and his two cats), who has
tastefully renovated an old
Victorian house and con-
verted it into a small inn.
The three bright, spacious
guest rooms have a particularly charming style about
them. Two of the rooms –
one with a queen-size bed
and another with two twin
beds – share a large bathroom. The third has a king-
size bed and a private bath.
The generous breakfasts are
served in a lovely dining
room.

Maisonneuve

For the location of the following hotels, please refer to p 210.

Gîte Olympique
$95 bkfst incl.
pb, tv, P
P2752 Boulevard Pie-IX, H1V 2E9
☎ *254-5423 or 888-254-5423*
≈ *254-4753*
www.dsuper.net/~olympic
Although it is located on the very busy Boulevard Pie-IX, Gîte Olympique offers five quiet rooms and a great view of the Olympic Stadium. There are two sitting rooms where guests can relax or meet other travellers. In summer, breakfast is served on a large terrasse out back.

Near the Airports

Mirabel Airport

Château de l'Aéroport-Mirabel
$115
≈, △, ◎, ℜ, ≡, ᓬ
12555 Rue Commerce, A4, J7N 1E3
☎ *476-1611 or 800-361-0924*
≈ *476-0873*
www.chateaumirabel.com
Directly accessible from Mirabel Airport, this hotel was built to accommodate travellers with early morning flights. Unlike its downtown cousins, this hotel's high season is from November to May. The rooms are very functional and comfortable.

Dorval Airport

Set in a rather unappealing industrial park, the following two hotels are of interest primarily for their proximity to Dorval Airport. Most of the guests are catching early morning flights.

Best Western Hôtel International
$99 bkfst incl.
◎, △, ≈, P, ℜ
13000 Chemin Côte-de-Liesse, H9P 1B8
☎ *631-4811 or 800-361-2254*
≈ *631-7305*
The rooms in the Best Western Hôtel International are pleasant and affordable. The hotel also offers an interesting service: after spending the night here, guests can park their car here for up to three weeks, free of charge. Free airport shuttle service available.

Montréal Aéroport Hilton
$159 bkfst incl.
482 rooms
bar, ◎, ≈, △, ℜ, P
12505 Côte-de-Liesse, H9P 1B7
☎ *631-2411 or 800-268-9275*
≈ *631-0192*
This Hilton has pleasant rooms but the main advantage is its proximity to the airport.

Ulysses's Favourite Restaurants

Montréal's finest dining:

Nuances	p 332
Toqué	p 322
Chez la Mère Michel	p 303
Les Caprices de Nicolas	p 302

For history buffs:

Le Festin des Gouverneurs	p 332
Gibby's	p 292
Le Vieux Saint-Gabriel	p 292
La Maison Pierre-du-Calvet	p 292
La Maison George Stephen	p 300

For the view:

| Club Lounge 737 | p 298 |
| Nuances | p 332 |

For the terrace:

La Moulerie	p 328
Chez Julien	p 300
Santropol	p 307

For the location:

| Hélène-de-Champlain | p 332 |

For Québec cuisine:

| Nuances | p 332 |
| Le Festin des Gouverneurs | p 332 |

For the romantic ambiance:

| Aux Baisers Volés | p 315 |

To see and be seen:

| L'Express | p 321 |
| Continental | p 319 |

Restaurants

M ontréal's reputation as far as food is concerned is enviable, to say the least; it is also well-deserved.

The culinary traditions of countries around the world are represented here by restaurants in all different sizes and price ranges. The best thing is that no matter what your budget, a memorable meal is always possible! The following listings are grouped according to location, in the same order as the tours in the "Exploring" chapter (see p 77), to make it easier for visitors to find those hidden treasures while they are exploring a particular area. An index by type of cuisine can be found in this chapter; each restaurant is also in the main index at the end of the guide.

$	=	less than \$10
$$	=	\$10 to \$20
$$$	=	\$20 to \$30
$$$$	=	more than \$30

Unless otherwise indicated, the prices in this guide are for a meal for one person, including taxes, but excluding drinks and tip.

Though you may have learned differently in your French classes, Quebecers refer to breakfast as *déjeuner*, lunch as *dîner*, and dinner as *souper*. Many restaurants offer a "daily special" (called *spécial du jour*), a complete meal for one price, which is usually less expensive than ordering individual items from the menu. Served only at lunch, the price usually includes a choice of appetizers and main dishes, plus coffee and dessert. In the evenings, a *table d'hôte* (same formula, but slightly more expensive) is also an attractive possibility.

"Bring Your Own Wine"

At certain restaurants, you can bring your own wine. This interesting phenomenon is a result of the fact that in order to sell alcohol, a restaurant must have an alcohol permit, which is very expensive. Restaurants that want to offer their clientele a less expensive menu opt for a special type of permit that allows their patrons to bring their own wine.

In most cases, a sign in the restaurant window indicates whether alcohol can be purchased on the premises or if you have to bring your own (*Apportez votre vin*).

Besides the alcohol permit, there is also a bar permit. Restaurants with only the alcohol permit can sell alcohol, beer and wine, but only accompanied by a meal. Restaurants with both permits can sell customers just a drink, even if they do not order a meal.

Cafés

Most Québécois take their coffee and espresso very seriously, as is evident by the popularity of the many charming little cafés with their friendly, relaxed atmospheres. Many have been around for years, and constitute an integral part of everyday life in the city's various communities. The gleaming coffee machines take centre stage, of course, but these little shops also serve excellent soups, salads or *croque-monsieurs* and, of course, croissants and desserts! On weekends, breakfast is usually served until early afternoon. For the addresses of some of these places, check the index within this chapter.

Index by
Type of Cuisine

Asian

Soy 318
Tampopo 315
Zyng 310

Belgian

Bières & Compagnie. . 316
Frite Alors 313, 326
L'Actuel 298
Le Petit Moulinsart . . . 290

Brazilian

Lélé da Cuca 314

Breton

Crêperie Bretonne
Ty-Breiz 319

Brunch and Breakfast

Ambiance 335
Aux Entretiens 311
Beauty's 304
Café Cherrier 319
Café Souvenir 326
Chez Claudette 313
Eggspectations . . 294, 326
Fruit Folie 313
Jardin du Ritz 297
La Croissanterie 326
Le Pélerin 310
Petit Alep 329
Toasteur 313

Cafés and Tearooms

Ambiance 335
Aux Entretiens 311
Bilboquet 326
Brioche Lyonnaise . . . 309
Brûlerie
Saint-Denis . . 293, 309, 312
Café Méliès 308
Café Rico 312
Café Romolo 326
Café El Dorado 312

Café Souvenir 326
Café Starbuck's 294
Calories 302
Fruit Folie 313
Kilo 304, 333
La Croissanterie 326
Le Paltoquet 327
Le Porté Disparu 313
Les Gâteries 309
Toi Moi et Café 327

Cajun

La Louisiane 325
Wienstein 'n' Gavino's
Pasta Bar Factory Co. . 299

Chicken and Ribs

Bar-B-Barn 302
Champs 306
Coco Rico 304
Laurier B.B.Q. 327

Chilean

La Chilenita 312

Chinese

Chez Chine 299
La Perle Szechuan . . . 337
Le Caveau Szechwan . 336
Le Wok de Szechuan . 331
Mr. Ma 300
Piment Rouge 301
Soy 318
Tampopo 315
Zen 301

Czech

Café Toman 294

Ethiopian

Le Nil Bleu 317

Fondue

Fondue Mentale 317
La Fonderie 330

Restaurants

French

Aux Deux Gauloises . .	324
Aux Baisers Volés	315
Bonaparte	292
Café du TNM	296
Café Cherrier	319
Café Ciné-Lumière . . .	306
Café de Paris	302
Chez Gauthier	298
Chez Lévesque	328
Chez Queux	292
Chez Georges	299
Chez la Mère Berteau .	333
Chez la Mère Michel . .	303
Continental	319
Côté Soleil	316
Festin des Gouverneurs	332
Gavroche	330
Grand Comptoir	296
Hélène de Champlain .	332
Jardin du Ritz	297
Julien	300
L'Académie	315
L'Entre-Miche	334
L'Estaminet	331
L'Express	321
La Prunelle	321
La Petite Marche	318
La Gargote	290
La Colombe	322
Laloux	320
Le Grain de Sel	334
Le 917	315
Le Bistro Gourmet . . .	303
Le Lutétia	300
Le Caveau	297
Le Flambard	320
Le Bistingo	327
Le Maistre	325
Le Paris	297
Le Petit Extra	333
Maison Pierre du Calvet	292
Nuances	332
Parchemin	298
Paris-Beurre	328
Persil Fou	317
Pistou	320
Planète	334
Sans Menu	335
Vieux Saint-Gabriel . . .	292

Fusion (blend of cuisines)

Anubis	311
Chu Chai	316
Claremont	324
Continental	319
Le Gourmand	336
Les Caprices de Nicolas	302
Marlowe	337
Mess Hall	325
Monkland Tavern	325
Planète	334
Toqué	322
Un Monde Sauté	318

German

Chez Better	288, 322

Greek

La Psarotaverna du	
Symposium	322
Le Jardin de Panos . . .	317
Mezze	307
Milos	328
Ouzeri	317

Hambugers

Cafétéria	306
Cage aux Sports	289
Champs	306
Frite Alors	313, 326
Green Spot	335
L'Anecdote	311
L'Avenue	319
La Paryse	335
Lesage J.B.	331
Moe's Deli & Bar   297, 334
Saloon	333
Shed Café	308

Health Food/Vegetarian

Aux Entretiens	311
Bio Train	288
Café America	335

Chu Chai 316
La Boulange
du Commensal 314
Le Gourmand 336
Le Pélerin 310
Le Commensal 294, 310, 324
Santropol 307

Hungarian
Café Roccoco 303

Ice Cream
Bilboquet 326
Crémerie Saint-Vincent 289

Indian
Ambala 314
Palais de l'Inde 307
Pique Assiette 302
Tandoori Village 306

Italian
Al Dente 324
Buona Notte 308
Café Italia 329
Casa Cacciatore 330
Cucina 306
Da Vinci 298
Euro Deli 304
Il Cicerone 331
Il Mulino 330
Il Mondo 331
Il Fornetto 336
L'Académie 315
L'Amalfitana . . . . ?
La Transition 325
La Sila 311
La Molisana 321
La Tarantella 330
La Spaghettata 328
La Fontanina 336
Le Piémontais 310
Le Latini 301
Mangia 294
Misto 320
Modigliani 321
Pasta Casareccia 323

Pasta Express 331
Pavarotti 290
Piazza Romana 337
Piccolo Diavolo 333
Poco Piu 320
Restorante-Trattoria
Carissima 321
Vieux Saint-Gabriel . . 292
Wienstein 'n' Gavino's
Pasta Bar Factory Co. . 299

Iranian
Byblos 312

Japanese
Azuma 308
Ginger 308
Jardin Sakura 297
Kaizen 303
Katsura 300
Mikado 311
Soto 299

Medieval
Auberge du
Dragon Rouge 329

Mediterranean
Côté Soleil 316
Modavie 290
Titanic 289

Mexican
Cactus 316
El Zaziummm 318
La Casa de Mateo . . . 289

Peruvian
La Selva 315

Pizza
Piazzetta 314
Pizzafiore 323
Pizzaïolle 327
Pizzédélic 307, 314, 324, 327
Pizzeria Napoletana . . 330

Polish
Stash's Café Bazar 290

Russian
Troïka 301

Seafood
Chez Delmo 290
Desjardins Sea Food . . 301
La Marée 293
La Moulerie 328
Maestro S.V.P. 309
Milos 328

Smoked Meat
Ben's Delicatessen . . . 293
Schwartz's Montréal
Hebrew Delicatessen . 304
Lester's 327
Moe's Deli & Bar   297, 334

Spanish
Casa Tapas 319
Don Miguel 307

Steak
Gibby's 292
L'Entrecôte Saint-Jean . 296
La Cabane 306
Magnan 336
Moishe's 309
Steak Frites 289

Swiss
La Raclette 321

Syrian
Petit Alep 329

Thai
Bato Thaï 333
Chao Phraya 307
Chu Chai 316
Le Goût de la Thaïlande 314
Pattaya 303
Thaï Grill 309
Thaï Express 304

Traditionnal Québécois
Binerie Mont-Royal . . . 312
Chez Claudette 313
Le P'tit Plateau 321

Tunisian
Le Kerkennah 331

Vietnamese
L'Escale à Saïgon 328

Vieux-Montréal

For the location of the following restaurants, please refer to p 81.

In summer, you'll have no trouble finding an ice-cream bar in Old Montreal – they're everywhere, especially around Rue de la Commune. Some even have terrasses.

Bio Train
$
Mon-Fri 5:30am to 5pm
410 Rue Saint-Jacques
☎842-9184
For health food, Bio Train is a favourite self-serve restaurant. At lunchtime, things move very quickly.

Chez Better
$
160 Notre-Dame Est
☎861-2617
The menu at Chez Better, a chain of restaurants, consists mainly of German sausages, French fries and sauerkraut. While the layout varies from one location to the next, the atmosphere is

always relaxed. This particular branch is inside an old house from the French Regime.

Crémerie Saint-Vincent
$
153 Rue St-Paul Est, at the corner of Rue St-Vincent

Only open in the summertime, the Crémerie Saint-Vincent is one of the rare spots in Montréal to enjoy excellent soft maple-syrup ice cream! The menu lists a wide variety of flavours.

Steak Frites
$
12 Rue Saint-Paul Est
☎*842-0972*

Business people crowd into Steak Frites at noon, where they feel perfectly comfortable despite the relatively small and noisy dining room. They come here for well-prepared steaks and French fries drenched in a variety of sauces.

Titanic
$
Mon-Fri 7am to 4pm
445 Rue Saint-Pierre
☎*849-0894*

Titanic is a very busy lunch spot located in a semi-basement. It offers a multitude of baguette sandwiches and Mediterranean-style salads, *feta* and other cheeses, smoked fish, *pâtés*, marinated vegetables... Delicious!

Cage aux Sports
$-$$
395 Rue Lemoyne
☎*288-1115*

The Cage aux Sports features an interesting decor strewn with an eclectic mix of bric-a-brac, some very imposing, like a plane! Spare ribs, chicken – very North American. Generous portions, inexpensive beer and friendly, efficient service. Major sporting events are shown on a giant screen.

Café Électronique
$$
1425 Blvd. René Levesque
☎*871-0307*

At the Café Électronique, you can enjoy all the wonders of technology while drinking a coffee or eating a snack. Of course, you have to pay for the time you spend on the computer. It costs around $5.50 to surf the Net for a half hour, or $4 to view a CD-Rom. Courses are offered on how to use the Internet and the CD-Roms.

La Casa de Mateo
$$
440 Rue St-Francois-Xavier
☎*844-7448*

Decorated with hammocks, cacti and Latin-American knick-knacks, La Casa de Mateo is a delightful Mexican restaurant. The food is typical but delicious nonetheless.

Chez Delmo
$$
Sat and Sun dinner only
211 Rue Notre-Dame Ouest
☎*849-4061*
The specialty of Chez
Delmo is fish and seafood.
The outstanding *bouilla-
baisse* is not to be missed.
The first room, with its two
long oyster bars, is the most
pleasant one.

Pavarotti
$$
408 Rue St-Francois-Xavier
☎*844-9656*
The Pavarotti belongs to Mr.
Mateo, who is also the
owner of the Mexican res-
taurant next door, La Casa
de Mateo (see above). This
establishment was named in
honour of the famous
Italian tenor. Traditional
Italian dishes figure on the
menu, to be savoured while
listening to selections from
Luciano Pavarotti's reper-
toire.

Stash's Café Bazar
$$
200 Rue St-Paul Ouest
☎*845-6611*
Stash's Café Bazar was
forced to move a street
corner away from its origi-
nal location in the shadow
of Notre-Dame Basilica after
a terrible fire. With a simple
decor, this charming little
Polish restaurant is the ideal
choice for delicious cheese-
stuffed pirogies, sausage
and sauerkraut. The vodka
is also excellent.

La Gargote
$$-$$$
351 Place D'Youville
☎*844-1428*
La Gargote is not what you
would expect from its
name, which means "a
cheap place to eat" in
French. Rather, it is a small
French restaurant that at-
tracts a regular clientele and
curious newcomers. The
decor is inviting, the cuisine
tasty, and the prices afford-
able.

Modavie
$$-$$$
1 Rue Saint-Paul Ouest
☎*287-9582*
You will recognize
Modavie, at the corner of
by its awning-covered win-
dows. Its beautiful decor,
both modern and antique,
creates a soothing atmo-
sphere. Mediterranean-style
Meat, pasta and fish dishes
are served.

Le Petit Moulinsart
$$-$$$
Sat and Sun dinner only
139 Rue St-Paul Ouest
☎*843-7432*
Le Petit Moulinsart is a
friendly Belgian bistro that
could easily pass for a small
museum devoted to the
characters of the *Tintin*
comic books by Georges
Rémi, a.k.a. Hergé. All sorts
of objects and posters re-
lated to the *Tintin* books

Cafés

In the last few years, "fast-food" cafés have been springing up everywhere in the United States and Canada, and Montréal has its fair share of them. Though these establishments are not nearly as charming as other local cafés, they offer a unique concept: some have take-out counters, some are Internet cafés, and all serve many different kinds of coffee, juices, ice-teas – even muffins and humongous deserts! The clientele is young and lively, and the décor is modern. You'll surely come across several of them while in Montréal, and some are open 24 hours. Take note that some cafés prohibit smoking. Here are a few locations:

Downtown

Café République	93 Rue Ste-Catherine Ouest
Presse Café	1374 Rue Ste-Catherine Ouest
	1263 Rue Ste-Catherine Est
Second Cup	1465 Rue Crescent
	262 Rue Ste-Catherine Ouest
	625 Rue Ste-Catherine Ouest
	1122 Rue Ste-Catherine Ouest
	1351 Rue Ste-Catherine Est

Around l'Hôtel-Dieu and Boulevard Saint-Laurent

Café République	3563 Boulevard St-Laurent
Second Cup	3695 Boulevard St-Laurent

Quartier Latin

Presse Café	1750 Rue St-Denis
Second Cup	1551 Rue St-Denis
Tribune Café	1567 Rue St-Denis

Plateau Mont-Royal

Espresso Mondo	4497 Rue St-Denis
Second Cup	4287 Rue St-Denis

Outremont

Café République	1051 Avenue Bernard
Second Cup	1275 Avenue Bernard
	3498 Avenue du Parc
	377 Avenue Laurier

Restaurants

decorate the walls, menus and tables of the establishment. Service is friendly, but slow. Besides the traditional dish of mussels and French fries, don't miss Colonel Sponz's sorbet and Capitaine Haddock's salad.

Bonaparte
$$$
443 Rue Saint-François-Xavier
☎*844-4368*
The varied menu of the French restaurant Bonaparte always includes some delicious surprises. The tables on the mezzanine offer a lovely view of Old Montreal.

Gibby's
$$$-$$$$
Dinner only
298 Place d'Youville
☎*282-1837*
Gibby's is located in a lovely, renovated old stable and its menu offers generous servings of beef or veal steaks served at antique wooden tables set around a glowing fire and surrounded by low brick and stone walls. In the summer months, patrons can eat comfortably outdoors in a large inner courtyard. All in all, an extraordinary decor, which is reflected in the rather high prices. Vegetarians beware.

Vieux Saint-Gabriel
$$$
Tue-Sat
426 Rue Saint-Gabriel
☎*878-3561*
The attraction of the Vieux Saint-Gabriel lies above all in its enchanting decor reminiscent of the first years of New France; the restaurant is set in an old house that served as an inn in 1754 (see p 92). The French and Italian selections from the somewhat predictable menu are adequate.

Chez Queux
$$$-$$$$
158 Rue Saint-Paul
☎*866-5194*
Ideally located in Old Montreal and overlooking Place Jacques-Cartier, Chez Queux serves classic French cuisine in the finest tradition. Refined service in an elegant setting guarantee a positive culinary experience.

Maison Pierre du Calvet
$$$$
Closed Sun and Mon
401 Rue Bonsecours
☎*282-1725*
The old jewel among Montréal restaurants, the Filles du Roi restaurant, has given way to a magnificent inn (see p 265) boasting one of the best dining rooms in the city. The establishment is particularly recommended for its delicious and imaginative French cuisine. Its menu,

based on game, poultry, fish and beef, changes every two weeks. The elegant surroundings, antiques, ornamental plants and discrete service further add to the pleasure of an evening meal here.

La Marée
$$$$
Sat and Sun dinner only
404 Place Jacques-Cartier
☎**861-9794**
Located on bustling Place Jacques-Cartier, La Marée has managed to maintain an excellent reputation over the years. The chef prepares fish and seafood to perfection. The dining room is spacious, so everyone is comfortable.

Downtown and the Golden Square Mile

For the location of the downtown restaurants, please refer to p 295.

If you're in the mood for a no-frills, quick bite to eat, keep the **many food stands** set up around the skating rink at the Amphithéâtre Bell in mind (*$*; *1000 Rue de la Gauchetière*). There is, among others, a Lebanese-food stand with good vegetarian food.

Ben's Delicatessen
$
900 Boulevard de Maisonneuve Ouest
☎**844-1000**
At the beginning of the century, a Lithuanian immigrant modified a recipe from his native country to suit the needs of workers, and thus introduced the smoked meat sandwich to Montréal, and in the process created Ben's Delicatessen. Over the years, the restaurant has become a Montréal institution, attracting a motley crowd from 7am to 4am. This is where people come when the bars close! The worn, Formica tables and photographs yellowed by time give the restaurant an austere appearance.

Brûlerie Saint-Denis
$
2100 Rue Stanley, in the Maison Alcan
☎**985-9159**
The Brûlerie Saint-Denis serves the same delicious coffee blends, simple meals and sinful desserts as the other two Brûleries. Though the coffee is not roasted on the premises, it does come fresh from the roasters on Saint-Denis (see also p 312).

Restaurants

Café Starbuck's
$
1171 Rue Ste-Catherine, Chapters bookstore, 2nd floor
☎843-4418

The Café Starbuck's, set in a corner of the downtown branch of Chapters has a lot going for it: there is of course the excellent coffee, and then there are the books! What better way to pass the time before the shops open or after they close than to find a good book or magazine (the magazine section is right next to the café) and savour a good cup of coffee? A selection of cakes, muffins and pre-made sandwiches are also available.

Café Toman
$
1421 Rue Mackay
☎844-1605

Café Toman is popular among students from the neighbouring universities. The menu features delicious Czech specialties, including cakes, soups and salads. Unfortunately, the restaurant closes early (*5pm*) and is closed on Sundays and Monday.

Eggspectations
$
1313 Boul. de Maisonneuve Ouest
☎842-3447

Eggspectations is an excellent spot for brunch. In addition to eggs, they have good waffles, crêpes and French toast, all topped with fruit and whipped cream and served in an eclectic decor and lively ambiance.

Van Houtte
$
Places des Arts

The Van Houtte at Place des Arts has a modern décor that blends well into its surroundings. It is a convenient place for a quick coffee, croissant or muffin before watching a show.

Le Commensal
$-$$
1204 McGill College
☎871-1480

Le Commensal is a buffet-style restaurant. The food, all vegetarian, is sold by weight. Le Commensal is open every day until 11pm. The inviting, modern decor and big windows looking out on the downtown streets make it a pleasant place to be (see p 310).

Mangia
$-$$
1101 Boulevard De Maisonneuve Ouest
☎848-7001

Mangia is a counter-shop and one of the few places in downtown Montréal where you'll find good, reasonably-priced meals to have in an attractive atmosphere or to go. Salads and pasta dishes, each more enticing than the last, are sold by weight, and sandwiches and more elaborate

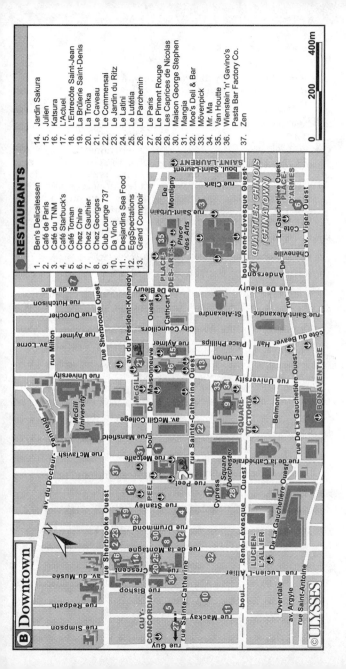

B Downtown

♦ RESTAURANTS

1. Ben's Delicatessen
2. Café de Paris
3. Café du TNM
4. Café Starbuck's
5. Café Toman
6. Chez Chine
7. Chez Gauthier
8. Chez Georges
9. Club Lounge 737
10. Da Vinci
11. Desjardins Sea Food
12. EggSpectations
13. Grand Comptoir

14. Jardin Sakura
15. Julien
16. Katsura
17. L'Actuel
18. L'Entrecôte Saint-Jean
19. La Brûlerie Saint-Denis
20. La Troika
21. Le Caveau
22. Le Commensal
23. Le Jardin du Ritz
24. Le Latini
25. Le Lutétia
26. Le Parchemin

27. Le Paris
28. Le Piment Rouge
29. Les Caprices de Nicolas
30. Maison George Stephen
31. Mangia
32. Moe's Deli & Bar
33. Mövenpick
34. Mr. Ma
35. Van Houtte
36. Wienstein 'n' Gavino's Pasta Bar Factory Co.
37. Zen

0   200   400m

© ULYSSES

meals like steak with bell peppers are also on the menu.

Mövenpick
$-$$
Place Ville-Marie

☎861-8181

Where do we start? Precisely the question you will ask the moment you enter Marché Mövenpick, a unique market-cafeteria-restaurant concept! But don't worry, the host/ess will reserve a table for you and explain the way things work. Once you understand, you will have many choices: there are stalls for many different kinds of food from around the world made with the freshest ingredients and in every price range. Just order something and get your passport stamped. The food is excellent for fast food and includes Asian soups, Indonesian *bami goreng* and custom-made pizzas; there are also fish, seafood, steak, soup, salad, desert and juice counters, a pub, a bar – even a French bistro serving the finest wines and steak tartare! The place can sometimes be a zoo and seats hard to find. The Swiss chain is currently expanding in North America.

Grand Comptoir
$-$$
Closed Sun and Mon evenings during the winter
1225 Place Phillips

☎393-3295

At lunchtime, the place to be is the Grand Comptoir, not for its decor, which is rather nondescript, but for the bistro menu at unbeatable prices.

L'Entrecôte Saint-Jean
$$
2022 Rue Peel

☎281-6492

The menu of L'Entrecôte Saint-Jean is very simple, and therefore inexpensive; it consists of rib-steak (*entrecôte*) prepared in a variety of ways.

☕ Café du TNM
$$
84 Rue Ste-Catherine Ouest

☎866-8668

The Café du TNM is a lovely addition to this somewhat run-down section of town. Sip a glass of wine or a coffee, or sample a dessert in the deconstructionist decor of the ground-floor dining room, or have a good meal upstairs in the atmosphere of a Parisian brasserie. The menu matches the decor: classic French bistro cuisine. Impeccable service, beautiful presentation and excellent food.

Jardin du Ritz
$$$
1228 Rue Sherbrooke Ouest
☎842-4212
The Jardin du Ritz is the perfect escape from the summer heat and the incessant downtown bustle. Classic French cuisine is featured on the menu, with tea served on a patio surrounded by flowers and greenery, next to the pond with its splashing ducks. Only open during the summer months, the Jardin is an extension of the hotel's other restaurant, Le Café de Paris (see p 302).

Jardin Sakura
$$
2114 Rue de la Montagne
☎288-9122
With a name like Jardin Sakura, diners might expect a more refined decor (*"Sakura"* is the beautiful flower on Japanese cherry trees). The menu offers decent Japanese cuisine, though the sushi is not always a success. The service is very attentive.

Moe's Deli & Bar
$$
1050 Rue de la Montagne
☎931-6637
Moe's Deli & Bar opened its doors on Rue de la Montagne just months before the new Molson Centre was inaugurated across the street and has since cashed in on the increasing popularity of the area. Smoked

meat, burgers and the like have made the reputation of this chain of restaurants. This particular one could even be called a "sports deli and bar." A festive atmosphere and young crowd set the tone (see also p 334).

Le Paris
$$
1812 Rue Sainte-Catherine Ouest
☎937-4898
If you like *boudin, foie de veau* or mackerel in white wine, Le Paris is the place to enjoy such French delicacies in a friendly and relaxed ambiance. As for the décor, well, it hasn't changed in years, besides a fresh coat of paint (the same colour of course) when and where required! The wine list is, however, quite respectable and up to date.

Le Caveau
$$-$$$
Sat and Sun dinner only
2063 Rue Victoria
☎844-1624
Le Caveau occupies a charming white house nestled between the downtown skyscrapers. The restaurant serves skilfully prepared, fine French cuisine.

Restaurants

L'Actuel
$$-$$$
Closed Sun
1194 Rue Peel
☎*866-1537*

L'Actuel, the most typically Belgian restaurant in Montréal, is always full for lunch and dinner. It has two large, fairly noisy and very lively dining rooms, where affable waiters hurry about among the clientele of business people. The restaurant serves mussels, of course, as well as a number of other specialties.

Da Vinci
$$-$$$
Closed Sun
1180 Rue Bishop
☎*874-2091*

Da Vinci is an established family restaurant that caters to an upscale crowd (a crowd that incidentally often includes a few hockey stars, past and present). The menu is classic Italian and though you won't find too many surprises on it, everything served is well-prepared with the finest of ingredients. The extensive wine list contains just the bottle to complement any meal. Rich, subdued lighting and beautifully set tables create a refined and inviting atmosphere.

Club Lounge 737
$$-$$$
Sat and Sun dinner only
1 Place Ville-Marie
☎*397-0737*

Located on the 42nd floor of Place Ville-Marie, the Club Lounge 737 boasts large windows allowing for an unobstructed view of Montréal and its surroundings. As for the menu, it offers various French-inspired dishes. Be warned that the prices here are as high as the restaurant is.

Chez Gauthier
$$-$$$
Closed Sun
3487 Avenue du Parc
☎*845-2992*

Chez Gauthier is a traditional bistro in the purest sense of the word. It's dining room is fitted with wainscotting. The food is excellent, including the desserts from the Pâtisserie Belge next door. Pleasant terrace.

Parchemin
$$-$$$
Closed Sun
1333 Rue University
☎*844-1619*

In the former rectory of the Christ Church Cathedral, the Parchemin is distinguished by its stylish decor and velvety atmosphere. Guests enjoy carefully prepared French cuisine, suitable for the finest of palates. For those with a well-lined purse, the six-course *ménu dégustation* is a real feast (*$43 per person*), while the four-course *table d'hôte*, with its wide range of choices, is also a treat.

Chez Georges
$$-$$$
1415 Rue de la Montagne
☎288-6181

Formerly located on Sherbrooke Street, Chez George recently moved to Rue de la Montagne, where it continues to serve its famous traditional and delicious French cuisine. Attentive and efficient service. This is a prized meeting place for the area's business people.

Wienstein 'n' Gavino's Pasta Bar Factory Co.
$$-$$$
1434 Rue Crescent
☎288-2231

Wienstein 'n' Gavino's Pasta Bar Factory Co. occupies a modern building that visitors and locals alike might swear had been part of the streetscape for years. The look is just as effective inside, where exposed brick walls, bright yet weathered Mediterranean floor tiles and ventilation ducts in the rafters give the place the feel of an old warehouse. Everything is on display here, in particular the feverish activity in the kitchen on the upper level. Each table receives a loaf of fresh French bread along with olive oil for dipping and

roasted garlic for spreading. Among the menu offerings, the pizzas are decent, if a little bland, but the pasta dishes are delicious, especially the Gorgonzola with dill. Red snapper in foil is another delectable treat.

Soto
$$$
500 Rue McGill
☎864-5115

In a large space within one of McGill Street's beautiful late-19th-century buildings, Soto serves top-notch Japanese fare befittingly presented as a feast for the eyes, which serves to prepare you for the treat awaiting your palate. Lunch specials allow you to sample a range of sushi, maki, sashimi or tempura dishes without inflating the bill. The food is pricier at night, but is there any such thing as good, low-priced Japanese cuisine?

Chez Chine
$$$
99 Avenue Viger Ouest
☎878-9888

Located at the edge of Chinatown, the Holiday Inn Select has one of the district's best restaurants, Chez Chine. Here, delicious Chinese specialties are served in an immense dining room next to the reception. Although the windowless space is somewhat impersonal, the décor is attractive. The tables are placed around an indoor pond, in the centre of which is a pagoda (with a large table in it). You can also reserve small private dining rooms, which are ideal for receptions.

Julien
$$$
Closed Sun
1191 Rue Union
☎*871-1581*

Julien is a Montréal institution, thanks largely to its *bavette à l'échalote* or steak with shallots, which is one of the best in the city. But it isn't just the *bavette* that attracts patrons, as each dish is more succulent than the last. For that matter, everything here is impeccable, from the service to the décor and even the wine list.

Katsura
$$$
2170 Rue de la Montagne
☎*849-1172*

At Katsura, located in the heart of downtown, visitors can savour refined Japanese cuisine. The main dining room is furnished with long tables, making this a perfect place for groups. Smaller, more inti mate rooms are also available.

Le Lutétia
$$$
Tue-Sat
1430 Rue de la Montagne
☎*288-5656*

The chic Victorian décor on display at the restaurant at Hotel de la Montagne, Le Lutétia, cannot fail to impress, nor can its menu, with all the classics of French cuisine: lamb chops, rib steak and filet mignon.

Maison George Stephen
$$$
Closed Jul and Aug
1440 Rue Drummond
☎*849-7338*

The Maison George Stephen houses the Mount Stephen Club, founded in 1884, which recently opened its restaurant to the public on Sundays, when it serves a musical brunch. The decor is from another time, with superb panelled walls adorned with 19th-century stained glass. You will have the privilege of treating both your palate and your ears to a feast, as classical music interpreted by conservatory students wafts through the air.

Mr. Ma
$$$
1 Place Ville-Marie (corner Cathcart and Mansfield)
☎*866-8000*

With two dining rooms, one that lets natural light in during the day, Mr. Ma makes Szechuan cuisine that is nothing extraordinary but offers good value for the money, especially for the downtown area. The seafood dishes are a good choice.

Troïka
$$$
2171 Rue Crescent
☎*849-9333*

Troïka epitomizes a typical Russian restaurant. Hanging tapestries, mementos, dark and intimate corners and live accordion music conjure up images of the old country. The food is authentic and excellent.

Desjardins Sea Food
$$$-$$$$
1175 Rue Mackay
☎*866-9741*

Desjardins Sea Food has long been one of the best seafood restaurants in Montréal. Everything is fresh and delicious and served in a refined atmosphere with plush decor where wall-to-wall carpeting, white napkins, flowers and crystal set the tone. Here, you can have a wonderful meal in a peaceful setting right in middle of the downtown, surrounded by big bay windows that let in a lot of light, and comfortably seated in padded high-backed chairs. Professional service, and though

prices are on the high side, the value is excellent.

Le Latini
$$$-$$$$
Sat and Sun dinner only
1130 Rue Jeanne-Mance
☎*861-3166*

The Italian restaurant Le Latini is known as much for its excellent, deliciously refined cuisine as for its elegant and exclusive ambience. The wine list is sure to please even the most discerning patrons.

Zen
$$$-$$$$
1050 Rue Sherbrooke Ouest, in the Omni Montréal Hotel
☎*499-0801*

The decor at Zen is modern minimalism to an extreme, and though it is far from cozy, it is exceptional; one might even find it conducive to a Zen experience. Each of the excellent Chinese dishes is beautifully presented. If you can't decide, opt for the "Zen Experience," an unlimited choice of smaller portions of the 40-odd dishes on the menu (*$27*).

Piment Rouge
$$$$
1170 Rue Peel
☎*866-7816*

The Piment Rouge prepares delicious Chinese and Szechuanese specialties, served in a pleasant setting. A visit to this restaurant guarantees a satisfied palate. The service is efficient and friendly.

Café de Paris
$$$$
1228 Sherbrooke Ouest
☎**842-4212**

The Café de Paris is the renowned restaurant of the magnificent Ritz-Carlton Kempinski. Its sumptuous blue-and-ochre decor is absolutely beautiful. The carefully thought-out menu is delicious.

✿ Les Caprices de Nicolas
$$$$
2072 Rue Drummond
☎**282-9790**

Les Caprices de Nicolas is one of the very best restaurants in Montréal, with highly innovative and very sophisticated French cuisine. There is an interesting arrangement whereby, for the price of a bottle of wine, you can sample different wines by the glass to accompany every course of the meal. The service is friendly and impeccable, and the décor is an indoor garden.

Shaughnessy Village

For the location of the following restaurants, please refer to p 143.

Calories
$
4114 Rue Sainte-Catherine Ouest
☎**933-8186**

Calories, which welcomes a noisy clientele late into the night, features delicious cakes served in generous portions.

Pique Assiette
$-$$
2051 Rue Sainte-Catherine Ouest
☎**932-7141**

Pique Assiette has an Indian-style décor and a quiet atmosphere. The lunchtime Indian buffet is well worth the trip. The menu lists excellent curries and Tandoori specialties. Guests can have as much *nan* bread as they please. Anyone with a weak stomach should stay away, because the food is very spicy. English beer washes these dishes down nicely.

Bar-B-Barn
$-$$
1201 Rue Guy
☎**931-3811**

The Bar-B-Barn serves sweet, delicious pork ribs cooked just right. The food is hardly refined, especially seeing as you have to eat it with your hands, but it appeals to many Montrealers. Those planning to come here on the weekend should prepare to be patient, since there is often a long wait.

Café Roccoco
$-$$
1650 Lincoln
☎*938-2121*
Café Roccoco is a charming little Hungarian restaurant mostly frequented by a Magyar-speaking clientele. The food is decent and served with lots of paprika. The pink and scarlet drapes and tablecloths give this place a cute Eastern European décor that would be made even more romantic with candles on each table. Excellent selection of cakes.

Pattaya
$$
1235 Rue Guy
☎*933-9949*
A small Thai restaurant, Pattaya has a simple, tasteful layout and serves good, exotic-tasting cuisine.

Le Bistro Gourmet
$$-$$$
2100 Rue Saint-Mathieu
☎*846-1553*
Le Bistro Gourmet is a pleasant little French restaurant where visitors can savour delicious dishes, always prepared with fresh ingredients and carefully served.

🐟 **Chez la Mère Michel**
$$$-$$$$
Sat, Sun and Mon dinner only
1209 Rue Guy
☎*934-0473*
Considered by many to be one of Montréal's best restaurants, Chez la Mère Michel is the definition of fine French dining. Inside a lovely old house on Guy Street are three exquisitely decorated, intimate dining rooms. Banquettes and chairs covered in richly printed fabrics welcome patrons to their elegantly set tables, and a cosy fireplace and profusion of plants set the mood. Chef Micheline creates delightful French regional specialties and an alternating five-course seasonal *table d'hôte* menu with market-fresh ingredients. The service is friendly and attentive. The wine cellar has some of the finest bottles in the city.

Kaizen
$$$$
4120 Rue Ste-Catherine O.
☎*932-5654*
The best Japanese restaurant in Westmount, Kaizen serves all the classics from this land of the rising sun The prices are high but the portions are gargantuan! The staff won't even mind if you share your plate.

Around the Hôtel-Dieu and Boulevard Saint-Laurent

For the location of the following restaurants, please refer to p 147.

Restaurants

Beauty's
$
93 Avenue du Mont-Royal Ouest
☎849-8883
Beauty's is known for its hearty, delicious brunches. The place is often crowded on weekend mornings. It is only open for breakfast, lunch and brunch.

Coco Rico
$
3907 Boulevard Saint-Laurent
☎849-5554
Coco Rico specializes in roast chicken, and is perfect for anyone on a tight budget. For as little as $2.99, treat yourself to a quarter chicken with salad. On Mondays and Tuesdays, whole roast chickens sell for $5.99.

Euro Deli
$
3619 Boulevard Saint-Laurent
☎843-7853
Euro Deli is where the hip St-Laurent crowd hangs out and is the best choice for a ready-made meal of pasta or pizza at any time of the day or night.

Kilo
$
5206 Boulevard Saint-Laurent
☎277-5039
Kilo looks like a contemporary fairy-tale house, with its aesthetically placed profusion of candies, grey-coloured walls, metal furnishings and high ceiling. A young, dynamic clientele can be found here at all hours, enjoying a sandwich or a piece of the establishment's famous gargantuan cakes. People don't come here to relax, but to mingle with the *beau monde*, the beautiful people!

Schwartz's Montréal Hebrew Delicatessen
$
3895 Boulevard Saint-Laurent
☎842-4813
Montréal is famous for its smoked meat and, according to many people, the best can be found at Schwartz's Montréal Hebrew Delicatessen. Patrons come here for a sandwich on the go and to rub elbows with carnivorous connoisseurs who often travel a long ways for this delicacy. The small establishment is not exactly welcoming, but authenticity is guaranteed.

Thaï Express
$
3710 Blvd. St-Laurent
☎287-9957
In a simple setting that strongly evokes a Thai atmosphere, choose from a menu that offers a host of combinations. The place is a sure bet, with all dishes prepared to order from fresh ingredients. Moreover, the open kitchen allows you to watch the cooks at work. Intrepid souls can order their dishes "spicy,"

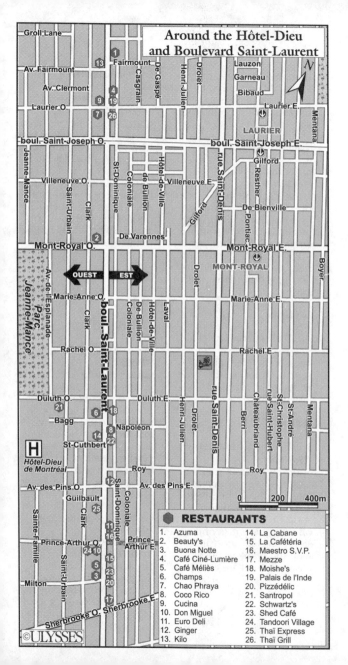

Around the Hôtel-Dieu and Boulevard Saint-Laurent

RESTAURANTS

1. Azuma
2. Beauty's
3. Buona Notte
4. Café Ciné-Lumière
5. Café Méliès
6. Champs
7. Chao Phraya
8. Coco Rico
9. Cucina
10. Don Miguel
11. Euro Deli
12. Ginger
13. Kilo
14. La Cabane
15. La Cafétéria
16. Maestro S.V.P.
17. Mezze
18. Moishe's
19. Palais de l'Inde
20. Pizzédélic
21. Santropol
22. Schwartz's
23. Shed Café
24. Tandoori Village
25. Thaï Express
26. Thaï Grill

©ULYSSES

though they are actually very mild compared to what you get in Bangkok. A good place for an inexpensive meal.

Tandoori Village
$
27 Rue Prince Arthur O.
☎842-8044
Located in the most modest of settings, but in a neighbourhood livened up by McGill University students, among others, Tandoori Village satisfies a growing number of clients with its delicious, affordable Indian cuisine.

La Cabane
$-$$
3872 Boulevard Saint-Laurent
The restaurant-bar La Cabane is the ideal place to savour a pint of amber ale and simple but mouth-watering dishes.

Champs
$-$$
3956 Boulevard Saint-Laurent
☎987-6444
Sport enthusiasts gather at Champs to enjoy simple meals and cold beer while watching their favourite sport on the giant screen or on one of the many television sets. The sports vary with the seasons: hockey, baseball, football, etc.

Café Ciné-Lumière
$$
5163 Boulevard Saint-Laurent
☎495-1796
Café Ciné-Lumière is decorated with the set of a Paris bistro left over from the Cité Ciné exposition. Old movies are shown on a giant screen. The comfortable atmosphere is a little trendy, but not too much! Earphones are provided for anyone who wants to listen to the movies. This is the ideal spot to enjoy a meal alone.

The food's quality however varies.

Cafétéria
$$
3581 Boulevard Saint-Laurent
☎849-3855
Cafétéria attracts young professionals, who come here for hamburgers and people-watching through the big picture windows that look onto Boulevard Saint-Laurent. The tasty, healthy vegetarian burger is definitely worth a try. The 1950s décor is the epitome of kitsch.

Cucina
$-$$
5134 Boulevard Saint-Laurent
☎495-1131
The Italian restaurant Cucina has an extremely austere décor and prepares delicious pizzas with local or international flavours.

Pizzédélic
$-$$
3509 Boulevard Saint-Laurent
☎282-6784

The restaurant Pizzédélic has a modern decor in a larger new space where clients go to see and to be seen, but the service is pretty slow and the music too loud. This is a good place to eat *nouvelle-cuisine pizza* made with quality ingredients and a thin crust. There is a large outdoor terrace in the back. See also p 314 and 324.

Santropol
$-$$
3990 Rue Saint-Urbain
☎842-3110

Popular with groovy diners of all ages, the Santropol serves enormous sandwiches, quiches and salads, always with plenty of fruits and vegetables. It is also known for its wide variety of herbal teas and coffees, great décor and fantastic terrace.

Chao Phraya
$$
50 Avenue Laurier Ouest
☎272-5339

Recently renovated, Chao Phraya has a very modern decor enhanced by big bay windows. Delicious Thai food.

Don Miguel
$$
20 Rue Prince Arthur Ouest
☎845-7915

In a setting that quickly transports you to some remote Spanish province, Don Miguel himself serves you delicious cuisine from his native land, such as the irresistible paellas. Patrons are offered some cultural immersion into the bargain, so feel free to brush up on your Spanish.

Mezze
$$
3449 Boulevard Saint-Laurent
☎281-0275

In a strip of restaurants where the establishments and their clientele are very pretentious, Mezze offers excellent Greek cuisine in a simple atmosphere. People come here to eat well, rather than show off their luxury cars in the parking lot. We can only hope that some of its neighbours will follow Mezze's example.

Palais de l'Inde
$$
5125 Boulevard Saint-Laurent
☎270-7402

The Palais de l'Inde is one of the many great Indian restaurants along Saint-Laurent near Rue Laurier. The menu includes a good selection of main dishes, which, though prepared with quality ingredients, lack originality. The service is a bit aloof.

Restaurants

Shed Café
$$
3515 Boulevard Saint-Laurent
☎*842-0220*
The Shed Café serves salads, hamburgers and desserts. The interior, which definitely plays a role in attracting the restaurant's clientele, is wacky and avant-garde. A down side, however, is the loud, indigestible music. The café is open until 3am every day.

Azuma
$$-$$$
Closed Sun
901 Rue Sherbrooke Est
☎*525-5262*
At the charming restaurant Azuma, visitors can sample Japanese cuisine. Reservations are recommended, as this restaurant is too small to seat all its customers. The service is polite and attentive.

Café Méliès
$$-$$$
3536 Boulevard Saint-Laurent
☎*847-9218*
Café Méliès followed Cinéma Parallèle into Ex-Centris (see p 150, 356), a new and modern building on Boulevard St-Laurent. Located on two floors, the café overlooks the street from its magnificent windows. Its cinematographic décor is impressive (notice the majestic staircase). The food is even better than it was in its old location farther north on St-Laurent.

Delicious sandwiches and hot dishes are served here, but you can also just have a glass of wine or a cup of coffee. Definitely worth checking out more than once!

Buona Notte
$$$
3518 Boulevard Saint-Laurent
☎*848-0644*
It is impossible to walk down Boulevard Saint-Laurent without noticing Buona Notte. And once up close, it is nearly impossible to resist the temptation of going inside. Buona Notte is Italy rediscovered, a combination of Little Italy and Soho, a piece of New York in Montréal. The prices are high, but then again, the typical clientele here doesn't seem to mind...

Ginger
$$$
16 Avenue des Pins Est
☎*844-2121*
A little ways off "The Main," Ginger serves sushi, rolls, *makis* and *sashimi*, as well as salads, dumplings and noodles. Its wide selection of refined Japanese cuisine is served in an atmosphere that is ethnic rather than uptight. The very attractive décor has a distinctively Asian flavour. Ginger also has a summer terrasse on Rue des Pins, which unfortunately is very noisy from the traffic on St-Laurent and des Pins.

Maestro S.V.P.
$$$
Sat and Sun dinner only
3615 Boulevard Saint-Laurent
☎*842-6447*
3017 Masson
☎*722-4166*
Maestro S.V.P is remarkable for the quality of its oyster bar, sea food and ultra-dynamic staff, who really seem to get in to the uplifting jazz music.

Moishe's
$$$
Dinner only
3961 Boulevard Saint-Laurent
☎*845-3509*
Moishe's serves what are without a doubt the best steaks in town. The secret of this deliciously tender meat lies in the aging process. One of the specialties is chopped liver and fried onions. The façade of Moishe's has been renovated as part of the initiative to beautify St-Laurent Boulevard.

🖾 **Thaï Grill**
$$$
5101 Boulevard Saint-Laurent
☎*270-5566*
It is no surprise that the Thaï Grill won a prize for its design. Patrons never grow weary of admiring the gold decor. Traditional Thai elements have been skilfully integrated into a modern environment that manages to maintain a quiet elegance despite the animation all around. The service

is friendly and attentive. The innovative food is based on traditional Thai cuisine and includes such dishes as green papaya salad with lime and exquisitely seasoned rice noodles with chicken.

Quartier Latin

For the location of the following restaurants, please refer to p 155.

Brioche Lyonnaise
$
1593 Rue Saint-Denis
☎*842-7017*
Brioche Lyonnaise is a pastry shop and café offering an extremely wide selection of pastries, cakes and sweetmeats, all the more appealing because everything really is as delicious as it looks!

Brûlerie Saint-Denis
$
1587 Rue Saint-Denis
☎*286-9159*
See also p 312

Les Gâteries
$
3443 St-Denis
☎*843-6235*
A stone's throw from Square Saint-Louis, this small café serves tasty light dishes like sandwiches, salads, as well as a healthy, flavourful daily menu. The dessert counter is literally overflowing with delicious

Restaurants

treats. The establishment, which has been open for several years, has the atmosphere of a neighbourhood café with an intimate, pleasant ambience created partially by low-key lighting. A terrace is open in the summertime.

La Paryse
$
302 Rue Ontario E.
☎842-2040
In a 1950s décor, La Paryse is regularly frequented by students, and by looking at its menu, you will understand why: delicious hamburgers and home fries are served in generous portions.

Le Pélerin
$
330 Rue Ontario Est
☎845-0909
Located near Rue Saint-Denis, Le Pélerin is a pleasant, unpretentious café. The wooden furniture, made to look like mahogany, and the works of modern art on exhibit create a friendly atmosphere that attracts a diverse clientele. This is the perfect place to grab a bite and chat with a friend. The service is attentive and friendly.

Le Commensal
$-$$
1720 Rue Saint-Denis
☎845-2627
The well-known, vegetarian restaurant Le Commensal, which has been a landmark at the corner of Rue Sherbrooke and Rue Saint-Denis for ages, recently moved to a new location a little further down Saint-Denis. It offers the same buffet menu of tasty, healthy dishes sold by weight. Its large bay windows in the front, brick walls and different levels lack warmth, but the fare is good and the atmosphere is relaxed.

Zyng
$-$$
1748 Rue St-Denis
☎284-2016
This branch of the Toronto chain of friendly noodle and *dim sum* restaurants brings flair to this overly commercial part of St-Denis. The flavours of China, Japan, Thailand, Korea and Vietnam meet and mix here, creating very original dishes.

Le Piémontais
$$
closed Sun
1145-A Rue de Bullion
☎861-8122
All true lovers of Italian cuisine know and adore this restaurant. The dining room is narrow and the tables are close together, making this place very noisy, but the soft, primarily pink décor, the kind, good humoured and efficient staff, and the works of culinary art on the

menu make dining here an unforgettable experience.

Mikado
$$

1731 Rue St-Denis

☎*844-5705*

This area has not weathered the years very well, but the worst seems to be over, and with its theatres, concert venues and cinemas right nearby, it is drawing locals who had once forsaken it. The Mikado has stayed the course and continues to serve the same excellent Japanese cuisine, with sushi and sashimi at the forefront. There are no fashionable trappings here and so much the better; even the prices don't follow the astronomical curve of other Japanese restaurants, some of which are obviously only taking advantage of the current trend for this type of cuisine! For that matter, true-blue Asians patronize this place in droves, a sure sign of its authenticity.

La Sila
$$$-$$$$
Sat and Sun dinner only

2040 Rue Saint-Denis

☎*844-5083*

La Sila serves traditional Italian cuisine in an elegant setting, which includes an inviting bar and an outdoor terrace for warm summer evenings. Fresh pastas cooked just right are topped with flawless sauces. The wine list boasts the finest

Italian vintages. Free parking.

Plateau Mont-Royal

For the location of the following restaurants, please refer to p 163.

L'Anecdote
$

801 Rue Rachel Est

☎*526-7967*

Serves hamburgers and vegetarian club sandwiches made with quality ingredients. The place has a 1950s-style décor, with movie posters and old Coke ads on the walls.

Anubis
$$

35 Avenue du Mont-Royal Est

☎*843-3391*

Head to Anubis for alternative cuisine. The atmosphere is warm, and on some evenings there is a singer.

Aux Entretiens
$

1577 Avenue Laurier Est

☎*521-2934*

A large room with only a few posters, an old tin ceiling and an atmosphere conducive to conversation awaits diners at Aux Entretiens. This neighbourhood café serves all sorts of sandwiches and salads.

Restaurants

Binerie Mont-Royal
$
367 Avenue Mont-Royal Est
☎285-9078
With its décor made up of
four tables and a counter,
the Binerie Mont-Royal
looks like a modest little
neighbourhood restaurant.
It is known for its specialty,
baked beans (*fèves au lard or
"binnes"*) and also as the
backdrop of Yves
Beauchemin's novel, *Le
Matou (The Alley Cat)*.

Brûlerie Saint-Denis
$
3967 Rue Saint-Denis
☎286-9158
Imports its coffees from all
over the world and offers
one of the widest selections
in Montréal. The coffee is
roasted on the premises,
filling the place with a very
distinctive aroma. The
menu offers light meals and
desserts (see also p 287 and
301).

Byblos
$
closed Mon
1499 Rue Laurier Est
☎523-9396
A small, very modest-looking restaurant whose walls
are decorated with Persian
handicrafts, Byblos appears
both simple and exotic. The
light, refined dishes are
marvels of Iranian cuisine.
The service is attentive and
friendly.

Café Rico
$
969 Rue Rachel E.
☎529-1321
www.caferico.qc.ca
Café Rico is a small coffee-
roasting joint whose policy
is to use fair-trade coffee
exclusively. So why not
drop by this charming Ra-
chel Street café, with its
casual decor consisting of a
few tables, a hammock and
plants, to smell and sample
its delicious blends. As an
accompaniment, you'll have
to make do with a simple
sandwich or biscuit, but in
compensation, you can
linger for hours in this con-
vivial setting that serves as a
gathering place for java
junkies with a social con-
science.

Café El Dorado
$
921 Avenue du Mont-Royal Est
☎278-3333
Where the Plateau's new
trendy crowd hangs out for
a coffee or a quick simple
meal, has a curvaceous
decor. El Dorado's desserts
are definitely worth a try.

La Chilenita
$
152 Rue Napoléon
☎286-6075
4348 Rue Clark
☎982-9212
La Chilenita is a small
bakery-restaurant that prepares superb *empanadas*.
Fresh pastries stuffed with
various ingredients such as

beef, sausage, tomatoes, eggplant, olives and cheese are served hot with a delicious homemade salsa. Latin American–style sandwiches and a few Mexican dishes are also served.

Chez Claudette
$
24 hrs/day, 7 days
351 Avenue Laurier Est
☎279-5173
A cozy family bistro, Chez Claudette is decorated with posters, a long counter and an open kitchen. Typical North American fare makes up the menu.

Frite Alors
$
closed Mon
1562 Avenue Laurier Est
☎524-6336
433 Rue Rachel
☎843-2490
See also p 326.

Fruit Folie
$
3817 Rue Saint-Denis
☎840-9011
Patrons flock to Fruit Folie for its spectacular breakfasts, which are not only delicious but also very affordable. You'll simply go crazy (*"folie"*) for their fruit-filled plates! The restaurant opens every day at 7am, but if you sleep in on Sundays and only arrive after 11am, expect to wait in line; this is especially so if you have your heart set on a terrace table. Fruit Folie also serves simple dishes such as pasta and salads for lunch and dinner.

Le Porté Disparu
$
957 Avenue Mont-Royal Est
☎524-0271
Le Porté Disparu is a friendly café-bistro that welcomes a chattery clientele of intellectuals into opulent surroundings, where they can also sit and read books off the shelves for hours on end. Besides shows on the weekends, Monday nights are animated by poetry readings that range from the conventional to the humorous. Parents should note that the back of the room features a play area for children.

Toasteur
$
Mon-Fri 7am to 4pm, Sat and Sun 7am to 5pm
950 Rue Roy
☎527-8500
Popular for its old-fashioned breakfasts and its brunches... in fact, it is closed in the evenings. If you are nostalgic for the old days when people started the day by eating enough protein, not to mention cholesterol, to fuel a full day of outdoor activity, this is the spot. Attractive décor with 1950s accents. Friendly service.

Restaurants

Ambala
$-$$
wine
3887 Rue Saint-Denis
☎ *499-0446*

Ambala is a typical Montréal Indian restaurant, with its affordable menu selections, its quality if predictable Indian cuisine, its English beers, its rare French wines and its cordial, reserved service. Beyond all of this though, it is the deliciously aromatic and exotic curries and tandooris that keep the faithful coming back.

La Boulange du Commensal
$-$$
5043 Rue Saint-Denis
☎ *843-7741*

Health-food lovers should stop in at La Boulange du Commensal for a nourishing but simple meal. Many Commensal products and the best muffins in town are sold here.

Le Goût de la Thaïlande
$-$$
wine
2229 Avenue du Mont-Royal Est
☎ *527-5035*

In search of good inexpensive Thai food? Try Le Goût de la Thaïlande, where exotic flavours and savoury dishes make up the menu.

L'Harmonie d'Asie
$-$$
wine
dinner only
65 Rue Duluth Est
☎ *289-9972*

L'Harmonie d'Asie is a tiny Vietnamese restaurant with a charming staff and a solid menu. Though the service is a bit slow, this ensures that things are properly prepared. The vegetarian dishes are composed of perfectly cooked, crunchy vegetables, and the meat and fish dishes are low-fat. The soups are especially tasty.

Lélé da Cuca
wine
$-$$
70 Rue Marie-Anne Est
☎ *849-6649*

Serves Mexican and Brazilian dishes. This cramped restaurant can only accommodate about 30 people, but exudes a relaxed and laid-back ambience.

Piazzetta
$-$$
4097 Rue Saint-Denis
☎ *847-0184*

Serves pizza made in the true Italian style, with a thin, crispy crust. The *prosciuto* and melon salad is worth a try. See p 327, 333.

Pizzédélic
$-$$
1250 Avenue Mont-Royal Est
☎ *522-2286*

Serves delicious thin-crust pizza with a delicious selection of toppings. The large windows are open in summer and let in a nice breeze (see also p 307 and 324).

La Selva
$-$$
wine
closed Sun and Mon dinner only
862 Rue Marie-Anne Est
☎*525-1798*

Inexpensive and good food is served at La Selva, a simple Peruvian restaurant. The place is often filled with regulars, and reservations are recommended.

Tampopo
$-$$
4449 Rue Mentana
☎*526-0001*

Tampopo's tiny space is a constant beehive of activity. A multitude of people from the Plateau and beyond come here at practically all hours of the day to chow down on good Asian food. Bountiful Tonkinese soups share menu space with a series of noodle dishes. Behind the counter, cooks sauté vegetables, meat and seafood done to a turn in huge woks. Take a seat on a small stool at the counter or on a floor mat at one of three low tables and be sure to savour the Oriental-style decor as well!

Le 917
$$
wine
dinner only
917 Rue Rachel Est
☎*524-0094*

For quality French cuisine at reasonable prices, try Le 917. The large mirrors on the walls, the close-set tables and the waiters in aprons create a bistro atmosphere that perfectly matches the cuisine. Giblets, kidneys and calf sweetbread are particularly well prepared here, and will melt in your mouth!

L'Académie
$$
wine
4015 Rue St-Denis
☎*849-2249*

Although the service provided for the masses may be deplorable, though no less efficient, the quality of the food served at this "academy," which recently rose from its ashes after a devastating fire., is noteworthy. Italian dishes stand alongside French selections, with occasional California accents thrown in for good measure. The lunch and dinner specials prove to be advantageous, especially as patrons can (indeed must!) bring their own wine. The main floor's long and narrow glassed-in dining room, strategically looking out on St-Denis and Duluth streets, also earns our stamp of approval.

Aux Baisers Volés
$$
closed Sun and Mon
371 Rue Villeneuve Est
☎*289-9921*

Aux Baisers Volés, which means "stolen kisses", truly lives up to its name. This cosy little restaurant is the ideal place for an intimate tête-à-tête over simply prepared dishes.

Bières & Compagnie
$$
4350 Rue Saint-Denis
☎844-0394

Let yourself be seduced by an excellent meal: sausages, grilled dishes, mussels, ostrich, bison and caribou burgers. Add to this one of the establishment's 115 local and imported beers, and you have everything you need to fully enjoy the musical ambiance this place has to offer.

Cactus
$$
4461 Rue Saint-Denis
☎849-0349

Prepares refined Mexican food. Though servings are small the ambiance is cosy and very pleasant. It's too bad that the service has lost its warmth of the old days. The restaurant's little terrace is very popular during the summer.

🌿 Chu Chai
$$
4088 Rue St-Denis
☎843-4194

Deserves praise for breaking the monotony and daring to be innovative. The Thai vegetarian menu is quite a surprise: vegetarian shrimp, vegetarian fish, and even vegetarian beef and pork. The resemblance to the real thing is so extraordinary that you will spend the evening wondering how they do it! The chef affirms that they really are made of vegetable-based products like seitan, wheat, etc. The delicious results delight the mixed clientele that squeezes into the modest dining room or onto the terrace. They have inexpensive lunch specials. You should also note that a recently opened fast-food counter can be found nearby. It's on the go but still quite good.

🛶 Côté Soleil
$$
closed Mon in winter
3979 Rue Saint-Denis
☎282-8037

Coté Soléil offers a consistently fresh menu that changes every day and never misses the mark. Excellent, occasionally inventive French cuisine is served at prices so affordable that this is probably the best value in the neighbourhood. The service is attentive and always friendly. There is a pleasant sidewalk terrace, and the décor is simple but inviting. The service is attentive and friendly, and the setting, although simple, is quite warm. In summer, two sunny terraces are opened up: one on the busy street and the other in the lovely garden.

Fondue Mentale
$$
dinner only
4325 Rue Saint-Denis
☎*499-1446*
Fondue Mentale is inside an old house, which, with its superb woodwork, is typical of Plateau Mont-Royal. As the restaurant's name suggests, fondue is the specialty here – and what a choice, each one more appetizing than the last! The Swiss fondue with pink pepper is particularly delicious.

La Gaudriole
$$
825 Avenue Laurier Est
☎*276-1580*
La Gaudriole is in cramped and somewhat uncomfortable quarters, but serves excellent "hybrid" French cuisine, which incorporates flavours from around the world. The menu is constantly changing, so the ingredients are always fresh, allowing chef Marc Vézina's creativity to shine through.

Le Jardin de Panos
$$
wine
521 Rue Duluth Est
☎*521-4206*
A Greek *brochetterie*, Le Jardin de Panos serves simple cuisine made with quality ingredients. Inside a house with a large terrace, this restaurant is extremely pleasant in the summer.

Le Nil Bleu
$$
3706 Rue Saint-Denis
☎*285-4628*
The amazingly delicious food at the Ethiopian restaurant is certainly worth the trip, if only to dine in the traditional manner, with your right hand on a choice of meat or vegetables rolled in an enormous crêpe, called *injera amharic*. There are some vegetarian dishes. The decor is extremely inviting.

Ouzeri
$$
4690 Rue Saint-Denis
☎*845-1336*
Ouzeri set out on a mission to offer its clientele refined Mediterranean cuisine, and succeeded. The food is excellent, and the menu includes several surprises, such as vegetarian *moussaka* and scallops with melted cheese. With its high ceilings and long windows, this is a pleasant place, where you'll be tempted to linger on and on, especially when the Greek music sets your mind wandering.

Persil Fou
$$
dinner only
4669 Rue Saint-Denis
☎*284-3130*
Facing the Théâtre du Rideau Vert, the friendly little French restaurant Persil Fou boasts an excel-

lent and well-priced table d'hôte menu.

La Petite Marche
$$
5035 rue St-Denis
☎*842-1994*

One of the few small café-style neighbourhood restaurants on St-Denis, a street that is becoming increasingly commercialized, La Petite Marche is a good place to have a reasonably priced meal in a casual atmosphere. The table-d'hôte menu is varied and offers generous portions of French- and Italian-inspired dishes. The service is courteous and efficient. Breakfasts available.

Soy
$$
3945 Rue Saint-Denis
☎*499-9399*

With its catchy name and logo featuring chopsticks and a wok, Soy is both intriguing and attractive. Upon entering this restaurant on the second floor of a Rue Saint-Denis building, you will discover a lovely setting of stained wood, eye-catching colours, brick walls and orchids, with a great atmosphere to boot. This restaurant offers Asian cuisine concocted by a most inspired and creative chef. From wonton soup to General Tao chicken to wok-sautéed rice noodles and dumplings, everything is finely prepared and

served. The top-notch service also deserves mention.

El Zaziummm
$$
1276 Laurier Est
☎*598-0344*
4525 Avenue du Parc
☎*499-3675*
51 Rue Roy Est
☎*844-0893*

El Zaziummm is unlike any other Mexican restaurant in Montréal. The decor is highly eccentric and includes, for example, an old bathtub used as a table and glass-top tables through which post cards and plane tickets half-buried in sand can be seen. The toilet paper rolls on each table and the countless knick-knacks placed haphazardly here and there confer an undeniable, though unusual, charm to the restaurant. The menu offers a long list of typical Mexican dishes prepared in new and original ways, although the service is about as slow as it gets..

Un Monde Sauté
$$-$$$
1481 av. Laurier E.
☎*590-0897*

This restaurant has an original concept. The concept is simple: an internationally inspired menu (mostly sautés, hence the name), an intimate and colourful décor, and unparalleled friendly service. An exotic place that will brighten up

even the coldest winter
days.

L'Avenue
$$-$$$
922 Avenue Mont-Royal Est
☎ 523-8780
L'Avenue has become a
sanctuary for the beautiful
people in search of hearty
meals. Arrive early to avoid
the line-up. The service is
attentive and polite.

Café Cherrier
$$-$$$
3635 Rue Saint-Denis
☎ 843-4308
The meeting place of forty-
something yuppies, the
terrace and dining room at
the Café Cherrier is always
packed. The bustling
French *brasserie* ambiance is
enjoyable. The menu fea-
tures respectable bistro-style
cuisine. A brunch is served
on weekends. The meeting
place *par excellence* of many
fortyish professionals, the
terrace and dining room of
Café Cherrier are always
packed. The atmosphere is
reminiscent of a French
brasserie, highly animated
and busy, which can lead to
fortuitous meetings. The
menu features bistro-type
meals that are generally
quite tasty, but the service
can be uneven.

Casa Tapas
$$-$$$
266 Rue Rachel Est
☎ 848-1063
Serves exquisite traditional
Spanish cuisine in its newly
extended room. *Tapas* are
little appetizers which the
Spanish eat mainly in the
late afternoon at the bar.
Combined, they are a meal
in themselves. Meals of
tapas are served here, so
you can taste a selection of
the specialties of this sun-
drenched country.

Continental
$$-$$$
closed noon
4169 Saint-Denis
☎ 845-6842
The staging is very subtle at
the Continental. Some evenings, the restaurant is posi-
tively charming, with its
attentive, courteous staff,
stylish clientele and a modern 1950s-style décor. The
varied menu ranks among
the best in Montréal and
includes a few surprises,
such as veal kidneys with
thyme and Asian crunchy
noodles.. The cuisine can
be sublime sometimes, and
the presentation of the
dishes is always excellent.

Crêperie Bretonne Ty-Breiz
$$-$$$
933 rue Rachel Est
☎ 521-1444
Crêperie Bretonne Ty-Breiz
serves wonderful crêpes,
both regular and whole
wheat, with a wide selec-

Restaurants

tion of stuffings. The décor is typical of northwestern France, but you might mistake it for Austrian or Swiss. Good wine list and desert – more crêpes! *Table d'hôte* menu for lunch and dinner during the week. Probably the best crêperie in Montréal and the best known.

Le Flambard
$$-$$$
851 Rue Rachel Est
☎596-1280

A pleasant bistro decorated with woodwork and mirrors, Le Flambard excels in the preparation of quality French cuisine. Though the place is charming, the narrow dining room and closely set tables offer little room for intimacy.

Laloux
$$-$$$
Sat and Sun dinner only
250 Avenue des Pins Est
☎287-9127

Set up inside a superb residence, Laloux resembles a chic and elegant Parisian-style bistro. People come here to enjoy nouvelle cuisine of consistently high quality, which is one of the best in Montréal. A reasonably priced *menu théâtre*, which includes three light courses is offered.

Misto
$$-$$$
929 Avenue Mont-Royal Est
☎526-5043

Misto is an Italian restaurant patronized by a hip clientele, who come here to savour delicious and imaginative Italian cooking. The décor features exposed brick walls and shades of green, and the noisy atmosphere and crowded tables only add to the ambience and the attentive and friendly service.

Pistou
$$-$$$
Sat and Sun dinner only
1453 Rue Mont-Royal Est
☎528-7242

With its large, high-ceilinged dining room and its modern décor, Pistou is certainly not cosy, not to mention that it is usually too packed to have a quiet conversation. But the noise isn't bothersome when amongst friends who tend to chat loudly. The menu lists some classics like salad with warm goat cheese and honey *(salade de chèvre chaud au miel)*, absolutely delicious, and steak tartar. Another good choice is the daily *table d'hôte*.

Poco Piu
$$-$$$
closed Mon
4621 Rue Saint-Denis
☎843-8928

Upon entering Poco Piu, you will be seduced by the

The Jacques-Cartier Bridge, which links the south shore of the St. Lawrence River to the island of Montréal, looks even more majestic in the sunrise.
- *Philippe Renault*

In both winter and summer, the port of Montréal welcomes giant cargo ships from all over the world.
- Philippe Renault

Colourful Victorian home such as these, with impossibly steep or contorted exterior staircases, hav become emblematic of Montréal. - *Patrick Escude*

In the city's parks, hockey is still one of the favourite sports enjoyed by young Montrealers. - Philippe Renault

plush yet relaxed atmosphere. The choice of dishes will certainly satisfy and send you on a delicious voyage through the wonders of Italian cuisine.

Le P'tit Plateau
$$-$$$
wine
closed Sun and Mon
330 Rue Marie-Anne Est
☎*282-6342*

A neighbourhood restaurant, Le P'tit Plateau offers a family atmosphere and attentive service. Simple and unpretentious cuisine.

La Raclette
$$-$$$
1059 Rue Gilford
☎*524-8118*

La Raclette is a popular neighbourhood restaurant on warm summer evenings, thanks to its attractive terrace. Menu choices like raclette (of course), salmon with *Meaux* mustard and cherry clafoutis are some of the other draws. Those with a hearty appetite can opt for the *menu dégustation*, which includes appetizer, soup, main dish, dessert and coffee.

Restorante-Trattoria Carissima
$$-$$$
222 Mont-Royal Est
☎*844-PATE (7283)*

Carissima is a fine Italian restaurant that opened in the fall 1998. The interior décor is done in dark wood, enhanced by a cosy fireplace

in the (smoking) dining room and large sliding windows facing Mont-Royal. Prices are reasonable and there is a table-d'hôte menu during the week. Good selection of deserts. Italian foodstuffs for sale are displayed on dark-wood shelves next to the kitchen.

🌴 L'Express
$$$
3927 Rue Saint-Denis
☎*845-5333*

A yuppie gathering place during the mid-1980s, L'Express is still highly rated for its locomotive dining-car decor and lively Parisian bistro atmosphere, which few restaurants have managed to recreate. In addition to the consistently appealing menu, the above-mentioned factors have earned this restaurant a solid reputation over the years.

Modigliani
$$$
1251 Rue Gilford
☎*522-0422*

Located off the beaten track, the Italian restaurant, with its abundance of plants, has an inviting atmosphere and decor. The food is original and consistently good.

La Prunelle
$$$
wine
327 Rue Duluth E.
☎*849-8403*

This is one of the best restaurants in the area, in a space that looks right out onto the street, which is especially pleasant in the summer. La Prunelle serves attractively presented, classic French cuisine with a few innovative touches. Patrons can even bring their own wine, a not-inconsiderable perk in a land where restaurant owners pay more for wine than do consumers. So dust off that good bottle you've been saving for a special occasion and enjoy a lovely evening at La Prunelle.

La Colombe
$$$
wine
554 Rue Duluth E.
☎849-8844

A hallmark veteran of the restaurant wars, La Colombe has long been welcoming patrons in a warm and intimate setting, and serving quality French "market" cuisine. Like its Duluth Street counterparts, this is a bring-your-own-wine establishment.

La Psarotaverna du Symposium
$$$
3829 Saint-Denis
☎842-0867

The blue and white decor and warm island spirit of the service at La Psarotaverna du Symposium transports guests instantly to the Aegean Sea. Fish (sea bream) and seafood are the specialties here. Try the delicious moussaka and *saganaki*. For dessert, make sure to sample the delicious, milk-based *galatoboureco*.

Toqué
$$$$
dinner only
3842 Rue Saint-Denis
☎499-2084

If you're looking for a new culinary experience, Toqué is without a doubt the place to go in Montréal. The chef, Normand Laprise, insists on having the freshest ingredients and manages the kitchen, where dishes are always prepared with great care, and are beautifully presented. Not to mention the desserts, which are veritable modern sculptures. The service is exceptional, the wine list good, the new decor elegant, and the high prices do not seem to deter anyone. One of the most original dining establishments in Montréal.

Westmount and Western Montréal

For the location of the following restaurants, please refer to p 168.

Chez Better
$
5400 Chemin de la Côte-des-Neiges
☎344-3971
See also p 288.

Westmount and Western Montréal

OUTREMONT

Barclay · Ducharne · Outremont
Van Horne · Lajoie
Bernard
Edouard-Montpetit
Université de Montréal
École polytechnique
av. Marie-Guyard
Cimetière Notre-Dame-des-Neiges
Mount Royal Cemetery
ch. de la Remembrance
Parc du Mont-Royal
Chalet de la Montagne · Belvédère Kondiaronk
av. Cedar · av. des Pins
MONTRÉAL Ouest
Dr. Penfield
Guy-Concordia
Sherbrooke · Atwater
Dorchester · boul. René-Lévesque O.
Autoroute Ville-Marie (20)
St-Antoine
St-Jacques
Place St-Henri · Lionel-Groulx
Georges-Vanier · St-Jacques · Lucien-L'Allier · Peel

Plamondon · Carlton
Van Horne
Westbury · Victoria · Légaré · Bourret · ch. de la Côte-des-Neiges
Côte-des-Neiges
Ste-Catherine
Université de Montréal · boul. Édouard-Montpetit
Lacombe
Côte-des-Neiges
Snowdon · ch. Queen-Mary
Oratoire Saint-Joseph
Parc Summit
Sunnyside
The Boulevard
Notre-Dame-de-Grâce
ch. de la Côte · St-Luc
Villa-Maria
av. Monkland
Notre-Dame-de-Grâce chemin
Westmount
Claremont · Grey · Claremont · Grosvenor · Roslyn · la · de · Décarie
Côte-St-Antoine
WESTMOUNT
Clarke · Greene
Sherbrooke Ouest
Parc Westmount · boul. De Maisonneuve Ouest
Vendôme · Ste-Catherine Ouest
St-Rémi
Autoroute Décarie · Earnscliffe · MacDonald · Isabella
Autoroute Décarie
Marcil · Wilson · St-Jacques
Canal de Lachine (15)

RESTAURANTS

1. Al Dente	5. La Pasta Casareccia	9. Le Maistre
2. Aux Deux Gauloises	6. La Transition	10. Mess Hall
3. Chez Better	7. Le Claremont	11. Monkland Tavern
4. La Louisiane	8. Le Commensal	12. Pizzafiore
		13. Pizzédélic

0 · 1 · 2km

©ULYSSES

Pasta Casareccia

$

5849 Rue Sherbrooke O.

☎483-1588

The bizarre red and yellow decor of Pasta Casareccia attracts a clientele of all different ages. The house specialty is fresh pasta. The service, provided by the

family that owns the place, is courteous and attentive.

Pizzafiore

$

3518 Lacombe

☎735-1555

Upon entering Pizzafiore, visitors will see the cook standing beside the wood-burning oven in which the pizzas are baked. He makes pizza for every taste, with every different kind of sauce, topped with the widest range of ingredients imaginable. This pleasant restaurant is often filled with locals and people from Université de Montréal.

Le Commensal
$-$$
3715 Chemin Queen Mary
☎**733-9755**
See p 294 and 310.

Pizzédélic
$-$$
5556 Monkland
☎**487-3103**
5153 Chemin de la Côte-des-Neiges
☎**739-2446**
An affirmation of Monkland's coming of age was the opening of a branch of the trendy pizzeria Pizzédélic. The same funky décor, great thin-crust pizza and eclectic choice of toppings have made this branch, one of the biggest, just as popular as the others (see also p 307 and 314).

Al Dente
$$
wine
5768 Avenue Monkland
☎**486-4343**
Well established on Monkland for many years, Al Dente is a popular and friendly Italian eatery. The menu features a good selection of pizzas, soups and fresh salads, as well as a list of pastas and accompanying sauces that you can mix and match. The décor is simple and the ambiance, laid back. Diners come here for the solid food and the no-fuss service.

Aux Deux Gauloises
$$
5195 Chemin de la Côte-des-Neiges
☎**737-5755**
The kitchen of this French restaurant churns out a wide variety of crêpes, each more delicious than the last. Pleasant ambience and friendly service.

Le Claremont
$$
5032 Rue Sherbrooke Ouest
☎**483-1557**
Opened in the early 1990s, the Claremont is a lively place, to say the least. A fine menu offers a wide range of choices from one of the best and freshest pestos around to a delicious and savoury mulligatawny soup. You might also prefer, as many here do, just to enjoy a drink and a platter of nachos with fresh salsa. The loud music rules this place out as a spot for a quiet dinner, but if you don't mind a little excitement, you won't be disappointed. The décor is enhanced by changing exhibits of works by local artists and photographers.

Mess Hall
$$
4858 Rue Sherbrooke Ouest
☎*482-2167*
With the same owners as
Saint-Laurent's trendy
Cafétéria (see p 306), Mess
Hall boasts a similarly strik-
ing decor, the *pièce de
résistance* being an exquisite
starburst chandelier in the
centre of the room. The
menu is both original and
standard with great salads,
burgers and pasta, as well
as a few more refined
dishes. Westmount's young
professionals come here to
see and be seen.

🪶 Monkland Tavern
$$-$$$
5555 Avenue Monkland
☎*486-5768*
Established in a genuine
neighbourhood tavern, The
Tavern restaurant is owned
by the same folks that run
the Claremont (see above)
and the Marlowe (see
p 337). A similar crowd of
young professionals flocks
to this place with its terrace
on the west end's latest
trendy avenue, Monkland.
The menu is limited, but is
complemented by ever-
changing daily specials.
Surely one of the best offer-
ings here is the *crostini*,
small slices of French bread
spread with *tapenade* and
topped with sun-dried to-
matoes and *bocconcini*
cheese, simply divine!

La Transition
$$
4785 Rue Sherbrooke Ouest
☎*933-1000*
The Italian bistro has been
catering to a local clientele
for over 10 years. Pleasant
lighting and the sounds of
jazz create a relaxing atmosphere. The menu is classic
Italian with a few innovative touches.

La Louisiane
$$-$$$
closed Mon
5850 Rue Sherbrooke Ouest
☎*369-3073*
A meal at La Louisiane is
like a trip to the Bayou.
You can start with a plate
of authentic hush puppies,
continue with something
spicy like crayfish *étouffée* or
shrimp magnolia and finish
up with an order of heav-
enly bananas Foster. Huge
paintings of New Orleans
street scenes adorn the
walls and the sounds of jazz
filling the air complete the
mood.

Le Maistre
$$-$$$
5700 Avenue Monkland
☎*481-2109*
Firmly established on
Monkland for many years,
Le Maistre serves French
cuisine that is always impeccable. The choice of
wines to accompany your
meal is always good and
well-priced. In the summer,
there is a lovely terrace

Restaurants

overlooking the excitement of the street.

Outremont

For the location of the following restaurants, please refer to p 179.

Bilboquet
$

1311 Avenue Bernard Ouest
☎*276-0414*

Ice-cream lovers of all ages flock to Bilboquet for the countless different flavours. This little café, located in the heart of Outremont, has a cute little terrace that is always full on summer evenings.

Café Romolo
$

272 Avenue Bernard Ouest
☎*272-5035*

People go to Café Romolo to talk endlessly while sipping delicious cafés au lait served Portuguese- and Spanish-style in tall glasses.

Café Souvenir
$

1261 Avenue Bernard Ouest
☎*948-5259*

Maps of large European cities like Paris decorate the walls of the Café Souvenir, literally Memory Café. The ambiance of a French café pervades this comfortable little restaurant, which is open 24 hours a day. Rainy Sundays bring out the droves of locals, for a quick coffee and chat. The menu is not extraordinary, but the meals are well prepared.

La Croissanterie
$

5200 Rue Hutchison
☎*278-6567*

La Croissanterie is one of those neighbourhood treasures that are so delightful to discover. Small marble tables, old-fashioned chandeliers and beautiful wood panelling make up a decor perfectly suited to leisurely breakfasts and intimate conversations when you wish time could stand still. The bright morning sun streams through large windows. This café almost seems like it came from a bygone era! Regulars include struggling artists and distracted intellectuals.

Eggspectations
$

198 av. Laurier Ouest
☎*278-6411*

See description p 294.

Frite Alors
$

5235 A Avenue du Parc
☎*948-2219*

Frite Alors is a re-creation of a typical *friterie belge*, a Belgian fry-stand, where patrons can stop by at any time of the day for fries and a sausage. Though service can be a bit slow, this is where you'll find some of the best fries in town (see also p 313).

Lester's
$
closed Sat evenings and Sun
1057 Avenue Bernard Ouest
☎276-6095

A Montréal institution, Lester's is famous for its smoked meat sandwiches. There is not much décor to speak of, creating a sterile and cold atmosphere, but no matter – it doesn't take long to eat a smoked-meat sandwich!

Le Paltoquet
$
closed Mon
1464 Avenue Van Horne
☎271-4229

Le Paltoquet is both a pastry shop and a café. Run by a friendly French couple, it serves delicious French sweets that will satisfy any sweet-tooth.

Toi Moi et Café
$
244 Avenue Laurier Ouest
☎279-9599

Toi Moi et Café is a charming place decorated in warm tones where hours can be spent sipping excellent coffee roasted on the premises. The café's Sunday brunches are extremely popular, so arrive early to avoid waiting in line.

Laurier B.B.Q.
$-$$
381 Avenue Laurier Ouest
☎273-3671

Laurier B.B.Q. has been a favourite of Montréal fami-

lies for years. The menu includes delicious, golden barbecued chicken. Meals are a bit expensive, however.

Pizzaïolle
$-$$
5100 Rue Hutchison
☎274-9349

Pizzaïolle was one of the first restaurants in Montréal to serve pizza cooked in a wood-burning oven. They also do the best job. The tables are a little close together, but the atmosphere is still very pleasant.

Piazzetta
$-$$
1105 Avenue Bernard Ouest
☎278-6465
See also p 314.

Pizzédélic
$-$$
370 Avenue Laurier Ouest
☎490-9599
See also p 307, 314 and 324.

Le Bistingo
$$
1199 Avenue Van Horne
☎270-6162

Avenue Van Horne is without a doubt one of the prettiest streets in Outremont. It is lined with some of the most charming bistros, of which Le Bistingo is among the most pleasant. The food is always delicious at this intimate establishment, which has only a few tables, large bay windows

Restaurants

and attentive service. The menu varies according to what fresh ingredients are available, which is why people come back again and again.

L'Escale à Saïgon
$$
Sat and Sun dinner only
107 Avenue Laurier Ouest
☎272-3456

The stark modern décor of this Vietnamese restaurant defies the stereotype, with a beautiful bar, stylized fans and exotic flowers. The cuisine is exquisite.

La Moulerie
$$
1249 Avenue Bernard Ouest
☎273-8132

If you like mussels (*moules* in French), check out La Moulerie for its elaborate menu and distinguished atmosphere. The menu includes mussels served in a variety of sauces, and also a section of other dishes entitled *j'haïs les moules* or "I hate mussels."

Paris-Beurre
$$
1226 Avenue Van Horne
☎271-7502

Though the menu at Paris-Beurre has remained unchanged for some time, the regulars keep coming back to savour the classic dishes that have stood the test of time, dishes like a *côté de boeuf* (beef) with mustard sauce, salmon with sorrel or

the delectable vanilla *crème brulée*, which is always a hit. Diners also delight in the attractive dining room, despite the drab view of Van Horne from the large bay windows.

Chez Lévesque
$$-$$$
1030 Avenue Laurier Ouest
☎279-7355

Laurier has several restaurants that have stood the test of time and maintained their enviable reputations, and Chez Levesque is one of them. Its menu includes traditional French dishes; there are no surprises but the food is high quality and always very tasty.

La Spaghettata
$$$
399 Avenue Laurier Ouest
☎273-9509

La Spaghettata is a large restaurant with a modern yet classic decor. Tables are set up on various different levels, creating the sensation that each table has its own private corner. The menu includes pasta and veal dishes.

Milos
$$$$
5357 Avenue du Parc
☎272-3522

Milos puts your standard Greek *brochetterie* to shame; this is real Greek cuisine. This establishment's reputation rests firmly with the quality of its exceptional selection of fresh fish and seafood from around the globe. The decor retains the air of the simple *psarotaverna* that this place started out as, but with a certain rustic elegance that appeals to a wealthy clientele. The portions are large, but if you have any room left, the traditional baklava is well worth it.

Little Italy

For the location of the following restaurants, please refer to p 189.

Café Italia
$
6840 Boulevard Saint-Laurent
☎495-0059
People don't go to the Café Italia for the décor, consisting of mismatched chairs and dominated by a large television, but for the comfortable atmosphere, the excellent sandwiches and most of all the cappuccino, considered by many to be the best in the city.

Petit Alep
$-$$
191 Rue Jean-Talon Est
☎270-9361
Mouhamara, tabouli, humus, wine leaves, shish-kebab, shish-taouk... is your mouth watering yet? All these Middle Eastern dishes are available at Petit Alep.

Called "little" because big brother Alep is right next door, this café-bistro mainly serves Syrian food that is absolutely delicious. Awaken your tastebuds with honey, oil or cayenne pepper. The place looks like a loft with its large garage door opening onto Rue Jean-Talon. Temporary exhibits adorn the wall and are sometimes interesting. The newspapers and magazines just might make you want to stay a while... Weekend brunch.

Auberge du Dragon Rouge
$$
8870 Rue Lajeunesse
☎858-5711
Located near the Crémazie Métro station, in the heart of a residential district, the Auberge du Dragon Rouge welcomes an eccentric mix of clients who come to taste typical medieval fare while enjoying period music played by troubadours. Not to be missed are the little *"pétaques"* (sliced potatoes cooked in oil, then sprinkled with cinnamon). On the second floor, the Échoppe du Dragon Rouge boutique sells medieval crafts; they also have a shop on Saint-Denis (see p 386).

Pizzeria Napoletana
$$
wine
189 Rue Dante
☎*276-8226*

Pizzeria Napoletana is small and nondescript but usually overrun with a large, lively crowd. These regulars keep coming back for the consistently good pastas and pizzas, not to mention that guests can bring their own wine and choose from an inexpensive menu.

La Tarantella
$$
184, rue Jean-Talon E.
☎*278-3067*

What distinguishes La Tarantella from other good Italian restaurants is its location. There is nothing more pleasant than eating a copious breakfast, savouring a delicious dinner or sipping a café au lait on the flowered terrace of this restaurant, which looks out on all the activity of the Jean-Talon market.

Gavroche
$$-$$$
closed Sun and Mon
dinner only
2098 Jean-Talon Est
☎*725-9077*

Gavroche is an intimate French restaurant with a devoted neighbourhood clientele that appreciates the beautifully presented classic French dishes. Friendly and professional service make for an enjoyable evening.

Casa Cacciatore
$$$
170 Rue Jean-Talon Est
☎*274-1240*

Casa Cacciatore has kept up Montréal's Italian culinary tradition for years near the Jean-Talon Market. The decor is warm and intimate with tablecloths, candles and professional service. The enticing menu lists various dishes such as pasta and quality meats carefully prepared by the chef.

Il Mulino
$$$
236 Rue Saint-Zotique Est
☎*273-5776*

Many of the well-to-do residents of Little Italy choose to eat at Il Mulino for its fine Italian cuisine.

Sault-au-Récollet

For the location of the following restaurants, please refer to p 193.

La Fonderie
$
closed Mon
10145 Rue Lajeunesse
☎*382-8234*

La Fonderie enjoys a solid reputation for its many delicious fondues.

Le Kerkennah
$
Sat and Sun
dinner only
1021 Rue Fleury Est
☎*387-1089*
Generous portions of Tunisian food are served at this neighbourhood restaurant.

Lesage J.B.
$
669 Rue Millen
☎*383-9217*
This is an excellent place to grab a quick no-frills meal: hot dogs, hamburgers and delicious fries make up the menu.

Pasta Express
$
1501 Rue Fleury Est
☎*384-3174*
Pasta Express, a little restaurant that serves unpretentious Italian cuisine, is frequented by neighbourhood residents. The pasta dishes are inexpensive and always delicious.

Le Wok de Szechuan
$
1950 Rue Fleury Est
☎*382-2060*
Le Wok de Szechuan, as you may have guessed, serves good Szechuan food to a Chinese and local clientele.

L'Estaminet
$$
1340 Rue Fleury Est
☎*389-0596*

L'Estaminet is a comfortable little café that serves salads, soups and desserts.

Il Cicerone
$$
679 Boulevard Henri-Bourassa Est
☎*388-3161*
Il Cicerone attracts mainly a business crowd, and a few locals in search of good Italian cuisine.

La Molisana
$$
1014 Rue Fleury Est
☎*382-7100*
The Italian restaurant La Molisana has a quiet atmosphere. The menu is not very original, consisting mainly of pasta dishes and pizza cooked in a wood-burning oven, but the food is good and the portions are generous. Musicians liven up weekend evenings with a few songs.

Il Mondo
$$-$$$
10724 Rue Millen
☎*389-8446*
Il Mondo is rather nondescript from the outside, but don't let first impressions fool you, because the menu includes some delicious dishes. Many say that this restaurant serves the best sauces in Montréal, and after just a few tastes, you'll be convinced. The service is attentive.

Restaurants

Île Sainte-Hélène and Île Notre-Dame

For the location of the following restaurants, please refer to p 197.

Festin des Gouverneurs
$$$$
☎879-1141

Festin des Gouverneurs creates feasts like those prepared in New France at the beginning of colonization. Characters in period costumes and traditional Québec dishes bring patrons back in time to these celebrations. The restaurant only serves groups and reservations are necessary.

Hélène de Champlain
$$$
Sat and Sun dinner only
☎395-2424

On Île Sainte-Hélène, the restaurant Hélène de Champlain lies in an enchanting setting, without question one of the loveliest in Montréal. The large dining room, with its fireplace and view of the city and the river, is extremely pleasant. Each corner has its own unique charm, overlooking the ever-changing surrounding landscape. Though the restaurant does not serve the fanciest of gastronomic cuisine, the food is very good. The service is courteous and attentive.

Nuances
$$$$
dinner only
Casino de Montréal, Île Notre-Dame
☎392-2708
☎800-665-2274 ext 4322

On the fifth floor of Montréal's Casino, Nuances is one of the best dining establishments in the city, perhaps even the country. Refined and imaginative, cuisine is served in a décor bathed in mahogany, brass, leather and views of the city lights. Of particular note on the menu are the creamy lobster *brandade* in flaky pastry (*brandade crémeuse de homard en millefeuille*), brochette of grilled quail (*brochette de caille grillée*), roast cutlet of duck (*magret de canard rôti*), tenderloin of Québec lamb (*longe d'agneau du Québec*) or striped polenta with grilled tuna (*polenta rayée entourée d'une grillade mi-cuite de thon*). The delectable desserts are each exquisitely presented. The plush and classic ambiance of this award-winning restaurant is perfect for business meals and special occasions. The casino also has four less expensive restaurants: **Via Fortuna** (**$$**), an Italian restaurant, **L'Impair** (**$**), a buffet, **La Bonne Carte** (**$$**), a buffet with *à la carte* service and **L'Entre-Mise** (**$**), a snack bar.

The Village

For the location of the following restaurants, please refer to p 203.

Kilo
$
1495 Rue Ste-Catherine Ouest
☎*596-3933*
(See p 304)

Saloon
$
1333 Sainte-Catherine Est
☎*522-1333*
Located in the heart of the gay village, Saloon has the same menu as Shed Café (see p 308), in a setting less like a shed and more like a saloon.

Piazzetta
$-$$
1101 Rue Sainte-Catherine Est
☎*526-2244*
See also p 314.

Bato Thaï
$$
Sat and Sun dinner only
1310 Rue Sainte-Catherine Est
☎*524-6705*
Bato Thaï boasts the prettiest décor of all of Montréal's Thai restaurants. Warmly painted walls and ceiling enclose the latest in design and style. The food is always good, even if the menu is a little too easy to decode: it amounts to little more than chicken, fish, shrimp, beef and vegetables, each prepared with a selection of the same sauces: coconut milk, peanut sauce, curry, etc. Unless you are there every week, this lack of variety is not a problem, especially considering the charming staff and relaxed mood of this temple of Thai cuisine.

Chez la Mère Berteau
$$
closed Mon
1237 Rue Champlain
☎*524-9344*
Located in a simple house, Chez la Mère Berteau is run by the owner, who waits on the tables, and his wife, who prepares the delicious meals. The wonderful flavours make you forget the small portions.

Le Petit Extra
$$
Sat and Sun dinner only
1690 Rue Ontario Est
☎*527-5552*
Le Petit Extra is a large European-style bistro and a distinguished spot for a good meal in a lively setting. There is a different table d'hôte each day. The clientele includes many regulars.

Piccolo Diavolo
$$
Sat and Sun dinner only
1336 Rue Ste-Catherine Est
☎*526-1336*
The warm decor of this Italian restaurant provides all the intimacy necessary for a pleasant, tête à tête

Restaurants

dinner. The service is discreet and efficient. Too bad that prices are so steep for such simple pasta dishes.

Planète
$$
1451 Rue Ste-Catherine Est
☎861-9999

Planète serves innovative fusion cuisine. The menu offers more than 30 choices of entrées from all five continents. One of the best restaurants in the Gay Village.

Amalfitana
$$-$$$
1381 Boulevard René-Lévesque Est
☎523-2483

With its busy decor, premises that are too small for the number of tables, and congenial and warmhearted service, Amalfitana retains an old-fashioned charm that is truly delightful. The emphasis here is on flawless Italian cuisine; each dish is a veritable feast for the palate, be it antipasti, *picata al limone*, rock lobster or tiramisu. To top it all off, the prices are very reasonable.

L'Entre-Miche
$$-$$$
Mon to Fri lunch, Thu to Sat dinner
2275 Sainte-Catherine Est
☎521-0816

A lovely modern decor and very high ceiling give this local French restaurant a touch of class. The service

is friendly, attentive and professional.

Le Grain de Sel
$$$
closed Sun and Mon, Tue and Wed evenings
2375 Rue Ste-Catherine Est
☎522-5105

Le Grain de Sel is a little French bistro serving an unpretentious *table d'hôte*. The delicious food is always fresh and beautifully prepared.

Maisonneuve

For the location of the following restaurants, please refer to p 210.

Le Goût de la Thaïlande
$-$$
6361 Rue Sherbrooke Est
☎252-7031
See also p 314.

Moe's Deli & Bar
$$
3950 Rue Sherbrooke Est
☎253-6637

Moe's Deli & Bar is particularly prized for its "happy hour," which fills up the bar; the restaurant is often just as crowded, however. The menu is extremely varied though we would recommend the salads, sandwiches and grilled specialties over most other menu items. Tempting dessert choices are available as well. The music is loud, the atmosphere, lively and the decor, reminiscent of an English pub. The Olympic Stadium is just a few steps away. See also p 297.

Little Burgundy and Saint-Henri

For the location of the following restaurants, please refer to p 217.

Ambiance
$
dinner only
1874 Rue Notre-Dame Ouest
☎*939-2609*
Ambiance is both a tea-room and an antique shop; the combination makes the décor particularly charming.

Café America
$
Mon-Fri 8am to 6pm
20 Rue des Seigneurs
☎*937-9983*
Café America boasts a large terrace giving onto the Lachine canal bicycle path. This is a pleasant stop for cyclists and those out on a stroll in the park. Quality dishes with a certain accent on health food is served in the old-fashioned décor of a renovated warehouse.

Green Spot
$
3041 Rue Notre-Dame Ouest,
☎*932-2340*
Green Spot is another shrine to the French fry that has established a solid rep-

utation among hot-dog and *poutine* connoisseurs. Everything reeks of grease and the décor is non-existent, but this just adds to the charm of the place... For fast-food fans only.

Sans Menu
$-$$
closed Sun and Mon
3714 Rue Notre-Dame Ouest
☎*933-4782*
Sans Menu is a tiny bistro that is just that – *sans menu*, which means without a menu. The choice of dishes changes every day, and can include rabbit, lamb, juicy steaks and pasta with a variety of original and innovative sauces. The décor is reminiscent of a plain old Chinese restaurant, but there is nothing boring about the food nor the friendly staff.

Pointe Saint-Charles and Verdun

For the location of the following restaurants, please refer to p 223.

Villa Wellington
$
closed Mon
4701 rue Wellington
☎*768-0102*
A Peruvian restaurant in Verdun? The Villa Wellington offers very tasty traditional Peruvian cuisine mainly composed of fish

Restaurants

and seafood. The portions are generous and the prices are reasonable.

Magnan
$$-$$$
2602 Rue Saint-Patrick Pointe-Saint-Charles
☎935-9647

Right in the heart of industrial Pointe-Saint-Charles is Magnan, one of the best-known taverns in Montréal. The house specialty is steak, ranging from 6 ounces to 22 ounces (170 grams to 625 grams) – hey, why not get your yearly ration of red meat in one shot? The high-quality beef and lobster festival attracts large crowds. Arrive by 11:30am to get a table for lunch.

West Island

For the location of the following restaurants, please refer to p 231 and p 233.

Lachine

Il Fornetto
$
1900 Boulevard Saint-Joseph
☎637-5253

Located near Lachine's marina, Il Fornetto is ideal for those who like taking after-dinner strolls – especially if that stroll is along the water and you've just eaten one of the generous portions of food served

here. With its noisy crowd and friendly service, the place is reminiscent of a trattoria. The pizzas cooked in the wood-burning oven are worth a try.

Le Caveau Szechwan
$$
798 Boulevard Saint-Joseph
☎639-1800

Chinese-food lovers should keep Le Caveau Szechwan in Lachine in mind.

La Fontanina
$$
closed Mon
3194 Boulevard Saint-Joseph
☎637-2475

For real Italian food, head to La Fontanin, located in a charming, renovated old house.

Pointe-Claire

Le Gourmand
$
42 Rue Sainte-Anne
☎695-9077

Located inside a beautiful old stone house, Le Gourmand is the perfect place for a hot soup for lunch on a crisp fall day, or a fresh salad and cool iced tea on a bright summer afternoon. The evening menu features French, Cajun and Californian dishes. You can also pick up some delicious fixings for a picnic by the lake at the deli counter.

The Marlowe
$$
981 Boulevard Saint-Jean
☎426-8713

The Marlowe, owned by the same folks as the Claremont (see p 324) and The Tavern (see p 325), is possibly one of the hippest resto-bars in the West Island. The menu offers a wide choice of interesting dishes; the dumplings with peanut sauce make a nice starter, while the smoked salmon sandwich or spinach salad are just two of the tasty possibilities for the next course. The desserts are equally inviting. As at its cousins to the east, the volume level can be high, so be prepared for a noisy evening.

Piazza Romana
$$
339 Lakeshore Road
☎697-3593

Piazza Romana is another favourite Italian restaurant in the Pointe-Claire village. Inside, the décor is quaint and modern, while a terrace is open outside during the warm summer months. The menu consists of a reliable choice of standard dishes.

Restorante Mirra
$$
Sat and Sun dinner only
252 Lakeshore Road
☎695-6222

Located inside a rambling old house by the water, Restorante Mirra boasts a solid reputation and a devoted following in this neck of the woods. Classic Italian cuisine is married with the latest trends and flavours to produce a mouth-watering menu. Service is friendly and courteous.

Dollard-des-Ormeaux

La Perle Szechuan
$-$$
Sat and Sun dinner only
4230 Boulevard Saint-Jean
☎624-6010

La Perle Szechuan is the most inviting of the scores of Szechuan places that have recently opened up in the West Island. The menu is extensive and features the usual dishes. An affordable buffet is served at lunch.

Traditional Music in Montréal

Closely linked to traditional Celtic music, the Québécois musical tradition is distinguished by wild rhythms and original melodies, and in Montréal, it happily cohabitates with the proud Irish traditions. Many pubs and cafés in the city give violinists, accordionists, flautists and guitarists the opportunity to play together every week, much to the delight of regulars. These jam sessions are a great way to hear the new carriers of tradition in a warm, friendly atmosphere.

Here are four popular addresses:

Le Verre bouteille
2112 Avenue Mont-Royal Est
☎*521-9409*
Québécois music
Tuesday nights

Le Sergent Recruteur
(microbrewery)
4650 Boulevard Saint-Laurent
☎*287-1412*
Celtic music
Every other Thursday

McKibbin's Irish Pub
1426 Rue Bishop
F*288-1580*
Irish music
Saturday, Monday and Tuesday

Hurley's
1225 Rue Crescent
F*861-4111*
Irish music
Saturdays in late afternoons

Entertainment

Montréal's reputation as a vibrant and unique North American city is well established.

Whether it be cultural activities, huge festivals, or simply the countless bars and nightclubs of all kinds, Montréal is a fascinating city with something for everyone. Sports enthusiasts will also get their fill with professional hockey and baseball, as well as the international sporting events that take place here each year.

Bars and Nightclubs

From sundown until early morning, Montréal is alive with the sometimes boisterous, other times more romantic rhythm of its bars. Crowded with people of all ages, there are bars designed to suit everyone's tastes, from the sidewalk bars along Rue Saint-Denis to the underground bars of Boulevard Saint-Laurent; from the crowded clubs on Rue Crescent to the gay bars in the "Village"; there are whole other worlds to discover.

Most bars do not have a cover charge (although in winter there is usually a mandatory coat-check). Expect to pay a few dollars to get into danceclubs on weekends. Québec nightlife is particularly lively – of course, it does not hurt that the sale of alcohol continues until 3am! Some bars remain open past this hour but serve only soft drinks. Drinking establishments that only have a tavern or brasserie permit must close at midnight.

Happy Hour ("5 à 7")

Bars in the downtown areas often offer two-for-one specials during "Happy Hour" (*usually from 5pm to 7pm*). During these hours you can buy two beers for the price of one, and drinks are offered at a reduced price. Some snack bars and dessert places offer the same discounts. A Québec law prohibits the advertising of these specials, so if you are interested, ask your waiter or waitress.

Vieux-Montréal

L'Air du Temps
194 Rue Saint-Paul Ouest ☎842-2003
L'Air du Temps ranks among the most famous jazz bars in Montréal. Located in the heart of Old Montréal, it has a fantastic interior décor with scores of antiques. As the place is often packed, it is a good idea to arrive early to get a decent seat. The cover charge varies according to the show. Call for information on upcoming acts.

Aux Deux Pierrots
104 Rue Saint-Paul Ouest ☎861-1270
A noisy, enthusiastic crowd is drawn to Aux Deux Pierrots to sing along with Québec variety singers. During summer, there is a pleasant outdoor terrace.

Isart
263 Rue Saint-Antoine Ouest ☎393-1758
A true cornerstone of the contemporary art scene, Isart is a dark bar that is spread over two storeys, with an art gallery and bar on the first floor and a lounge furnished with comfortable couches on the second. Recent performers have included Andy Milne, a Canadian jazz pianist known in the avant-garde and M-Base scenes. Local bands present their new gems here and attract a crowd of 18- to 30-year-old fans who come for experimental, trip-hop, jazz and trance music. There are sometimes exhibitions of contemporary art, everything from collage to oils. Coming here won't break the bank, either – drinks cost next to nothing.

Downtown and the Golden Square Mile

Altitude 717
1 Place Ville-Marie
If you are one of those people who love reaching

high places, you must ascend to the top of Place Ville-Marie. On the 44th floor, Altitude 717 is jam-packed on weekend evenings, especially on Thursday and Friday when a clientele of young professionals in their 30s comes here for drinks before dinner. The comfortable room and its two terraces offer breathtaking views of the city and the river that unquestionably justify the place's popularity. Later at night, clubbers have to climb another storey to the 45th floor to dance the night away at Altitude 727, a hip club. Finally, there is the Restaurant Club Lounge 737 (see p 298) on the 46th floor.

Biddle's
2060 Aylmer
☎842-8656
If you like jazz and want to tuck into some good chicken and spareribs, Biddle's will be right up your alley. Charles Biddle is there almost every evening with his double bass and a few musicians to play for you while you dine. You can also just come for a drink.

Carlos & Pepes
1420 Rue Peel
☎288-3090
Carlos & Pepes, patronized by a predominantly English crowd in their 20s, has two floors, the first of which is a Tex-Mex restaurant. The second floor is equipped with TVs that keep fans up-to-date on their preferred spectator sport.

Funkytown
1454 A Rue Peel
☎282-8387
Downtown, Funkytown is frequented by a twenty-something clientele nostalgic for the sounds of the 1980s. The disco ball hanging from the ceiling, the illuminated floor, and the disco and rock music mixed with current hits make this a great place to dance and perhaps make new acquaintances.

Les Foufounes Électriques
87 Rue Sainte-Catherine Est
☎844-5539
Les Foufounes Électriques is a fantastic, one-of-a-kind bar/dance club/pick-up joint. The best bar in Québec for dancing to alternative music, it attracts a motley crowd of young Montrealers, ranging from punks to medical students. The decor, consisting of graffiti and strange sculptures, is wacky, to say the

least. Don't come here for a quiet night.

The Hard Rock Café
1458 Rue Crescent
☎*987-1420*

The famous Hard Rock Café is decorated with objects once owned by highly acclaimed musicians. It has a relatively small dance floor. Get there early on the weekend, or you'll find yourself waiting in line to get in.

Hurley's Irish Pub
1225 Rue Crescent
☎*861-4111*

Discreetly tucked away south of Rue Sainte-Catherine among the innumerable Crescent Street restaurants and bars, Hurley's Irish Pub succeeds in recreating an atmosphere worthy the most traditional of Irish pubs, thanks largely to the excellent amateur Irish folk musicians and the world-famous Guinness stout.

Luba Lounge
2109 Rue de Bleury
☎*288-5822*

For a relaxing evening comfortably seated with a glass of porto, try Luba Lounge, which features a DJ and bands a couple of nights a week. This place is packed with 20- to 30-year-olds on Fridays, partly because there is no cover charge.

Peel Pub
1107 Sainte-Catherine Ouest
☎*844-6769*

The most popular place in town for sports and draught beer fans. If you have a victory to celebrate, a defeat to mourn, or simply feel like letting loose, head on over to Peel Pub. Special events are held here every night, and there are a number of prizes to be won.

Le Sherlock
1010 Rue Sainte-Catherine Ouest
☎*878-0088*

A very lovely décor, reminiscent of an English pub, including busts of Sherlock Holmes. It is also very big and very popular! Everything, however, is quite expensive, and the restaurant is not recommended. About 15 pool tables are also at the disposal of customers.

The Sir Winston Churchill Pub
1459 Rue Crescent
☎*288-3814*

An English-style bar, the Sir Winston Churchill attracts crowds of singles who come here to cruise and meet people. It has pool tables and a small dance floor.

Speakeasy
1426 Rue Bishop
☎*288-1580*

This is the place for scotch drinkers. The establishment offers about 20 single malts that are favourites of busi

The Rave Scene

If you like electrifying and pounding dancefloors, go to an after-hours club, which are always packed. The party atmosphere will leave you spinning for days! Eccentricity goes at these places, where dancing is the main attraction.

The crowd is generally young and friendly. Opening and closing hours vary (between 2am and 9am) from place to place. Since the sale of alcohol is prohibited after 3am, water, juice and smart drinks are served at after-hours clubs.

Here are some places where you can rave... at your own risk!

Back Street
1459 St-Alexandre

Blade
1296 Amherst

Daylight
1254 rue Stanley

Red Lite
1955 Notre-Dame-de-Fatima, Laval

Sona
1439 rue de Bleury

Stéréo
858 Ste-Catherine Est

Entertainment

ness people during happy hour. Students invade the spot later to talk leisurely over the quiet background music in this attractive, den-like bar.

Thursday's
1449 Rue Crescent
☎288-5656
Thursday's bar is very popular, especially among the city's English-speaking population. It is a favourite meeting place for business people and professionals.

Upstairs
1254 Rue Mackay
☎931-6808
Located in the heart of downtown Montréal, Upstairs hosts jazz and blues shows seven days a week. During summer, the walled terrace behind the bar is a wonderful place to take in the sunset.

The Old Dublin Pub
1219A Rue University
☎861-4448
An Irish pub with live Celtic music and an impressive selection of draught beer.

Woody's Pub
1234 Rue Bishop
☎954-0771
If you're between the ages of 22 and 26, Woody's Pub could well be the place for you. On its three levels, an English clientele comes to chat, have drinks and let loose on the small dance floor. Current hits and disco classics fill the air at this little place, where cruising, albeit subtle, is the name of the game.

Around the Hôtel Dieu

Allegra
3523A Boulevard Saint-Laurent
☎845-4337
Next door to Di Salvio's, the private salons and velvet curtains of the Allegra are a veritable haven for those who prefer a quiet evening with a vintage cigar, available here for anywhere between $3 and $30. Wanna-bes clad in jeans and sneakers will be turned away.

Bacci
3553 Boulevard Saint-Laurent
☎287-9331
Bacci has about 30 pool tables, as well as a varied but mediocre menu. That's not what people come here for, however: a pleasure-hungry crowd packs in here to chat, cruise, fall in love and drink beer, which is unfortunately quite expensive.

Le Balattou
4372 Boulevard Saint-Laurent
☎845-5447
Dark, smoky, jam-packed, hot, hectic and noisy, Le Balattou is without a doubt the most popular African nightclub in Montréal. On weekends, the cover charge is $7 (including one drink).

Shows are presented only during the week, when the cost of admission varies.

Belmont sur le Boulevard
4483 Boulevard Saint-Laurent, corner of Avenue Mont-Royal
☎*845-8443*
A clientele composed mainly of junior executives crowds into the Belmont sur le Boulevard. On weekends, the place is literally overrun with customers.

Les Bobards
4328 Boulevard Saint-Laurent, corner of Avenue Marie-Anne
☎*987-1174*
Les Bobards, an unassuming neighbourhood bar, is the perfect location for people-watching along Saint-Laurent while enjoying one of the many beers on tap. All-you-can-eat peanuts are another reason to stop in, and the inevitable shells covering the floor add colour and charm to the place.

Café Campus
57 Prince Arthur
☎*844-1010*
Forced to move from its location in front of the Université de Montréal, Café Campus has settled into a large place on Rue Prince Arthur. Over the years, it has become a Montréal institution. The décor is still quite plain. Good musicians frequently perform here.

Bar Saint-Laurent
3874 Boulevard Saint-Laurent
☎*844-4717*
A motley crowd frequents the noisy Bar Saint-Laurent every weekend to drink pitchers of beer and dance to classic rock 'n' roll or old school punk music. A great place if you're looking for a little drama, but don't expect a peaceful night.

Swimming
3643 Boulevard Saint-Laurent
☎*282-7665*
The entrance to Swimming leads through the dilapidated vestibule of a building dating back to the beginning of the century, making the view from the third floor of this gigantic pool room even more striking. The large rectangular bar and endless rows of pool tables and players are surrounded by glazed concrete columns, deliberately emphasized and topped by strange polyhedrons. The old tin ceiling is a reminder of both the industrial city of the early 20th century and the building's original purpose.

Quartier Latin

Baloo's
403 Rue Ontario Est
☎*843-5469*
At the corner of Ontario and Saint-Denis is Baloo's, a very appealing drinking hole with a very friendly

Entertainment

staff, frequented by a crowd mainly in their 20s. Low prices on beer and shooters are their specialty, as the bartender will be sure to point out. French and English rock, alternative, rhythm and blues are played here. A second bar and a dance floor are open for partiers from Thursday to Saturday, when rock bands also play. The establishment also has a pool table, a football game and a few televisions tuned either to sporting events or The Simpsons.

Les Beaux Esprits
2073 Rue Saint-Denis
☎844-0882
A bar with a modest décor, Les Beaux Esprits hosts good jazz and blues shows.

Café Sarajevo
$$
2080 Clark
☎284-5629
Café Sarajevo hosts gypsy bands on Thursdays, Fridays and Saturdays, and jazz musicians the rest of the week. The crowd is a mix of bohemian students and, of course, Yugoslavians, and the decor is straight out of a bar in that country. While sipping a beer or a glass of red Hungarian wine, why not try some Balkan specialities, such as *bourek* (meat and filo pastry roll), *pleckavica* (hamburger) and *cevapcici* (meatballs) served with

ajvar (red pepper spread). There is a patio out back that is pleasant during the summer. Meet Osman, the charismatic owner, who bears an uncanny resemblance to Sean Connery! Closed Mondays. Cover charge later in the evening for performances.

Café Chaos
1635 and 1637 Rue Saint-Denis
☎844-1301
Set on two storeys, the co-operatively run Café Chaos attracts a packed crowd of young, energetic students who like to chat about music and life in general. The music here includes every imaginable style: garage, rock, surf, alternative, new wave, techno-industrial, etc. Local musicians present their newest creations four nights a week, beginning at about 9pm. Groups like Caféine and WD-40 made their debuts here and are still regulars. The establishment also serves mainly vegetarian cuisine Monday to Friday from noon to 10pm. The second floor has an unpretentious décor; the ambience is perfect for conversation, except on nights when the music from downstairs is too loud. Nevertheless, come early to enjoy the happy hour from 4pm to 7pm. There is also a back terrace that seats 75.

Le Cheval Blanc

809 Rue Ontario Est
☎*522-0211*

Le Cheval Blanc is a Montréal tavern and micro-brew-
ery that does not appear to
have been renovated since
the 1940s; hence its unique
style! Excellent beers are
brewed on the premises.

Île Noire

342 Rue Ontario Est
☎*982-0866*

The Île Noire is a beautiful
bar in the purest Scottish
tradition. The abundance of
precious wood used for the
décor gives the place a cosy
charm and sophisticated
atmosphere. The knowl-
edgeable staff guide guests
through the impressive list
of whiskeys. The bar also
has a good selection of
imported draught beer.
Unfortunately, the prices
are high.

Jello Bar

151 Rue Ontario Est
☎*285-2621*

Jello Bar is strewn with an
unusual mix of furniture
and knick-knacks straight
out of the suburban living
rooms of the 1960s and
1970s. The bar serves a
selection of 32 different
martini cocktails to be
sipped to the mellow
sounds of jazz or blues.
Great musical acts are regularly booked.

Le Medley

1170 Rue Saint-Denis
☎*842-6557 (bar)*
☎*842-SHOW (show information)*

Many of the big names in
the music business have
performed at Le Medley.
Indeed, such musicians as
Bob Walsh, Jimmy James
and other notable blues
singers have attracted large,
enthusiastic crowds. Artists
from south of the border
such as Marilyn Manson
and icons of a not-too-dis-
tant past like Chuck Berry
and James Brown have
come here to perform their
classics. Spread out over
two floors, Le Medley offers
lots of room, both seated
and standing, and the beer
flows freely.

L'Ours Qui Fume

2019 Rue Saint-Denis
☎*845-6998*

Hear ye! Hear ye! Fans of
the songs and poetry of
Québec commune at L'Ours
Qui Fume. Local writers
and musicians drop in here
to discuss, sometimes quite
loudly, their most recent
artistic discoveries, or simply to relax. Decorated with
photographs of these same
artists, this extremely appealing little place, which
occasionally presents live
music, is well worth checking out.

Entertainment

P'tit Bar
3451 Rue Saint-Denis
☎ *281-9124*

Right opposite Square Saint-Louis, the P'tit Bar is the perfect place to discuss literature, philosophy, photography, etc. The former hangout of the late Gérald Godin, a celebrated Québec poet, this place will appeal to fans of French music. Photo exhibits make up the sober decor.

Quartier Latin Pub
318 Rue Ontario Est
☎ *845-3301*

The Quartier Latin Pub serves a variety of draught and bottled beers. Decorated with photographs of Montréal, this pub is a pleasant place to kick back and relax to the sounds of acid-jazz and soul. A thirty-something clientele comes here to chat about business, music, etc. The place was completely renovated in the summer of 1996, and its elegant new look is sure to please even the most sophisticated visitors.

Saint-Sulpice
1682 Rue Saint-Denis
☎ *844-9458*

The Saint-Sulpice occupies all three floors of an old house and is tastefully decorated. Its front and back terraces are perfect places to make the most of summer evenings.

Plateau Mont-Royal

Bacci
4205 Rue Saint-Denis
☎ *844-3929*
see p 344

Bily Kun
354 Rue Mont-Royal Est
☎ *845-5392*

The second bar opened by the "Cheval Blanc" microbrewery, Bily Kun offers a wide selection of beers, including the excellent and reasonable house brand. With an original décor of mounted ostrich necks, this place has a friendly and very lively atmosphere.

Bleu est Noir
812 Rue Rachel Est
☎ *524-4809*

A motley young crowd ranging in age from 18 to 30 lets loose on the dance floor at Bleu est Noir. Underground classics from the 1980s mix it up with the latest hits of today's pop darlings until late into the night.

Le Boudoir
850 Avenue du Mont-Royal Est
☎ *526-2819*

The inviting atmosphere at Le Boudoir is sure to appeal to a broad audience. A variety of movie posters adorn the walls, giving the place a distinctive character. It has a pool table and a foosball table, and hosts

live folk and blues bands
every Tuesday.

Diable Vert
4557 Rue Saint-Denis
☎**849-5888**
The Diable Vert is the place
to go to let loose on a large
dance floor. Because it is
very popular with students,
there might be a lineup.
Cover charge is $2 (includ-
ing coat-check) on Wednesday and Thursday nights
and $3 on Friday and Satur-
day nights.

Dogue
4177 Rue Saint-Denis
☎**845-8717**
The Dogue is the ideal
place to dance, dance,
dance! The music, which
ranges from Elvis classics to
the latest Rage Against the
Machine hit, gratifies a
rather young, high-spirited
crowd thirsting for cheap
beer. There are two pool
tables, which are a bit in
the way, but keep the pool
sharks entertained. The
place is jam-packed seven
days a week, so you are
strongly advised to get
there early.

Inspecteur Épingle
4051 Rue Saint-Hubert
☎**598-7764**
Another good place for a
beer and some great blues
is Inspecteur Épingle. This
tavern, which became fa-
mous as a regular (less so
now) hangout of controversial Québec singer Plume

Latraverse, books good
local blues musicians.

Passeport
4156 Rue Saint-Denis
☎**842-6063**
Passeport is very dark and
intimate. A twenty-some-
thing crowd comes here to
dance to 1980s tunes or
simply have a beer with
friends. This unpretentious
place gets packed on the
weekend, especially during
summer.

Sofa
451 Rue Rachel Est
☎**285-1011**
Sofa invites you into a
lounge atmosphere where a
crowd between the ages of
20 and 35 comes to sip port
and scotch. As the name
indicates, this establishment
is scattered with comfortable plush couches that are
perfect for enjoying a drink
with old friends and new
acquaintances. A small
stage allows some local
bands (Jazz Pharmacy, Blue
Continentals, Ouaouaron)
to take the audience into
the worlds of jazz, soul and
R&B.

El Zaz Bar
4297 Rue Saint-Denis
El Zaz Bar is owned by the
same people who run the
Zaziumm restaurants. There
is a small popular dance
floor where the crowd can
let loose to almost every
style of music, from French
crooners to disco, salsa and

Entertainment

techno. The unusual decor, composed of a multitude of mismatched objects, even includes the shell of a Volkswagen van. The service is nothing to write home about, but if you are interested in a change of scenery, this is the place to go!

The Zinc Café Bar

1148 Avenue Mont-Royal Est ☎523-5432

Looking for a good place to talk about everything and nothing while enjoying a *picon bière*? The Zinc Café Bar is an inviting place that serves a variety of unusual drinks.

Westmount and Western Montréal

Crocodile

5414 Rue Gatineau
☎733-2125

At Crocodile, the clientele is mostly made up of young professionals who come here to dance to popular music, have a few drinks and to see and be seen. The restaurant offers a standard menu in the early evening.

Grande Gueule

5615a Chemin-de-la-Côte-des-Neiges
☎733-3512

The Grande Gueule, located right near the Université de Montréal, has a light menu, cheap draught beer and four pool tables. A number

of board games are also available. On Mondays, you can play pool for free when you buy a drink.

Ye Olde Orchard

5563 Monkland Avenue
☎484-1569

Ye Olde Orchard is a neighbourhood pub and restaurant in the heart of the increasingly trendy Monkland Village. It attracts a primarily local crowd of regulars who meet for a pint (or two) in casual, relaxed surroundings.

The six local micro-brews and six imported beers on tap are the perfect accompaniment to a burger or a plate of fish 'n chips. And for the connoisseur, there is a choice of 30 single malt whiskeys. Live Celtic, blues or pop music is featured from Saturday to Tuesday nights. Friendly servers in kilts.

Typhoon Lounge

5752 Monkland Avenue, corner of Wilson
☎482-4448

Come sip a beer on the comfy couches at Typhoon Lounge, which hosts jam sessions on Monday nights. Lounge music takes over on Tuesdays and Saturdays, while Wednesdays are devoted to favourites from the 70s and 80s, Thursdays feature reggae and ska, and Saturdays play world beat.

Outremont

Fûtenbulle
273 Avenue Bernard Ouest
☎*276-0473*
The Fûtenbulle is frequented by a varied crowd. Besides the simple menu, patrons can choose from one of the largest selection of beers in Montréal.

Set
5301 Boulevard Saint-Laurent
☎*270-9311*
The Set is a small cozy bar, decorated with antiques. The pleasant choice of music is always at just the right volume so as not to interfere with conversation. This is a popular spot on weekends.

Little Italy

Whisky Café
5800 Boulevard Saint-Laurent
☎*278-2646*
The Whisky Café is so conscientiously decorated that even the men's bathrooms are a strange tourist attraction. The warm colours used in a modern setting, the tall columns covered with woodwork and pre-1950s-style chairs all create a sense of comfort and elegance. The well-off, well-bred clientele consists of a gilded youth between the ages of 20 and 35.

Gay Bars and Nightclubs

Bar Exotica
$2; Thu to Sun 10pm to 3am
417 Rue Saint-Pierre
☎*281-1773*
Bar Exotica is the only gay Latino disco in Montréal and will transport clients from Old Montréal to Guadalajara or Acapulco. Frequented by a largely Québécois crowd, it plays a mix of fashionable American hits and *muy caliente* Latino tunes. There are a lot of hips wiggling here, especially during the hot tropical numbers. Lots of fun!

Cabaret l'Entre-Peau
1115 Rue Sainte-Catherine Est
☎*525-7566*
Cabaret l'Entre-Peau puts on transvestite shows. The place attracts a lively, mixed clientele.

Sisters
1333 Rue Sainte-Catherine Est, 2nd floor
☎*522-4717*
Sisters is for women, lesbian, bi or straight (men are refused admission, except on Tuesday). The latest mainstream hits get things moving and shaking on the dance floor.

Entertainment

Sky Pub
1474 Rue Sainte-Catherine Est
☎529-6969

Sky Pub, the busiest gay bar in Montréal, boasts a refined, cozy and elegant decor. A profusion of wood and inspired lighting have made this place popular since its opening. The loud and uninspired music, however, leaves a bit to be desired. In the summer there is people-watching on the terrace facing Sainte-Catherine. With its three or four dance floors that each play a different type of music (alternative, commercial, techno, retro, etc.), the two-storey club rivals Unity as Montréal's largest gay club. Obviously, in such an immense place, there is more than one atmosphere. The crowd is mostly young and the cover charge changes frequently. Note: At press time, the Sky Pub was closed for renovations but scheduled to reopen shortly.

Unity
Thu to Sun 10pm to 3am
In the summer, the bar and
terrace open every day at 4pm.
1171 Rue Sainte-Catherine E
☎523-4429

Unity is a large gay club frequented by a mainly male crowd of all ages. Its architecture is very interesting with different levels including a mezzanine from which you can watch the dance floor and the en-

trancing light show. In addition to the main dance floor, there are also two other dance floors, including the Bamboo, where the music tends to be quieter, and another featuring the trendiest of tunes. On the main floor, there is now a lovely bar decorated with plenty of woodwork and carefully thought-out lighting. For warm summer nights there is a huge rooftop terrace.

Stéréo
858 Rue Ste-Catherine East

Young members of the gay community who go to sleep in the wee hours of the morning don't miss the chance to drop by Stéréo on the weekend. This after-hours club opens at 2am and is well known for the quality of its sound equipment… you guessed it: it's loud! The clientele here is hip and quite young.

Fun and Games

Laser Quest (*7$/15 min.; 1226 Rue Ste-Catherine Ouest,* ☎393-3000) will thrill young people of all ages who relish interactive science-fiction games. Two teams battle it out with laser light guns in a labyrinth spread out over three floors.

Located on Île Sainte-Hélène, **La Ronde** amusement park is chock-full of world-class roller coasters, Ferris wheels and rides that will delight thrill-seekers young and old (see p 199).

With 2,700 slot machines and 100 gaming tables (blackjack, roulette, baccarat, poker, etc.), the **Casino de Montréal** *(free admission, every day 24 hours, Métro île Sainte-Hélène and Bus No. 167, ☎392-2746)* is without a doubt a major player in the city's nightlife. Following the addition of a new wing in the former Québec pavilion in 1996, the casino is now one of the 10 biggest casinos in the world in terms of its gaming equipment. A cabaret show, also added in 1996, has seen the likes of Liza Minelli, André-Philippe Gagnon and Jean-Pierre Ferland to name but a few, and has brought a new vitality to the place.

Cultural Activities

Montréal has a distinct cultural scene. All year round, there are shows and exhibitions, which enable Montrealers to discover different aspects of the arts. Accordingly, shows and films from all over the world, exhibitions of all different styles of art, and festivals for all tastes and ages are presented here. The free

weekly newspapers *Voir, Ici, The Mirror* and *Hour* sum up the main events taking place in Montréal.

Theatres and Concert Halls

Prices vary greatly from one theatre to the next. Most of the time, however, there are discount rates for children, students and seniors.

Agora de la danse
840 Rue Cherrier
☎525-7575
Métro Sherbrooke

Centaur Theatre
453 Rue Saint-François
☎288-3161

Espace Libre
1945 Rue Fullum
☎521-4191

Le Cabaret
2111 Boulevard Saint-Laurent
☎845-2014
Métro Saint-Laurent

Monument National
1182 Boulevard Saint-Laurent ☎871-9883
Métro Saint-Laurent

Place des Arts
260 Boulevard de Maisonneuve Ouest
☎285-4200
☎842-2112 *(for the box office)*
Métro Place-des-Arts
The complex contains five performance spaces: Salle Wilfrid-Pelletier, Théâtre

Entertainment

Maisonneuve, Théâtre Jean-Duceppe, Théâtre du Café de la Place and the Cinquième Salle, opened in 1992. The **Orchestre Symphonique de Montréal** (*for subscription information call ☎849-0269, otherwise call the Place des Arts box office*) and **Grands Ballets Canadiens** (*for subscription information call ☎842-9951, otherwise call the Place des Arts box office*) both perform in the main hall.

Saidye Bronfman Centre
5170, ch. de la Côte-Sainte-Catherine
☎*739-7944*

Spectrum
318 Rue Sainte-Catherine Ouest
☎*861-5851*
Métro Place-des-Arts
Shows usually begin around 11pm. Count on at least $10 to get in. Shows after 11pm are usually free during the Jazz Festival.

Theâtre La Chapelle
3700 Rue Saint-Dominique
☎*843-7738*

Théâtre d'Aujourd'hui
3888 Rue Saint-Denis
☎*282-3900*
Métro Sherbrooke

Théâtre Denise-Pelletier
4353 Rue Sainte-Catherine Est
☎*253-8974*
Métro Papineau, Bus 34

Théâtre Espace GO
4890 Boulevard Saint-Laurent
☎*271-0813*
Métro Laurier, Bus 51

Théâtre de Verdure
Parc Lafontaine
☎*872-2644*
Métro Sherbrooke
Set up in the heart of the Parc Lafontaine, the Théâtre de Verdure puts on free open-air shows all summer long.

Théâtre des Deux Mondes
7285 Rue Chabot
☎*593-4417*

Théâtre du Gesù
1200 Rue de Bleury
☎*861-4036*
Métro Place-des-Arts

Théâtre La Licorne
4559 Rue Papineau
☎*523-2246*

Théâtre du Nouveau Monde
84 Rue Sainte-Catherine Ouest
☎*866-8668*
Métro Place-des-Arts

Théâtre Olympia
1004 Rue Sainte-Catherine Est
☎*287-7884*

Théâtre du Rideau Vert
4664 Rue Saint-Denis
☎*844-1793*
Métro Laurier

Théâtre de Quat'Sous
100 Avenue des Pins Est
☎*845-7277*
Métro Sherbrooke

Théâtre Saint-Denis
1594 Rue Saint-Denis
☎*849-4211*
Métro Berri-UQAM

Usine C
1345 Avenue Lalonde
☎*521-4493*
Métro Beaudry

Ticket Sales

There are three major ticket agencies in Montréal that sell tickets for shows, concerts and other events over the telephone. Service charges, which vary according to the show, are added to the price of the ticket. Credit cards are accepted.

Admission
☎*(514) 790-1245*
☎*800-361-4595*

Telspec
☎*(514) 790-2222*

Information on the Arts

Info-Arts (Bell)
☎*790-ARTS (2787)*
☎*800-280-2787*.
This service provides information on current cultural and artistic events in the city.

Museums

Permanent exhibits at most museums are free on Wednesday evenings between 6pm and 9pm. Special rates are available for temporary exhibits during the same period. Call ahead to check. See the "Exploring" chapter for descriptions of various museums.

Movie Theatres

Montréal has many movie theatres; here is a list of the major downtown theatres. Special rates are offered on Tuesdays and for matinees. The regular price of a ticket is $8.50 (except at repertory theatres).

The following show films in French:

Berri
1280 Rue Berri
☎*849-3456*
Métro Berri-UQAM

Le Parisien
480 Rue Sainte-Catherine Ouest
☎*866-3856*
Métro McGill

Le Quartier Latin
305 Rue Émery, corner of Saint-Denis
Métro Berri-UQAM
☎*849-4422*

Entertainment

The following show films in English:

Centre Eaton
705 Rue Sainte-Catherine Ouest
☎985-5730

Paramount
977 Rue Sainte-Catherine Ouest
☎866-0111

The following are repertory theatres:

La Cinémathèque Québécoise
335 Boulevard de Maisonneuve Est
☎842-9763
shows films in French
Métro Berri-UQAM

Cinéma du Parc
3516 av. Du Parc
☎281-1900
The Cinéma du Parc is *the* place to see international, indie and cult flicks. The selection is impressive, with three theatres showing different films all day. Everything from B-movies to the latest Cannes entries. Pick up their detailed, informative schedule at any downtown café or bar. Students and seniors pay less.

Ex-Centris
3536 Boulevard St. Laurent
☎(514) 847-3536
French and English
Ex-Centris is fast becoming a Montréal cultural institution. The brainchild of a local media guru, this theatre/café/architectural gem is host to numerous festivals and media events. Aside from the fantastic films screened here, highlights include an enormous rotating clock in the lobby, reflective metal bathrooms, and a unique, televised ticket-buying experience!

Impérial
1430 Rue de Bleury
☎848-0300
Métro Place-des-Arts
This is the oldest movie theatre in Montréal, and by far the most beautiful.

Imax
at the Vieux-Port de Montréal, on Rue de la Commune, corner of Boulevard Saint-Laurent
☎496-4629
Films are presented on a giant screen (see p 102).

Office National du Film (National Film Board)
1564 Rue Saint-Denis
☎496-6895
A *cinérobothèque* allows several people to watch NFB films at once. A robot, the only one like it in the world, loads each machine. The complex is dedicated to Québec and Canadian cinema.

Cultural Centres

Cultural centres have been established to help young artists all over Montréal practice their crafts on a more professional level and to promote their work. In order to make these exhibits and shows accessible to all, admission is free. Schedules of the specific exhibits at these Maisons de la Culture are published in the "Show" section of *The Gazette* newspaper every Friday.

Chapelle Historique du Bon Pasteur
100 Rue Sherbrooke Est
☎872-5338

Côte-des-Neiges
5290 Chemin de la Côte-des-Neiges
☎872-6889

Frontenac
2550 Rue Ontario Est
☎872-7882

La Petite Patrie/Rosemont
6707 Avenue de Lorimier
☎872-1730

Maisonneuve
4120 Rue Ontario Est
☎872-2200

Marie-Uguay
6052 Rue Monk
☎872-2044

Mercier
8105 Rue Hochelaga
☎872-8755

Notre-Dame-de-Grâce
3755 Rue Botrel
☎872-2157

Plateau Mont-Royal
465 Avenue du Mont-Royal Est
☎872-2266

Maison du Pressoir
10865 Rue du Pressoir
☎872-8749

Festivals

During summer, festival fever takes hold of Montréal. From May to September, the city hosts a whole series of festivals, each with a different theme. One thing is certain – there is something for everyone. As the summer season draws to a close, the events become less frequent.

The **Présence Autochtone** will be celebrating its 10th anniversary in June 2000. The festival screens First Nations' films, including some world-wide premieres, and gives you the chance to meet some of the filmmakers. Theatre, music and dance performances are also held, as are public lectures and on-site painting demonstrations.

The most important festival of its kind in North America, **La Mondial de la Bière (Montreal Beer Festival)** (*$8; 6415 Rue Écores, first floor,* ☎722-9640, ≈722-8467, *http://festivalmondialbiere.qc.ca*) beer festival is now in its fifth year. This event is held on Île Notre-Dame from June 8 to the 17, 2000 and gives you the chance to taste some of the 200 beers from around the world. To encourage responsible drinking, the samples are served in 3- to 4-ounce cups, paid for with coupons (*70¢ per coupon*). For *$13*, you can get an "Event Passport," which grants free admission for 10 days of the event. The "VIP Passport" (*$35*) is valid for one day and lets you into the VIP tasting lounge, as well as seminars and workshops. Real beer fans can go all out and get the 10-day VIP Passport (*$125*), which includes access to the VIP tasting lounge, seminars and workshops.

The magical **Cirque du Soleil** (*adult $25.25-$49.50, child $17.75-$34.50,* ☎ *790-1245, 800-361-4595 or 800-678-5440*) performs a new show in Montréal practically every year for a few weeks, and it is sure to amaze and delight. This internationally renowned troupe from Québec has made a name for itself with its innovative approach to this traditional form, drawing on theatrical traditions from around the world, and above all from the realm of the imagination.

In 2000, the **Concours International d'Art Pyrotechnique / International Fireworks Competition** (☎*872-6222*) starts around mid-June and ends in late July. The world's top pyrotechnists present high-quality pyro-musical shows every Saturday in June and every Sunday in July. Montrealers crowd to the La Ronde amusement park (*tickets cost $28, $29 or $30; call* ☎ *790-1245 or 800-361-4595*), on the Pont Jacques-Cartier or alongside the river (both at no cost) to admire the spectacular blossoms of flame that colour the sky above the city and last for over half an hour.

During the **Festival International de Jazz de Montréal** (☎*871-1881*), hundreds of shows set to the rhythm of jazz and its variations are presented on stages erected around Place des Arts. From June 28 to July 9 2000, this part of the city and a fair number of theatres are buzzing with activity. The event offers people an opportunity to take to the streets and be carried away by the festive atmosphere of the fantastic, free outdoor shows that attract Montrealers and visitors in large numbers.

Humour and creativity are highlighted during the **Festival Juste pour Rire / Just for Laughs Festival** (☎*845-3155 or 790-HAHA*), which will be held from July 13 to the 23 2000. Theatres host comedians from a variety of countries for the occasion. Théâtre Saint-Denis presents shows consisting of short performances by a number of different comedians. Outdoor activities take place in the Quartier-Latin, on Rue Saint-Denis south of Rue Sherbrooke, which is closed to traffic.

The **FrancoFolies** (☎871-1881) are organized to promote French-language music and song. From July 27th to August 5th 2000, artists from all Francophone countries (Europe, Africa, French Antilles, Québec and French Canada) will perform, providing spectators with a unique glimpse of the world's French musical talent.

The **Fêtes Gourmandes** (5$/person; ☎861-8241), which usually takes place in August on Île Notre-Dame, is the perfect opportunity to sample gastronomic goodies from Québec, the rest of Canada and several other countries. Over a kilometre of international tables are set up, allowing visitors to taste and discover exotic flavours from all over the world.

At the end of the summer, the **Festival International des Films du Monde / World Film Festival** (☎848-3883) takes over various Montréal movie theatres. During this competition, films from different countries are presented to Montréal audiences. At the end of the competition, prizes are awarded to the most praiseworthy films. The most prestigious category is the Grand Prix des Amériques. During the festival, films are shown from 9am to midnight, to the delight of movie-goers across the city. An outdoor screening takes place at Place des Arts every night during the festival. Outdoor shows are also presented at the Place des Arts.

Winter's cold does not preclude the festival spirit; it merely provides an opportunity to organize another festival in Montréal, this time to celebrate the pleasures and activities of this frosty season! The **Fête des Neiges de Montréal** takes place on Île Notre-Dame, from the end of January to mid-February. Skating rinks and giant toboggans are available for the enjoyment of Montréal families. The snow-sculpture competition also attracts a number of curious onlookers.

Fête des Neiges de Montréal

Entertainment

Spectator Sports

Centre Molson
1250 Rue de la Gauchetière
☎989-2841
In the fall, the hockey games of the famous Montreal Canadiens hockey team start in the new Centre Molson. There are 42 games during the regular season followed by the playoffs, semi-finals and the Stanley Cup.

Stade Olympique
4141 Avenue Pierre-de-Courbertin
☎846-3976
Spring signals the beginning of baseball season. The Expos play against the various teams of the National Baseball League at the Olympic Stadium.

Major Events

The **Tour de-l'Île** usually takes place in June. The event can accommodate a maximum of 45,000 cyclists, who ride together for some 65km around the island of Montréal. Registration begins in April, and costs $22 for adults and $9 for children under 11 and senior citizens.

Registration forms are available at Canadian Tire stores (in Québec) and from **Tour de l'île de Montréal** (*1251 Rue Rachel Est, H2J 2J9*, ☎521-8687).

Mid-June is marked by an international event that captivates a large number of fans from all over North America – the **Grand Prix Air Canada** (*to reserve seats, call* ☎350-0000), which takes place at the Circuit Gilles Villeneuve on Île Notre-Dame. This is without question one of the most popular events of the summer. During these three days, it is possible to attend a variety of car races, including the roaring, spectacular Formula One competition.

In August, the best tennis players on the international circuit take part in the **Coupe Rogers et AT&T Canada** (women) and **Tennis Masters Series** (men) events. The women's event is held on even years. For more information, call ☎273-1515 and to purchase tickets, call ☎790-1245.

Shopping

Whether it be original Québec creations or imported articles, Montréal's shops sell all sorts of merchandise, each item more interesting than the last.

To assist you in your shopping, we have prepared a list of shops with exceptionally high-quality, original or inexpensive products.

E*n vente*" and "*en solde*" both mean on sale, therefore the price is reduced.

The Underground City

The 1962 construction of Place Ville-Marie, with its underground shopping mall, marked the origins of what is known today as the underground city. The development of this "city under the city" was accelerated by the construction of the Métro, which opened in 1966. Soon, most downtown businesses and office buildings, as well as a few hotels, were strategically

linked to the underground pedestrian network and, by extension, to the Métro.

Today, the underground city, now the largest in the world, has five distinct sections. The first lies at the very heart of the Métro system, around the Berri-UQAM station, and is connected to the buildings of the Université du Québec à Montréal (UQAM), the Galeries Dupuis and the bus station. The second stretches between the Place-des-Arts and Place-d'Armes stations, and is linked to Place des Arts, the Musée d'Art Contemporain, Complexe Desjardins, Complexe Guy Favreau and the Palais des Congrès, forming an exceptional cultural ensemble. The third, at the Square-Victoria station, serves the business centre. The fourth, which is the busiest and most important one, encompasses the McGill, Peel and Bonaventure stations. It includes the La Baie department store; the Promenades de la Cathédrale, Place Montréal Trust and Cours Mont-Royal shopping centres, as well as Place Bonaventure, 1000 de la Gauchetière, the train station and Place Ville-Marie. The fifth and final area is located in the commercial section around the Atwater station; it is linked to Westmount Square, Collège Dawson and Place Alexis Nihon.

Fashion

The fashion industry is flourishing in Montréal. The city is a multi-ethnic crossroads where Québecois and Canadian designers show their latest creations alongside those from the United States, Italy, France and elsewhere. Streets like Saint-Denis, Laurier, Saint-Laurent and Sherbrooke stand out for the numerous boutiques that line their sidewalks. A visit to the shops is sure to turn up something that is just your size.

Shopping Centres and Department Stores

Several downtown shopping centres and department stores offer a good selection of clothing by well-known fashion designers, including Jean-Claude Chacok, Cacharel, Guy Laroche, Lily Simon, Adrienne Vittadini, Mondi, Ralph Lauren and many others.

Holt Renfrew
1300 Rue Sherbrooke Ouest
☎842-5111

Ogilvy
1307 Rue Sainte-Catherine Ouest
☎842-7711

Place Montréal Trust
1600 Avenue McGill College
☎843-8000

Place Ville-Marie
5 Place Ville-Marie
☎861-9393

Westmount Square
4 Westmount Square
☎*932-0211*

Simons (*677 Ste-Catherine O.*)
has been part of the Qué-
bec City shopping land-
scape since 1840. In 1999,
the chain finally opened a
store in Montréal, some-
thing many were waiting
years for! This large, attractively designed department
store sells clothes for men,
women and children in
many shapes and styles.
Fashion accessories and
bedding are also sold here.

Certain other department
stores carry *haute couture*
lines in various price
ranges. These stores also
carry Canadian designs,
such as those by Simon
Chang, Michel Robichaud
and Alfred Sung, as well as
fashions by foreign designers like Mondi, Jones New
York and Adrienne Vittadini. Leather goods can also
be found at respectable
prices.

The Bay
Square Phillips (on Rue Sainte-
Catherine Ouest)
☎*281-4422*
When shopping for sports-
wear, sweaters, jeans, shirts
and other casuals, adults of
all ages appreciate the comfortable, reasonably priced
clothing at Gap, Jacob, Be-
do, America and Tristan et
Iseut.

Clothing

Womenswear

Artefact
4117 Rue Saint-Denis
☎*842-2780*

La Cache
2185 Rue Crescent
☎*842-0276*
3941 Rue Saint-Denis
☎*842-7693*
1051 Avenue Laurier Ouest
☎*273-9700*
1353 Avenue Green
☎*935-4361*
La Cache is a Canadian
chain of quality clothing
stores. Their clothes are
handmade in India from
colourful and original fabrics. The same attractive
material, with patterns
inspired by traditional
Indian themes, is used to
make matching bedding
and household articles.

Henriette L.
1031 Avenue Laurier Ouest
☎*277-3426*
You don't have to go to
extremes to find an original:
you are sure to find one at
Henriette L. in Outremont.

Mains Folles
4427 Rue Saint-Denis
☎*284-6854*
The attractive bas-reliefs in
the storefront at Mains
folles are just the beginning.
The real reason for shop-

ping here is the beautiful apparel: colourful dresses, skirts and shirts imported from Bali. There is also a small selection of jewellery that complements the clothing.

Océan
4413B Rue Saint-Denis
☎*848-8980*

Revenge
3852 Rue Saint-Denis
☎*843-4379*
Not every inspired creation comes from Paris. Revenge sells lovingly crafted originals and accessories created by talented Quebec designers for both men and women.

Silo
4255 Rue Saint-Denis
☎*845-5944*
Silo is a good place on Saint-Denis Street for clothes – at good prices.

Menswear

Downtown Montreal has exceptionally fine clothing stores for the well-dressed man. **Eccetera…& Co** (*1440 Rue Peel,* ☎*845-9181*), **Uomo** (*1452 Rue Peel,* ☎*844-1008*), **Il n'y a que deux** (*1405 Rue Crescent,* ☎*843-5665*), **Revenge** (*see above*) and **Dubuc: mode de vie** (*4451 Rue Saint-Denis,* ☎*282-1424*) are among the best. For a more sporty look there's **Old**

River (*1115 Rue Sainte-Catherine Ouest,* ☎*843-7828*).

Pierre, Jean, Jacques
50 Avenue Laurier
☎*270-8392*
After several years in business on trendy Rue Saint-Denis, the friendly owner of the men's clothing store Pierre, Jean, Jacques has moved to the more exclusive Avenue Laurier. Highly professional, she gives good advice to male customers of any age. Don't be shy to ask her for help when trying to find the perfect something to wear.

Hats

For any kind of hat in any size, shape or colour, here are two great places to look in Montreal:

Chapofolie
3944 Rue Saint-Denis
☎982-0036

Henri Henri
189 Rue Sainte-Catherine Est
☎*288-0109*

Lingerie

Looking for something lacy? **Deuxième Peau** (*4457 Saint-Denis,* ☎*842-0811*), **Lyla** (*1087 Avenue Laurier Ouest,* ☎*271-0763*) and **Madame Courval** (*4861 Rue Sherbrooke Ouest,* ☎*484-5656*) have lovely selections of lingerie. They also sell bathing suits.

Furs

Well known for years as a place to buy furs, Montreal has designers who create the most up-to-date fashions from the most luxurious pelts.

Desjardins Fourrure
325 Boulevard René-Lévesque Est
☎ *288-4151*

Fourrure Oslo
2863A Boulevard Rosemont
☎ *721-1271*

McComber
402 Boulevard De Maisonneuve Ouest
☎ *845-1167*

Boots

Top Western
4268 Rue Saint-Denis
☎ *843-6069*
For stylish cowboy boots, go to Top Western.

Jeans

All kinds of jeans are available in Montreal, often at lower prices than in Europe.

Levi's
705 Rue Sainte-Catherine Ouest, in the Centre Eaton
☎ *286-1574*
1241 Rue Sainte-Catherine Ouest
☎ *288-8199*
For those who won't wear anything but Levi's will love these two shops that sell this brand exclusively.

Pantalon Supérieur
69 Rue Sainte-Catherine Est
☎ *842-6969*
Pantalon Supérieur doesn't look like much from the outside, but people say it has the lowest prices on Levis in the city.

Children's Wear

Enfants Deslongchamps
1007 Avenue Laurier Ouest
☎ *274-2442*
Parents who want to spoil their children will love Enfants Deslongchamps. This store doesn't cater to the budget- minded!

Chez Fiou
3922 Rue Saint-Denis
☎ *844-0444*
Chez Fiou, has clothing for infants and children up to eight years old. The owner is familiar with the childrenswear business and sells attractive clothing from well-known manufacturers.

Peek a Boo
807 Rue Rachel Est
☎*890-1222*
6252 Saint-Hubert
☎*270-4309*
is an attractive Second-hand children's clothing and accessory store. Everything you need for pampering baby, from pajamas to baby carriers, is available in good condition at affordable prices.

Pom'Canelle
4860 Rue Sherbrooke Ouest
☎*483-1787*
is another good spot for dressing the little ones.

Outdoor Equipment

L'Altitude
4140 Rue Saint-Denis
☎*847-1515*
L'Altitude has a new store on Plateau Mont-Royal. It is small but full of tents, backpacks, hiking boots, clothing, etc. The salespeople are friendly and knowledgeable.

L'Aventurier
1610 Rue Saint-Denis
☎*849-4100*
L'Aventurier, in a large open area inside the enormous Quartier Latin movie theatre complex, sells all sorts of gear for outdoor activities by famous brand names including the Québec brand, Chlorophylle. L'Aventurier specializes in

nautical sports, and the canoes and kayaks that decorate the store are for sale. They will make you want to climb in and start paddling!

Azimut
1781 Rue Saint-Denis
☎*844-1717*
1189 Place Phillips
☎*866-1616*
Azimut stores sell outdoor clothing and apparel by popular brand names such as Kanuk, which has been in business in Québec for over 15 years. They also sell other top-of-the-line clothing and sports equipment: tents, backpacks, rain gear, etc.

La Cordée
2159 Rue Sainte-Catherine Est
☎*524-1106*
La Cordée opened in 1953 to outfit the Boy Scouts and Girl Guides of Québec. Now they serve just about anyone who wants the best quality outdoor equipment. Renovated and expanded in 1997, the store is the largest of its kind in Montréal, and its layout and design make it a very pleasant place to shop.

Kanuk
485 Rue Rachel Est
☎*527-4494*
Kanuk manufactures backpacks, sleeping bags and outerwear. You can buy their merchandise at their huge outlet, located right

above the factory. Kanuk winter coats come in various styles and are extremely warm.

La Maison des Cyclistes
1251 Rue Rachel Est
☎*521-8356*
La Maison des Cyclistes as its name implies, has a lot of equipment for cyclists, including guides, maps and small accessories: a real help in exploring Montréal and Québec by bicycle.

Le Yéti
5127 Boulevard Saint-Laurent
☎*271-0773*
Le Yéti is a large, attractive store that sells bicycles, as well as outdoor clothing and accessories.

Bookstores

Montréal has both French and English bookstores. Books from Québec, the rest of Canada and the United States are available at reasonable prices. Books from Europe are slightly more expensive because of import costs. Anyone interested in Québécois literature will find a large selection in Montréal stores.

General

Archambault (French)
500 Rue Sainte-Catherine Est
☎*849-6201*

Champigny (French)
500 Rue Sainte-Catherine Est
4380 Rue Saint-Denis
☎*844-2587*

Chapter's
1171 Rue Sainte-Catherine Ouest
☎*849-8825*

Indigo
Place Montréal Trust
☎*281-5549*

Librairie Gallimard (French)
500 Rue Sainte-Catherine Est
3700 Boulevard Saint-Laurent
☎*499-2012*

Librairie Paragraphe
2220 McGill College
☎845-5811

Librairie Renaud-Bray (French)
500 Rue Sainte-Catherine Est
5252 Chemin de la Côte-des-Neiges
☎*342-1515*
4301 Rue Saint-Denis
☎*499-3656*
5117 Avenue du Parc
☎*276-7651*

Coles
Place Ville-Marie
☎*861-1736*
Promenades de la Cathédrale
☎*289-8737*

Specialty Bookstores

Capitaine Québec
1837 Rue Sainte-Catherine Ouest
☎*939-9970*
Comic books.

Librairie ABYA-YALA
4555 Boulevard Saint-Laurent
☎*849-4908*
French, English, Spanish
and Portugese books about
and from the Americas.

Librairie Allemande
3488 Chemin de la Côte-des-Neiges
☎*933-1919*
German books.

Librairie l'Androgyne
3636 Boulevard Saint-Laurent
☎*842-4765*
Gay, lesbian and feminist
literature.

Librairie Biosfaire
4571 Rue Saint-Denis
☎*985-2467*
New Age and spirituality.

Librairie Boule de Neige
4433 Rue Saint-Denis
☎*849-0959*
Esoteric and New Age
books.

Librairie C.E.C. Michel Fortin
3714 Rue Saint-Denis
☎*849-5719*
Education and languages.

**Librairie du Centre Canadien
d'Architecture**
1920 Rue Baile
☎*939-7028*
Architecture and design.

Librairie Double Hook
1235A Avenue Green
☎*932-5093*
Canadian literature.

Librairie Dupont et Dupond
271 Avenue Duluth Est
☎*844-2939*
Comic books.

Librairie Italiana
6792 Boulevard Saint-Laurent
☎*277-2955*
Italian books.

Librairie Las Américas
10 Rue Saint-Norbert
☎*844-5994*
Spanish, mainly Latin American books.

**Librairie du Musée des
beaux-arts**
1368 Rue Sherbrooke Ouest
☎*285-1600, extension 350*
Art books.

Librairie Olivieri
5200 Rue Gatineau
☎*739-3639*
Foreign literature, science,
art.

Librairie Olivieri
185 Rue Sainte-Catherine Ouest
☎*847-6903*
Contemporary art books.

Librairie Renaud-Bray Jeunesse
5219 Chemin de la Côte-des-Neiges
☎*342-1515*
Children's books.

Librairie Ulysse
4176 Rue Saint-Denis
☎*843-9447*
560 Avenue du Président-Kennedy
☎*843-9447, ext. 2243*
Travel guides.

Maison de la Bible Promenades de la Cathédrale
625 Rue Sainte-Catherine Ouest
☎848-9777
Religion.

McGill University Bookstore
3420 McTavish
☎398-7444
Academic and general.

Mélange Magique
1928 Ste-Catherine Ouest
☎938-1458
Mélange Magique specializes in New Age and spirituality. They also sell tarot cards, incense, charms and other esoteric items. There is even an in-house psychic!

Nicholas Hoare Ogilvy
1307 Rue Sainte-Catherine Ouest
☎844-8244
1366 Greene Avenue Westmount
 ☎934-6046
Art and literature. Great coffee-table books!

Stage Librairie de Théatre Book Shop
2123 Sainte Catherine Ouest
☎931-7466
Stage Librairie de Théatre Book Shop for theatre buffs and aspiring actors.

Used Books

Bibliomania Bookshoppe
1841A Sainte Catherine Ouest
☎933-8156
Bibliomania Bookshoppe has an extensive and eclectic stock of books, including some collectables.

Cheap Thrills
2044 Metcalfe
☎844-8988
1433 Bishop
☎844-7604
As its name suggests, Cheap Thrills has quality used books at more than reasonable prices. A broad range of used CDs is also sold, and both locations have a laid-back and friendly atmosphere that makes browsing a real pleasure.

SW Welch
3878 Boulevard Saint-Laurent
☎848-9358
Though it is far from the most atmospheric of Montréal's used bookstores, SW Welch is conveniently located on the Main and has a wide selection, ranging from literature to religion, mysteries and science fiction. A bit pricey.

You're sure to make some real finds at the small, cozy **Westcott Books** (*2065 Sainte Catherine Ouest,* ☎846-4037), which is only one of several excellent used bookstores in the area. The **Argo** (*1915 Sainte Catherine Ouest,* ☎931-3442) is an equally appealing little place, just a few doors down.

The Word
469 Milton
☎845-5640
Specializing in art, literature and philosophy, is tucked away in a small, timeworn store reminiscent of the Left

Bank. If you want to do more than browse, be prepared to pay cash, since bank and credit cards are not accepted here – the owner even tallies up the total by hand!

Newspapers and Magazines

Maison de la Presse Internationale
550 Rue Sainte-Catherine Est
☎842-3857
1393 Rue Sainte-Catherine Ouest
☎844-4508
4261 Rue Saint-Denis
☎289-9323

Maps, Atlases and Travel Guides

Librairie Ulysse
4176 Rue Saint-Denis
☎843-9447
560 Avenue du Président-Kennedy
☎843-7222
1001 Square Dorchester
☎843-9447, ext. 2243
Ulysses has a large selection of city and road maps as well as travel guides.

Quatre points cardinaux
551 Rue Ontario Est
☎843-8116
For topographic maps of Quebec, drop into Quatre points cardinaux.

Stationery

Aux Papiers Japonais
24 Fairmount Ouest
☎276-6863
The art of making paper is still very popular at Aux Papiers Japonais, which sells paper with textures unlike any others: perfect for origami or fancy letters. The staff can explain how to make certain shapes or characters, and paper-making courses are sometimes given.

Carton
4068 Rue Saint-Denis
☎844-9663
For an original little gift, swathed in tissue paper and elegantly wrapped, go to Carton, where they never run out of ideas. Don't forget the greeting card!

Essence du papier
4160 Rue Saint-Denis
☎288-9691
Olgivy
1307 Rue Sainte-Catherine Ouest
☎844-8244
Onion skin, tissue, stationery and wrapping paper: every kind of paper imaginable is available at Essence du papier. Postcards, ribbons, famous brand-name pens – even inkwells and feathers are sold here!

For any kind of greeting card try **Artz 'n Cardz** (*The*

Faubourg, 1616 St. Catherine Ouest, ☎939-0079).

Farfelu
843 Avenue du Mont-Royal Est
☎528-6251
Still searching for the perfect gift wrapping? Try Farfelu. It's packed with coloured ribbons, wrapping paper, and anything else to embellish that special something.

Westmount and Outremont
also have specialty paper shops: **Origami** (*1369 Avenue Greene,* ☎938-4688) and **Papillote** (*1126 Avenue Bernard,* ☎271-6356), and **Papeterie Westmount** (*4887 Sherbrooke Ouest,* ☎481-2575)

Music

The following megastores have the largest selection of compact discs of all musical genres at the lowest prices:

Archambault Musique
500 Rue Sainte-Catherine Est
☎849-6201
or
175 Rue Sainte-Catherine Ouest,
Place des Arts
☎281-0367

HMV
1010 Rue Sainte-Catherine Ouest
☎875-0765

Music World
150 Rue Sainte-Catherine Ouest,
Complexe Desjardins
☎845-7796

Sam the Record Man
399 Rue Sainte-Catherine Ouest, at the intersection with Saint-Alexandre
☎281-9877

The following smaller stores specialize in second-hand compact discs or certain kinds of music:

Cheap Thrills
2044 Rue Metcalfe
☎844-8988
1433 Bishop
☎844-7604
Cheap Thrills has a large selection of new and used jazz CDs. They also have a large collection of new and used vinyl.

Hibiscus Records
288 Rue Sainte-Catherine Ouest
☎393-4090
Hibiscus Records has the largest selection of international music.

Rayon Laser
3656 Boulevard Saint-Laurent
☎848-6300
Rayon Laser is the place to go for new and used alternative CDs.

Annexe
1035 Rue Sainte-Catherine Ouest

Primitive
3828 Rue Saint-Denis
☎845-6017

Shopping

Primitive carries rare and imported vinyl, as well as CDs. An unbeatable selection of 1980s/New Wave albums, and everything else from Garage to French pop to soul. A nice collection of vintage magazines too.

Le Pick-Up
4383 Rue Saint-Denis
☎287-9484
Similar to Primitive, Le Pick-Up also sells used vinyl and CDs. Great prices and an excellent selection of alternative music from the better part of the 20th century!

Disquivel
1587 Boulevard Saint-Laurent
☎842-1607
Impossible to miss because of its bizarre window displays, Disquivel is another great record store, specializing in indie/art-rock vinyl and CDs. An added bonus is the soundproof "electronica" room at the back.

Noize
3697 Boulevard Saint-Laurent
Located in a loft above Second Cup, Noize takes full advantage of its space. Complete with rentable dj booths, couches and live turntable action, it should serve as a model for all other record stores. Boasting a thorough selection of music of all genres (techno, motown, hip hop, break beats, indie, 80s...), Noize also hosts the occasional live show. Definitely de-

serves a place in Montréal history.

Musical Instruments

Steve's Music Store
51 Rue Saint-Antoine Ouest
☎878-2216
For years now, Steve's Music Store has been the place to go for musical instruments and accessories. Despite its popularity and reputation for quality, the shop does not accept credit cards.

Electronics

Radio Shack
Place Montréal Trust, 1500 Avenue McGill College
☎499-9922
Need a handy calculator to add up the shopping bills, a Walkman to get away from it all, a new telephone cord, or a battery for a toy? These items and more are available at Radio Shack.The displays are neatly arranged – efficiency's the word!

Future Shop
470 Rue Sainte-Catherine Ouest
☎393-2600
When it comes to colour televisions, computers and other electronic appliances, one establishments claims to have the lowest prices: Future Shop They frequently do have bargains, but shop around a bit before buying.

Téléboutique Bell
Place Alexis-Nihon
1500 Avenue Atwater
Galeries Dupuis
1475 Rue Saint-Hubert
When it comes to tele-
phones, it's best to consult
the experts at Téléboutique
Bell.

On Boulevard Saint-Laurent,
between Rue Ontario and
Rue Sherbrooke, several
stores sell all kinds of electronic equipment. Bargain-
ing is in order; count on
getting 10% to 20% off the
listed price.

Computers

The latest computers, software, printers, books and
other computer products
can be purchased at the
following stores:

Crazy Irving
1219 Square Phillips
☎398-0737

Dumoulin Informatique
8251 Rue Saint-Hubert
☎385-1777
2050 Boulevard Saint-Laurent
☎288-7973

Micro Boutique
6615 Avenue du Parc
☎270-4477
Macs.

Softmagic Computer Software
9760 Boulevard Henri-Bourassa Ouest
☎335-0195

Camelot Info
1191 Square Phillips
☎861-5019
1 Place Ville-Marie
☎861-7400
Books only

CD-ROM Dépot
7275 Rue Sherbrooke Est
Radisson Métro, Room 155
☎353-1015

Arts and Crafts

Québec Crafts

Québec art is produced by
artists from many cultures:
French and English Cana-
dian, Mohawk, Cree, Inuit,
and others. Each year in
December at **Place
Bonaventure** (*901 Rue de La
Gauchetière Ouest*), these
artists display and sell their
work in a giant exposition
hall; this event is called "Le
Salon des métiers d'art du
Québec." If you miss the
show, **Le Rouet** (*84 Saint-
Paul Est,* ☎*954-0276; 1500
Avenue McGill College,*
☎*843-5235 or 289-0803*) sells
sculptures, pottery and
ceramics by several Québec
artists. For First Nations'
crafts, the **A'Nowara** (*350 Rue
St-Paul,* ☎*398-0710*) boutique is worth a visit.

Guilde Canadienne des Métier d'Art
2025 Rue Peel
☎ *849-6091*
Guilde Canadienne des Métier d'Art has a shop that sells French and English Canadian hand-crafted objects. As well, there are two small galleries that deal in Inuit and other native art.

Le Chariot
446 Place Jacques-Cartier
☎ *875-6134*
Le Chariot exhibits fantastic art works by Inuit and other native peoples, which are also sold here. It is really worth visiting just to take a look!

Quai des Arts
7 Rue de La Commune
☎ *285-2733*
In the Vieux-Port, Quai des Arts doesn't greet ships, but rather curious visitors who come for the highly original hand-crafted objects for sale here.

International Crafts

Giraffe
3997 Rue Saint-Denis
☎ *499-8436*
From Africa, the cradle of humanity, striking masks, dazzling fabrics and fascinating hand-crafted objects are all available at Giraffe, a shop where the merchandise is irresistibly appealing.

Mexico Lindo
230 Rue Saint-Paul Ouest
☎ *845-5068*
Discover the treasures of Mexico: wooden, ceramic, silver and glass hand-crafted objects at Mexico. Lindo.

Galerie Ima
3839 -A Rue Saint-Denis
☎ *499-2904*
Iranian artisans chisel, decorate and weave small, delicate treasures with geometric designs in bronze, silk, wood and mother-of-pearl. Some art objects from this far-away country are sold at Galerie Ima.

Art Galleries

Art galleries are everywhere in Montreal. It is hard to describe them since they vary according to the exhibition held. It is better to go there in person and let the art works speak for themselves.

Galerie Dominion
1438 Rue Sherbrooke Ouest
☎ *845-7471*

Galerie Claude Lafitte
1270 Rue Sherbrooke Ouest
☎ *842-1270*

Galerie Jean-Pierre Valentin
1434 Rue Sherbrooke Ouest
☎ *849-3637*

Waddington & Gore
1446 Rue Sherbrooke Ouest
☎847-1112

Galerie Clarence Gagnon
301 St-Paul Est
☎875-2787

For glassworks, there is
only one place in town:

Elena Lee
1428 Rue Sherbrooke Ouest
☎844-6009
For contemporary and
modern art:

Galerie Clark
1591 Rue Clark
☎288-4972

Galerie Michel-Ange
430 Rue Bonsecours
☎875-8281

Galerie Oboro
4001 Rue Berri
☎844-3250

Galerie Samuel Lallouz
4295 Boulevard Saint-Laurent
☎849-5844

Galerie Simon Blais
4521 Rue Clark, Suite 100
☎849-1165

Galerie Skol
460 Rue Sainte-Catherine Ouest
Bureau 511
☎398-9322

Galerie Trois Points
372 Rue Sainte-Catherine Ouest
☎866-8008

Community cultural centres
and the Université du Québec à Montréal (UQAM)
also host exhibitions of
various Québec artists.

Art Supplies

Charcoal, pastels, tempera,
sketchbooks, India ink,
easels and other materials
for your masterpiece:

Omer DeSerres
334 Rue Sainte-Catherine Est
☎842-6637
or
2134 Sainte-Catherine Ouest
☎938-4777

Pavillon des Arts
1763 Rue Saint-Denis
☎284-2911

Antique and Second-Hand Shops

In Montréal, antique and
secondhand stores offer a
wide variety of colourful
merchandise. Stroll along
Rue Sherbrooke in West-
mount and explore the
many antique shops. For
less expensive items, try the
secondhand stores on Rue
Notre Dame near Guy. Here
are some places for beautiful antique furniture:

David S. Brown
2125 Rue de la Montagne
☎844-9866

Shopping

Henrietta Anthony
4192 Rue Sainte-Catherine Ouest
☎935-9116

Petit Musée
1494 Rue Sherbrooke Ouest
☎937-6161

Rue Duluth, between Boulevards St. Laurent and St. Denis, is chock full of craft shops selling everything from antiques to funky creations by individual artists.

Home Décor

Arthur Quentin
3960 Rue Saint-Denis
☎843-7513
For entertaining in style, Arthur Quentin has the finest selection of dishware, table linens and kitchen accessories – everything from garlic crushers to sugar tongs!

Open only Thursday to Saturday, the little **Atelier** (*Thu to Fri 10am to 6pm, Sat 10am to 5pm; 4247 Rue Saint-André*, ☎843-7513) on Rue Saint- Andre is a discount store for Arthur Quentin (see above) and the **Bleu Nuit** shops (see p 366) on Saint-Denis. It is a great spot for reasonably priced items to decorate your home.

Artisans du Meuble Québécois
88 Rue Saint-Paul Est
☎866-1836

The craftspeople at Artisans du Meuble Québécois create new, antique-looking furniture that blends in well with the decor of modern houses.

Jeune d'ici
134 Avenue Laurier Ouest
☎270-5512
Children, as well as adults, deserve lovely furniture. Jeune d'ici has functional and imaginative items for children.

La Cache
2185 Rue Crescent
☎842-0276
3941 Rue Saint-Denis
☎842-7693
1051 Avenue Laurier Ouest
☎273-9700
1353 Avenue Green
☎935-4361
La Cache sells lovely objects for the home, including linen.

Caplan Duval 2000
5800 Boulevard Cavendish
☎483-4040
Caplan Duval 2000 has a wide choice of crystal vases, glassware and china to complete your trousseau.

Côté Sud
4338 Rue Saint-Denis
☎289-9443
Whether your decorating style is baroque, classical or more exotic, Côté Sud will suit your taste. Furniture, mirrors, draperies and wall hangings, stylish doorknobs, bathroom carpets,

dishes and candle holders... the list goes on!

Interversion
4349 Rue Saint-Denis
Interversion has three stories full of furniture and other crafts made in Québec. These lovely, affordably priced objects are contemporary, yet timeless, and most are made out of wood. They add originality and creativity to any home.

Maison d'Émilie
1073 Avenue Laurier Ouest
☎277-5151
It is hard to leave Maison d'Émilie empty-handed. The exquisite table linens and settings, glassware, china and kitchen accessories are tempting and sometimes costly.

Ma Maison
1 Westmount Square
☎933-0045
For beautiful and affordable table settings, your best bet is Ma Maison.

MDI Multi Design International
273 Avenue Laurier Ouest
☎277-0052
MDI Multi Design International sells designer kitchenware (by Alesi, Dansk, and others) perfect for ultra-modern stainless-steel kitchens.

Nordsouth Inc.
50 Rue Saint-Paul Ouest
☎288-1292

Nordsouth Inc. is chock full of modern furniture and other household items by Québec designers.

Zone
4246 Rue Saint-Denis
☎845-3530
5014 Rue Sherbrooke Ouest
☎489-8901
Looking for the perfect gift and fresh out of ideas? Head straight for Zone where off-beat key chains, stylish candle holders, Art Deco soap dishes and mood-enhancing lamps will inspire you!

Linen

Bleu Nuit
3913 Rue Saint-Denis
☎843-5702
Suffering from the bedtime blues? The pretty cotton sheets at Bleu Nuit will hush you right to sleep. A bit pricey.

Carré Blanc
3999 Rue Saint-Denis
☎847-0729
White includes all the colours in the spectrum, which are all available at Carré Blanc, in affordably priced sheets and pillowcases that will give you a good night's sleep.

Décor Marie Paule
1090 Avenue Laurier Ouest
☎273-8889
From hot colours to cool pastels, Décor Marie Paule

has down comforter covers and sheets to match.

The Linen Chest
625 Rue Sainte-Catherine Ouest
Promenades de la Cathédrale
☎*282-9525*
The Linen Chest is the "supermarket" of bedding.

Posters

À L'Affiche
4415 rue Saint-Denis
☎*845-5723*
To plaster your walls with movie posters, go to À L'Affiche.

For reproductions of Renoirs, Van Goghs, Fortins or Borduas check out **l'Atelier 68** (*5170 Boulevard Saint-Laurent,* ☎*276-2872*) or **Galerie Montréal Images** (*3854 Rue Saint-Denis,* ☎*284-0192; 3620 Boulevard Saint-Laurent,* ☎*842-1060*).

Florists

Say it with flowers!

Fauchois Fleurs
3933A Rue Saint-Denis
☎*844-4417*

Fleuriste Pourquoi Pas
3629 Boulevard Saint-Laurent
☎*844-3233*

Madame Lespérance
1135-A Laurier Ouest
☎*277-2173*

Marcel Proulx
3835 Rue Saint-Denis
☎*849-1344*

Marie Vermette
801 Rue Laurier Est
☎*272-2225*

Westmount Florist
360 Avenue Victoria
☎*488-9121*

Here are two shops that not only sell flowers and plants but also pretty terracotta vases from Mexico, Thailand and Indonesia:

Alpha
230 Rue Peel
☎*935-1812*

Caméléon Vert
1300 Rue Saint-Antoine Ouest
☎*937-2481*

Food

Specialty Grocers

L'Aromate
1106 Avenue du Mont-Royal Est
☎*525-1514*
L'Aromate sells seasonings, spices, herbs, jams, jellies, ketchups as well as decorative objects to spice up the kitchen.

Atlantic Meat and Delicatessen
5060 Chemin de la Côte-des-Neiges
☎*731-4764*
Atlantic Meat and Delicatessen is a German grocery

popular for its traditional foods like sauerkraut and sausages.

Boulangerie Monsieur Pinchot
4354 Rue de Brébeuf
☎522-7192
Boulangerie Monsieur Pinchot is just the place to stock up for an impromptu picnic off the bicycle path. This charming old-fashioned bakery has delicious quality products.

How can you speak of Montréal bakeries without mentioning bagels?! Montréal is famous internationally for these kosher little breads, and they are probably the best bagels in the world. Whether this is true or not, they are certainly delicious and much loved. Many bakeries, especially in Outremont and Mile-End, make several varieties of them made in a wood-burning oven. Among these are the **Fairmount Bagel Bakery** (*74 Fairmount O.*, ☎277-0667), open 24hrs, and the **Bagel Shop** (*158 St-Viateur O.*, ☎270-2972).

Faubourg Saint-Catherine
1616 Rue Sainte-Catherine Ouest
☎939-3663
Faubourg Saint-Catherine is a small, modern shopping complex near Guy-Concordia Métro that has different specialty shops selling excellent quality foods.

La Foumagerie
1375 Rue Sherbrooke Ouest
☎527-3327
La Foumagerie boasts a large assortment of cheeses, including different kinds of brie, goat's milk and raw milk cheese.

Le Fromentier (*1375 Avenue Laurier Est*, ☎272-2702) is an old-fashioned bakery that makes many different kinds of bread, each more delicious than the last. Although the place has recently expanded, you can still watch the bakers at their ovens. Their bread is sold in many supermarkets and grocery stores throughout the city. There is also an excellent cheese shop located here with the very original name of **Maître Affineur Maître Corbeau** (☎528-3293) (which means Master Fox and Master Raven – from *the Raven and the Fox*, a fable by French writer Jean de la Fontaine).

Fromagerie Hamel
220, rue Jean-Talon E.
☎272-1161
There is a panoply of little shops worth mentioning around the Jean-Talon Market. One of these is the Fromagerie Hamel, one the best cheese shops in the city, which is known for the fine quality and wide selection of its products, as well as its excellent service. Definitely try their cheeses if offered. Despite the lineup,

Shopping

the staff always sees to customers' every need.

Gourmet Laurier
1042 Avenue Laurier Ouest
☎274-5601

The Gourmet Laurier grocery store has a large selection of cheeses.

Maison des Pates Fraîches
865 Rue Rachel
☎527-5487

Maison des Pates Fraîches sells quality Italian food: cheese, olives and capers, cold cuts, biscotti and gelati as well as delicious fresh pasta and savoury sauces. Here you can buy all the ingredients for concocting a quick, delicious homemade meal. Also, tasty hot dishes that cost next to nothing are prepared on the premises.

Marché Andes
4387 Boulevard Saint-Laurent
☎848-1078

Marché Andes sells dishes like *salsa, empanadas, tortillas,* as well as other Latin-American products.

Milano
6862 Boulevard Saint-Laurent
☎273-8558

In the heart of little Italy, Milano is a large grocery store that has a whole range of European products from fresh pasta to chocolates, including prosciuto and provolone. The delicious pannetones (Italian bread cakes) hanging from the ceiling provide and an interesting décor.

The **Première Moisson** bakery cannot really be called an artisanal bakery because it is a chain of shops. However, each one prepares fresh delicious baked goods daily, straight from, if you please, a wood-burning oven! Meats, cakes, chocolates and delicious ready-made dishes are also sold here. Première Moisson also has stores in Montréals's three public markets, as well as the Gare Centrale and 1271 Bernard Ouest.

La Queue de Cochon
1328, av. Laurier E.
☎527-2252

Fine gourmets will definitely like the excellent products at La Queue de Cochon, a small artisanal *charcuterie* (butcher shop). A variety of terrines and sausages such as *boudin blanc* and *boudin noir* (white-pudding and blood-pudding sausages), as well as several prepared dishes, are available here. Pork products are obviously the speciality here, and after the owner (from Vendée, France) and his family tell you all about them, you won't want to leave without buying something!

La Vieille Europe
3855 Boulevard Saint-Laurent
☎842-5773
For European products such as salami, smoked bacon, chorizo, vegetable sausages, foie gras and olives, a visit to La Vieille Europe is a must. They have an incredible selection of cheeses at unbeatable prices, as well as an excellent choice of coffees.

Chinatown is the place to shop for Chinese food (*de la Gauchetière and Boulevard St-Laurent below Boulevard René Lévesque, Place d'Armes métro*).

Health Food

Rachelle-Berry
505 Rue Rachel Est
☎524-0725
4660 Boulevard Saint-Laurent
2510 Rue Beaubien Est
Originally located at the corner of Rachel and Berri, Rachelle- Berry now has two other stores in the city. These are large grocery stores that sell natural products such as food, vitamins and cosmetics.

Tau
4238 Rue Saint-Denis
☎843-4420
Tau sells a vast array of soaps, health products, bulk foods, organically grown fruit and vegetables, as well as prepared dishes. In short, they have everything neces-

sary to maintain good health.

Optimum
630 Sherbrooke Ouest
☎845-1015
Optimum is the largest natural health food and beauty store in Montréal, and therefore has a huge selection. Their products are often on special.

Farmers Markets

Montréal still has public markets where local farmers come to sell their produce. Imported products are also available at these two.

Marché Atwater
138 Avenue Atwater

Marché Jean Talon
7075 Rue Casgrain

Pâtisseries
(Pastry Shops)

Brioche Lyonnaise
1593 Rue Saint-Denis
☎842-7017
At the Brioche Lyonnaise, delicious pastries and coffee can be enjoyed right on the premises. But don't worry – there are plenty left to bring home!

Shopping

Pâtisserie Belge
3487 Avenue du Parc
☎*845-1245*
1075A Avenue Laurier Ouest
☎*279-5274*
Belgian in name only,
Pâtisserie Belge offers a
wide assortment of little
morsels made of chocolate,
cream and mousse, and
many other almost sinful
delights that add the perfect
finishing touch to a meal.

Pâtisserie de Nancy
5655 Avenue Monkland
☎*482-3030*
Pâtisserie de Nancy is
prized by neighbourhood
residents who love good,
hot, buttery croissants on
Saturday and Sunday morn-
ings. Many other treats are
available.

Duc de Lorraine
5002 Chemin de la Côte-des-Neiges
☎*731-4128*
The Duc de Lorraine is another classic Montréal
pâtisserie that has captivated
the taste buds of many local
gourmets thanks to its delicious Grand Marnier glazed
treats and almond crois-
sants.

Pâtisserie de Gascogne
6095 Boulevard Gouin Ouest
☎*331-0550*
4825 Rue Sherbrooke Ouest
☎*932-3511*
237 Avenue Laurier Ouest
☎*490-0235*
For years, the Pâtisserie de
Gascogne has been consid-
ered one of the city's best.

The new location on Laurier
Street is easy to reach and
has tables where you can
have a coffee and pastry.
Miroir Cassis and *Indulgent*,
popular French nouvelle-
cuisine desserts, are their
specialty.

Pâtisserie Bruxelloise
860 Avenue du Mont-Royal Est
☎*523-2751*
Pâtisserie Bruxelloise sells
excellent chocolates, cakes,
pastries and other delicious
creations.

Chocolate and Candy

Au Festin de Babette
4118 Rue Saint-Denis
☎*849-0214*
In summer, the terrace at
Au Festin de Babette is a
charming spot to sip an
espresso or savour a sorbet
or ice cream. In winter,
there is a veritable treasure
trove to browse through
indoors: marvellous olive
oils, exotic preserves, fla-
vourful condiments and
many other delightful items.
Their mouth-watering Bel-
gian pralines are simply to
die for! Exquisite! Pleasant
service.

Succulent Belgian pralines
are also available at
Daskalides (*5111 Avenue du
Parc,* ☎*272-3447*) and
Léonidas (*605 Boulevard de
Maisonneuve Ouest,*
☎*849-2620*).

Neuhaus
1442 Rue Sherbrooke Ouest
☎*849-7609*
For a few dollars more,
Belgian-chocolate lovers
will be lured to Neuhaus
*where the scrumptious morsels
are more elegantly presented.*

Godiva (*Ogilvy, 1307 Rue
Sainte-Catherine Ouest,
☎849-4789*) and **Source au
Chocolat** (*Cours Mont-Royal,
1455 Rue Peel, ☎499-1731*)
both sell fine chocolates.

Pâtisserie Bruxelloise
860 Avenue du Mont-Royal Est
☎*523-2751*
(see to the left) Pâtisserie
Bruxelloise sells delicious
chocolate made on the premises and in the finest Belgian tradition.

Confiserie Louise Décarie
4424 Rue Saint-Denis
☎*499-3445*
Children of all ages will like
the colourful displays of
candy, soft caramels, barley
sugar and other sweet de-
lights at Confiserie Louise
Décarie.

Pâtisserie Chez Gaumont
3725 Rue Wellington
☎*768-2564*
For quality candy sold by
the pound, go to Pâtisserie
Chez Gaumont.

Special Occasions

Gift Shops

Montréal's museum gift
shops are almost like museums in themselves. They
sell various reproductions
lovely enough to embellish
any home. Here are two to
remember:

**Boutique du Musée d'Art
Contemporain** (*185 Rue
Sainte- Catherine Ouest,
☎847-6226*).

**Boutique du Musée des
Beaux-Arts de Montréal** (*1390
Rue Sherbrooke Ouest,
☎285-1600*).

However, there are many
other places with great gift
ideas:

Cartier
1498 Rue Sherbrooke Ouest
☎*939-0000*
What can be said about
Cartier that hasn't already
been said? Exquisite jewellery, china and beautiful
decorative objects at exorbi-
tant prices.

Céramique art-café
4201, Rue St-Denis
☎*848-1119*
95 rue de la Commune E.
☎*868-1611*
If you are looking for an
original gift, at the Céramique art-café you can paint a

Shopping

clay object yourself while comfortably seated and enjoying a light meal or a drink. The experienced staff is there to help you. This is probably the most personalized gift you can get!

La Mouette Rieuse
4418 Rue Saint-Denis
☎*843-4851*
La Mouette Rieuse sells comic-strip figures of characters like Tin Tin and Le Marsupilami. They may seem expensive, but each one is a masterpiece of craftsmanship.

Wine connoisseurs should definitely stop in at **Millesimes** (*3901 Rue Saint-Denis*, ☎*284-2613*) or **Bacchus Collection** (*1231 Avenue Bernard Ouest*, ☎*273-3104*), where a large selection of accessories for wine cellars is available. Wine-tasting glasses are also sold here.

Mimosa Pinsons
1224 Rue Bernard
☎*277-8645*
Mimosa Pinsons is one of a kind in Montréal. Instead of the endlessly reproduced art works commonly sold in stores, they sell old engravings, made from works that can date back over a century. There are some veritable masterpieces among them!

Kamikaze
4156 Rue Saint-Denis
☎*848-0728*
A tiny boutique by day, Kamikaze becomes a lively bar by night (Le Passeport). It offers fashionable costume jewellery (earrings, necklaces and other imaginative creations) and clothing (scarves, hosiery and hats).

Senteurs de Provence
4077 Rue Saint-Denis
☎*845-6867*
Senteurs de Provence sells Provençal soaps, aromatic oils, potpourris, perfumes, fabrics and many other charming items from this Mediterranean region.

The Body Shop (*1 Place Ville Marie*, ☎*397-1343; 1008 St. Catherine Ouest*, ☎*397-0345*) and **Fruits and Passion** (*4163 St. Denis*, ☎*282-9406*) sell fruit-flavoured soaps, perfumes, bath oils and other beauty products. The Body Shop is known for its environmental awareness.

Sex Shops

La Capoterie
2061 Rue Saint-Denis
☎*845-0027*
Every fantasy goes at La Capoterie, the only shop of its kind in Montréal. There are coloured, fluorescent and even fruit-flavoured condoms that come in all

sizes. Kinky types should not miss it!

Priape

1311 Rue Sainte-Catherine Est
☎521-8451

When love is gay the place to go is Priape for accessories and erotic literature. You'll even find articles to wear in drag!

Jewellery Stores

Birks

1240 Square Phillips
☎397-2511

A veritable Montréal institution, Birks has beautiful jewellery such as diamond engagement rings, wedding bands and anniversary gifts.

Agatha

1054 Avenue Laurier Ouest
☎272-9313

For fancy costume jewellery in silver or molten glass, check out Agatha.

For designer jewellery, take a peek at **Kyose** (*Cours Mont-Royal, Rue Sainte-Catherine Ouest*, ☎849-6552) or **Oz Bijoux** (*3955 Rue Saint-Denis*, ☎845-9568).

Games and Toys

La Cerf-Volanterie

224 Rue Saint-Paul Ouest
☎845-7613

To buy a kite, why not go to the experts? La Cerf-Volanterie custom-makes them for everyone. On summer weekends, customers can try out their kite-flying skills at the Quai de l'Horloge or the Quai Jacques-Cartier in Old Montréal.

Coin du Cheminot

5290 Rue Belanger Est
☎728-8443

Model train collectors should check out Coin du Cheminot.

Franc Jeu

4152 Rue Saint-Denis
☎849-9253

Pinocchio and Capucine, Babar and Milou will delight children at Franc Jeu, which has a vast assortment of toys for all ages from birth to ninety-nine.

Unicef

Mon-Sat 10am to 5pm
4474 Rue Saint-Denis
☎288-1305

Run by volunteers, the non-profit Unicef shop, sells greeting cards, gifts and many children's toys to benefit this United Nations organization. When buying a present for a child, why not help a less fortunate child at the same time?

Valet de Coeur

4408 Rue Saint-Denis
☎499-9970

Playing is not only for children, and Valet de Coeur has games for everyone,

Shopping

from three-dimensional puzzles, Chinese checkers and chess sets to a variety of parlour games.

Victoire Victorine
4859 Rue Sherbrooke Ouest
☎486-7814

Victoire Victorine has a wonderful selection of educational toys and stuffed teddy bears in quality plush.

Travel Accessories

Jet-Setter
66 Avenue Laurier Ouest
☎271-5058

Whether you are planning a weekend in Quebec City, two weeks in the Dominican Republic or a sabbatical year in a remote paradise, Jet-Setter has suitcases, trunks and backpacks to meet your travel needs.

Pet Stores

The following stores have everything to help care for animal companions: food in bulk, sweaters, winter booties, down-filled wicker baskets and much more.

L'Heure Manger
4310 Rue de la Roche
☎521-9491

Little Bear
4025 Rue Sainte-Catherine Ouest
☎935-3425

Maxime Bailey
6165 Monkland
☎369-2499

Pattes a Poil
404 Rue Gifford
☎282-9886

Medieval Boutiques

Excalibur
277 Rue de la Commune Est
☎393-7260
4400 Rue Saint-Denis
☎843-9993

Excalibur has an impressive selection of armour, swords, hats, costumes, books and many other articles inspired by the period from the Middle Ages to the Renaissance.

L'Échoppe du Dragon Rouge
8870 Rue Lajeunesse
☎858-5711
3804 Rue Saint-Denis
☎840-9030

L'Échoppe du Dragon Rouge sells replicas of medieval objects.

Glossary

GREETINGS

Hi (casual)	*Salut*
How are you?	*Comment ça va?*
I'm fine	*Ça va bien*
Hello (during the day)	*Bonjour*
Good evening/night	*Bonsoir*
Goodbye, See you later	*Bonjour, Au revoir, à la prochaine*
Yes	*Oui*
No	*Non*
Maybe	*Peut-être*
Please	*S'il vous plaît*
Thank you	*Merci*
You're welcome	*De rien, Bienvenue*
Excuse me	*Excusez-moi*
I am a tourist.	*Je suis touriste*
I am American (m/f)	*Je suis Américain(e)*
I am Canadian (m/f)	*Je suis Canadien(ne)*
I am British	*Je suis Britannique*
I am German (m/f)	*Je suis Allemand(e)*
I am Italian (male/female)	*Je suis Italien(ne)*
I am Belgian	*Je suis Belge*
I am Swiss	*Je suis Suisse*
I am sorry, I don't speak French	*Je suis désolé(e), je ne parle pas français*
Do you speak English?	*Parlez-vous anglais ?*
Slower, please.	*Plus lentement, s'il vous plaît.*
What is your name?	*Quel est votre nom?*
My name is...	*Je m'appelle...*
spouse (m/f)	*époux(se)*
brother, sister	*frère, soeur*
friend (m/f)	*ami(e)*
son, boy	*garçon*
daughter, girl	*fille*
father	*père*
mother	*mère*
single (m/f)	*celibataire*
married (m/f)	*marié(e)*
divorced (m/f)	*divorcé(e)*
widower/widow	*veuf(ve)*

DIRECTIONS

Is there a tourism office near here?	*Est-ce qu'il y a un bureau de tourisme près d'ici?*
There is no...	*Il n'y a pas de...,*
Where is...?	*Où est le/la ... ?*
straight ahead	*tout droit*
to the right	*à droite*
to the left	*à gauche*
beside	*à côté de*

near	*près de*
here	*ici*
there, over there	*là, là-bas*
into, inside	*à l'intérieur*
outside	*à l'extérieur*
far from	*loin de*
between	*entre*
in front of	*devant*
behind	*derrière*

GETTING AROUND

airport	*aéroport*
on time	*à l'heure*
late	*en retard*
cancelled	*annulé*
plane	*l'avion*
car	*la voiture*
train	*le train*
boat	*le bateau*
bicycle	*la bicyclette, le vélo*
bus	*l'autobus*
train station	*la gare*
bus stop	*un arrêt d'autobus*
The bus stop, please	*l'arrêt, s'il vous plaît*
street	*rue*
avenue	*avenue*
road	*route, chemin*
highway	*autoroute*
rural route	*rang*
path, trail	*sentier*
corner	*coin*
neighbourhood	*quartier*
square	*place*
tourist office	*bureau de tourisme*
bridge	*pont*
building	*immeuble*
safe	*sécuritaire*
fast	*rapide*
baggage	*bagages*
schedule	*horaire*
one way ticket	*aller simple*
return ticket	*aller retour*
arrival	*arrivée*
return	*retour*
departure	*départ*
north	*nord*
south	*sud*
east	*est*
west	*ouest*

CARS

for rent	*à louer*
a stop	*un arrêt*
highway	*autoroute*
danger, be careful	*attention*
no passing	*défense de doubler*
no parking	*stationnement interdit*
no exit	*impasse*
stop! (an order)	*arrêtez!*
parking	*stationnement*
pedestrians	*piétons*
gas	*essence*
slow down	*ralentir*
traffic light	*feu de circulation*
service station	*station-service*
speed limit	*limite de vitesse*

MONEY

bank	*banque*
credit union	*caisse populaire*
exchange	*change*
money	*argent*
I don't have any money	*je n'ai pas d'argent*
credit card	*carte de crédit*
traveller's cheques	*chèques de voyage*
The bill please	*l'addition, s'il vous plaît*
receipt	*reçu*

ACCOMMODATION

inn	*auberge*
youth hostel	*auberge de jeunesse*
bed and breakfast	*gîte*
hot water	*eau chaude*
air conditioning	*climatisation*
accommodation	*logement, hébergement*
elevator	*ascenseur*
bathroom	*toilettes, salle de bain*
bed	*lit*
breakfast	*déjeuner*
manager, owner	*gérant, propriétaire*
bedroom	*chambre*
pool	*piscine*
floor (first, second...)	*étage*
main floor	*rez-de-chaussée*
high season	*haute saison*
off season	*basse saison*
fan	*ventilateur*

SHOPPING

open	*ouvert(e)*
closed	*fermé(e)*
How much is this?	*C'est combien?*
I would like...	*Je voudrais...*

I need...	J'ai besoin de...
a store	un magasin
a department store	un magasin à rayons
the market	le marché
salesperson (m/f)	vendeur(se)
the customer (m/f)	le / la client(e)
to buy	acheter
to sell	vendre
t-shirt	un t-shirt
skirt	une jupe
shirt	une chemise
jeans	un jeans
pants	des pantalons
jacket	un blouson
blouse	une blouse
shoes	des souliers
sandals	des sandales
hat	un chapeau
eyeglasses	des lunettes
handbag	un sac
gifts	cadeaux
local crafts	artisanat local
sun protection products	crèmes solaires
cosmetics and perfumes	cosmétiques et parfums
camera	appareil photo
photographic film	pellicule
records, cassettes	disques, cassettes
newspapers	journaux
magazines	revues, magazines
batteries	piles
watches	montres
jewellery	bijouterie
gold	or
silver	argent
precious stones	pierres précieuses
fabric	tissu
wool	laine
cotton	coton
leather	cuir

MISCELLANEOUS

new	nouveau
old	vieux
expensive	cher, dispendieux
inexpensive	pas cher
pretty	joli
beautiful	beau
ugly	laid(e)
big, tall (person)	grand(e)
small, short (person)	petit(e)
short (length)	court(e)
low	bas(se)
wide	large

narrow	*étroit(e)*
dark	*foncé*
light (colour)	*clair*
fat (person)	*gros(se)*
slim, skinny (person)	*mince*
a little	*peu*
a lot	*beaucoup*
something	*quelque chose*
nothing	*rien*
good	*bon*
bad	*mauvais*
more	*plus*
less	*moins*
do not touch	*ne pas toucher*
quickly	*vite*
slowly	*lentement*
big	*grand*
small	*petit*
hot	*chaud*
cold	*froid*
I am ill	*je suis malade*
pharmacy, drugstore	*pharmacie*
I am hungry	*j'ai faim*
I am thirsty	*j'ai soif*
What is this?	*Qu'est-ce que c'est?*
Where?	*Où?*
fixed-price menu	*table d'hôte*
order courses separately	*à la carte*

WEATHER

rain	*pluie*
clouds	*nuages*
sun	*soleil*
It is hot out	*Il fait chaud*
It is cold out	*Il fait froid*

TIME

When?	*Quand?*
What time is it?	*Quelle heure est-il?*
minute	*minute*
hour	*heure*
day	*jour*
week	*semaine*
month	*mois*
year	*année*
yesterday	*hier*
today	*aujourd'hui*
tomorrow	*demain*
morning	*le matin*
afternoon	*l'après-midi*
evening	*le soir*
night	*la nuit*
now	*maintenant*

never	*jamais*
Sunday	*dimanche*
Monday	*lundi*
Tuesday	*mardi*
Wednesday	*mercredi*
Thursday	*jeudi*
Friday	*vendredi*
Saturday	*samedi*
January	*janvier*
February	*février*
March	*mars*
April	*avril*
May	*mai*
June	*juin*
July	*juillet*
August	*août*
September	*septembre*
October	*octobre*
November	*novembre*
December	*décembre*

COMMUNICATION

post office	*bureau de poste*
air mail	*par avion*
stamps	*timbres*
envelope	*enveloppe*
telephone book	*bottin téléphonique*
long distance call	*appel outre-mer*
collect call	*appel collecte*
fax	*télécopieur, fax*
telegram	*télégramme*
rate	*tarif*
dial the regional code	*composer le code régional*
wait for the tone	*attendre la tonalité*

ACTIVITIES

recreational swimming	*la baignade*
beach	*plage*
scuba diving	*la plongée sous-marine*
snorkelling	*la plongée-tuba*
fishing	*la pêche*
recreational sailing	*navigation de plaisance*
windsurfing	*la planche à voile*
bicycling	*faire du vélo*
mountain bike	*vélo tout-terrain (VTT)*
horseback riding	*équitation*
hiking	*la randonnée pédestre*
to walk around	*se promener*
museum or gallery	*musée*
cultural centre	*centre culturel*
cinema	*cinéma*

TOURING

river	*fleuve, rivière*
waterfalls	*chutes*
viewpoint	*belvedère*
hill	*colline*
garden	*jardin*
wildlife reserve	*réserve faunique*
peninsula	*péninsule, presqu'île*
south/north shore	*côte sud/nord*
town or city hall	*hôtel de ville*
courthouse	*palais de justice*
church	*église*
house	*maison*
manor	*manoir*
bridge	*pont*
basin	*bassin*
dam	*barrage*
workshop	*atelier*
historic site	*lieu historique*
train station	*gare*
stables	*écuries*
convent	*couvent*
door, archway, gate	*porte*
customs house	*douane*
locks	*écluses*
market	*marché*
canal	*canal*
channel	*chenal*
seaway	*voie maritime*
museum	*musée*
cemetery	*cimitière*
mill	*moulin*
windmill	*moulin à vent*
hospital	*Hôtel Dieu*
high school	*école secondaire*
lighthouse	*phare*
barn	*grange*
waterfall(s)	*chute(s)*
sandbank	*batture*
neighbourhood, region	*quartier*

NUMBERS

1	un	22	vingt-deux
2	deux	23	vingt-trois
3	trois	24	vingt-quatre
4	quatre	25	vingt-cinq
5	cinq	26	vingt-six
6	six	27	vingt-sept
7	sept	28	vingt-huit
8	huit	29	vingt-neuf
9	neuf	30	trente
10	dix	40	quarante
11	onze	50	cinquante
12	douze	60	soixante
13	treize	70	soixante-dix
14	quatorze	80	quatre-vingt
15	quinze	90	quatre-vingt-dix
16	seize	100	cent
17	dix-sept	200	deux cents
18	dix-huit	500	cinq cents
19	dix-neuf	1,000	mille
20	vingt	10,000	dix mille
21	vingt-et-un	1,000,000	un million

Index

19th- and 20th-century
European Art
(Vieux Montréal) 124
Académie Querbes
(Outremont) 181
Accommodations 261
    Auberge Alternative 264
    Auberge de
        Jeunesse 266
    Auberge de la
        Fontaine 279
    Auberge de l'Hôtel
        de Paris 275
    Auberge des
        Glycines 276
    Auberge du
        Vieux-Port 264
    B & B Bienvenue . 278
    Bed & Breakfasts . 262
    Best Western Hôtel
        International ... 281
    Camping 263
    Casa Bella 269
    Centre Sheraton . 271
    Chasseur Bed and
        Breakfast 276
    Château de l'Aéroport-
        Mirabel 281
    Château Versailles 270
    Collège Jean-de-
        Brébeuf 279
    Comfort Suites ... 269
    Concordia University
        Student
        Residences .. 266
    Courtyard Marriott 270
    Crowne Plaza Métro
        Centre 277
    Days Inn Montréal
        Centre-Ville 277
    Delta Centre-Ville . 266
    Delta Montréal ... 272
    Dorval Airport ... 281

Accommodations (cont.)
    Douillette et
        Chocolat 280
    Fairmont La Reine
        Elizabeth 273
    Four Points Sheraton 272
    Gîte du Parc
        Lafontaine 278
    Gîte du Vieux
        Montréal 264
    Gîte Olympique .. 281
    Gîte Sympathique 279
    Gîte Turquoise ... 280
    Golden Square Mile 266
    Holiday Inn Select
        Mtl Centre-Ville .. 271
    Hôtel Best Western
        Ville-Marie 271
    Hôtel de la
        Montagne 270
    Hôtel de l'Institut . 277
    Hôtel de Paris ... 276
    Hôtel des Gouverneurs
        Place Dupuis .. 278
    Hôtel du Fort 275
    Hôtel du Nouveau
        Forum 269
    Hôtel du Parc ... 271
    Hôtel Inter-
        Continental 265
    Hôtel Terrasse
        Royale 279
    Hôtel Wyndham .. 272
    Jardin d'Antoine . 276
    Loews Hôtel Vogue 274
    Lord Berri 277
    L'Abri du Voyageur 268
    Maisonneuve ... 281
    Maison Pierre du
        Calvet 265
    Manoir Ambrose . 268
    Manoir LeMoyne
        All Suite Hotel .. 274
    Manoir Sherbrooke 275

Accommodations (Cont.)
Marmelade 269
Marriott - Residence
Inn Montréal . . 270
Marriott Château
Champlain 272
McGill University . . 266
Mirabel Airport . . 281
Montréal Aéroport
Hilton 281
Novotel 272
Omni Montréal . . 274
Outremont 279
Passants du
Sans-Soucy 264
Pierre et Dominique 275
Plateau Mont-Royal 278
Quartier Latin 275
Queen Elizabeth
Hotel 273
Riche Bourg 274
Ritz-Carlton
Kempinski 273
Saint André 280
Shaughnessy Village 274
The Village 280
Travellers With
Disablties 263
Travelodge Montréal
Centre 269
Université de
Montréal 280
University
Residences 263
UQÀM Residences 275
Vacances Canada 4
Saisons 278
Vieux-Montréal . . 264
YMCA 268
Adventure packages . . 259
Agora de la Danse
(Plateau Mont-Royal) 165
Airports 48
Alcohol 69
Amphithéâtre Bell
(Vieux-Montréal) . . . 108

Antique and
Second-Hand Shops . 375
Architecture Garden
(Shaughnessy Village) 145
Around the Hôtel Dieu 146
Bars and Nightclubs 344
Restaurants 303
Art and Crafts 373
Auberge Saint-Gabriel
(Vieux-Montréal) 92
Avenue Bernard
(Outremont) 183
Avenue Bloomfield
(Outremont) 181
Avenue Greene
(Mont Royal and
Westmount) 177
Avenue Laurier
(Outremont) 180
Avenue Laval
(Quartier Latin) 154
Avenue Maplewood
(Outremont) 185
Avenue McDougall
(Outremont) 182
Avenue McGill College
(Downtown) 111
Avenue Seymour
(Shaughnessy Village) 144
Bain Morgan
(Maisonneuve) 215
Banking 60
Banks 61
Banque de Montréal
(Vieux-Montréal) 83
Banque Laurentienne
(Little Burgundy and
Saint-Henri) 221
Banque Molson
(Vieux-Montréal) 82
Banque Royale
(Vieux-Montréal) 82
Bars and Nightclubs
Allegra 344
Altitude 717 340
Around the
Hôtel Dieu 344

Bars and Nightclubs *(cont.)*
  Aux Deux Pierrots   340
  Bacci 344, 348
  Baloo's 345
  Bar Exotica 351
  Bar Saint-Laurent . 345
  Belmont sur le
    Boulevard 345
  Biddle's 341
  Bily Kun 348
  Bleu est Noir 348
  Cabaret l'Entre-Peau 351
  Café Campus 345
  Café Chaos 346
  Café Sarajevo 346
  Carlos & Pepes . . . 341
  Crocodile 350
  Diable Vert 349
  Dogue 349
  Downtown 340
  El Zaz Bar 349
  Funkytown 341
  Fûtenbulle 351
  Gay Bars and
    Nightclubs 351
  Golden Square Mile 340
  Grande Gueule . . 350
  Hard Rock Café . . 342
  Hurley's Irish Pub   342
  Île Noire 347
  Inspecteur Épingle   349
  Isart 340
  Jello Bar 347
  L'Air du Temps . . 340
  Le Balattou 344
  Le Boudoir 348
  Le Cheval Blanc . . 347
  Le Medley 347
  Le Sherlock 342
  Les Beaux Esprits . 346
  Les Bobards 345
  Les Foufounes
    Électriques 341
  Little Italy 351
  Luba Lounge 342
  L'Ours Qui Fume . 347
  Mont Royal 350

Bars and Nightclubs *(cont.)*
  Old Dublin Pub . . 344
  Outremont 351
  Passeport 349
  Peel Pub 342
  P'tit Bar 348
  Quartier Latin Pub   348
  Saint-Sulpice 348
  Set 351
  Sir Winston Churchill
    Pub 342
  Sisters 351
  Sky Pub 352
  Sofa 349
  Speakeasy 342
  Stéréo 352
  Swimming 345
  Thursday's 344
  Typhoon Lounge . 350
  Unity 352
  Upstairs 344
  Vieux-Montréal . . 340
  Western Montréal . 350
  Westmount 350
  Whisky Café 351
  Woody's Pub 344
  Ye Olde Orchard . 350
  Zinc Café Bar 350
Basilique Notre-Dame
  (Vieux-Montréal) 85
Bateau Mouche
  (Vieux-Montréal) 92
Bay, The (Downtown)   114
Beer 70
Belding-Corticelli silk
  mill (Pointe St-Charles
  and Verdun) 226
Belvedere
  (Vieux Montréal) . . . 122
Belvédère Camilie-Houde
  (Mont-Royal and
  Westmount) 167
Bibliothèque Municipale
  de Montréal (Plateau
  Mont-Royal) 165
Bibliothèque Nationale
  (Quartier Latin) 157

Index

Bicycle Rentals 253
Biodôme (Maisonneuve) 214
Biosphere (Île Sainte-
   Hélène and Île
   Notre-Dame) 199
Bird-Watching 254
Bookstores 367
Boulevard Mont-Royal
   (Outremont) 186
Boulevard Saint-Laurent
   Restaurants 303
Boulevard Saint-Laurent
   (Downtown) 116
Boulevard Saint-Laurent
   (Little Italy) 190
Boulevard Saint-Laurent
   (Vieux-Montréal) 92
Brasserie Dawes
   (West Island) 236
Business Hours 64
Caisse Populaire
   (Little Burgundy and
   Saint-Henri) 221
Canadian Centre for
   Architecture
   (Vieux-Montréal) . . 144
Canadian National
   railyards (Pointe-Saint-
   Charles and Verdun) 227
Canal de Lachine
   (Vieux-Montréal) 91
Canals and Gardens
   (Île Notre-Dame) . . . 200
Car rentals 56
Casa d'Italia (Little Italy) 187
Caserne de Pompiers no 1
   (Maisonneuve) 216
Caserne de Pompiers no 15
   (Pointe-Saint-Charles
   and Verdun) 227
Caserne de Pompiers
   no 31 (Little Italy) . . 190
Casino (Île Notre-Dame) 200
Cathedral of St. Peter
   and St. Paul
   (The Village) 206

Cathédrale Marie-Reine-
   du-Monde
   (Downtown) 108
Cathédrale Schismatique
   Grecque Saint-Nicolas
   (Montréal) 96
Centre Canadien
   d'Architecture
   (Shaughnessy Village) 144
Centre d'Accueil et
   d'Interprétation du
   Canal de Lachine . 234
Centre d'Histoire de
   Montréal
   (Vieux-Montréal) . . . 89
Centre de Commerce
   Mondial
   (Vieux-Montréal) . . . 79
Centre de Divertissements
   Metaforia
   (Downtown) 112
Centre Eaton
   (Downtown) 112
Centre Infotouriste
   (Downtown) 105
Centre Molson
   (Downtown) 107
Chalet du Mont Royal
   (Mont Royal and
   Westmount) 169
Champ-de-Mars
   (Vieux-Montréal) . . . 95
Chapelle Mariale
   Notre-Dame-de-
   L'Assomption
   (Saint-Laurent) . . . 243
Chapelle Notre-Dame-
   de-Bonsecours
   (Vieux-Montréal) 97, 98
Chapelle Notre-Dame-de-
   Lourdes
   (Quartier Latin) . . . 158
Château Dufresne
   (Maisonneuve) 211
Château Ramezay
   (Vieux-Montréal) 96

Chelsea Place
(Golden Square Mile)   138
Chemin de la Côte-Sainte-
Catherine (Outremont) 180
Chemin Senneville
(Pointe-Claire)   241
Chemin Senneville
(Sainte-Anne-de-
Bellevue)   241
Children   73
Chinatown (Downtown) 118
Christ Church Cathedral
(Downtown)   113
Church of St. Andrew
and St. Paul
(Downtown)   102
Church of St. James
The Apostle
(Golden Square Mile)   140
Church of the Ascension of
Our Lord (Mont Royal
and Westmount) . .   175
Cimetière Notre-Dame-des-
Neiges (Mont Royal
and Westmount) . .   173
Cinema   39
Cinéma Corona (Little
Burgundy and
St-Henri)   220
Cinéma Excentris
(Around the
Hôtel-Dieu) . . .   150
Cinémathèque Québécoise
(Quartier Latin)   158
Circuit Gilles-Villeneuve
(Île Notre-Dame) . . .   201
City Hall (Westmount)   176
Climate   65
Clos Saint-Bernard
(Outremont)   183
Collection of Canadian Art
(Vieux Montréal) . . .   126
Collège de Saint-Laurent
(Saint-Laurent)   244
Collège du Mont-Saint-
Louis (Sault-au-
Récollet)   194

Collège Rachel (Plateau
Mont-Royal)   166
Collège Sophie-Barat
(Sault-au-Récollet) . .   192
Colonne Nelson
(Vieux-Montréal)   94
Complex of the Soeurs des
Saints-Noms-de-Jésus-
et-de-Marie   184
Complexe Desjardins
(Downtown)   116
Computers   373
Concert Halls   353
Concordia University
(Golden Square Mile) 139
Conseil des Arts de la CUM
(Around Hôtel-Dieu)   151
Consulates   42
Contemporary Art
collection
(Vieux Montréal) . . .   124
Cours Le Royer
(Vieux-Montréal)   87
Cours Mont-Royal
(Downtown)   104
Couvent de Lachine
(Lachine)   235
Couvent des Soeurs de
Marie-Réparatrice
(Outremont)   187
Couvent des Sœurs Grises
(Shaughnessy
Village)   145
Cross-country
skiing   257
Cultural activities   353
Cultural centres   356
Currency   62
Cycling   252
Dawson College
(Shaughnessy
Village)   142
Disabled people   71
Dollard-des-Ormeaux
Restaurants   337
Dorval Airport   48

Downtown 100
   Accommodations . 266
   Bars and Nightclubs 340
   Restaurants 293
Drugs 73
Eaton department store
  (Downtown) 112
École des Hautes Études
  Commerciales
  (Quartier Latin) . . . 159
École Le Plateau
  (Plateau Mont-Royal) 165
École Madonna Della
  Difesa (Little Italy) . . 190
École Sainte-Brigide
  (The Village) 206
École Sainte-Julienne-
  Falconieri (Little Italy) 188
Écomusée du Fier Monde
  (The Village) 204
Ecomuseum (Morgan
  Arboretum) 248
Ecomuseum (Sainte-
  Anne-de-Bellevue) . . 240
Economy 32
Édifice Ernest-Cormier
  (Vieux-Montréal) 92
Édifice Godin
  (Around Hôtel-Dieu) . 152
Édifice Grothé
  (Around Hôtel-Dieu) . 152
Édifice Sun Life
  (Downtown) 106
Église de l'Immaculée-
  Conception (Plateau
  Mont-Royal) 162
Église de la Visitation
  (Sault-au-Récollet) . . 192
Église des Saints-Anges
  Gardiens (Lachine) . 235
Église du Gesù
  (Downtown) 114
Église du Très-Saint-
  Nom-de-
  Jésus(Maisonneuve) 216
Église Madonna Della
  Difesa (Little Italy) . . 188

Église Notre-Dame-des-
  Sept-Douleurs
  (Verdun) 230
Église Saint-Charles
  (Pointe-Saint-Charles
  and Verdun) 226
Église Saint-Gabriel
  (Pointe-Sainte-Charles
  and Verdun) 225
Église Saint-Henri
  (Little Burgundy and
  Saint-Henri) 220
Église Saint-Irénée
  (Little Burgundy and
  Saint-Henri) 220
Église Saint-Jean-Baptiste
  (Plateau Mont-Royal) 166
Église Saint-Jean-
  Baptiste-de-LaSalle
  (Maisonneuve) . . . 215
Église Saint-Laurent
  (Saint-Laurent) 243
Église Saint-Léon
  (Mont Royal and
  Westmount) 177
Église Saint-Pierre-Apôtre
  (The Village) 205
Église Saint-Sauveur
  (Quartier Latin) 160
Église Saint-Viateur
  (Outremont) 181
Église Saint-Zotique
  (Little Burgundy and
  Saint-Henri) 221
Église Sainte-Anne
  (Sainte-Anne de
  Bellevue) 241
Église Sainte-Brigide
  (The Village) 206
Église Sainte-Cunégonde
  (Little Burgundy,
  Saint-Henri) 219
Église Sainte-Geneviève
  (Sainte-Geneviève) . 242
Église St-Joachim, the
  Mill and the Convent
  (Pointe-Claire) 238

Electricity 73
Electronics 372
Embassies 42
Emergencies 57
Entertainment 339
    Bars and Nightclubs 339
    Cultural Activities . 353
    Cultural Centres . . 356
    Festivals 357
    Fun and Games . . 352
    Information on
      the Arts 355
    Major Events 360
    Movie Theatres . . 355
    Museums 355
    Spectator Sports . . 360
    Ticket Sales 355
Entrance formalities . . . 42
Erskine & American
  United Church
  (Downtown) 102
Esplanade Émilie-Gamelin
  (Quartier Latin) 159
European Decorative Arts
  (Vieux Montréal) . . . 122
Ex-Centris Cinema
  (around Hôtel-Dieu) . 150
Exchange rates 60
Experimental Farm
  (Sainte-Anne-de-
    Bellevue) 240
Exploring
    Tour A:
      Vieux-Montréal . . . 77
    Tour B: Downtown 100
    Tour C: Montreal
      Museum of
      Fine Arts 118
    Tour D: The Golden
      Square Mile 129
    Tour E: Shaughnessy
      Village 141
    Tour F: Around the
      Hôtel-Dieu 146
    Tour G: Quartier
      Latin 153

Exploring (cont.)
    Tour H: Plateau
      Mont-Royal 160
    Tour I: Westmount
      and Western
      Montreal 167
    Tour J: Outremont 178
    Tour K: Little Italy 187
    Tour L:
      Sault-au-Récollet 191
    Tour M: Île Sainte-
      Hélène et Île
      Notre-Dame . . 195
    Tour N: The Village 201
    Tour O:
      Maisonneuve . . . 208
    Tour P: Little Burgundy
      and Saint-Henri 218
    Tour Q: Pointe-Saint-
      Charles and
      Verdun 224
    Tour R: The West
      Island 232
Fashion 362
Faubourg Sainte-Catherine
  (Shaughnessy Village) 146
Ferme Écologique du
  Cap Saint-Jacques . . . 249
Ferme Outre-Mont
  (Outremont) 182
Ferme Saint-Gabriel
  (Pointe-Saint-Charles
    and Verdun) 228
Festivals 357
Fire Station (Little
  Burgundy and
  Saint-Henri) 221
Folklore 74
Food 378
Former Cinéma Corona
  (Little Burgundy and
  Saint-Henri) 220
Former First Presbyterian
  Church (Around the
  Hôtel-Dieu) 149
Former hôtel de ville
  (Maisonneuve) . . . 215

Former Military Cemetery
(Île Ste-Hélène
and N.-D.) 199
Former Monastère
Sainte-Croix
(Sainte-Geneviève) . 242
Fort de l'Île
Sainte-Hélène
(Île Ste-Hélène) . . . 198
Fort Rolland
(Lachine) 236
Fur Trade at Lachine
National Historic Site
(Lachine) 235
Galleries of Ancient
Cultures
(Vieux Montréal) . . 124
Garden Court
(Outremont) 183
Gare Centrale
(Downtown) 111
Gare Dalhousie
(Vieux-Montréal) . . . 97
Gare Maritime Iberville
(Vieux-Montréal) . . . 91
Gare Viger
(Vieux-Montréal) . . . 97
Gare Windsor
(Downtown) 106
Gay and Lesbian Life . . 71
Gay Village 204
George-Étienne-Cartier
National Historic
Site (Vieux-Montréal) . 96
Glass Court
(Vieux-Montréal) . . . 124
Golden Square Mile . . 129
Accommodations . 266
Bars and Nightclubs 340
Restaurants 293
Golf 256
Grain silos
(Vieux-Montréal) . . . 91
Grand Séminaire
(Shaughnessy Village) 141

Grand Trunk houses
(Pointe-Saint-Charles
and Verdun) 228
Guided tours 58
Habitat '67 (Île Sainte-
Hélène and Île
Notre-Dame) 196
Hairdresser 74
Health 65
Hiking 250
History 14
Between the
Two Wars 26
From 1960 to Today 29
Fur Trade
(1665-1760) 18
Industrialization and
Economic Power
(1850-1914) 24
Origins 15
Renewed Growth
(1945-1960) 27
Transitional Years
(1763-1850) 22
Ville-Marie
(1642-1665) 16
Holt Renfrew
(Downtown) 103
Home Decor 376
Hôpital Général des Soeurs
Grises (Montréal) . . . 90
Hôpital Notre-Dame
(Plateau Mont-Royal) 165
Hospice Auclair
(Plateau Mont-Royal) 166
Hôtel de Ville
(Outremont) 183
Hôtel de Ville
(Vieux-Montréal) . . . 95
Hôtel-Dieu (Around
the Hôtel-Dieu) . . . 149
Île des Sœurs (Pointe-Saint-
Charles and Verdun) 230
Île Notre-Dame 200
Restaurants 332
Île Sainte-Hélène 195
Restaurants 332

Imax 356
In-line Skating 256
Insectarium
    (Maisonneuve) . . 209, 211
Institut de Tourisme et
    d'Hôtellerie du Québec
    (Quartier latin) . . . 153
Institut des Sourdes-
    Muettes (Plateau
    Mont-Royal) 165
Insurance 68
Inuit Art collection
    (Vieux-Montréal) . . . 128
iSci centre
    (Vieux Montréal) 88
Jardin Botanique
    (Maisonneuve) 209
Just for Laughs Museum
    (Around Hôtel-Dieu) 152
La Cité Complex
    (Around the
    Hôtel-Dieu) 149
Lachine Canal National
    Historic Site (Pointe-
    Saint-Charles) 226
La Ronde (Île
    Sainte-Hélène and
    Île Notre-Dame) . . . 199
Lac aux Castors
    (Mont Royal and
    Westmount) 172
Language 31, 67
Laundromats 74
Le Bocage
    (Pointe-Claire) 239
Le Château (Downtown) 103
Linton (Downtown) . . 100
Literature 37
Little Burgundy 218
        Restaurants 335
Little Italy 187
        Bars and Nightclubs 351
        Restaurants 329
Lock (Sainte-Anne-
    de-Bellevue) 241

Macdonald College
    (Sainte-Anne-
    de-Bellevue) 240
Maison Alcan
    (Downtown) 104
Maison André Legault,
    dit Deslauriers
    (Dorval) 237
Maison Antoine-Pilon
    (Pointe-Claire) 238
Maison Atholstan
    (Downtown) 104
Maison Baumgarten
    (Golden Square Mile) 132
Maison Baxter
    (Downtown) 103
Maison Brown (Dorval) 237
Maison Clarence-de-Sola
    (Golden Square Mile) 137
Maison Clermont (Little
    Burgundy and
    St-Henri) 224
Maison Cormier
    (Golden Square Mile) 138
Maison David-Dumouchel
    (Sault-au-Récollet) . . 192
Maison de l'Arbre
    (Maisonneuve) . 209, 211
Maison de l'OACI
    (Vieux-Montréal) 79
Maison de Radio-Canada
    (The Village) 205
Maison des Cyclistes . . 252
Maison du Meunier (Parc-
    Nature de l'Île-de-la-
    Visitation) 250
Maison du Pressoir (Parc-
    Nature de l'Île-de-la-
    Visitation) 250
Maison du Pressoir
    (Sault-au-Récollet) . . 194
Maison d'Ailleboust-
    de-Manthet
    (Sainte-Geneviève) . 242
Maison Forget
    (Downtown) 103

Index

Maison Fréchette
   (Quartier Latin) 156
Maison Frederick Barlow
   (Dorval) 237
Maison Hamilton
   Golden Square Mile) 136
Maison Hans Selye
   (Around the
   Hôtel-Dieu) 148
Maison Henry V.
   Meredith (Golden
   Square Mile) 133
Maison Hosmer (Golden
   Square Mile) 137
Maison J.B. Aimbault
   (Outremont) 184
Maison James Ross
   (Golden Square Mile) 133
Maison James Thomas
   Davis (Golden Square
   Mile) 136
Maison John Kenneth L.
   Ross (Golden Square
   Mile) 133
Maison Linton (Golden
   Square Mile) 139
Maison Lyall (Golden
   Square Mile) 139
Maison Minnie Louise
   Davis (Dorval) 237
Maison Mortimer B.
   Davis (Golden
   Square Mile) 135
Maison Notman
   (Around Hôtel-Dieu) 151
Maison Papineau
   (Vieux-Montréal) 98
Maison Picard
   (West Island) 236
Maison Pierre-du-Calvet
   (Vieux-Montréal) 98
Maison Quesnel
   (West Island) 236
Maison Raymond
   (Golden Square Mile) 138
Maison Rodolphe-Forget
   (Golden Square Mile) 137

Maison Shaughnessy
   (Shaughnessy Village) 144
Maison Simon Fraser
   (Sainte-Anne-de-
   Bellevue) 240
Maison Stephen (Golden
   Square Mile) 140
Maison William
   Alexander Molson
   (Golden Square Mile) 129
Mainsonneuve 208
   Accommodations . 281
   Restaurants 334
Marché Atwater (Little
   Burgundy and
   Saint-Henri) ... 224
Marché Bonsecours
   (Vieux-Montréal) 99
Marché Jean-Talon
   (Little Italy) 191
Marché Maisonneuve
   (Maisonneuve) 215
Masonic Temple
   (Shaughnessy Village) 141
McCord Museum of
   Canadian History
   (Vieux-Montréal) .. 130
McGill University (Golden
   Square Mile) 130
Medieval boutiques .. 386
Merchants Manufacturing
   Company (Little Bur-
   gundy-Saint-Henri) 222
Milestone (Mont Royal
   and Westmount) ... 176
Mirabel Airport 49
Molson Bank
   (Vieux-Montréal) 82
Molson Brewery
   (The Village) 207
Monastère des
   Pères du Très-
   Saint-Sacrement
   (Plateau Mont-Royal) 161
Money 60
Mont Royal 167
   Bars and Nightclubs 350

Mont-Saint-Louis
(Quartier Latin) 156
Montcalm
(Outremont) 183
Montreal Diocesan
Theological College
(Around Hôtel-Dieu) 148
Montreal High
School (Around the
Hôtel-Dieu) 148
Montréal métro
(Vieux-Montréal) 110
Montréal Museum of
Fine Arts
(Downtown) .. 102, 118
Monument National
(Downtown) 117
Monument to Maisonneuve
(Vieux-Montréal) 83
Monument to the Patriots
(Faubourg à M'Lasse) 208
Morgan Arboretum ... 248
Morrice Hall (Downtown)
Around the
Hôtel-Dieu 132
Moulin Fleming
(Lachine) 233
Mount Royal Club
(Downtown) 104
Mount Royal Park 169
Mount Royal Protestant
Cemetery (Mont Royal
and Westmount) .. 169
Mouth of the Canal de
Lachine (Lachine) .. 234
Movie Theatres 355
Musée d'Archéologie de la
Pointe-à-Callière 88
Musée d'Art
(Saint-Laurent) 244
Musée d'Art Contemporain
(Downtown) 115
Musée David M. Stewart
(Île Ste-Hélène and
N.-D.) 198
Musée de la Basilique
(Vieux-Montréal) 86

Musée de Lachine
(Lachine) 234
Musée des Arts
Décoratifs de Montréal
(Downtown) 102
Musée des Beaux-Arts
de Montréal 118
Musée des Hospitalières
(Around Hôtel-Dieu) 150
Musée Juste Pour
Rire (Around the
Hotel-Dieu) 152
Musée Marc-Aurèle-Fortin
(Vieux-Montréal) 90
Musée Marguerite-
Bourgeoys
(Vieux-Montréal) ... 98
Musée Marguerite-
d'Youville (Shaughnessy
Village) 146
Musée McCord
d'Histoire Canadienne
(Golden Square Mile) 130
Museum of Decorative
Arts (Downtown) ... 102
Museums 74
Music 371
National Film Board of
Canada
(Quartier Latin) ... 158
Newspapers 74
Northern Electric factory
(Pointe-Saint-Charles
and Verdun) 227
Numismatic Museum
(Vieux-Montréal) 84
Office National du Film
(Quartier Latin) 157
Ogilvy's department store
(Golden Square Mile) 140
Old Masters collection
(Vieux Montréal) .. 122
Old Port
(Vieux-Montréal) 91
Olympic Village
(Maisonneuve) 212

Oratoire Saint-Joseph
   (Mont Royal and
      Westmount)   173
Ouimetoscope
   (The Village)   204
Outdoor equipment . .   366
Outdoors   247
      Outdoor Activities   250
      Parks   247
Outremont   178
      Accommodations .   279
      Bars and Nightclubs   351
      Restaurants   326
Palais de Justice
   (Vieux-Montréal)   92
Palais des Congrès
   (Downtown)   118
Parc Angrignon   247
Parc Beaubien
   (Outremont)   182
Parc de la Cité du Havre
   Île Ste-Hélène and
      N.-D.)   196
Parc de la Presse
   (Vieux-Montréal) . .   84
Parc des Îles   248
Parc du Mont-Royal . .   247
Parc Hélène-de-Champlain
   (Île Sainte-Hélène)   196
Parc Jarry   248
Parc Jeanne-Mance . . .   247
Parc Joyce (Outremont)   184
Parc Lafontaine (Plateau
   Mont-Royal) .   161, 247
Parc Maisonneuve . . .   248
Parc Monk (Lachine) . .   234
Parc Morgan
   (Maisonneuve) . . .   216
Parc Murray (Mont Royal
   and Westmount)   176
Parc Nature de L'Anse-à-
   l'Orme (Sainte-Anne-
      de-Bellevue) . . .   241
Parc Nature du Bois-de-
   Liesse
      (Sainte-Geneviève) 243

Parc Nature du Cap-Saint-
   Jacques (Sainte-Anne-
      de-Bellevue) . . .   241
Parc Outremont
   (Outremont)   181
Parc René-Lévesque
   (Lachine) 234, 247
Parc-Nature de l'Anse-à-
   l'Orme   249
Parc-Nature de
   l'Île-de-la-
      Visitation . . .   194, 294
Parc-Nature de la
   Pointe-aux-Prairies   250
Parc-Nature du Bois-de-
   l'île-Bizard   249
Parc-Nature du Bois-de-
   Liesse   249
Parc-Nature du Cap
   Saint-Jacques   249
Parcs-Nature   249
Parisian Métro railing
   (Vieux-Montréal) .   79
Parkland (Outremont) .   184
Parks   248
      Parc Angrignon . .   247
      Parc des Îles   248
      Parc du Mont-Royal   247
      Parc Jarry   248
      Parc Jeanne-Mance   247
      Parc Lafontaine . .   247
      Parc Maisonneuve   248
      Parc René-Lévesque   247
      Parc-Nature de
         l'Anse-à-l'Orme .   249
      Parc-Nature de
         l'Île-de-la-Visitation 249
      Parc-Nature de la
         Pointe-aux-Prairies 250
      Parc-Nature du Bois-
         de-l'île-Bizard . .   249
      Parc-Nature du Bois-
         de-Liesse   249
      Parc-Nature du Cap
         Saint-Jacques . . .   249

Passport 42
Pavillon Jacques-Cartier
    (Vieux-Montréal) . 99
Pavillon Marie-Victorin
    (Outremont) 185
Pavillon Vincent d'Indy
    (Outremont) 185
Pensionnat du Saint-Nom-
    de-Marie
    (Outremont) . . . 185
Pensionnat Notre-Dame-
    des-Anges
    (Saint-Laurent) . . 243
Pet stores 386
Pets 73
Pharmacie Gauvin
    (The Village) 206
Pharmacies 74
Pilon Clothing Store
    (The Village) 202
Pitfield House
    (Parc-Nature du
    Bois-de-Liesse) . 250
Place Alexis-Nihon
    (Shaughnessy
    Village) 144
Place Bonaventure
    (Downtown) 110
Place Charles-de-Gaulle
    (Plateau Mont-Royal)162
Place d'Armes
    (Vieux-Montréal) . . 83
Place d'Youville
    (Vieux-Montréal) . . 89
Place des Arts
    (Downtown) 115
Place du 6-décembre-1989
    (Mont-Royal) 175
Place du Canada
    (Downtown) 106
Place du Quartier Latin
    (Quartier Latin) . . 159
Place Dupuis
    (The Village) 202
Place Émilie-Gamelin
    (Quartier latin) . . 159

Place Jacques-Cartier
    (Vieux-Montréal) . 93
Place Montréal Trust
    (Downtown) 111
Place Royale
    (Vieux-Montréal) . . 87
Place Saint-Henri
    (Little Burgundy
    and Saint-Henri) 221
Place Vauquelin
    (Vieux-Montréal) . . 95
Place Ville-Marie
    (Downtown) 111
Plage de l'Île
    Notre-Dame
    (Île Notre-Dame) 201
Planétarium Dow
    (Downtown) 108
Plateau Mont-Royal . . . 160
    Accommodations . . 278
    Bars and Nightclubs 348
    Restaurants 311
Plaza Saint-Hubert
    (Little Italy) 188
Pointe Saint-Charles . . 224
    Restaurants 335
Pointe-à-Callière, Montréal
    Musuem of
    Archaeology and
    History 88
Pointe-Claire
    Restaurants 336
Politics 32
Pont Jacques-Cartier
    (Île Ste-Hélène and
    Notre-Dame) . . . 198
Pont Jacques-Cartier
    (The Village) 207
Portrait 13
Post offices 63
Practical Information . . . 41
Pre-Columbian Art
    (Vieux-Montréal) . 128
Prints and Drawings
    (Vieux-Montréal) . 128
Prison du Pied-du-Courant
    (The Village) . . . 208

Promenade du Père
    Marquette
        (Lachine) 234
Promenades de la
    Cathédrale
        (Downtown) . . 113
Public holidays 64
Public transportation . . . 53
Quai Jacques-Cartier
(Vieux-Montréal) 94
Quartier Latin 153
    Accommodations . 275
    Bars and
        Nightclubs 345
    Restaurants 309
Québec cuisine 65
Québec pavilion (Île
Sainte Hélène) 201
Queen Elizabeth Hotel 111
Rafting 255
Ravenscrag (Golden
    Square Mile) 136
Redpath Museum
(Golden Square Mile) . 132
Religion 75
René-Lévesque Park . . 247
Restaurant Hélène-de-
    Champlain
        (Île Ste-Hélène) . 199
Restaurants 283
    Al Dente 324
    Amalfitana 334
    Ambala 314
    Ambiance 335
    Anubis 311
    Auberge du Dragon
        Rouge 329
    Aux Baisers Volés 315
    Aux Deux
        Gauloises 324
    Aux Entretiens . . . 311
    Azuma 308
    Bar-B-Barn 302
    Bato Thaï 333
    Beauty's 304
    Ben's Delicatessen 293
    Bières & Compagnie 316

Restaurants (cont.)
    Bilboquet 326
    Binerie Mont-Royal 312
    Bio Train 288
    Bonaparte 292
    Brioche Lyonnaise 309
    Brûlerie Saint-
        Denis . 293, 312, 309
    Buona Notte 308
    Byblos 312
    Cactus 316
    Café America 335
    Café Cherrier 319
    Café Ciné-Lumière 306
    Café de Paris 302
    Café du TNM 296
    Café El Dorado . . 312
    Café Italia 329
    Café Méliès 308
    Café Rico 312
    Café Roccoco 303
    Café Romolo 326
    Café Souvenir . . . 326
    Café Starbuck's . . 294
    Café Toman 294
    Cafétéria 306
    Cage aux Sports . 289
    Casa Cacciatore . . 330
    Casa Tapas 319
    Champs 306
    Chao Phraya 307
    Chez Better 322
    Chez Chine 299
    Chez Claudette . . 313
    Chez Delmo 290
    Chez Gauthier . . . 298
    Chez Georges . . . 299
    Chez la Mère
        Berteau 333
    Chez la Mère
        Michel 303
    Chez Lévesque . . . 328
    Chez Queux 292
    Chu Chai 316
    Club Lounge 737 . 298
    Coco Rico 304
    Continental 319

Restaurants *(cont.)*

Côté Soleil 316
Crémerie Saint-
  Vincent 289
Crêperie Bretonne
  Ty-Breiz 319
Cucina 306
Desjardins Sea Food 301
Don Miguel 307
Downtown 293
Eggspectations 294, 326
El Zaziummm . . . 318
Euro Deli 304
Festin des
  Gouverneurs 332
Fondue Mentale . . 317
Frite Alors
  (Outremont) 326
Frite Alors
  (Plateau
    Mont-Royal) . . 313
Fruit Folie 313
Gavroche 330
Gibby's 292
Ginger 308
Golden Square
  Mile 293
Green Spot 335
Hélène de
  Champlain 332
Il Cicerone 331
Il Fornetto 336
Il Mondo 331
Il Mulino 330
Île Notre-Dame . . 332
Île Sainte-Hélène . 332
Jardin du Ritz 297
Jardin Sakura 297
Julien 300
Kaizen 303
Katsura 300
Kilo (Boulevard
  Saint-Laurent) . . 304
Kilo (The Village) 333

Restaurants *(cont.)*

L'Actuel 298
L'Anecdote 311
L'Avenue 319
L'Entre-Miche 334
L'Entrecôte
  Saint-Jean 296
L'Escale à Saïgon . 328
L'Estaminet 331
L'Express 321
La Bonne Carte . . 332
La Boulange du
  Commensal 314
La Cabane 306
La Casa de Mateo . 289
La Chilenita 312
La Colombe 322
La Croissanterie . . 326
La Fonderie 330
La Fontanina 336
La Gargote 290
La Gaudriole 317
La Louisiane 325
La Marée 293
La Moulerie 328
La Paryse 310
La Perle Szechuan 337
La Petite Marche . 318
La Psarotaverna du
  Symposium 322
La Raclette 321
La Selva 315
La Sila 311
La Spaghettata . . . 328
La Tarantella 330
La Transition 325
Laloux 320
Laurier B.B.Q. . . . 327
Le 917 315
Le Bistingo 327
Le Bistro Gourmet 303
Le Caveau 297
Le Caveau
  Szechwan 336
Le Claremont 324
Le Commensal
  (Downtown) . . . 294

Index

Restaurants *(cont.)*

Le Commensal
  (Quartier Latin) . 310
Le Commensal
  (Western Montréal)324
Le Flambard 320
Le Gourmand . . . 336
Le Goût de la
  Thaïlande
  (Maisonneuve) . . 334
Le Goût de la
  Thaïlande (Plateau
  Mont-Royal) 314
Le Grain de Sel . . 334
Le Jardin de Panos 317
Le Kerkennah . . . 331
Le Latini 301
Le Lutétia 300
Le Maistre 325
Le Nil Bleu 317
Le P'tit Plateau . . . 321
Le Paltoquet 327
Le Paris 297
Le Pélerin 310
Le Petit Extra 333
Le Petit Moulinsart 290
Le Piémontais . . . 310
Le Porté Disparu . 313
Le Wok de
  Szechuan 331
Lélé da Cuca 314
Les Caprices de
  Nicolas 302
Les Gâteries 309
Lesage J.B. 331
Lester's 327
Little Burgundy . . 335
Little Italy 329
L'Académie 315
L'Entre-Mise 332
L'Harmonie d'Asie 314
L'Impair 332
Maestro S.V.P. . . . 309
Magnan 336
Maison George
  Stephen 300

Restaurants *(cont.)*

Maison Pierre du
  Calvet 292
Maisonneuve 334
Mangia 294
Marlowe 337
Mess Hall 325
Mezze 307
Mikado 311
Milos 328
Misto 320
Modavie 290
Modigliani 321
Moe's Deli & Bar
  (Downtown) . . . 297
Moe's Deli & Bar
  (Maisonneuve) . . 334
Moishe's 309
Monkland Tavern . 325
Mövenpick 296
Mr. Ma 300
Nuances 332
Outremont 326
Ouzeri 317
Palais de l'Inde . . 307
Paris-Beurre 328
Pasta Casareccia . . 323
Pasta Express 331
Pattaya 303
Pavarotti 290
Persil Fou 317
Petit Alep 329
Petit Extra 333
Piazza Romana . . . 337
Piazzetta
  (Outremont) . . . 327
Piazzetta (Plateau
  Mont-Royal) 314
Piazzetta
  (The Village) . . . 333
Piccolo Diavolo . . 333
Piment Rouge . . . 301
Pique Assiette . . . 302
Pistou 320
Pizzafiore 323
Pizzaïolle 327

Restaurants *(cont.)*
Pizzédélic
. . . . 307, 327, 314, 324
Pizzeria Napoletana 330
Planète 334
Poco Piu 320
Restorante Mirra . . 337
Restorante-Trattoria
Carissima 321
Saint-Henri 335
Saloon 333
Sans Menu 335
Santropol 307
Sault-au-Récollet . 330
Schwartz's Montréal
Hebrew
Delicatessen . . . 304
Shaughnessy Village 302
Shed Café 308
Soto 299
Soy 318
Stash's Café Bazar 290
Steak Frites 289
Tampopo 315
Tandoori Village . 306
Thaï Express 304
Thaï Grill 309
Titanic 289
Toasteur 313
Toi Moi et Café . . 327
Toqué 322
Troïka 301
Un Monde Sauté . 318
Van Houtte 294
Via Fortuna 332
Villa Wellington . . 335
Wienstein 'n' Gavino's
Pasta Bar
Factory Co. . . . 299
Zen 301
Zyng 310
Ritz-Carlton Kempinski
(Downtown) 103
Rivoli and Château
Cinemas (Little Italy) . 188
Royal Bank
(Vieux-Montréal) 82

Royal Victoria College
(Around the
Hôtel-Dieu) 148
Royal York
(Outremont) 184
Rue Cherrier (Plateau
Mont-Royal) 165
Rue Coursol (Little
Burgundy and
Saint-Henri) 218
Rue Crescent
(Downtown) 103
Rue Dalcourt
(The Village) 206
Rue Prince-Arthur
(Around Hôtel-Dieu) 151
Rue Prince-Arthur
(Quartier Latin) 154
Rue Saint-Amable
(Vieux-Montréal) 94
Rue Saint-Augustin
(Little Burgundy and
Saint-Henri) 222
Rue Saint-Denis (Plateau
Mont-Royal) 165
Rue Saint-Jacques
(Vieux-Montréal) 82
Rue Saint-Paul
(Vieux-Montréal) 99
Rue Sainte-Catherine
(Downtown) 112
Rue Sainte-Émilie
(Little Burgundy
and Saint-Henri) . . . 222
Rue Sainte-Rose
(The Village) 205
Safety 70
Sailin 256
Saint-Henri 218
Restaurants 335
Saint-Jacques (Quartier
Latin) 156
Sainte-Cunégonde
city hall 219
Salle Claude-Champagne
(Outremont) 185

Salle Émile-Legault
  (Saint-Laurent) 244
Salle Pierre-Mercure
  (Quartier Latin) . 158
Sault-au-Récollet 191
  Restaurants 330
Senior Citizens 71
Shaughnessy Village . . 141
  Accommodations . 274
  Restaurants 302
Shopping
  Antique and second-
    hand shops 375
  Art and crafts 373
  Bookstores 367
  Computers 373
  Electronics 372
  Fashion 362
  Food 378
  Home decor 376
  Medieval boutiques 386
  Music 371
  Outdoor equipment 366
  Pet stores 386
  Special occasions . 383
  Stationery 370
  Travel accessories 386
  Underground City 361
Simons (Downtown
  and Golden
  Square Mile) 363
Skating 257
Special Occasions 383
Spectator Sports 360
Square Cabot
  (Shaughnessy
  Village) 144
Square Dorchester
  (Downtown) 105
Square Phillips
  (Downtown) 113
Square Phillips
  (Vieux-Montréal) . . . 113
Square Saint-Henri (Little
  Burgundy and
  Saint-Henri) 220

Square Saint-Louis
  (Quartier Latin) 153
Square Sir-Georges-
  Étienne-Cartier
  (Saint-Henri) 221
Square Victoria
  (Vieux-Montréal) . . . 79
Square Viger
  (Quartier Latin) 159
St. Andrew's United
  Church (West Island) 236
St. George's Anglican
  Church (Downtown) 106
St. James United Church
  (Downtown) 114
St. Jude's Church
  (Little Burgundy and
  Saint-Henri) 219
St. Patrick's Basilica
  (Downtown) 115
St. Stephen's Anglican
  Church
  (West Island) 235
Stade Olympique
  (Maisonneuve) . . 212
Stationery 370
Statue of Queen Victoria
  (Vieux-Montréal) . 79
Stewart Hall
  (Pointe-Claire) 238
Swimming 254
Tax refunds for
  non-residents 66
Taxes 66
Taxis 52
Télé-Métropole
  (The Village) 206
Telecommunications . . . 63
Telegrams 75
Tennis 256
Terrasse Saint-Denis
  (Quartier Latin) . 156
Théâtre Denise Pelletier
  (Maisonneuve) 216
Théâtre National
  (The Village) 204

Théâtre Outremont
(Outremont) 183
Théâtre Saint-Denis
(Quartier Latin) 157
Theatres 353
Ticket sales 355
Time zone 63
Tipping 67
Tour 1000 (Downtown) 108
Tour BNP (Downtown) 112
Tour CIBC (Downtown) 105
Tour de la Bourse
(Vieux-Montréal) 78
Tour de l'Horloge
(Vieux-Montréal) 99
Tour de l'Île 252
Tour de Montréal
(Maisonneuve) . . 214
Tour IBM-Marathon
(Downtown) 106
Tour Lévis (Île
Ste-Hélène and
Île Notre-Dame) . . . 198
Tourist information 45
Travel accessories 386
Tropique Nord (Île Ste-
Hélène and Île
Notre-Dame) 196
Underground City
(Downtown) . . . 104, 361
Union Française
(Quartier Latin) 160
Univers Maurice
"Rocket" Richard
(Maisonneuve) . . 214
Université de Montréal
(Mont Royal and
Westmount) 174
Université du Québec à
Montréal (Quartier
Latin) 158
Verdun
Restaurants 335

Vieille douane
(Vieux-Montréal) 87
Vieux palais de justice
(Vieux-Montréal) . 93
Vieux Séminaire
(Vieux-Montréal) 86
Vieux-Montréal 77
Accommodations . 264
Bars and Nightclubs 340
Restaurants 288
Vieux-Port de Montréal
(Vieux-Montréal) . 91
Vieux-Verdun
(Pointe Saint-Charles
and Verdun) 229
The Village 201
Accommodations . 280
Restaurants 333
Villa Préfontaine
(Outremont) 185
Weather 75
West Island 232
Restaurants 336
Western Montréal 167
Bars and Nightclubs 350
Restaurants 322
Westmount 167
Bars and Nightclubs 350
Restaurants 322
Westmount Library
(Mont Royal and
Westmount) 177
Westmount Park 177
Westmount Square
(Mont Royal and
Westmount) 178
Windsor (Downtown) . 105
Wine 69
World Trade Centre
(Vieux-Montréal) 79

Order Form

Ulysses Travel Guides

- ☐ Acapulco ..... $14.95 CAN / $9.95 US
- ☐ Alberta's Best Hotels and Restaurants ... $14.95 CAN / $12.95 US
- ☐ Arizona– Grand Canyon ..... $24.95 CAN / $17.95 US
- ☐ Atlantic Canada $24.95 CAN / $17.95 US
- ☐ Beaches of Maine $12.95 CAN / $9.95 US / $10.95 US
- ☐ Belize .... $16.95 CAN / $12.95 US
- ☐ Boston .... $17.95 CAN / $12.95 US
- ☐ British Columbia's Best Hotels and ... $14.95 CAN / Restaurants $12.95 US
- ☐ Calgary ...... $17.95 CAN / $12.95 US
- ☐ California ..... $29.95 CAN / $21.95 US
- ☐ Canada .... $29.95 CAN / $21.95 US
- ☐ Cancún & ..... $19.95 CAN / Riviera Maya $14.95 US
- ☐ Cape Cod, ... $24.95 CAN / Nantucket and Martha's Vineyard $17.95 US
- ☐ Cartagena ..... $12.95 CAN / (Colombia) $9.95 US
- ☐ Chicago ...... $19.95 CAN / $14.95 US
- ☐ Chile .... $27.95 CAN / $17.95 US
- ☐ Colombia ..... $29.95 CAN / $21.95 US
- ☐ Costa Rica .... $27.95 CAN / $19.95 US
- ☐ Cuba .... $24.95 CAN / $17.95 US
- ☐ Dominican .... $24.95 CAN / Republic $17.95 US
- ☐ Ecuador and .. $24.95 CAN / Galápagos Islands $17.95 US
- ☐ El Salvador .... $22.95 CAN / $14.95 US

- ☐ Guadalajara ... $17.95 CAN / $12.95 US
- ☐ Guadeloupe ... $24.95 CAN / $17.95 US
- ☐ Guatemala .... $24.95 CAN / $17.95 US
- ☐ Havana ...... $16.95 CAN / $12.95 US
- ☐ Hawaii .... $29.95 CAN / $21.95 US
- ☐ Honduras ..... $24.95 CAN / $17.95 US
- ☐ Huatulco– .... $17.95 CAN / Puerto Escondido $12.95 US
- ☐ Inns and Bed & Breakfasts in Québec .... $14.95 CAN / $10.95 US
- ☐ Islands of the .. $24.95 CAN / Bahamas $17.95 US
- ☐ Las Vegas ..... $17.95 CAN / $12.95 US
- ☐ Lisbon .... $18.95 CAN / $13.95 US
- ☐ Los Angeles ... $19.95 CAN / $14.95 US
- ☐ Los Cabos .... $14.95 CAN / and La Paz $10.95 US
- ☐ Louisiana ..... $29.95 CAN / $21.95 US
- ☐ Martinique .... $24.95 CAN / $17.95 US
- ☐ Miami .... $9.95 CAN / $12.95 US
- ☐ Montréal ..... $19.95 CAN / $14.95 US
- ☐ New Orleans .. $17.95 CAN / $12.95 US
- ☐ New York City . $19.95 CAN / $14.95 US
- ☐ Nicaragua ..... $24.95 CAN / $16.95 US
- ☐ Ontario ...... $27.95 CAN / $19.95 US
- ☐ Ontario's Best Hotels and Restaurants ... $27.95 CAN / $19.95 US
- ☐ Ottawa–Hull ... $17.95 CAN / $12.95 US

☐ Panamá . . . . . . $24.95 CAN $17.95 US	☐ San Francisco . . $17.95 CAN $12.95 US
☐ Peru . . . . $27.95 CAN $19.95 US	☐ Seattle . . . . $17.95 CAN $12.95 US
☐ Phoenix . . . . . . $16.95 CAN $12.95 US	☐ St. Lucia . . . . . . $17.95 CAN $12.95 US
☐ Portugal . . . . . . $24.95 CAN $16.95 US	☐ St. Martin $16.95 CAN and St. Barts $12.95 US
☐ Provence & the $29.95 CAN Côte d'Azur $21.95US	☐ Toronto . . . . . . $18.95 CAN $13.95 US
☐ Puerto Plata– . . $14.95 CAN Sosua $9.95 US	☐ Tunisia . . . . $27.95 CAN $19.95 US
☐ Puerto Rico . . . $24.95 CAN $17.95 US	☐ Vancouver . . . . $17.95 CAN $12.95 US
☐ Puerto Vallarta . $14.95 CAN $9.95 US	☐ Washington D.C. $18.95 CAN $13.95 US
☐ Québec . . . . . . $29.95 CAN $21.95 US	☐ Western Canada $29.95 CAN $21.95 US
☐ Québec City . . . $17.95 CAN $12.95 US	

budget.zone

☐ Central America $14.95 CAN $10.95 US	☐ Western Canada $14.95 CAN $10.95 US

Ulysses Travel Journals

☐ Ulysses Travel Journal (Blue, Red, Green, Yellow, Sextant) . . . . $9.95 CAN $7.95 US	☐ Ulysses Travel Journal (80 Days) . . . . . $14.95 CAN $9.95 US

Ulysses Green Escapes

☐ Cycling in France $22.95 CAN $16.95 US	☐ Hiking in the . . $19.95 CAN Northeastern U.S. $13.95 US
☐ Cycling in . . . . $22.95 CAN Ontario $16.95 US	☐ Hiking in . . . . . $19.95 CAN Québec $13.95 US
☐ Ontario's Bike . $19.95 CAN Paths and Railtrails $14.95 US	☐ Hiking in . . . . . $22.95 CAN Ontario $16.95 US

Ulysses Conversation Guides

☐ French for . . . . $9.95 CAN Better Travel $6.50 US	☐ Spanish for Better Travel in in Latin America $9.95 CAN $6.50 US

Title	Qty	Price	Total

Name:		Subtotal	
		Shipping	$4 CAN $3 US
Address:		Subtotal	
		GST in Canada 7%	
		Total	

Tel: Fax:

E-mail:

Payment: ☐ Cheque ☐ Visa ☐ MasterCard

Card number_____

Expiry date_____

Signature_____

ULYSSES TRAVEL GUIDES

4176 Saint-Denis,
Montréal, Québec,
H2W 2M5
☎(514) 843-9447
Fax: (514) 843-9448

305 Madison Avenue,
Suite 1166,
New York, NY 10165

Toll-free: 1-877-542-7247
Info@ulysses.ca
www.ulyssesguides.com